INTERVENTIONS: NEW STUDIES IN MEDIEVAL CULTURE

Ethan Knapp, Series Editor

Fragments for a History of a Vanishing Humanism

EDITED BY MYRA SEAMAN and EILEEN A. JOY

The Ohio State University Press • Columbus

Copyright © 2016 by The Ohio State University.
All rights reserved.

Library of Congress Cataloging-in-Publication Data
Names: Seaman, Myra, editor. | Joy, Eileen A., 1962– editor.
Title: Fragments for a history of a vanishing humanism / edited by Myra Seaman and
  Eileen A. Joy.
Other titles: Interventions (Columbus, Ohio)
Description: Columbus : The Ohio State University Press, [2016] | "2016" | Series:
  Interventions : new studies in medieval culture | Includes bibliographical references and
  index.
Identifiers: LCCN 2016006037| ISBN 9780814213049 (cloth ; alk. paper) | ISBN 0814213049
  (cloth ; alk. paper)
Subjects: LCSH: Humanism. | Humanism in literature. | Literature—Philosophy. |
  Literature, Medieval—History and criticism. | Identity (Psychology) in literature. |
  Human-animal relationships—Philosophy. | Animals (Philosophy) | Aesthetics.
Classification: LCC B821 .F695 2016 | DDC 809/.93384—dc23
LC record available at http://lccn.loc.gov/2016006037

Cover design by Laurence J. Nozik
Text design by Juliet Williams
Type set in Minion Pro

∞ The paper used in this publication meets the minimum requirements of the American
National Standard for Information Sciences—Permanence of Paper for Printed Library
Materials. ANSI Z39.48-1992.

9 8 7 6 5 4 3 2 1

CONTENTS

Acknowledgments   vii

Introduction: The Work, or the Agency, of the Nonhuman
in Premodern Art   1
ANNA KŁOSOWSKA and EILEEN A. JOY

Part I   ***Singularities, Species, Inter/faces***

1. Paleolithic Representations of Human Being at Chauvet
and Rouffignac   33
JEFFREY SKOBLOW

2. Eros, Event, and Non-Faciality in Malory's "The Tale of Balyn
and Balan"   51
EILEEN A. JOY

3. The Book of Hours and iPods, Passionate Lyrics, and Prayers:
Technologies of the Devotional Self   65
TIM SPENCE

4. What *Does* Language Speak? Feeling the Human with Samuel
Beckett and Chrétien de Troyes   95
DANIEL C. REMEIN and ANNA KŁOSOWSKA

Part II   ***Human, Inhuman, Spectacle***

5. Aninormality   129
JEFFREY JEROME COHEN

6. Humanist Waste   151
MICHAEL A. JOHNSON

7 How Delicious We Must Be / Folcuin's Horse and the Dog's
   Gowther, Beyond Care   175
   KARL STEEL

8 Excusing Laius: Freud's Oedipus, Sophocles' *Oedipus Rex*,
   and Lydgate's Edippus   193
   DANIEL T. KLINE

Coda: The Trick of Singularity: *Twelfth Night,* Stewards
of the Posthuman, and the Problem of Aesthetics   223
   CRAIG DIONNE

   Bibliography   245
   About the Contributors   267
   Index   271

ACKNOWLEDGMENTS

FIRST AND FOREMOST, the contributors to this volume have our deepest gratitude for their boundless patience while we wrestled this volume into print, a process that required nearly eight years. Academic labor takes forms often impossible to reckon, and for every book that is published, many more creep along with great anguish for the authors and editors involved, sometimes languishing and falling off the desk altogether. There is no way to account for the books that never get written, or that get started but are never finished, and one wishes that these abandoned projects might be included among our scholarly labors. Suffice to say that there were times in the past eight years when it felt as if this book might not see the light of day. Yet thanks to the generous diligence of this volume's contributors, who remained attached to the project even when it seemed destined to remain only an idea, and to the commitment of The Ohio State University (OSU) Press, who first expressed their interest in the project in 2008, this volume—which the editors believe signifies an important premodern intervention into contemporary critical post/humanist studies—now thankfully rests in your hands.

The volume initially grew out of multiple conversations at various conferences, seminars, and symposia from 2005 through 2008, which also led to a special issue of the *Journal of Narrative Theory* on "Premodern to Modern Humanisms: The BABEL Project" published in Summer 2007. For their contributions to organizing and participating in and otherwise shepherding these earlier conversations and journal issue (which laid the groundwork for this present volume), we wish to extend our heartfelt appreciation to the authors in this volume and also to Maria Bachman, Kimberly Bell, Doryjane Birer, Justin Brent, Holly Crocker, Michael Harper, Deirdre Joy, Betsy McCormick, Michael Edward Moore, Christine Neufeld, Robin Norris, Dana Oswald, Mary Ramsey, Teresa Reed, Nelljean Rice, LeAnne Teruya, Michael Uebel, and Valerie Vogrin.

The editors wish also to express their thanks to Malcolm Litchfield, former Acquisitions Editor of OSU Press, for first green-lighting the volume; to Ethan Knapp for encouraging us to submit the manuscript to OSU Press's

Interventions: New Studies in Medieval Culture book series in the first place and for never losing faith in the volume's significance; and to Eugene O'Connor, and editorial and design staff, at OSU Press for overseeing the volume's review and final production phases with such elegant care. Thanks are also due to the two anonymous reviewers who provided us with such insightful and helpful comments for revision (any remaining infelicities being our own), and to Norman James Hogg for donating his photograph for the cover. Finally, the editors wish to thank each other for what has now been fifteen years of sustaining friendship and collaboration. We dedicate this volume to the memory of Cynthia (Cindy) Ho (d. 2014), who always encouraged and supported BABEL's projects and who always approached life and scholarship with a sense of joyful adventure. She is sorely missed from our company.

INTRODUCTION

The Work, or the Agency, of the Nonhuman in Premodern Art

ANNA KŁOSOWSKA and EILEEN A. JOY

> The "human," we now know, is not now, and never was, itself.
> —Cary Wolfe

LACRIMAE RERUM: PREMODERN SOURCES FOR A THEORY OF NONHUMAN SENSIBILITY

In a famous ballad on the theme of *ubi sunt* (in a sense, "where has everything gone?"—the classic lament for the passing of time and the inevitable fading of life), fifteenth-century poet François Villon chose for his refrain the image of the snows of yesteryear. Snow's transformative and impermanent miracle could be a Northern European version of cherry blossoms: "But where are yesteryear's snows?" ["Mais où sont les neiges d'antan?"]. Lending snow, beautiful and ephemeral, the same intensity as that which inhabits the names of vanished queens and beauties, Villon alchemically turns melted snow into *lacrimae rerum,* or "thingly tears," making explicit the agency of things and the important role things play in the human realization, performance, and reliving of existential, sweet, and inescapable sorrow, to the point that sorrow and things become one with each other.

When Aeneas weeps at the depictions of the Trojan War in Carthage, he enjoins his companion Achates to rally and let his fears dissolve, since even this faraway nation will empathize with their plight: these, he says, "are thingly tears, and the mortal things touch the mind" (Virgil, *Aeneid*, 1.462: "sunt lacrimae rerum et mentem mortalia tangunt").[1] Since Virgil, the expression *lacrimae rerum* ["thingly tears"] has marked that sweet and sad entanglement of the mind and emotions with things—not necessarily warlike things, although the line is often quoted on military monuments. Virgil's passage is famously multivalent, and its gnomic half-line is usually cited out of context. Symptomatically, one classicist explicating *lacrimae rerum* called upon Ezra Pound's observation that truly great literature is "language charged with meaning to the utmost possible degree," concluding that "the passage, of course, cannot be translated."[2] All agree that this famous line's enigmatic nature lends it a "sense of wondrous beauty and pathetic dignity," and "many would be disposed to quote [it] as the *best* verse in Latin poetry."[3] Here are some readings that have been given to the Latin verse over the years:

> Tears for things, tears of things, tears that the things shed, things worthy of tears. Tears are powerful and their effects are material, so that tears can as well be called material things and considered real. The universe of material things sheds tears for us in the face of our acute misery. These images would wring tears out of stone. Sorrow and tears are implicit in men's affairs or things. Nothing (or no thing) is free of tears. Depicted on the wall are events (things) that bring on tears; these are tear-inducing things. We all cry at the same things; great tragedies move us whether or not they happen to us and ours or to distant others.

The line's fruitful multiplicity of meanings is exactly what inspires the later echoes.

Lacrimae rerum—the classical, premodern, and modern precursor of our speculative materialisms, post/humanisms, and *past*humanisms—are not a narrowly premodern European concept. Take *mono no aware* ["the affective

---

1. David Wharton, "*Sunt lacrimae rerum*: An Exploration in Meaning," *Classical Journal* 103 (2008): 259–79.

2. John Wright, "*Lacrimae rerum* and the Thankless Task," *Classical Journal* 62.8 (1967): 365–66 [365–67].

3. Robert Yelverton Tyrrell, *Latin Poetry: Lectures Delivered in 1893 on the Percy Turnbull Memorial Foundation in John Hopkins University* (Boston: Houghton Mifflin, 1895), 147; partially cited by Arthur L. Keith, "A Virgilian Line," *Classical Journal* 17.7 (1922): 398 [398–402].

and aesthetic force of things in the world"], a theoretical concept and practical precept that permeates Japanese culture of the Heian period (794–1185). The sensitivity, empathy, or enchantment to, of, and by things [*mono*] is used as a critical term describing the heightened awareness of the ephemeral nature [*mojo*] of things, combined with a sense of wistfulness and an almost glad sorrow inspired by the consideration of transience evoked by objects, where understanding and feelings merge.[4] *Aware* is the ability to be moved. Sorrow, pathos, or sadness are associated with *aware* (where *aware* = "alas!"), but primarily the term refers to an intense impression (where *aware* = "sigh," "Oh!", and "Ah!").[5] The viewings of the moon and picnics of the cherry blossom season [*hanami*], a tradition noted as early as the third century, are permeated with *mono no aware*, as the cherry blooms [*sakura*] move like a fantastical, impermanent, earthbound cloud across the archipelago in a stately and inexorable wave. Since the rise of modern scholarship on Japanese literature, especially the contributions of Motoori Norinaga (1730–1801), examples of *mono no aware* are often drawn from the eleventh-century *Tale of Genji*, whose author, Lady Murasaki, often used the expression nominally, as when we say, "He has a certain *je ne sais quoi*." It was also Norinaga who emphasized the Heian period commonplace that, when the awareness of things is particularly intense, only sharing poetry or narratives that result from this feeling, and moving others as powerfully as one is moved, may bring relief.[6] For us, the themes of *mono no aware* and *lacrimae rerum* participate in a premodern genealogy of the nonhuman as a work of art and the work or agency of the nonhuman in art, the topic of the essays assembled in this volume.

POST/HUMANISM AND THE CRISIS OF THE HUMAN/ITIES

The idea of enchantment with the world, and with its vibrant materialities, and with thingly tears guided us as we approached this collection, conceived

---

4. Tomiko Yoda, "Fractured Dialogues: *Mono no aware* and Poetic Communication in the *Tale of Genji*," *Harvard Journal of Asiatic Studies* 59.2 (1999): 524 [523–57]. Yoda adds: "*Mono no aware* refers to a profound feeling with which one spontaneously responds to a myriad of things and occurrences in the world. To 'know *mono no aware*' refers to one's ability to have such a feeling for certain objects on an appropriate occasion" (526). See also Kazumitsu Kato, "Some Notes on *Mono no Aware*," *Journal of the American Oriental Society* 82.4 (1962): 558–59, and Mark Meli, "'Aware' as a Critical Term in Japanese Poetics," *Japan Review* 13 (2001): 67–91.

5. Motoori Norinaga, *The Poetics of Motoori Norinaga: A Hermeneutical Journey*, trans. Michael F. Marra (Honolulu: University of Hawai'i Press, 2007), 174.

6. Yoda, "Fractured Dialogues," 527.

as one possible answer to Judith Butler's question, "What qualifies as a human, as a human subject, as human speech, as human desire?"[7] and also to Edward Said's provocation, in the context of the humanities, that

> as scholars and teachers we believe we are right to call what we do "humanistic" and what we teach "the humanities." [Yet,] are these still serviceable phrases, and if so, in what way? How then may we view humanism as an activity in light of its past and probable future?[8]

For a long while now, there has been a significant turn both *to* and *beyond* the human (or, the liberal humanist subject) in aesthetic, historical, philosophical, sociological, and more scientific studies—a turn, moreover, which is also often accompanied by a nod to post-*histoire,* or the "end of history." Thus, we might revise Butler's question to something like, "What qualifies as a post/human and what is at stake in this qualification?" This poses a great challenge to those concerned with the future of humanistic letters and education, especially when, as John Caputo writes, "one has lost one's faith in *grand récits,*" and "being, presence, *ouisa,* the transcendental signified, History, Man—the list goes on—have all become dreams." As Caputo writes, "We are in a fix, except that even to say 'we' is to get into a still deeper fix. We are in the fix that cannot say 'we,'" and yet, "the obligation of me to you and both of us to others ... is all around us, on every side, tugging at our sleeves, calling on us for a response."[9] Caputo expressed these sentiments (which are also worries) in 1993, but they accord well with the anxieties of the editors of the 2007 issue of *The Hedgehog Review* on "Human Dignity and Justice," who were concerned that "transcendent accounts of why the lives of all persons should be valued" no longer "make sense," and therefore, "one might ask whether a rhetoric of human dignity can be sustained and whether calls [in numerous human rights discourses] to honor the dignity of every individual can gain traction." Is it possible any longer "to sustain justice without the idea of human dignity, or a similar concept?"[10]

In relation to these concerns and anxious questions, multiple post/human (and nonhuman, inhuman, ahuman, and even *post*-posthuman) disciplines

---

7. Quoted in "Changing the Subject: Judith Butler's Politics of Radical Resignification" (interview with G. A. Olson and L. Worsham), in *The Judith Butler Reader,* ed. Sarah Salih (Oxford: Blackwell, 2004), 356 [325–56].

8. Edward Said, *Humanism and Democratic Criticism* (New York: Columbia University Press, 2004), 7.

9. John D. Caputo, *Against Ethics: Contributions to a Poetics of Obligation with Constant Reference to Deconstruction* (Bloomington: Indiana University Press, 1993), 6.

10. "Introduction: Human Dignity and Justice," *Hedegehog Review* 9.3 (2007): 5 [5–6].

have (for a while now) been in full swing in the fields of the arts, humanities, social sciences, and sciences.¹¹ In 2006, the National Humanities Center (NHC) announced a three-year project, "Autonomy, Singularity, Creativity: The Human and the Humanities," which sought to "crystallize a conversation already begun" by "a small but growing number of philosophers, literary scholars, and other humanistic thinkers" whose thought and studies have "turned to the work of computational scientists, primatologists, cognitive scientists, biologists, neuroscientists, and others" in an attempt to "gain a contemporary understanding of human attributes that have traditionally been described in abstract, philosophical, or spiritual terms."¹² The NHC wanted to consider the possible ramifications of the *approaching* "posthuman era" by bringing into conversation with these humanists the scientists who have been turning their attention to questions typically reserved for the humanists—questions, moreover, that have to do with "the nature of human identity; the legitimate scope of agency in determining the circumstances or conditions of one's life;

---

11. See, for example, most recently, Rosi Braidotti, *The Posthuman* (Cambridge: Polity, 2013); Claire Colebrook, *Death of the Posthuman: Essays on Extinction, Vol. 1* (Ann Arbor, MI: Open Humanities Press/MPublishing, 2014); Noreen Giffney and Myra J. Hird, eds., *Queering the Non/human* (Hampshire, UK: Ashgate, 2008); Richard Grusin, ed., *The Nonhuman Turn* (Minneapolis: University of Minnesota Press, 2015); Patricia MacCormack, ed., *The Animal Catalyst: Toward a Human Theory* (London: Bloomsbury, 2014); Cary Wolfe, *What Is Posthumanism?* (Minneapolis: University of Minnesota Press, 2009); and Joanna Zylinska, *Minimal Ethics for the Anthropocene* (Ann Arbor: Open Humanities Press/MPublishing, 2014). The recent turns to "new materialisms," "speculative realism," and "object-oriented" studies have given fresh impetus as well to the longer-standing post/human turn. See, for example, Stacy Alaimo, *Bodily Natures: Science, Environment, and the Material Self* (Bloomington: Indiana University Press, 2010); Jane Bennett, *Vibrant Matter: A Political Ecology of Things* (Durham, NC: Duke University Press, 2010); Ian Bogost, *Alien Phenomenology, or What It's Like to Be a Thing* (Minneapolis: University of Minnesota Press, 2012); Levi Bryant, *The Democracy of Objects* (Ann Arbor, MI: Open Humanities Press, 2011); Levi Bryant, Nick Srnicek, and Graham Harman, eds., *The Speculative Turn: Continental Materialism and Realism* (Melbourne: re.press, 2011); William E. Connolly, *The Fragility of Things: Self-Organizing Processes, Neoliberal Fantasies, and Democratic Activism* (Durham, NC: Duke University Press, 2013); Diana Coole and Samantha Frost, eds., *New Materialisms: Ontology, Agency, and Politics* (Durham, NC: Duke University Press, 2010); Graham Harman, *Prince of Networks: Bruno Latour and Metaphysics* (Melbourne: re.press, 2009) and *The Quadruple Object* (Hants, UK: Zero Books, 2011); Quentin Meillassoux, *After Finitude: An Essay on the Necessity of Contingency*, trans. Ray Brassier (London: Bloomsbury, 2010); Timothy Morton, *Realist Magic: Objects, Ontology, Causality* (Ann Arbor: Open Humanities Press/MPublishing, 2013) and *Hyperobjects: Philosophy and Ecology after the End of the World* (Minneapolis: University of Minnesota Press, 2013); Steven Shaviro, *The Universe of Things: On Speculative Realism* (Minneapolis: University of Minnesota Press, 2014); and Tom Sparrow, *The End of Phenomenology: Metaphysics and the New Realism* (Edinburgh: Edinburgh University Press, 2014).

12. National Humanities Center, "Autonomy, Singularity, Creativity: A Project of the National Humanities Center," *National Humanities Center*, May 2007, http://onthehuman.org/archive/more/.

the relation of cognition to embodiment; the role of chance, luck, or fate; the definition of and value attached to 'nature'; and the nature and limits of moral responsibility."[13] From 2006 through 2009, the NHC offered residential fellowships and convened symposia and seminars that brought together humanists and scientists to engage in a more comprehensive dialogue on the following three "distinct but related areas":

(1) *Human autonomy,* which entails the capacity for self-determination, self-awareness, and self-regulation that is central to our conceptions of free will and moral accountability;
(2) *Human singularity,* on which our privileged place in the order of being, distinct from animals on the one hand and from machines on the other, is premised;
(3) *Human creativity,* through which mankind demonstrates its capacity for representation and expression, and which many take to be the distinctive feature of the human species.[14]

These objectives make clear that the NHC focused its energies on three areas that are distinctly related to what might be called an ongoing "crisis" of the (supposed) stability and centrality of the liberal, sovereign human subject within the realm of so-called human affairs (having to do with morality, governance, sovereignty, freedom, the arts, etc.), which are also traditionally held to underpin the mission and projects of the human/ities, and the university more largely.

According to Katherine Hayles, who helped to usher in the post/human turn[15] and who served as a Senior Fellow in NHC's Project, "The humanities have always been concerned with shifting definitions of the human," so "the human has always been a kind of contested term." But for Hayles, "what the idea of the posthuman evokes that is not unique to the twentieth century, but became much more highly energized in the twentieth century, is the idea that technology has progressed to the point where it has the capability of fundamentally transforming the conditions of human life."[16] As Hayles elaborated:

---

13. Ibid.
14. Ibid.
15. See N. Katherine Hayles, *How We Became Posthuman: Virtual Bodies in Cybernetics, Literature, and Informatics* (Chicago: University of Chicago Press, 1999) and *My Mother Was a Computer: Digital Subjects and Literary Texts* (Chicago: University of Chicago Press, 2005), among other works.
16. Quoted in Don Solomon, "Interview with N. Katherine Hayles: Preparing the Humanities for the Post Human," *National Humanities Center,* May 2007, http://onthe human.org /archive/more/interview-with-n-katherine-hayles/.

Even though "one of the deep ideas of the humanities is that the past is an enduring reservoir of value, and that it pays us rich dividends to know the past," there are some things "that have never happened before in human history. . . . We've never had the possibility for manipulating our own genome in a generation as opposed to 150 generations. We never had the possibility for individually manipulating atoms as in nanotechnology, and so forth."[17]

The post/human condition, then, in some respects (and according to some), is thoroughly modern because of its dependence, partly, on technological and medical innovations that could not have even been imagined in the past. It has to be stated that in many post/humanist discourses that have been circulating within the university, whether in the humanities or the sciences, the scholarship of those who work in premodern periods (such as classical antiquity, late antiquity, the Middle Ages, and the Renaissance) is often not considered relevant to the discussion—even when that scholarship is concerned, as some of it definitively has been, with issues of the human and the animal, self and subjectivity, cognition and theory of mind, singularity and networks, corporality and embodiment, bare life and sociality, flesh versus machine, and so on. In more recent years, this has been changing, however, with monographs, essay collections, and journal issues in premodern studies that play a prominent and influential role in the post/human turn.[18] Nevertheless, the question of historical difference remains something of a problematic.

---

17. Ibid.

18. See, for example, Jeffrey Jerome Cohen, ed., *Animal, Vegetable, Mineral: Ethics and Objects* (Brooklyn, NY: punctum books, 2012); idem, *Inhuman Nature* (Brooklyn: punctum books, 2014); Jeffrey Jerome Cohen and Lowell Duckert, eds., "Ecomaterialism," special issue, *postmedieval: a journal of medieval cultural studies* 4.1 (2013); Jean E. Feerick and Vin Nardizzi, eds., *The Indistinct Human in Renaissance Literature* (New York: Palgrave Macmillan, 2012); Stefan Herbrechter and Ivan Callas, *Posthumanist Shakespeares* (New York: Palgrave Macmillan, 2012); Eileen A. Joy and Christine Neufeld, eds., "Premodern to Modern Humanisms: The BABEL Project," special issue, *Journal of Narrative Theory* 37.2 (2007); Eileen A. Joy and Craig Dionne, eds., "*When Did We Become Post/human?*" special issue, *postmedieval: a journal of medieval cultural studies* 1.1/2 (2010); J. Allan Mitchell, *Becoming Human: The Matter of the Medieval Child* (Minneapolis: University of Minnesota Press, 2014); The Petropunk Collective [Eileen A. Joy, Anna Kłosowska, Nicola Masciandaro, and Michael O'Rourke], eds., *Speculative Medievalisms: Discography* (Brooklyn, NY: punctum books, 2013); Laurie Shannon, *The Accommodated Animal: Cosmopolity in Shakespearean Locales* (Chicago: University of Chicago Press, 2013); Karl Steel, *How to Make a Human: Animals and Violence in the Middle Ages* (Columbus: The Ohio State University Press, 2011); Karl Steel and Peggy McCracken, eds., "The Animal Turn," special issue, *postmedieval: a journal of medieval cultural studies* 2.1 (2011); Henry S. Turner, *Shakespeare's Double Helix* (London: Bloomsbury, 2008); and Julian Yates, *Error, Misuse, Failure: Object Lessons from the English Renaissance* (Minneapolis: University of Minnesota Press, 2002).

So, for example, in an early prospectus (circa 2007) for the Posthumanities book series at the University of Minnesota, series director Cary Wolfe argued that post/humanism cannot be glossed with reference to terms like "post-industrialist" or "post-structuralist" or "post-modern," for "the question of 'posthumanism' is more complicated than any of these [other 'post-isms'], because it references not just chronological progression (what comes *after* the industrial, the modern, and so on) but also takes on fundamental ontological and epistemological questions that are not reducible to purely historical explanation." Indeed, it was Wolfe's hope when inaugurating the series that the books would draw "renewed attention to the difference between *historicity* and 'historicism' that seems to have been largely elided or avoided in much recent work in the humanities."[19] The series, then, is "not 'against' history, of course, but against historicism in its more unreflective and problematic forms." The imprint has since published 33 books, none of which are exclusively focused on premodern subjects, although some of the books do tangentially touch upon those,[20] and thus, regardless of its claims to reject the overly simplistic construct of "what comes after" and to aim for a more complex historiography, the series nevertheless remains somewhat stuck in the chrono-landscape of contemporary thought and life, and its "historicism" is not very deep. Its prospectus also overlooks the fact that for quite a while now, in premodern studies, but also in cultural and historiographical studies, *much* work has actually been done to attend to the differences between historicity and historicism.[21]

---

19. The prospectus for University of Minnesota's Posthumanities book series, authored by Cary Wolfe, is no longer available online, but was first accessed and transcribed by us in October 2007.

20. Such as Tom Tyler, *Ciferae: A Bestiary in Five Fingers* (Minneapolis: University of Minnesota Press, 2012).

21. See footnote 28 for the relevant works in premodern studies, and in the field of cultural studies and history, see (as just a small sampling) F. R. Ankersmit, *Historical Representation* (Stanford, CA: Stanford University Press, 2002); Roger Chartier, *On the Edge of a Cliff: History, Language, Practices*, trans. Lydia G. Cochrane (Baltimore: Johns Hopkins University, 1996); Andreas Huyssens, *Present Pasts: Urban Palimpsests and the Politics of Memory* (Stanford: Stanford University Press, 2003) and *Twilight Memories: Marking Time in a Culture of Amnesia* (New York: Routledge, 1995); Dominick LaCapra, *Writing History, Writing Trauma* (Baltimore: Johns Hopkins University Press, 2001); Peter Osborne, *The Politics of Time: Modernity and the Avant-Garde* (London: Verso, 1995); Eric L. Santner, *Stranded Objects: Mourning, Memory and Film in Postwar Germany* (Ithaca, NY: Cornell University Press, 1993); and Hayden White, *The Content of the Form: Narrative Discourse and Historical Representation* (Baltimore: Johns Hopkins University Press, 1990). It should be noted as well that practically the entire oeuvre of the historians initially attached to the *Annales, Histoire, Sciences Sociales* journal (founded in 1929)—such as Marc Bloch, Lucien Febvre, and Fernand Braudel, among others—also attended to the divide between historicity and historicism, although this is not always acknowledged in current work on chronicity and historiography.

Nevertheless, it is precisely to Wolfe's hope of a theoretical post/humanism that would pay better attention to the *difference* between historicity and an unreflective historicism, and to Hayles's assertion that certain aspects of the post/human can only ever be modern (or, driven by certain post-nineteenth-century technologies), that our volume of essays, *Fragments For a History of a Vanishing Humanism*, addresses itself. After all, Wolfe himself has argued that "the human is not now, and never was, itself,"[22] and scholars in medieval studies *have* explored the question of the relation between the post/human (or never-human) and the past—a question that has been explored, for example, by Jeffrey Jerome Cohen in his book *Medieval Identity Machines*, where he writes that even in the Middle Ages human identity was, "despite the best efforts of those who possess[ed] it otherwise—unstable, contingent, hybrid, discontinuous."[23] In all times and places, as Cohen has argued elsewhere, being human really means "endlessly 'becoming human.' It means holding an uncertain identity, an identity that is always slipping away from us,"[24] and this resonates with Hayles's idea that human subjectivity emerges from and is integrated "into a chaotic world rather than occupying a position of mastery and control removed from it."[25] More specifically, we want to continue filling in (and further complicating) what we believe has been a definitive lacuna or gap in post/humanist studies more generally: the absence of a theoretically rigorous *longer* (premodern) historical perspective. Many of the contemporary discourses on post/humanism have mainly focused on the ways in which new findings and developments in fields such as biotechnology, neuroscience, and computing have complicated how we believe we are enacting our human "selves," ushering in the language of crisis over the supposed destabilization of the category "human" in its biological, social, and political aspects (the futurist-dystopic view).[26] Or, they have concentrated on a theoretical reform of

---

22. Cary Wolfe, "Introduction," in *Zoontologies: The Question of the Animal*, ed. Wolfe (Minneapolis: University of Minnesota Press, 2003), xiii [ix–xxiii].

23. Jeffrey Jerome Cohen, *Medieval Identity Machines* (Minneapolis: University of Minnesota Press, 2003), xxiii.

24. Jeffrey Jerome Cohen, "Afterword: An Unfinished Conversation about Glowing Green Bunnies," in *Queering the Non/human*, eds. Giffney and Hird, 373–74 [363–75].

25. Hayles, *How We Became Posthuman*, 291.

26. For one of the best examples of the "crisis," or dystopic, perspective, see Francis Fukuyama, *Our Posthuman Future: Consequences of the Biotechnology Revolution* (New York: Farar, Straus and Giroux, 2002). See also Zygmunt Bauman, *Liquid Modernity* (Cambridge: Blackwell, 2000); Benjamin Bratton, *The Stack: On Software and Sovereignty* (Cambridge, MA: MIT Press, 2015); Kenneth Gergen, *The Saturated Self: Dilemmas of Identity in Contemporary Life* (New York: Basic Books, 1991); Benjamin Noys, *Malign Velocities: Accelerationism and Capitalism* (Hants, UK, 2014); Eugene Thacker and Alexander Galloway, *The Exploit: A Theory of Networks* (Minneapolis: University of Minnesota Press, 2007); Paul Virilio, *The Information Bomb*,

a humanistic tradition of thought (from the Renaissance through modernity) believed to have produced, in Iain Chambers' words, an oppressive "history of possessive subjectivism" (the critical philosophical view).[27] Or, finally, in some circles (primarily scientific but also cultural studies), the same post/human turn has led to a language of hope and (even occasionally giddy) elation over all of the ways in which we—whatever "we" might be—might finally be able to escape or somehow make less vulnerable or more extensively enjoyable the death-haunted "trap" of our all-too-human bodies (the futurist-utopic view).[28]

But what is missing from most of these discourses, even when they claim to address the question of history, historicism, or historicity, are the incorporated dialogue of scholars who have a deep expertise in premodern studies (antiquity through the Middle Ages). While the past is often invoked and (often crudely) drawn in contemporary theory, it is rarely visited via the route of, or *unsettled* by, actual scholarship in premodern studies—scholarship that in recent years has been deeply concerned with issues of the status of the human and, in a theoretically sophisticated manner, also calls into question the "straight" teleologies and causal explanations of a traditional, or in Wolfe's

---

trans. Chris Turner (London: Verso, 2000); and Langdon Winner, *The Reactor and the Whale: The Search for Limits in an Age of High Technology* (Chicago: University of Chicago Press, 1987).

27. Iain Chambers, *Culture after Humanism: History, Culture, Subjectivity* (London: Routledge, 2001), 4. For an excellent overview of "critical humanisms," see Martin Halliwell and Andy Mousley, *Critical Humanisms: Humanist/Anti-Humanist Dialogues* (Edinburgh: Edinburgh University Press, 2003). See also Tzvetan Todorov, *The Imperfect Garden: The Legacy of Humanism* (Princeton, NJ: Princeton University Press, 2002).

28. On the futurist-utopic (or more affirmative) view, in both scientific and cultural studies, see especially Jean Baudrillard, *The Ecstasy of Communication*, trans. Bernard and Caroline Schultze (New York: Semiotext(e), 1988); Nick Bostrom, *Superintelligence: Paths, Dangers, Strategies* (Oxford: Oxford University Press, 2014) and "Why I Want to Be a Posthuman When I Grow Up," in *Medical Enhancement and Posthumanity*, eds. Bert Gordijn and Ruth Chadwick (Dordrecht: Springer, 2008), 107–37; Rosi Braidotti, *Metamorphoses: Towards a Materialist Theory of Becoming* (Cambridge: Polity Press, 2002); Gilles Deleuze and Félix Guatarri, *A Thousand Plateaus: Capitalism and Schizophrenia*, trans. Brian Massumi (Minneapolis: University of Minnesota Press, 1987); Judith Halberstam and Ira Livingston, "Introduction: Posthuman Bodies," in *Posthuman Bodies*, ed. Halberstam and Livingston (Bloomington: Indiana University Press, 1995), 1–19; Donna Haraway, "A Cyborg Manifesto: Science, Technology, and Socialist-Feminism in the Late Twentieth Century," in *Cyborgs, and Women: The Reinvention of Nature*, ed. Haraway (New York: Routledge, 1991), 149–82, and *When Species Meet* (Minneapolis: University of Minnesota Press, 2007); Eduardo Kac, *Signs of Life: Bio Art and Beyond* (Cambridge, MA: MIT Press, 2007); Ray Kurzweil, *The Age of Spiritual Machines: When Computers Exceed Human Intelligence* (New York: Viking, 1999) and *The Singularity Is Near: When Humans Transcend Biology* (New York: Viking, 2005); Hans Moravec, *Mind Children: The Future of Robot and Human Intelligence* (Cambridge, MA: MIT Press, 1988); Lee Silver, *Remaking Eden: Cloning and Beyond in a Brave New World* (New York: Avon, 1997); and Gregory Stock, *Redesigning Humans: Our Inevitable Genetic Future* (Boston: Houghton Mifflin, 2002).

terms an unreflective, historicism.[29] Neither is this is a scholarship that Hayles worries might adopt the "attitude that there's nothing that has happened or could happen that has not already happened in the past," but rather, that these studies pose the Middle Ages, in the words of Jeffrey Jerome Cohen, as an "interminable, difficult middle" that stresses "not difference (the past as past) or sameness (the past as present)," but "temporal interlacement, the impossibility of choosing alterity or continuity."[30] Although seemingly wholly "Other," the past in these studies is "lodged deep within social and individual identity, a foundational difference at the heart of the selfsame" and could even be described as a kind of "unbounded" space-time that is generative of human identity through a "constant movement of irresolvable relations that constitute its traumatic effect, an ever-expanding line that arcs back through what has been even as it races toward what it shall be."[31] But these are lines of critical thought that, for a while now, have been mainly confined to conversations among premodernists (who might be discussing with each other, for example,

---

29. Regarding a medieval studies that subverts traditional historicist teleologies, see Kathleen Biddick, *The Shock of Medievalism* (Durham, NC: Duke University Press, 1998); Glenn Burger and Steven F. Kruger, introduction in *Queering the Middle Ages*, eds. Burger and Kruger (Minneapolis: University of Minnesota Press, 2001), xi–xxiii; Jeffrey Jerome Cohen, "Introduction: Midcolonial," in *The Postcolonial Middle Ages*, ed. Cohen (New York: Palgrave Macmillan, 2000), 1–17, and "Time's Machines," in *Medieval Identity Machines*, 1–34; Andrew Cole and D. Vance Smith, eds., *The Legitimacy of the Middle Ages: On the Unwritten History of Theory* (Durham, NC: Duke University Press, 2010); Kathleen Davis, *Periodization and Sovereignty: How Ideas of Feudalism and Secularization Govern the Politics of Time* (Philadelphia: University of Pennsylvania Press, 2008); Kathleen Davis and Nadia Altschul, eds., *Medievalisms in the Postcolonial World: The Idea of the "Middle Ages" Outside Europe* (Baltimore: Johns Hopkins University Press, 2009); Carolyn Dinshaw, *Getting Medieval: Sexualities and Communities, Pre- and Postmodern* (Durham, NC: Duke University Press, 1999) and *How Soon Is Now? Amateur Readers, Medieval Texts, and the Queerness of Time* (Durham, NC: Duke University Press, 2012); L. O. Aranye Fradenburg, *Sacrifice Your Love: Psychoanalysis, Historicism, Chaucer* (Minneapolis: University of Minnesota Press, 2002); Amy Hollywood, *Sensible Ecstasy: Mysticism, Sexual Difference, and the Demands of History* (Chicago: University of Chicago Press, 2001); Bruce Holsinger, *The Premodern Condition: Medievalism and the Making of Theory* (Chicago: University of Chicago Press, 2005); Bruce Holsinger and Ethan Knapp, "The Marxist Premodern," *Journal of Medieval and Early Modern Studies* 34.3 (2004): 463–71; Eileen A. Joy, "Like Two Autistic Moonbeams Entering the Window of My Asylum: Chaucer's Griselda and Lars von Trier's Bess McNeill," *postmedieval: a journal of medieval cultural studies* 2.3 (2011): 316–28; Eileen A. Joy, Myra J. Seaman, Kimberly Bell, and Mary Ramsey, eds., *Cultural Studies of the Modern Middle Ages* (New York: Palgrave Macmillan, 2007); Elizabeth Scala and Sylvia Federico, eds., *The Post-Historical Middle Ages* (New York: Palgrave Macmillan, 2009); D. Vance Smith, "Irregular Histories: Forgetting Ourselves," *New Literary History* 28.2 (1997): 161–84; and Paul Strohm, "Postmodernism and History," in *Theory and the Premodern Text*, ed. Strohm (Minneapolis: University of Minnesota Press, 2000), 149–62.

30. Cohen, "Introduction: Midcolonial," 5.

31. Ibid.

"old" versus "new" historicist approaches to their subjects of study), and they do not always productively connect with the work of humanists (or scientists) working in disciplines concerned with more contemporary or post/human subjects, and who might view the too distant past as either beside or *opposite* the point. This is not to say that scholars working in premodern studies are not ever seeking a more cross-disciplinary or contemporary-minded audience. Some of them are, and in pointed fashion, especially in the past several years.[32]

It was partly with the idea of both a post/human Middle Ages and an *approaching* post/human era—neither of which can be free of concepts, identities, and social forms that are always both dead and alive at once—that this volume was initially conceptualized. We also formulated the following as initiatory and guiding questions for our contributors:

- How does the concept (or reality) of the post/human impact the ways we develop our notions of humanism, both past and present?
- How do the various historical traditions of humanism (classical, medieval, and early modern) productively and antagonistically intersect with more modern antihumanisms?
- In what ways might premodern and more modern studies, with respect to the vigorous debates over the value (or lack thereof) of the liberal humanities, form productive alliances across the Enlightenment divide?
- What is the role of the individual, singular person in relation to concepts of humanism, past and present?
- What is the role of language and literature in relation to being, body, and mind, past and present?
- Is it true, as some have argued, that the individual (and a concomitant emphasis on phenomenological inwardness) is a product of modernity (or, at least, of the post-Enlightenment), or has the human self, constructed in philosophy and other arts, always been "deep"? Or, conversely, has the "depth" of human persons always been an illusion?

---

32. For example, the mission and projects of the BABEL Working Group (http://babelworkinggroup.org) have been pitched in this direction. See, for example, the journal *postmedieval: a journal of medieval cultural studies*, edited by Eileen A. Joy, Myra Seaman, and Lara Farina, which dedicated its inaugural issue in 2010 to the post/human turn and is in continual dialogue with scholars across a wide variety of fields and temporal periods (see footnote 17). See, also, in recent medieval cultural studies, Jeffrey Jerome Cohen, ed., *Prismatic Ecology: Ecotheory beyond Green* (Minneapolis: University of Minnesota Press, 2013); Dinshaw, *How Soon Is Now?*; L. O. Aranye Fradenburg, *Staying Alive: A Survival Manual for the Liberal Arts* (Brooklyn, NY: punctum books, 2013); The Petropunk Collective, *Speculative Medievalisms*; Cole and Smith, eds., *Legitimacy of the Middle Ages*; and E. R. Truitt, *Medieval Robots: Mechanism, Magic, Nature, and Art* (Philadelphia: University of Pennsylvania Press, 2015).

- How does the interplay between singular corporealities and social "bodies" affect our understanding of what it means to be human, both in the past and in the present?
- What is the role of the Other (or, more generally, alterity) in our conceptions of humanism and "being human," past and present?
- Is humanism a philosophy, or set of ideas, or a historically situated sociocritical practice that has lost its *raison d'etre*, such that it is time for a new humanism or no humanism at all? Or is it time to reclaim a new "critical humanism" in new modes of address and analysis?

This last question has special prominence in our collective project. There is no doubt that humanism—especially of the variety in which, in Iain Chambers's words, "the human subject is considered sovereign, language [is] the transparent medium of its agency, and truth [is] the representation of its rationalism"—has a terrible reputation and has been responsible for some of the worst atrocities perpetrated in history.[33] Furthermore, we are aware that any attempt to recuperate humanism *now* may always come too late if, as Foucault supposes in the conclusion to *The Order of Things*, "man" has already been "erased," like "a face drawn in sand at the edge of the sea."[34] Yet even the most compelling antihumanist texts—such as Cary Wolfe's *What Is Posthumanism?* or Karl Steel's *How to Make a Human*—continue, in Kate Soper's terms, to "secrete" humanist rhetoric.[35] There is a certain dependence of anti- or post/humanist discourses upon the space (and languages) of the university humanities, where, as Derrida has written, the principle of unconditionality "has an originary and privileged place of presentation, of manifestation, of safekeeping" as well as its "space of discussion and reelaboration." And all of this

> passes as much by way of literature and languages (that is, the sciences called the sciences of man and culture) as by way of the nondiscursive arts, by way of law and philosophy, by way of critique, by way of questioning—where it is a matter of nothing less than rethinking the concept of man, the figure of humanity in general, and singularly the one presupposed by what we have called, in the university, for the last few centuries, the Humanities.[36]

---

33. Chambers, *Culture after Humanism*, 2–3.
34. Michel Foucault, *The Order of Things: An Archaeology of the Human Sciences* (London: Tavistock, 1966), 387.
35. Kate Soper, *Humanism and Anti-Humanism* (London: Hutchinson, 1986), 182.
36. Jacques Derrida, "The University without Condition," in Derrida, *Without Alibi*, ed. and trans. Peggy Kamuf (Stanford, CA: Stanford University Press, 2002), 207 [202–37].

In this sense, we might practice what Martin Halliwell and Andy Mousley have termed a critical or "baggy" humanism that "takes the human to be an open-ended and mutable process."[37] And like Halliwell and Mousley, we might develop a *new* or *post*/humanism that is "both a pluralistic and a self-critical tradition that folds in and over itself, provoking a series of questions and problems rather than necessarily providing consolation or edification for individuals when faced with intractable economic, political, and social pressures."[38] This is a humanism that acknowledges, with Chambers, that "being in the world does not add up, it never arrives at the complete picture, the conclusive verdict. There is always something more that exceeds the frame we desire to impose."[39]

A heretofore *under*developed consideration of the deep past in the post/humanist project is where we locate our point of entry into the ongoing conversation, but the (post/human) present always provides for us the pressing questions. We are therefore intensely invested, as Fernand Braudel was in the 1950s, in the idea that

> nothing is more important, nothing comes closer to the crux of social reality, than [the] living, intimate, infinitely repeated opposition between the instant of time and that time which flows only slowly. Whether it is a question of the past or of the present, a clear awareness of this plurality of social time is indispensable to the communal methodology of the human sciences.[40]

As regards our more narrow purview in this volume—literature, history, philosophy, narrative and critical theory, and the arts—we are especially concerned with developing, from a long or "slow" historical perspective, a critical post/humanism that would explore: (1) the significance (historical, sociocultural, psychic, etc.) of human expression, and affectivity, especially as that expression is enmeshed in various ecologies; (2) the impact of technology and new sciences on what it means to be a human self; (3) the importance of art and literature to defining and enacting human selves; (4) the importance of history in defining and re-membering the human; (5) the artistic plasticity of the human; (6) the question of a human collectivity or human "join": what is the value *and* peril of "being human" or "being post/human" together? and

---

37. Halliwell and Mousley, *Critical Humanisms*, 2.
38. Ibid., 16.
39. Chambers, *Culture after Humanism*, 2.
40. Fernand Braudel, "Histoire et sciences sociale: La longue durée," trans. Sarah Matthews, in *Histories: French Constructions of the Past*, ed. Jacques Revel and Lynn Hunt (New York: The New Press, 1995), 117 [115–45].

finally, (7) the constructive *and* destructive relations (aesthetic, historical, and philosophical) of the human to the nonhuman.

Following the example of the important three-volume collection edited by Michel Feher in 1989, *Fragments for a History of the Human Body*,[41] our volume is styled as a gathering of fragments *toward* a history of a humanism that could never be rendered in any sort of monolithic totality, especially if one is convinced (as we are) by the value of a discontinuist historicism in which history is always unfinishable and each temporal period is noncoincident with itself. This is to say, no era can be perfectly captured in our hermeneutic nets as there is never any "pure" or "whole" period to be captured that isn't already riven by its own contradictions and lack of self-knowledge, especially with regard to the active suppression of the fact that the past always inhabits the present (often in uncanny ways), and that the "contemporary" is never really the radical "break" with the past that it often believes itself to be. As Dominick LaCapra has cautioned, each period is always "beset with its own disruptions, lacunae, conflicts, irreparable losses, belated recognitions, and challenges to identity,"[42] and part of the aim of our volume is to make this state of affairs more visible, especially with regard to the supposedly postmodern genesis of the post/human. Similar to Feher and company's aim to provide the broadest and most temporally and geographically varied coverage of the human body's discontinuist history, while also insisting that that same human body is always constructed, always a social formation, and always representational, we too insist on the always provisional and contingent formations of the human, and of various humanisms, over time, while also aiming to demonstrate the different ways in which these formations emerge (and also disappear) in different times and places. There can thus be no "total history" of this state of affairs as it plays itself out in differing historical contexts, but nevertheless, we can see at the same time that defining what "the human" is has always been an agon—always an ongoing, never finished social-cultural-political project. We say also a "vanishing" humanism, mainly to denote the ways in which, as noted above, the foundations of the liberal humanist subject have been roundly critiqued and dismantled in many university discourses, and thus, appears as a "vanishing" figure in the contemporary scene. Indeed, following Foucault's assertion in *The Order of Things* that "man" is an invention of a more recent date than most believe, our volume aims also to demonstrate that the contours of the human figure and the humanisms attached to that figure have always

---

41. Michel Feher, ed. (with Ramona Naddaff and Nadia Tazi), *Fragments for a History of the Human Body*, 3 vols. (Cambridge, MA: Zone Books, 1989).

42. Dominick LaCapra, *History and Memory after Auschwitz* (Ithaca, NY: Cornell University Press, 1998), 24.

been—on both sides of the so-called Enlightenment divide—indeterminate, contestable, slippery, and ephemeral. Post/humanism, as philosophy and also methodology, would best be framed, we believe, by an attention to longer and discontinuist, historical perspectives.

The volume is divided into two sections: the first part (Singularity, Species, Inter/faces) focuses on critical issues that circulate around questions of human "singularity" and human "species," with faces, visages, facades, and/or interfaces serving as the most explicit thought props through which each author approaches the question of human being and human becoming, as well as the undoing of the human. The second part of the volume (Human, Inhuman, Spectacle) concentrates on the relations of the human to the inhuman and the difficulties attendant upon maintaining any sort of line between the two, especially vis-à-vis the analysis of certain aesthetic (and often surreal) spectacles designed to provoke wonder and horror, and to also destabilize the human as a figure of so-called "rational" and/or "humane" impulses. Although all of the essays in the book can be read productively in relation to each other (because each essay, in one form or another, takes up the question of the status—epistemological, ontological, psychic, historical, cultural, aesthetic, and so on—of the human being), the division of the book's contents has been structured to highlight, in the first section, the historical and critical problematics surrounding the attempts (both in the past and the present) to delineate "the human" as a singularity (whether as an individual or as a unique species), and in the second section, to foreground the ethical and cultural dilemmas that arise when the human is marked off from, but also merges with, what is supposedly nonhuman or inhuman. Each section begins with what might be called the most historically mute period—the so-called "prehistoric" (the chapters by Jeffrey Skoblow and Jeffrey Jerome Cohen, respectively)—and then includes chapters that consider instants and events of modern critical thought and/or culture (such as, for example, Claude Romano's "evential" hermeneutics, the surrealist biology of Roger Caillois, the iPod, Freud, Derrida's turn to the animal, biopolitical theory, George Lucas's *THX 1138*, and Samuel Beckett's *Molloy*) in relation to the slower currents of premodern thought and culture that still inhere in the present (such as, for example, the heroic quest, the devotional manual, the Oedipus myth, the chivalric romance, historical saga, and the idealized Lady of troubadour poetry). Finally, the essay by Craig Dionne on Shakespeare, the post/human, and aesthetics constitutes the cautionary cultural-materialist coda to the volume, alerting us, after immersion in the contents of this volume, that while we "must not turn our backs to the subaltern stories outside the manor" (the post/human), we "must [also] be mindful not to aestheticize . . . bare life." In other words, to speak of the post/human (if even in literary texts) is to call attention to forms of life more broadly, and also to *liveliness* and processes of *living,* and thus we must be careful to consider the material ("on the ground") conditions that undergird our theorizing, for *living* itself (human and otherwise) is at stake.

PART I: SINGULARITIES, SPECIES, INTER/FACES

Jeffrey Skoblow opens his discussion of palaeolithic images at Chauvet and Rouffignac in France with a timeline. The paintings and engravings, some 13,000 years old, resemble others extant from the period throughout Europe that are 35,000–40,000 years old. By comparison, the earliest tools, such as a symmetrical hand ax, are 100,000 years old, and Skoblow judiciously suggests we should include them in the catalogue of human representations. Also, 80,000-year-old burials that associate ochre with human remains imply the existence, at that time, of the belief that there is another, or a parallel, life in addition to the present one.

All these manifestations exist in a near-vacuum: we know little about the contexts that surround them. Thus, these human representations are not unlike things or animals: as Georges Bataille phrased it, "Whatever has no meaning for itself is a thing."[43] However closely we attend to them, the results of our efforts are meager. And yet, some paradigms emerge. For instance, the vast majority of portraits bear "no apparent figuratively human dimension: the delicate and expressive muzzles of horses, aurochs and lions, bison and mammoth eyes, horses' manes and bison beards and so on" predominate (48). With more schematic images, such as dots or V-shapes, interpretation is guesswork. A pointy shape can be thingly, animal, or female: "an arrow, a bird track, or a vulva" (49, quoted from Bahn, 159–60). What does that teach us about the human? Skoblow warns that even the modest categories—male/female, animal/human, whole/fragment—used to group these images may be anachronistic. But, as he consoles us, at her most vulnerable, the prehistoric human is also the most recognizable: we can easily embrace undecidability.

Skoblow describes what it was like to be in the caves themselves:

Mammoths, horses, bison, rhinos, and ibex required us to walk around in circles and backwards with our heads back, looking up and spinning to keep the images straight, to see them in their orientations as they crisscrossed and

---

43. Georges Bataille, *Death and Sensuality: A Study of Eroticism and the Taboo,* trans. Mary Dalwood (New York: Walker and Company, 1962), 157.

overlapped and spread across in their rough arc. All are filled with calm, even the ibex running with legs at full stretch, many with eyes that look back at you. Our guide answered questions and by way of wrapping up on the way back, he said, as I understood him, that "of the people who made these things we know nothing but one thing: they are us"—or he may have said "we are them" which, if not exactly the same, amounts to the same thing: what could only be called human. (47–48)

We might say that the cave visitors, then and now, as in Japanese literary contexts, "look like they know *mono no aware*"—that is, they look like poets. We can imagine that cave space filled with sighs: *aware cho* ["to sigh after being stirred by something"].

Eileen A. Joy's "Eros, Event, and Non-Faciality in Malory's 'Tale of Balyn and Balan'" never departs from that sigh-poem space of shared awareness. In *De civitate dei*, Augustine wrote that, unlike all other living creatures and animals, God chose to create the entire race of man from only one individual to bind humans "not only by similarity of nature, but . . . affection."[44] Against Augustine's optimism, Joy argues, most contemporary social theorists—for example, Zygmunt Bauman, Ulrich Beck, Elisabeth Beck-Gernsheim, Anthony Giddens, Scott Lash—regard the late modern individual, as opposed to the premodern person, as cut loose from social bonds. She does not even retain, as a remainder, her own intact selfhood—whatever "intact" might mean. Lash calls her "a combinard" who "puts together networks, constructs alliances, makes deals," and lives in a world of risk and precariousness.[45]

Joy argues that the human has always been in the process of coming unstuck from the consolations of local times and places, and tightly woven family groups, partly because the idea of the heroic individual mastering the world—whether the knight in Camelot or the financier on Wall Street—has been essential to the valorization of the human subject, while at the same time, that same heroic individual can only ever really succeed or fail on the terms set by the group from which she is always coming undone. In Malory's *Morte darthur*, Joy's test case, Balyn, "the knight with two swords," is a medieval combinard just as multi-local and non-linear as Bauman's "liquid modernity." Joy asserts that this contradicts the accounts of the supposedly monolithic and

---

44. Robert Flint, *The Philosophy of History in Europe*, vol. 1. London: William Blackwood and Sons, 1874.

45. Scott Lash, "Foreword: Individualization in a Non-Linear Mode," in *Individualization: Institutionalized Individualism and Its Social and Political Consequences*, eds. Ulrich Beck and Elisabeth Beck-Gernsheim and trans. Patrick Camiller. London: Sage Publications, 2002, ix [vii–xiii].

unified premodernity that acts as a backdrop against which, to paraphrase Carolyn Dinshaw, the modern and postmodern "groovily emerge."[46]

Joy argues that "almost all of our notions of time and temporality are insufficient to [its] weirdness and ungraspability . . . what might be called time's continual and dissonant 'forking'" (55). She reaches out to philosopher Claude Romano's "evential hermeneutics" to argue for a conception of the human person as a type of queer location (a "highly localized site of awareness" in the terminology of medieval historian David Gary Shaw[47]) that is always in the process of "becoming" through the "impersonal events of the world" that never cease "happening" to it (60). In this scenario, Balyn becomes "a nascently (or proto-)modern human individual" who is "thrust, through *aventure*, into the 'compulsive and obligatory self-determination' of a certain alienating *past*modernity" (56). Balyn is not so much a preexisting (and stably human) identity, as he is "a break within the flow" of the "absolute consciousness" (60) of the assemblage of Camelot, especially when caught in the flux of the events of his narrative, which he can never know in advance. Here, there is no becoming-human, only a "*taking place*" in a becoming-world (64).

Tim Spence's "The Book of Hours and iPods, Passionate Lyrics and Prayers" weaves parallels between two media platforms—the medieval prayer book and the personal music device playlist. For Spence, the overarching issue that brings the prayer book and iPods together is "the personal verification and comfort that stems from the habitual use of devotional technologies" (80). Prayers and contemporary songs are also alike in that both rely on a limited vocabulary of personal suffering, particularly in love and love-longing," both forms are intentionally composed in a highly lyrical manner, filled with pathos, and both can be used at will by individual agents to manipulate moods.

Spence divides history into three periods—medieval, modern, and digital—as he compares prayer manuals and mp3 players, devotional songs and rock-n-roll lyrics, all as technologies that individualize us and "allow us

---

46. Dinshaw writes: "Radical hybridity of postmodern identities is bought at the cost of the medieval. Merely displacing rather than eliminating totality (as Paul Strohm has remarked in relation to other postmodern theorists), [Homi] Bhabha produces via a convenient and simplified Benedict Anderson a binary modernist narrative of history—produces a dense, obvious (and white) Middle Ages against which the arbitrary modern groovily emerges—though he routinely critiques such binary narratives in decrying 'teleology and holism.' And this totalizing force applies pressure elsewhere in Bhabha's work; it is no coincidence (at least to this queer medievalist) that his treatment of an undifferentiated, homogeneous distant past intersects with his treatment of sexuality": Carolyn Dinshaw, "Queer Relations," *Essays in Medieval Studies* 16 (1999): 93 [79–94].

47. David Gary Shaw, *Necessary Conjunctions: The Social Self in Medieval England* (New York: Palgrave Macmillan, 2005), 12.

immediate access to our private passions" (91). The twelfth-century Victorines (Hugh, Adam, and others) were instrumental in composing and propagating prayers on Christ's Passion and other practices, later anthologized in the Books of Hours, allowing practitioners to interact "with their prayer books to discover appropriate material for their prayers and meditations, either scripted or original" (69). These practices involved "complex technologies—some cognitive, some concrete," including books, decorations, architectural spaces, calendars, and clocks (69).

Just beyond the edge of the historical density of these technologies, ca. 1500, Spence locates the birthplace—or perhaps more accurately, the College House—of Mr. Cogito, the character in Zbigniew Herbert's poems who embodies "the ironic contrast between an individual borne aloft in an untimely manner by his inner thoughts and the chaotic circumstances in which he finds himself, a world always just outside of the thinking being's control" (71). As Spence argues, "Mr. Cogito replaced Mr. Oratio—or the medieval deference to devotional prayer—at the moment introspective meditation stopped producing prayers and began producing subjective analysis for the self-reflective individual's independent self" (71).

To console herself in her untimely predicament, today's Mlle Cogito participates in a field of technologies that mirror the medieval Mr. Oratio's: "a network of technologies . . . woven together to form a very intimate and sensual relationship between the individual user and a larger, corporate body of being" (72). If for Mr. Oratio that corporation was ecclesiastic, for Mlle Cogito it is, perhaps less glamorously, capitalist. Spence skillfully and dizzyingly juxtaposes the Beguines and the band the Weather Underground, the rosary and the iPod, Goliards and college students, *Carmina Burana* and the band Public Enemy, the mystic Richard Rolle and the band Modest Mouse, dying in a tavern and overdosing, the Word made Flesh and the Digital Age Word that "has become electric." Spence concludes that the study of medieval prayer rituals renders more accessible certain aspects of the digital age that are obscured because of our immersion in them, especially the corporatization of private emotions and the role of the conveyances in habituating our emotions to function within a larger corporate structure that is both "omnipresent and invisible" (88).

Daniel Remein and Anna Kłosowska, in "What *Does* Language Speak: Feeling the Human with Samuel Beckett and Chrétien de Troyes," read *Perceval* (ca. 1165) and *Molloy* (1951) near to each other. Following Heidegger and structuralism, they ask: if language speaks, what is the status of the human—human desire and subjectivity? Perceval and Molloy both have an interesting time naming themselves: their similarities rift the space-time of literary and intellectual history, but the essay is still careful to "not wrest what it calls away from the re/moteness."[48]

Remein and Kłosowska argue that it is the very moment when Molloy and Perceval realize and say aloud their names that a strange infatuation or erotic fixation on an object emerges, recalling the Japanese principle of *mono no aware*, or the Virgilian *lacrimae rerum*, mentioned earlier in this introduction. In Molloy's case, this fixation "amounts to a potential incident of public inanimaphiliac intimacy with a bicycle that seems mechanically impossible" (99). Rather more sublimely, Perceval is transfixed by the procession of a candelabra, a bleeding lance, and the grail. Again, in a striking parallel to the principles of *mono no aware*, Perceval is punished for failing to ask questions about the condition of the Fisher King and thus failing to share his story, the sharing of which is portrayed as the only form of relief for what ails not only the king but also an entire kingdom, turned into a wasteland. Passing from Heidegger to Lacan, Deleuze, and Graham Harman's speculative materialism, Kłosowska and Remein borrow from Reza Negarestani the phrase "complicity with anonymous materials"[49] to point out three similarities between *Perceval* and *Molloy*. First, the narrative structure and content, from the description of the objects (radiance and light) to the hero's naming. Second, the objects in the narratives are not part of nature but rather they are semiautonomous, "somewhere in between tool and matter" (106). Third, these same objects short-circuit the grand isolation of humans from the world of nonhumans.

Remein and Kłosowska use Graham Harman's term *allure*, a "touch without touching," to describe the object's fetching agency. No longer inert or inhuman, Harman's object is radiant matter that, as in medieval physics, sends out beams that effect a cure or provoke longing, passion, and madness. Kłosowska and Remein ask what allure/relation is between the radiant matter, and the being, at the moment of naming—in terms of how they relate to what we would *want* to call human, and they conclude that poetry is the "erotic radiance of language caught on and besotted by fragments" (125). Second, they claim that Chrétien writes enough episodes of erotic co-operations or hybridizations with nonhuman matter to be reclaimed as a Beckettian modernist *avant la lettre*. Reading Chrétien, they submit, is the best training to take pleasure in Beckett—to laugh, frolic, and absurdly giggle as we imagine Molloy with his red rubber bicycle bulb, instead of shrinking from this and other Beckettian texts as if they were grey clouds dripping dour pessimism.

---

48. Martin Heidegger, *Poetry, Language, Thought*, trans. Albert Hofstader (New York: Harper, 1971), 196.

49. Reza Negarestani, *Cyclonopedia: Complicity with Anonymous Materials* (Melbourne: re.press, 2008).

PART II: HUMAN, INHUMAN, SPECTACLE

In "Aninormality," Jeffrey Jerome Cohen asks: what is the role of nonhuman agents in art? Take, for example, the three drops of blood on the snow in Chrétien's *Perceval* or the famous winter scene in *Sir Gawain and the Green Knight*: no amount of research on "Ricardian kingship or contemporary Welsh-English relations" (132) (the human and historical context) can explain their intensity, but neither can research on snowflakes or goose blood (the nonhuman context). Cohen turns to Roger Caillois's 1934 essay on the praying mantis: intrigued by the mantis that plays dead, Caillois notes that her behavior inspires a strange situational lyricism in the driest entomological accounts.[50] Caillois concludes that myths are not only inspired by social phenomena but also by striking natural ones: a slight instance of nonhuman agency, but agency nonetheless. This serves as Cohen's departure point for a consideration of the nonhuman as it is bound up with the human in medieval fabulist art.

Cohen highlights a passage in Caillois's writing on stone,[51] where Caillois talks of the intensities of various agents in three "kingdoms"—geological, vegetal, animal. To each kingdom's particular density corresponds a particular wavelength, speed, or frequency of its art, and since the art is set at different speeds, the mutual reading of each kingdom's art produces the effect of a blurred presence. If we really concentrate our attention, as Caillois and Cohen urge, that presence can be brought out in sharper relief. They both invoke the term *commonality* to represent this network of mutually recognizable (if blurry) yet also imperfectly perceived signals of nonhuman agents that together make up the "aesthetics of the universe."[52] For Caillois, the "mobilizing element" of this commonality across kingdoms is beauty, a general "innate lyricism," a shared "universal syntax."[53] "Natural fantasy" is another name Caillois gives to that nonhuman agency.[54] Caillois does not propose an "evolutionary, cultural or symbolic use value" (140) for nonhuman agency; instead, suggests Cohen, Caillois's idea is that impulse, mobility, or agency are the normal states of the three kingdoms—what Cohen labels their *aninormality*, a suitcase word that brings together the ideas of the animal and the anomalous to break up the definition of normalcy.

---

50. Roger Caillois, "The Praying Mantis: From Biology to Psychoanalysis," in *The Edge of Surrealism: A Roger Caillois Reader* (Durham, NC: Duke University Press, 2003), 66–81.

51. Roger Caillois, *The Writing of the Stones*, ed. Marguerite Yourcenar, trans. Barbara Bray (Charlottesville: University of Virginia Press, 1985).

52. Ibid., 49.

53. Ibid., 104.

54. Ibid., 84.

Against the anxiety that thinking in terms of the nonhuman is tantamount to thinking unkindly or unethically, with "pessimism, even misanthropy" (139), Cohen argues that posthumanism is not less but more caring in trying to "view the world through a less anthropocentric lens" (139). Cohen locates "medieval aninormality" (140) at work in Geoffrey of Monmouth's *History of the Kings of Britain* (ca. 1136) and also in the work of Marie de France (ca. 1160), who weaves a lyrical world of human-animal and human-object hybrids: man-wolf, man-osprey, talking deer, not to mention adventure plots that turn on bits of cloth, knots, and sticks. Cohen's attention to the final image of the earth, in whose porous cavities the heroine of Marie de France's *Yonec* discovers slumbering lovers ready to spring into action in yet-unnarrated stories that mirror her own, helps us to see what Cohen means by inhuman art: the transformative potentiality of stories that always already inheres in the geological crevasses of their landscapes.

In "Humanist Waste," Michael A. Johnson challenges the periodization where Renaissance humanism overcomes the medieval, and postmodern posthumanism overcomes the Enlightenment humanist subject. The Middle Ages, in this periodization, bears persistent material traces of "concepts, identities, and social forms that are always both dead and alive at once" (152). Because "dead and alive at once" has a decidedly excremental ring to it, Johnson's critique of periodization logically focuses on waste. Johnson cites two sides of one particular debate over periodization: representing the medieval troubadour tradition as "proto-humanist," or as antihumanist or inhuman—a tradition, as Johnson points out, "in which a persistent metaphorics of excrement troubles the question of the human" (152). Johnson looks, in medieval and more modern contexts, at technologies of waste disposal, literary and philosophical metaphors of waste, the complex interplay of individual and community "haunted by animal excrement" (152), and waste as a metaphor for a loss of meaning.

Johnson first takes us through the psychoanalytics of excrement. He explains that according to Lacan (via Žižek), the problem of waste disposal is linked to interiority and the distinction between human and animal: humans face shit disposal as a problem, while for animals, lacking an 'interior' of the sort humans experience, shit—this exteriorization of what was once interior—poses no problems. For Freud, the degree of separation from waste—through different means of disposal, repression, and sublimation—is a measure of civilization. Repression may go too far, as in the science fiction dystopian commonplace of the food pill that eliminates eating and waste, perceived negatively as the "imposition of an inhuman exteriority" (154) that is accompanied by other measures that erase interiority and individuality.

A similar example that Johnson turns to is George Lucas's film *THX 1138*, where the protagonist "inserts his wages, in the form of a colored dodecahedron, into a toilet-like device, as though to eliminate the process of consumption and waste altogether" (154), the "toilet" serving as "a vestigial trace of its original function," an absurd scenario that explains why later *THX* cannot mourn his mate: *THX* and others have "no interior, no 'private self,' *because they do not shit*" (155).

Parallel to Karl Steel's discussion of the superlative deliciousness of human flesh (see below), Johnson studies texts that laud the superiority of human excrement. This excellence notwithstanding, waste also stands in metaphorically for a collapse of difference, hierarchy, and value. Johnson guides us through Baudrillard, Freud, and Alenka Zupančič's reading of Lacan, to focus on Lacan's Seminar VII on sublimation, a point (many scholars agree) when Lacan moves from mostly abstract and structuralist language to a more embodied image of subjectivity. Johnson shows that troubadour poetry frequently combines the excremental, the animal, and the feminine, while at the same time these poems "plug up" the Lady's "explosive and filthy materiality through the technological prosthetics of writing" (166). With Lacan, Johnson uses the "scene" of *fin'amors* as a pattern that may help us rethink the human in and against this late-capitalist paradigm we currently inhabit.

Karl Steel's "How Delicious We Must Be / Folcuin's Horse and the Dog's Gowther, Beyond Care" looks at medieval discourses of anthropophagy as a ground of distinction between humans and animals, demonstrating that the binary is never successfully fixed in place. While most treatments of medieval anthropophagy use it as a metaphor—of profanation of the Host; of excessive cruelty or illegitimate government; of the painful formation of subjectivity, allowing psychoanalytic discussions—such metaphorical readings partly efface the visceral horror that Steel aims to restore.

The distinction between flesh and meat is like the distinction between human and animal, the animate—literally, "ensouled," or possessed of a soul or *anima*—and the inanimate. To show how blurry that distinction is, Steel summarizes Christian theories of life, including the commonplace understanding brought to the fore in Giorgio Agamben's *Homo Sacer* that animals possess mere biological life, *zoe* rather than *bios*.[55] The distinctive human characteristics that animals lack are usually defined as reason, language, and soul. Paradoxically, since the humans are superior to animals, their flesh must taste

---

55. See Agamben's introduction to *Homo Sacer: Sovereign Power and Bare Life*, trans. Daniel Heller-Roazen (Stanford: Stanford University Press, 1998).

better than animal flesh. This rather too literal appreciation for human superiority is explicit, as Steel shares, in many medieval texts, including Poggio Bracciolini's tale of a teenage serial killer, a fifteenth-century hunting manual of Edward of York, the story of king Cadwallo in Geoffrey of Monmouth's *History*, the Middle English romance *Richard Coer de Lyon*, the *Chanson d'Antioche*, Marco Polo's account of Japanese customs, and John Mandeville's similar account of the people of Lamore, which all describe human flesh as "the most restorative and most delicious" of meats (176).

Steel asks: what work does the distinction between eating animal and human flesh do? He suggests that the distinction is not intrinsic but rather constructed, a "carnophallogocentrism," as Derrida called it in *The Animal That Therefore I Am*.[56] This makes the horror of anthropophagy seem less noble: not a horror of violating the human, but a horror of violating the human privilege, human "exemption from routine violence." Next, Steel examines medieval alternatives, wherein "medieval people could imagine other relations to the animal, less concerned with violence and saving human privilege" (185). Noting that Cary Wolfe in *Animal Rites* discounts the meaning of such examples for the cultural paradigm because they are exceptions that confirm the rule—"the logic of the pet . . . the individual who is exempted from the slaughter in order to vindicate, with exquisite bad faith, a sacrificial structure"[57]—Steel argues against Wolfe by focusing on two texts where exceptions to the sacrificial economy are never explicitly claimed to serve some purpose, but rather seem to be "interruptions of economy" (idylls or utopias, even stories of companionship): Folcuin of Lobbes's story of a horse that led the funeral procession of its saintly master and afterward refused to carry anyone, and also the Middle English romance *Sir Gowther*, whose hero commits heinous crimes, after which the Pope prescribes as a penance a diet of food snatched from a dog's mouth. A greyhound feeds him "whyte loafe" until Gowther is ready to "forthe gon"—fight and snatch food forcibly from other dogs—in a three-day "hillside idyll" (188). In such stories, says Steel, we learn to "suspend ourselves between two impossibilities: the unjustifiable need to defend ourselves from the appetite of others, and the dizzying fact of temporary mattering, our own and others, within a near universal indifference, where we must make cuts to care, even if what we protect takes no notice of us at all" (192).

---

56. Jacques Derrida, *The Animal that Therefore I Am*, ed. Marie-Louise Mallet, trans. David Wills (New York: Fordham University Press, 2008), 93.

57. Cary Wolfe, *Animal Rites: American Culture, the Discourse of Species, and Posthumanist Theory* (Chicago: University of Chicago Press, 2003), 104.

Daniel Kline's essay, "Excusing Laius: Freud's Oedipus, Sophocles' *Oedipus Rex*, and Lydgate's Edippus," shows how the focus of Lydgate's story, different from Sophocles', can allow us to read the story of Oedipus differently from Freud, more along the lines of Emmanuel Lévinas's critique of Freud. Kline examines the genesis of Freud's theory of the Oedipal complex, citing Lévinas's critique of psychoanalysis as the "end result" of a rationalism—in other words, a humanism—that fails to account for realities more profound than ourselves and that are, ultimately, beyond our intentions. For Kline,

> Freud's Oedipal complex isolates aggression in the child and obfuscates parental responsibility for that violence in much the same way *Oedipus Rex* seems to condemn Oedipus. Thus, the father's violence against the child and the necessity of that violence in constituting the patriarchal family is relocated from age to youth, from external world to internal fantasies, and from the social realm to the intrapsychic. (194)

And yet, in the Oedipus story, "the Sphinx's riddle inheres in the paradox of aging and of retaining identity or sameness within temporal difference" (194). To push against this forgetting of the riddle and against making actual violence in Oedipus only a symbol, and at that, the relatively benign symbol of the social apprenticeship of the healthy individual, Kline underlines that "the Oedipus narrative begins not with the child's violence against the parents, but with attempted infanticide" (195), and he thus shows that Freud's account of Oedipus was a very particular choice, given his knowledge of other versions of the story.

Unlike the Sophocles version that assumes our knowledge of the backstory, medieval versions provide "prologues" to the episodes of patricide and incest, somewhat decentering the latter episodes crucial to Sophocles and Freud. Freud dismissed postclassical versions as religious rewritings that were supposed to inspire piety. Kline walks us through Freud's library in London, stopping at Léopold Constans's 1881 volume on twelfth-century French renditions of Oedipus that Freud heavily marked on almost every page, indicating that medieval versions of the story influenced Freud's thinking on the Oedipal Complex.

As Kline explains, Lydgate's *Siege of Thebes* is likewise based on these French renditions, and Kline attends to the ways in which Lydgate baroquely expanded the encounter with the Sphinx. This provides Kline grounds for a Lévinasian reading that "dismantles the hierarchy of father over son, of parent over child, by observing that the father's exteriority, most clearly present in the other who calls the father to responsibility, is found in, but is not reducible to, the child" (221). Lydgate's "generous and humane" (216) account of Oedipus emphasizes the responsibilities inherent in the parent-child relationship. Conversely, in Lydgate, somewhat surprisingly to modern critics, the horror of incest and patricide committed by Oedipus is not emphasized as much. As Kline suggests, that again allows us to think of Lydgate along the lines of Lévinas and not Freud: "If Freud sees Oedipus as the universal human subject, the autonomous individual who acts in history, Lydgate's Edippus is the exemplary individual who is tethered to" history (222). Lydgate's Lévinasian Oedipus is a creature of "change, not stasis; is embedded in culture, not isolated; adapts to the vagaries of age and change; and remains firmly wedded to the warp and woof of history" (222).

In the volume's cautionary coda, "The Trick of Singularity: *Twelfth Night*, Stewards of the Posthuman, and the Problem of Aesthetics," Craig Dionne reflects on the crisis of the humanities and asks, how are literature and culture relevant if they do not "directly speak to the complexity of the modern world?" (224). Dionne closes with an indelible image from Trevor Nunn's film version of *Twelfth Night*: Feste is banished to the dark world outside. The spectator, placed in the same dark space as Feste, observes the wedding feast through the glowing warm windows of the manor. Dionne enjoins those of us invested in the posthuman turn to not "turn our backs to the subaltern stories outside the manor" (243). We must be mindful of our responsibility to shape a more just society in economic and practical senses.

Dionne opens by evoking Robert Scholes's 2004 MLA presidential address, "The Humanities in a Post-Human World," concerned with religious fundamentalism and the so-called "pragmatic" or "real" neoconservative politics, as well as economics not invested in practices of care. Against the association of the term *posthuman* with these neoconservative political and fanatical religious values that go against the humanities, Dionne defines *posthumanism* as a label for a constellation of theorists and social critics working on the same problem but from positions within different critical discourses, including cyborg theory, informatics, systems theory, queer studies, the turn to the body and to animal rights, new materialism and the turn to ontology, theories coalesced around the BABEL Working Group, and scholars such as Cary Wolfe, Katherine Hayles, Cora Diamond, Ian Hacking, Ralph Acampora, Judith Butler, and others.

In *Twelfth Night*, Dionne sees an already postmodern play that hinges on the problem of defining a singular identity in the face of modernity's blurring of identities, as opposed to a humanist reading of the play as a rehearsal of "Renaissance melancholy or self-consuming love" (228). Among others, Dionne reads Malvolio as "a crude parody of Tudor humanist learning that is meant to bolster traditional venues of social ascension through courtly service" (234) and shows that Malvolio is the exponent of the unorganic, posthuman concept of the subject. Lastly, Dionne sees Malvolio's story as a parable of the academic. Malvolio's contradictory use of materialist language that "speaks us" and individual agency at the same time presages our own plight: "the problem of establishing an aesthetics of difference during a time of great economic, political, and ecological instability—a strangely familiar reminder for humanists that our own professional longing to return to aesthetics might replay something of a return of the repressed" (227).

Dionne closes with an image of reversible consciousness, like the chamois glove that can be turned inside out. If Frederic Jameson's *A Singular Modernity* attributes to film as a medium the rise of the postmodern experience of and preoccupation with contingency—a moviegoer emerging into the bright light experiences the shock of contingency—Dionne notes *Twelfth Night*'s obsession with this problem. We may have brought it to new heights—for example, "in a world of digitalized textual production—out-sourced and team-written texts that appear on the computer screen in a stream from a placeless nowhere"—but the problem was always already there in Orsino's "manic love," "a miming of the itinerant identity that appropriates its oscillating emotional states and shifting standpoints as a form of courtly pastime" (240). It was already there in the figure of Feste and the play's obsession with contingency and bare life, which should force us to examine the conditions of our posthumanist work in our own "manor."

ALL THE WAY TO THE VEGAN DEMON

Jean de la Fontaine (1621–95) once wrote: "If a lute played by itself, I would run away, although I passionately love music."[58] La Fontaine says this à propos of a scene in Apuleius's *Psyche*, which he translated, where the young woman, Psyche, marries a powerful man whom she cannot see, Cupid, and lives in a castle surrounded by a post/human kind of opulence and love: a castle filled with invisible servants and musicians. The tableau of post/human musical performance is so insufferable for La Fontaine that he adds harp-playing nymphs to explain where the music comes from. But anyone who has seen Jean

---

58. Jean de la Fontaine, "Preface," *Amours de Psiché et de Cupidon* (Paris: Claude Barbin, 1669), n.p. This phrase is picked up in André Gide's *Journal* (13 October 1927).

Cocteau's 1946 film *La Belle et la bête* is aware that charm and grace, desire and pleasure don't need human agents: a partly human beast, rows of moving disembodied hands, and other human fragments all contribute to a breathtaking love story. In La Fontaine's own seventeenth century, extended thought experiments relegated humans to insignificance, as in a reflection on cabbage in Cyrano de Bergerac's famous science fiction novel, *State and Empire of the Moon* (1657). Bergerac's protagonist encounters a vegan Demon so particular that he will only eat those vegetables that died of natural causes. Harvesting a live cabbage, wounding it with a knife, would have been unconscionable and unnatural:

> Is not this cabbage, as you are, a part of Nature? Is she—Nature—not the mother of both of you equally? It even seems to me that she made provisions with a greater urgency for the vegetative rather than for the reasonable kind, since she left the engendering of men to the caprice of their fathers who can, as they please, engender them or not: a stricture with which she did not, however, choose to afflict the cabbage: because instead of leaving the germination of the sons to the fathers' discretion, as if she were more apprehensive that the cabbage race might die out than the human race, she constrained them willy nilly to give being to one another, and not at all as it is with men, who only engender children by caprice, and who can only engender twenty at the most throughout their lifetime; while cabbages can produce four hundred thousand per head. To say that Nature loved man more than cabbage is to tickle yourself to make yourself laugh. . . . add that man cannot be born without sin . . . while we know full well that the first cabbage had never offended its Creator.[59]

And then, in the Demon's imaginary account, the cabbage speaks. That, as Joanna Zylinska insists, is a neat way to think about the ethics of the post/human turn. "What if x responded?" can be a useful touchstone in theorizing the ethics of the nonhuman. As Zylinska says, when we dismantle the hierarchy, we open the possibility of a better ethics. An ethics that is open ended, based on "a prior demand on those of us who call themselves humans to respond to the difference of the world critically and responsibly, without taking recourse all too early to pre-decided half-truths."[60] As we follow Zylinska,

---

59. Cyrano de Bergerac, *Histoire comique des etats et empire de la lune*, in *Oeuvres*, vol. 2 (Amsterdam: Jacques Desbordes, 1709), 83–85.

60. Joanna Zylinska, "Bioethics Otherwise, or, How to Live with Machines, Humans, and Other Animals," in *Telemorphosis: Theory in the Era of Climate Change*, vol. 1, ed. Tom Cohen (Ann Arbor: Open Humanities Press/MPublishing), 2012. (203–25).

let us take comfort in the familiarity of the thought exercise that allows us to imagine "x" responding, a post/human exercise that by far predates what we call modernity, as this volume well attests.

Thought experiments, texts, narratives, and other ways to think *with*, and not merely *about*, nonhumans are collected in the chapters of this volume. These chapters amount to something like cognitive engineering, because they allow us to think a little farther beyond ourselves. And, we inherit these thought experiments from a premodern world that extends all the way to the bear nests in prehistoric caves. Moving closer to the present, these thought experiments extend to vegan Aristoxenus and succulent vegetarian Pythagoras; moving closer still, to the medieval Marie de France, whose protagonists fall for avian boyfriends; to the three drops of goose blood that make Chretien's Perceval think about Blancheflor; to the greyhound who feeds a knight; and all the way to the scientific revolution of the 1650s when Bergerac's super-vegan Demon converses with cabbage. Was there resistance to these thought experiments? Yes, as La Fontaine's alteration of the myth of Cupid and Psyche shows. Did the post/human imagination always exist in explicit, self-aware and mainstream ways? To that question, we offer a resounding "yes"—not least because much of post/human thought seems to correlate with an ethical imperative to not diminish and avariciously contract the world, but rather to expand the scope of human sympathy and ethical being.

PART I

Singularities, Species, Inter/faces

CHAPTER 1

Paleolithic Representations of Human Being at Chauvet and Rouffignac

JEFFREY SKOBLOW

> Whatever has no meaning for itself is a thing.
> —Bataille

WHAT DOES IT MEAN "to be human"? What does "human" mean? What is "human"?

Bataille says that "to some extent the originality of the [Kinsey] Reports" on human sexuality "is that they discuss sexual conduct as one discusses things"; but something "could only be thought of as a thing," he notes, "if we had the power to abolish it and to go on living as if it did not exist."[1] The question of "the human" poses similar problems. Defining the word ourselves—and who else *would* define it?—ultimately amounts to circular thinking, the word used in its own definition. The "human," at least, is clearly not something we can imagine ourselves doing without and carrying on as if nothing had changed.

---

1. Georges Bataille, *Erotism: Death and Sensuality*, trans. Mary Dalwood (San Francisco: City Lights Books, 1986), 152, 158.

Another way to say this is that the concept "human" remains ever unfixed, never defined but always in dynamic process of self-definition—it is a commonplace to say so, perhaps, at least in certain contemporary critical circles. For Cary Wolfe, for instance, the category of "the human" is so deeply unstable that "the ontological difference between human and animal" becomes "more or less permanently unsettle[d]," leaving only "a palpable nostalgia for the human."[2] "The species distinction between *Homo Sapiens* and everything else," Wolfe goes on, is not "automatically coterminous" with "the theoretical, ethical, and political question of the subject"; in other words, "the human" is not reducible to—and is even to some extent misrepresented by—any system of thought (theoretical, ethical, political) with which we might try to apprehend it.[3] Thus the term or concept of "the human" remains open, not only virtually endlessly plastic but hardly even definable or conceivable, like Lacan's sex: "The sexual relation cannot be written.... Everything that is written is based on the fact that it will be forever impossible to write the sexual relation as such."[4] All reflections on the "sexual," as on the "human," however coolly rational and systematic they may be, are subject to a kind of ontological implosion: our perspective on the problem is helplessly entangled; we'll never get it off us. What this means for scholarship on the subject is dizzying to contemplate (dizzying to the point of nauseating, at times, the snake consuming its own tail). At the very least, we could say, the form and voice of such scholarship should be more than usually reflective upon itself and on the fragility of its claims. Whatever in the way of form or voice might be taken for granted, can be examined and recast in the always renewed exchange between writer and reader. Writing and reading, like the sexual and the human, are ever-unfixable terms, conceptions of ourselves we cannot think our way out of. Detachment is not a possibility. Old news.

The earliest (surviving) representations of human being—that is, images of human bodies or parts of human bodies—are dated now between 35,000 and 40,000 years ago, unless one considers (as well one might) a symmetrical hand ax from 100,000 (or for that matter a million) years ago to be a representation of the human in a more abstract sense. The earliest *figurative* representations that survive are dated around 35,000–40,000 BP (Before Present), and in Europe (which is where most of the oldest evidence has been found, for reasons having to do in part with climate and with sources of economic

---

2. Cary Wolfe, *Animal Rites: American Culture, the Discourse of Species, and Posthumanist Theory* (Chicago: University of Chicago Press, 2003), 48.

3. Ibid., 1.

4. Quoted in Peggy Phelan, *Unmarked: The Politics of Performance* (London and New York: Routledge, 1993), 6.

investment in research), they seem to coincide with the encounter between *Homo sapiens sapiens* and *Homo neanderthalensis* (or *Homo sapiens neanderthalensis*), as if a certain level of self-reflection required a type of Self reflected in the form of an Other. These earliest images of humans are contemporaneous with the earliest figurative representations of other creatures as well. Some of these representations at this earliest point are three-dimensional objects, such as the "hybrid figure that is half woman, half lion" (although Paul Bahn says "opinions differ as to whether it is male or female") from Hohlenstein-Stadel, Germany—a lion's head on an upright, bipedal body carved in mammoth ivory—or the "apparent phallus sculpted on root of a bovid incisor tooth";[5] and some images are engraved or drawn/painted on rock wall. Chauvet Cave, located in the Ardèche region of southeast France, provides one of the earliest and most spectacular cases of the latter, with reference both to Paleolithic parietal art generally and to human representation in particular.

Chauvet was decorated over the course of six thousand years, with the most intense artistic activity apparently concentrated in two periods of a thousand or so years each, the first beginning 32,000 BP and the second ending around 26,000 BP, according to Carbon 14 measurements judged to be "coherent."[6] Human representation is scarce and fragmentary, relative to the representations of animals with which the cave abounds—horses, rhinos, lions, aurochs, mammoth, ibex, bison, bear, hyena, musk ox, deer, and reindeer (and one owl); but these few images have an intensity of placement and treatment that, on top of their scarcity and their subject, demands attention. According to the French team directed by Jean Clottes, "There are six . . . depictions that are indisputably human" in Chauvet, in addition to other possible "anthropomorphous anatomical segments," as well as "six complete hand prints and five red hand stencils" and hundreds of palm prints (some of them "covered in ochre") and dots apparently made by fingers, all found throughout the cave.[7] Of these six indisputable figures, five are described as "pubic triangles on the cave's walls," four of which stand more or less alone, "isolated from any other anatomical segment," the fifth of which "is associated with other elements of the body . . . and, quite certainly," Yanik Le Guillou affirms, "with a complex,

---

5. Randall White, *Prehistoric Art: The Symbolic Journey of Humankind* (New York: Harry N. Abrams, 2003), 73, 74; Paul Bahn and Jean Vertut, *Journey through the Ice Age* (Berkeley: University of California Press, 1997), 100.

6. Jean Clottes et al., *Chauvet Cave: The Art of Earliest Times*, trans. Paul Bahn (Salt Lake City: University of Utah Press, 2003), 32.

7. Ibid., 167, 164. Jean Clottes is perhaps the preeminent contemporary expert on Paleolithic art. The recent discovery of Chauvet in 1994, and the pristine condition in which its discoverers left it, have provided an unparalleled opportunity to make the most careful and intensive study of the space, which Clottes was the natural choice to supervise and direct.

exceptional, even fundamental composition in the minds of those who came to draw it at the end of the cave," "a composite being, half-man and half-animal, nicknamed the 'Sorcerer' since its discovery" that is the sixth human figure.[8] All six of these figures appear at one extreme end of the cave, in the End Chamber and the adjacent Megaloceros Gallery, with the fifth "pubic triangle" and its associated "Sorcerer" (which, on the basis of dating nearby images, would appear to belong to the first period of activity in the cave)[9] placed for maximum impact, hanging down from the "ceiling" of the cave on a pendant spur of rock facing the left wall of the End Chamber: both wall and pendant spur are instantly visible upon entering the space, and the extraordinary panels of images on the wall—lions, rhinos, mammoths, mostly, with bison and horse represented as well—which wrap around behind the "composite being" give the human figure(s) the appearance of a witness or master of ceremonies.

Of the pubic triangles, "three are engraved and two are black," but otherwise the treatment is "very similar. All are drawn about 1.80 m (almost 6 feet) above the floor, and are of similar dimensions, slightly bigger than lifesize." "A strongly curving line forms the . . . upper contour. A continuous line or two unjoined lines . . . indicate the fold of the groin. The upper junction of these lines [is] open, or closed, . . . [t]he vulvar cleft. . . clearly indicated by a vertical line" and "the cleft. . . then engraved, [the] incision . . . marked so strongly that it removed both the black pigment and the rock's yellow surface film."[10] Such images come down to us throughout the Paleolithic era, and along with the widespread appearance of sculpted female figurines across Eurasia from southern France to the Urals around 28,000 BP (and beginning as early as 40,000 BP, as we have recently learned), they clearly indicate a deep preoccupation with the "female"; this is not necessarily the same question as the "human," although their apparent conflation is suggestive. The "female" may be an earlier conception than the "human" or the first form in which the "human" appears, to judge from this earliest evidence. Or, put another way: the human is always gendered, evidently impossible to conceive otherwise without ceasing to be human, which would tend to support both Bataille's and Lacan's claims with which I began. There is no consideration of the human without "the sexual relation," just as there would appear at this earliest point to be no consideration of human being without its relation to (if not enclosure within) "animal being." But beyond this, what the earliest human visitors to Chauvet meant or understood by these images remains a mystery.

---

8. Ibid., 167, 170.
9. Ibid., 33.
10. Ibid., 167.

The "Sorcerer" and the pubic form "associated with other elements of the body" are in some ways less fragmentary images than the other "pubic triangles," although not necessarily less disembodied. In this case, "the pubis is clearly marked" but "the legs, with fleshy thighs, end as points," "the feet are missing," and "all of the upper part of the body is absent"; indeed, for some time after the discovery of the image in 1994, it remained unseen, and only "quite recently," after "photographing all faces of the pendant," was it "noticed that this vulva was not isolated, but associated with two legs that evoke the bottom of a woman's body."[11] The other or related figure, "the so-called Sorcerer," consists of a powerfully drawn bison head, with vivid eye, curving horns, and a sensitive muzzle, as if leaning over the pubic triangle or about to drink from the bowl of its curved upper line; and a hump that rises behind the head, then curves downward giving the figure a distinctly "upright stance" with tapered human legs (or as Clottes says, "what have been interpreted as human legs"), again without feet or ends of any kind.[12] There is a distinctly human arm, with faintly visible but distinct fingers (the observation is by Le Guillou) hanging down in ordinary human posture—this arm following the line of the leg to one side of the pubis, as if the hand were resting on the bison-figure's own knee, as if the bison-figure and the pubis shared a leg.

What is human? On the evidence of these images from Chauvet, "the human" is marked by gender and/or sexual identity, and by relations to animal being that are at once a matter of blurred boundaries and sharp distinctions. These features of Paleolithic art have been clear at least since Andrei Leroi-Gourhan's work in the 1950s and 1960s, in which he posits a strict correlation between genders and specific animals (e.g., horses—even female horses—are "male," bison are "female"), reading their arrangements in relation to one another in the caves as an extended mythos or narrative of gender—even if the specific claims he makes (e.g., horses are "male" etc.) have been largely discredited as an overly systematic and conjectural explanation.[13] Humanity, animality, sexuality: these are at least some of the topics of Chauvet, although it is important to remember as always that these are *our* (contemporary) topics and may or may not approximate what Paleolithic human beings were thinking when they made or viewed these images.

---

11. Ibid., 170, 142.
12. Ibid., 140, 142, 170.
13. See André Leroi-Gourhan, *Treasures of Prehistoric Art* (New York: Abrams, 1966) and *Les religions de la Prèhistoire* (Paris: Presses Universitaires de France, 1964); for the best brief account in English of Leroi-Gourhan's theories, see Clayton Eshleman, *Juniper Fuse: Upper Paleolithic Imagination and the Construction of the Underworld* (Middletown, CT: Wesleyan University Press, 2003).

Figures such as "The Sorcerer"—that is, animal heads on human bodies—also come down to us throughout the Paleolithic; if not as numerous as the pubic triangles or the female figurines, they are still one of the signature features of this 25,000-year tradition. They have been understood by some to represent a sort of shaman figure, which seems an altogether fair hypothesis taken loosely—that is, taking it as given that these "combined" images are not necessarily literal representations of Paleolithic shamans, in the same way that the images of animals are not necessarily literal representations of animals—knowing as we do nothing (or next to nothing) about the systems of signification within which these images were made and first seen. (It would be like trying to understand an image of the Virgin Mary without knowledge of Christianity, monotheism, or even the notion of a god or gods.) David Lewis-Williams, along with Jean Clottes and Clayton Eshleman, has presented this "shamanic" reading most forcefully as a way of understanding Paleolithic art generally, backed by extensive research into contemporary and historical shamanic cultures and phenomena. Jean-Pierre Mohen has said, however, "that such figures are neither sorcerers nor shamans, but imaginary beings with their own distinct identity . . . [not] wearing masks or disguises . . . [but] composite, semi-divine creatures."[14] Whether these figures are depictions of shamans or less representational figures engaged in some shamanic activity, exploring some human-animal threshold, the general point would seem to hold that they "suggest a merged perception of humans and the animal kingdom."[15] Other figures deeply suggest this as well: we have the famous figure of the Scene in the Shaft at Lascaux (17,000 BP)—a stick-figure human with a bird-head mask of some kind and a staff seemingly topped by a bird or bird-handle, lying as if prostrate stiff before a large, powerfully drawn, semi-eviscerated bison—and the dancing upright bison of Gabillou (17,000 BP) and hybrid human-bison figures of Trois-Frères (16,000 BP), one a "hopping bison-headed man with female figure inside of him," along with another "Sorcerer" or "combined figure" at Trois-Frères, one of the most famous images in Paleolithic art, a "humanlike figure, with its head obliterated and wearing deer antlers," which "has adopted a quadruped posture leaving its sexual organs clearly visible beneath a long, somewhat equine looking tail."[16] All of these plainly suggest that, at the very least, concepts of humanity and animality were in dialogue with one another. Other figures come into play as well, not clearly

---

14. Jean-Pierre Mohen, *Prehistoric Art: The Mythical Birth of Humanity*, trans. John Tittensor (Paris: Pierre Terrail, 2002), 183.

15. Clottes et al., *Chauvet Cave*, 203.

16. Eshleman, *Juniper Fuse*, 155; Mohen, *Prehistoric Art*, 183.

shamanic though clearly transformative, such as the "bison-women" of Pech-Merle, which date from somewhere between 26,000 and 13,000 BP (Bahn calls these figures "probably Solutrean," that is, some 18,000–22,000 BP)—four drawings in proximity to one another, in which "a bison outline appears to be gradually transformed into a schematic female in profile"—or, in El Castillo, the bison upright on its own bison legs, half of it shaped naturally by the rock and half of it painted around 13,000 BP, a figure human in nothing except its posture.[17] What all of these figures mean, or meant, how they functioned (if that's the right word) for their artists (if that's the right word) and for others who saw them in the Paleolithic caves, again, will probably never be known in any but a most conjectural way, a matter of arguments accounting for details, rather than anything "indisputable." It would seem safe to say that religion, or what we call religion, is involved somehow—that is, some conception of an afterlife, or perhaps more precisely, an other-life (burials, often showing ochre in association with the skeletal remains, have been dated as early as 90,000 BP, with several well-substantiated claims reaching back even further, and were likely a long-established practice by the time of Chauvet)—though what "religion" means in any specific sense here does not reveal itself.

The earliest appearance of an image of the human head (without hybrid-animal form) may date, like Chauvet, to the Aurignacian period, which begins roughly 35,000 BP, with a female head carved in mammoth ivory, the so-called Lady (or Venus) of Brassempouy, although the dating and even the authenticity of this object have been questioned. More certainly with the Gravettian period, beginning around 28,000 BP, we see the representation of human heads proliferate, in general associated with the female figurines mentioned earlier, that is, as heads on bodies sculpted or carved out of ivory or various kinds of stone. The majority of these figures are faceless, their heads mere round balls, although several contain or display head coverings that may evoke hair or some other material. The Brassempouy figure is unusual although not unique in this regard, having both an elaborate head covering and the marked indications of a face: a fully sculpted nose and brow ridges, cheekbones and chin. All lack feet as well, like the pendant figure in Chauvet's End Chamber, and most lack indications of arms, emphasizing instead a sense of corpus as a whole, almost like a (slightly elongated) ball manifest in breasts, belly, buttocks, thighs. These figures too would seem to have participated in some elaborate ritual system—many, as at Dolní Věstonice (27,000 BP) in the Czech Republic and Avdeevo (21,000 BP) on the Russian Plain, were found buried

---

17. Eshleman, *Juniper Fuse*, 165; Bahn and Vertut, *Journey Through the Ice Age*, 192.

in pits arranged in relation to living spaces—the details of which are largely unrecoverable.

What Eshleman says of one cave in the French Dordogne, dated around 13,000 BP, certainly applies to Paleolithic representations of human beings more generally: "The human figurations in Combarelles as a whole are open to wide interpretation because of their indeterminacy." He goes on: "Many look as if they were done in the dark. Lines straggle this way and that. Some of them suggest anatomical shapes, but never depict the human figure as a finished or closed unit, with a bounding line separating it from its environment. The Combarelles figures, more than any others, present hominids as wispy creatures, as unstable as fog."[18] To the extent that these figures are particularly difficult to read, as they are sometimes carved faintly in rock wall already heavily marked by natural grooves and striations, the characterization ("more than any others") is apt, although the claim as a whole ("indeterminacy," "wispy," "unstable") would seem to apply to the whole range of Paleolithic depictions of human being, making Combarelles merely one (astonishing) variation on a general condition. The faces that begin to appear (somewhat enclosed, though never what you would call finished forms) in the Magdalenian period, beginning around 18,000 BP, share the same condition. From this point forward we begin to see human faces a bit more consistently, and on a wider range of supports (including cave walls), seemingly more varied in context—but here the picture gets, if anything, even more indecipherable.

How can we even begin to look at these faces? To begin with, we must remember that the process of getting to these Paleolithic faces—the earliest of ourselves we can look in the eye, so to speak—is a difficult one (both complicated and complex, that is, both composed of many steps and, at its root, not simply defined or definable) and that this difficulty, this process, is part of the meaning, or the being, that these representations hold for us. The difficulty is both practical—that is, getting to where the images are, in order to see them—and conceptual. Alphonso Lingis's meditations on symbiosis and interrelatedness among all creatures, and on the artificiality and precariousness of all category boundaries between and within all beings, argue this very point, not with regard to Paleolithic representations of faces, but as it were to all faces (and bodies), represented or actual, prehistoric or contemporary. Lingis speaks of

> the human form and the non-human, vertebrate and invertebrate, animal and vegetable, conscious and unconscious movements and intensities in us

---

18. Eshleman, *Juniper Fuse*, 153.

*that are not yoked to some conscious goal or purpose that is or can be justified
in some capitalist program for economic growth or some transcendental or
theological fantasy of object-constitution or creativity seated in us.*[19]

"Our muscular and vertebrate bodies," he goes on, "transubstantiate into ooze, slime, mammalian sweat, and reptilian secretions, into minute tadpoles and releases of hot moist breath nourishing the floating microorganisms of the night air," and these boundary blurrings extend, for Lingis, even to our relations with "household utensils, tools, and machines."[20] Given these conditions of existence, the very notion of "the human" becomes a makeshift affair, ever-fluctuating in its parameters; within such a conceptual landscape, "to seek out a face," Lingis writes, "is to put a question to it," which "is already an order, a command"—that is, already a kind of presupposed answer or set of expectations as to what we will find in the face. These expectations, however, can never be true to the full range and complexity of the object in all its "movements and intensities."[21]

Language itself, of course, is part of the problem here, since to speak at all is to make distinctions, as between human and nonhuman, or human and "toucans and wolves, jellyfish and whales," which do not exist beyond the constructed system of meanings within which they have currency.[22] Eshleman's chief thesis, in fact, is that Paleolithic art represents the protracted anxiety in human development with regard to this separation of the human from the animal—or our earliest consciousness of this separation, related perhaps in part to the development of hunting technology (spear throwers) that allowed killing at long(er) distances. Language is the mark of this separation as well as its engine: the subject here is literally unspeakable.

Yet the images in the caves remain and compel us to find ourselves in them. Difficult to access and vexed in conception or not, our recognition of them in the sensory immediacy of the encounter is instantaneous and complete, as if to look at them is to say: I made that.

Each cave presents its particular difficulties and irreducible materialities. At Rouffignac, now, you board a little train that sits on thin tracks and makes a quiet noise as it rides along on its electric engine, and you descend about a mile into the cave—a journey that is at once into deep time and (how could

---

19. Alphonso Lingis, "Animal Body, Inhuman Face," in *Zoontologies: The Question of the Animal*, ed. Cary Wolfe (Minneapolis: University of Minnesota Press, 2003), 166 [165–82], my emphasis.
20. Lingis, "Animal Body," 172, 167.
21. Ibid., 179, 166.
22. Ibid., 168.

it be otherwise) as contemporary as can be. The caves themselves shape the story of what humans have done in them for thousands of years, in part by providing a further sense of scale, in that the caves themselves are very much older still, spaces to which human presence comes very late and with a powerful sense of entering another world beyond our own time, somehow obscurely underlying the world we live in, day and night normally. These are the spaces in which the paintings and markings are seen, and from which they are inseparable. At Rouffignac, the cave is long and regularly shaped, with even, rounded dimensions—in my memory, a tube through the rock. It reaches down a long way at a gentle angle and then turns sharply to the right and goes a long way at the same steady slope, then branches into two more irregular, widening and narrowing galleries before trickling off into tight crevices and small chambers below and beyond. Water running over millions of years, and millions of years gone, carried rock down into fine grains and jumbles, clogging the ends of the passages out of sight; I imagine it a river, for the round regular breadth of the passage, the flow of the walls as I remember them, though the process is more likely to have been "longue et insidieuse," in Jean Plassard's words, "essentielement chimique, . . . une dissolution des matières carbonatées [dans] la roche" ["long and insidious," "essentially chemical . . . a dissolution of carbonate materials in the rock"].[23] The rock itself, exposed now as the walls and ceiling and floor of the cave, is said to have been laid down in the Cretaceous Period, some eighty million years ago, when the place was under a sea that, some fifteen million years later, had withdrawn under the force of tectonic and climatic changes. The water that hollowed the rock is said to have begun flowing around sixty-five million years ago and to have flowed for sixty million or more—there is water still in some of the more inaccessible reaches of the lower chambers and passages. Thousands upon thousands of generations of cave bears, over dozens of thousands of millennia, had found the space open and habitable to them, apparently three distinct species of them, all gone for thousands of years before humans first came upon the place thirteen thousand years ago. The bears left what look like small, smooth craters, some nearly a meter deep and several meters wide, along a whole stretch just off the main channel, what the scientists call nests, produced by all those millennial generations of bears turning circles before bedding down to sleep through deep long winters. The bears also left claw marks on the walls, *griffades d'ours* in the once soft clay about the level of a tall man's head or a little higher.[24] In some places,

---

23. Jean Plassard, *Rouffignac: Le Sanctuaire des Mammouths* (Paris: Editions du Seuil, 1999), 14; translations mine.

24. Ibid., 16.

the lines made by humans cross these *griffades d'ours*, which resemble one of the basic hash-mark patterns of the human engravings, naturally enough, which can easily make the bears appear to be one type of inspiration among others for those who decorated the cave. By the time of Rouffignac, people had been gouging and painting cave walls for over 20,000 years and must have had many and complex sources of inspiration; but these crossed lines, man-made and bear-made, do suggest at least a kind of dialogue, maybe a momentary one, in the act of one line encountering another, if not a foundational inspiration at least a side-conversation within the larger project of decorating the wall. Bumps and concavities and curving edges of the rock are also frequently incorporated into images painted throughout the Paleolithic (as noted earlier with reference to El Castillo), often appearing to be what suggests the image in the first place. Sometimes, in other words, the conversation seems to be not with animals but with the rock—the cave—itself.

The maps supplied by the Plassards show areas of the cave where the track does not reach, where nobody goes now except very rarely a very few, carefully selected people (scientists, photographers), and where works of great beauty remain: the entire branching formation of the Galerie du Plafond aux Serpentines and the Salon Rouge, as well as the further reaches of both Galerie Breuil and the chamber beyond the Grand Plafond.[25] Rouffignac has four images of human heads, and none of these is visible from the track, although some are in crevices off the central chamber of the Grand Plafond, where visitors can step off the train and gaze up at the great display overhead. One of these unseen images is called the Great Being: a human profile facing left, drawn in black and near life-size, with a bison above and a bison below it also in black but not to scale, among other bison and mammoths, six of each, and a horse.[26] The bison below the human head is horizontal and stationary, the one above drawn vertically, its forehooves spread ramping, its head taut, its back and hindquarters not shown. The Great Being may resemble a kind of thought emerging from the head of the bison grazing at rest, below, and giving rise to the bison above it, with its different step, a different fire in its eye. The Great Being would appear to be an androgynous figure, or rather, an ungendered figure almost mistakable for a skull, all the matter of a few deft lines: a slightly crumpled, egg-shaped braincase with no representation of hair or other individualizing features, an overlarge eye and a blunt nose, a mouth curving in a

---

25. The Plassards are the family that owns the land near the town of Rouffignac under which the cave is found; they have been its caretakers and chief students, and the main disseminators of what we know about the place.

26. Plassard, *Rouffignac*, 58, 86; see also Marie-Odile and Jean Plassard, *Visiter la Grotte de Rouffignac* (Luçon: Editions Sud Ouest, 1995), 28.

long slow grin, perhaps, of stupefaction or benediction, benign and spooky all at once. The gaze is forward and inward at once. This Being, with the mammoths and bison and horse around it, is to be found in the well at the edge of the Grand Plafond, dozens of meters down and difficult of access. In one of the three photos I have of the Great Being, lit somewhat differently, a formation of rock seems to take the shape of its nose, more prominent but in the right position and of reasonable proportions, and the other, drawn nose takes the form of a squiggle mouth.[27] The long line that had been the mouth becomes a jaw, and the jawline an indication of the neck. Issues of lighting seem clearly to be critical in the encounter with cave art, but again, what specific forms this encounter took in terms of flickering movement and shadow casting, is impossible to read anymore.

The second and third heads at Rouffignac appear together at the end of one of the far reaches of the Galerie Breuil, just at the point beyond which the people of the Magdalenian seem not to have penetrated. They are referred to in the literature as Adam and Eve, although no gender markings in this case are evident.[28] (While gender markings are often prominent in human representations—as in animal representations—throughout the Paleolithic, many representations of heads alone are not so marked.) Both again are heads in profile, facing each other, both more fully grotesque or schematic, more cartoonish doodle, than the Great Being, and both etched rather than painted, simple outlines transfigured in some scene of weird mirth. The head on the left is bigger, over two feet tall, with a crumpled, egg-shaped dome like the Great Being, but facing the other way, with a comically elongated and sharply *retroussé* nose, a blank mouth open in a permanent grin, a chinless flap of a jaw like a puppet, and one big eye shaped like a broken kidney. The smaller head faces this eye as an infant may be held to face a parent, but with no eye itself. It has a more smoothly rounded dome, in fact a "visage tout en rondeur" ["very round face"], a somewhat less grotesque but still absurd nose, and a similarly empty mouth appearing a bit less rapacious, perhaps, than the other.[29] They seem to be laughing and nodding together or in a shared dream of their mouths working, just heads with mouths and noses. In the photo of the Great Being in which its nose is seen to be figured in rock, not drawn but a facet of the rock wall catching the light, that nose resembles these noses, more burlesque riff than design, pliant appendages to go with the empty receptacles of the mouths of Adam and Eve. Human digital scratch marks resembling

---

27. Idem, *Visiter la Grotte*, 28.
28. Idem, *Rouffignac*, 58.
29. Ibid., 59.

griffades d'ours cross in horizontal bands of two or three below the seeming scene, crossing the lines of the larger head itself in some places, most noticeably at what would appear to be its sinuous horizontal throat, and just touching the base of a line of the smaller head at what would appear to be the back of a disproportionately long neck.

The fourth head I've only heard described.[30] It is to be found in another far branch of the Galerie Breuil, not at but near the end of the explored area, like Adam and Eve and the Great Being on the verge of a darkness apparently never entered. A third far branch of the Galerie Breuil ends with a frieze of tectiform shapes, like an arrow pointing upward from a base, another unusual configuration at the limit of Magdalenian discovery, which Rouffignac shares with several nearby caves: Font-de-Gaume, Les Combarelles, Bernifal. In the case of the fourth anthropomorph, as Plassard calls it, what lies beyond, before darkness, is only an especially spare mammoth, a black line from the top of the trunk over the dome of the head and the hump and slope of the back, with a dash of an eye and a flap of an ear, one of the figures farthest from the exterior world. The human head is apparently hardly elaborated at all, marked only by a deep mouth and a treatment of the back of the skull that don't permit identifying the engraved figure as any other kind of animal. This head, alone among the four, belongs to a body with extremities, which is, however, even more fully schematized, a body and extremities otherwise fully without detail, appearing to be crawling, or creeping, from a small hollow ("un petit gouffre"), or what might be translated as a chasm or abyss, in the wall.[31] In what direction is not indicated. The mammoth beyond faces left.

Thus end the three main branches at the end of the central passageway of the Galerie Breuil. The ends of the other main passageways are also unseen by riders on the little train at Rouffignac. Beyond the Grand Plafond at the point where the cave branches further is a figure known as the Pharaoh, which is generally considered among the bison, but which bears distinct humanoid elements in its face: an engraved profile facing right of a blunt bison face from the stylized hump rising behind the forehead, with two curving horns done in good perspective, down the slope of the nose and the chin, to a prominent beard jutting forward.[32] (The hump, which can resemble a Pharaoh's headgear, and the hieratic profile of the beard, suggest the figure's name.) A similar beard can be found on an exquisite bison drawn in black near the center of the Grand Plafond, but there, the presence of forelegs and the less ambiguous

---

30. Ibid.
31. Ibid.
32. Ibid., 51.

indication of a back, behind the hump, make clear the nature of the animal in spite of its seemingly human eyebrow and expressive mouth. With the Pharaoh, no legs are indicated, and the line made with a single finger moving back from the chin-beard recedes quickly as if the line of a sinuous thrusting horizontal throat, more elongated than on the bearded bison of the Grand Plafond, more like the throat of the large laughing head in the Galerie Breuil. And with the Pharaoh, the line of the back crosses some other digital doodles, three fingers together in a meandering pattern, or two fingers, and a single such line crosses the entire figure at the forehead, between the horns. Apparently these doodles precede the Pharaoh, although at one point of crossing at least the evidence is ambiguous, whereas the doodles around the laughing head seem to have come after the head itself. The eye of the Pharaoh can appear to be oriented frontally, which has a particularly transforming effect. Further mammoths, a tiny bison, and what might be a saiga antelope lie beyond.

Another head, which Plassard classifies among the indeterminables, appears to lie right along the track of the train in the main channel where two blind galleries branch off and back, not far from the cave entrance; I have no memory of having seen it on either of my visits to Rouffignac (1997 and 2006). Plassard gives no photo but a line sketch, which suggests that the original may be less visible than other engraved figures. He calls it the bearded head, *la tête barbue,* and notes its resemblance both to human and to beast in a frontal view, the eyes well centered and close to the nose, evoking the Sorcerer of the grotte des Trois-Frères, or the Gabillou figure of the dancing upright bison. It has upright ears of unequal sizes and two upright horns, not of a bison, and is situated between two *gravures de mammouths,* suggesting the figuration of one bison among mammoths seen elsewhere at Rouffignac, as in the passage beyond the Pharaoh. It is not clear and would seem impossible to determine if any of these images, especially the fourth anthropomorph, for instance, represents a finished product of a foreseen end, or an unfinished product, or not a question of finish at all, rather the trace of a process in which it is subsumed. Nor is it clear why the anthropomorphic figures so systematically lack the kind of precision and nuance of the animal figures for which Paleolithic art is justly renowned, nor what any of it means.

The young man at Rouffignac who was our guide in 1997 (or 18 BP), and perhaps drove the engine as well, wore a nondescript green parka and talked more or less continuously all the way down and, as I recall it, most of the way back up, explaining features of the cave, stopping to point out curiosities and reveal spectacles. He may have been one of the Plassards himself. His voice was quiet and vibrant, and I understood almost everything he said even if I can reproduce only the tiniest bit of it, from the very end. I remember him getting off the train from time to time and walking toward the wall explaining something to us while we watched, and I remember him at one point turning off the light to show us what the utter darkness of the cave was like, and sitting in silence for a moment, which was not very long but deep. We saw the famous friezes, and I remember people gasping as we pulled into view of the rhinos and mammoths. I had never seen them even in photos before or heard them described; they would appear, and the train would stop and the light be shined upon them. He showed us the three rhinoceros trotting left to right the way we came, drawn in black silhouette on a band of creamy stone that seems to float above another band, very white, on the wall, with modern graffiti of the last two centuries or so blackening the ceiling just above, and nineteenth-century names scratched into the backs of two of the rhinos. He had us turn our heads to see the witty horse's head peering from above and behind the rhinos, drawn in black profile on an ochre outcropping of silex, not visible normally until one is on the way back out: this creature too has a very human eye directed forward and a nose and mouth resembling a teddy bear. Plassard specifically says that this image is not shown on the tour, but his statement may be out of date.[33] Our guide showed us, too, the ten mammoths facing one another just a little further on along the same wall, as if a panel made for viewing, drawn in black with tusks and trunks, broad creamy backs seeming to rise from a white fog. Some of them overlap, and the two that meet from left and right almost seem to merge into a single creature or other being. The overall effect is peaceful in the extreme. There was something else our guide pointed out in the Galerie Breuil on the opposite wall, at least I seem to recall so though I don't remember what, and the map shows nothing clearly. We must have been shown the Mammoths of the Discovery, as they are called, because they were the first ones seen in 1956: an engraved pair facing one another and the two other pairs a little further on, facing one another over a fifth in the middle, a fragmentary frontal view of diminished size on the way to the Grand Plafond, although I have no memory of having seen them. He showed us the great swirling dream of the Grand Plafond. I remember as if in a dream getting off the little train and walking about a bit under the great round panel, spun with creatures in a crescent moon scattered across it. I remember the ceiling being white, although Plassard's photos show something even lovelier: a richly mottled creamy tan, against which the black line drawings of mammoths, horses, bison, rhinos, and ibex required us to walk around in circles and backward with our heads back, looking up and spinning to keep the images straight, to see them in their orientations as they

---

33. Ibid., 6.

crisscrossed and overlapped and spread across in their rough arc. All are filled with calm, even the ibex running with legs at full stretch, many with eyes that look back at you. Our guide answered questions, and by way of wrapping up on the way back, he said, as I understood him, that "of the people who made these things we know nothing but one thing: they are us"—or he may have said "we are them" which, if not exactly the same, amounts to the same thing: what could only be called human.

Human faces, heads, and bodies throughout the Paleolithic are striking in their indeterminacy. Chauvet and Rouffignac represent respectively the earliest and one of the latest examples of a tradition that runs for twenty-five millennia, including various other traditions at particular times and in particular places and spaces, but consistent across all of these variations is the human figure's peculiar position as a being at once both set apart and strongly identified in relation to other animal beings. This recalls, again, Eshleman's hypothesis that cave art as a whole tells the story of our agonic human separation from the animal being we nevertheless retain, a psychosexual, religiosocial crisis that takes in and moves through shamanic transformation as well as Hiroshima and Auschwitz; it is worth pointing out, too, that Eshleman's hypothesis is presented as a collage of poetry and short prose pieces of a variety of registers—scholarly, personal, narrative, and so on—as if (as seems to be the case) merely analytic, expository prose were an inadequate (perhaps even inappropriate) vessel. The "missing" faces (not to mention heads) of the Paleolithic are striking precisely for our hunger to see them, no doubt, but also for the incredibly vivid and detailed attention paid to animal faces, as in the Pharaoh (only one among countless other examples), most with no apparent figuratively human dimension: the delicate and expressive muzzles of horses, aurochs and lions, bison and mammoth eyes, horses' manes and bison beards, and so on. There is clearly no lack of observational skill, and no lack of technical know-how when it came to tricks of representation. The incredible sophistication of Chauvet's images, among the very earliest yet discovered, would indicate a long tradition extending further back still, in which such skills and tricks would have been developed. Still, these skills and the full range of these tricks are not in evidence when it comes to faces and heads recognizably (to us) human. Some figures from the middle and late Magdalenian—as at La Marche, and Riparo de Vado all'Arancio around 14,000 BP—begin to show elements of portraiture, as if particular individuals were being depicted (a common sensation with regard to the animal figures from Chauvet onward), but even here the figures are unelaborated, distinctive schema rather than shocking triumphs of verisimilitude; and the figures from La Marche are found engraved on stone plaquettes covered with obscuring masses of other lines, requiring the faces to be discerned—if discerning them was ever the object—with more than the usual degree of conjecture.[34]

But while it is impossible *not* to consider these matters of faces and heads (not to mention bodies), perhaps this is in the end the wrong way to approach the question, wishing to approach an understanding of Paleolithic conceptions of the "human"—if putting it that way, saying even that much, is not already too fragmented a notion, something we might be able to imagine ourselves without. The first human figurations we looked at—the pubic triangles of Chauvet—are themselves subject to question, as Paul Bahn reminds us, demonstrating the difficulty of interpreting or even identifying human images from this period generally:

> Huge numbers ... are ambiguous, unfinished or simply unidentifiable—quite apart from the vast quantities of apparently non-figurative motifs. Some designs are interpreted according to personal choice—for example, a simple "V" with a central line may be described as a "trident" but interpreted as an arrow, a bird track or a vulva. And of course all or none of these may be correct.[35]

Vulvas specifically, Bahn says, "are remarkably hard to find in Ice Age art. If one allows that the only definite specimens are those found in context—that is, in full female figures—all the rest are interpretations. ... Some of these motifs look more like horse-hoof or bird-foot prints, and it would not be surprising if the artists played with such ambiguities of form."[36] "Such interpretations," Bahn adds, "are fairly 'literal,' but simple motifs can have multiple possible meanings—for example, among Australia's Walbiri people a circle can denote a hill, tree, campsite, circular path, egg, breast, nipple, entrance into or exit from the ground, or a host of other things."[37] Drawing another analogy to contemporary hunter-gatherer culture, he notes that, "in Brazil, two triangles drawn apex to apex means a fish vertebra to the Bororó, while to the Desana they denote a quiver for curare arrows!"—which would clearly suggest ample room for variation over 25,000 years in the function of similar, fundamental images, with many interpretations and associations coming into play at various times and in various places.[38] Remarkable continuity of forms and

---

34. Paul G. Bahn, *The Cambridge Illustrated History of Prehistoric Art* (Cambridge: Cambridge University Press, 1998), 159–60.
35. Ibid., 180.
36. Ibid., 174.
37. Ibid., 180.
38. Ibid.

remarkable variation in their interpretation would seem to be one signature of these early representations, with regard both to abstract forms (triangles, dots, other small arrangements of lines) and to more fully elaborated images, like handprints, animal figures, and the hybrid "Sorcerer" figures, although again, what we can say with certainty about Paleolithic interpretations is minimal.

Perhaps questions of completeness, fragmentariness, wholeness—particularly when it comes to Paleolithic imagery, and specifically images of humans—only beg the question. (The question being: what is human? For we would have to "know" what "human" is, if we were to designate some image as "fragmentary" or "complete.") It is difficult to find a description that applies to any representation of a "whole body" that doesn't apply as well to a head, face, or pubic triangle, each one a self-contained whole in a web of further relations: all images leave out inessential visual details, claim the part for the whole, as surely as a handprint on the wall, or, for that matter, a digital squiggle left in soft clay. Clive Gamble tells us that metaphor—the part for the whole, in this case—comes even before language, so this dimension of interpretation reaches way back indeed.[39] Questions of what is fragmentary or partial, or complete or whole—that is to say, definitions of human identity and being—are precisely what we cannot resolve when it comes to Paleolithic art. This radical conceptual instability remains with us, is available to us in spite of many years of fuller access to thoughts and works of human culture (lost and otherwise) and, of course, in spite of the certainties that accrue with the advent of writing. In some sense the Paleolithic has not ended.

---

39. Clive Gamble, *Origins and Revolutions: Human Identity in Earliest Prehistory* (Cambridge: Cambridge University Press, 2007), 88.

CHAPTER 2

Eros, Event, and Non-Faciality in Malory's "The Tale of Balyn and Balan"

EILEEN A. JOY

> To lose our fascinating and crippling expressiveness might be the precondition for our moving within nature, moving as appearances registering, and responding to the call of, other appearances.
>
> —Leo Bersani and Ulysse Dutoit, *Forms of Being: Cinema, Aesthetics, and Subjectivity*

ACCORDING TO ANTHONY GIDDENS, "One of the most obvious characteristics separating the modern era from any other period preceding it is modernism's extreme dynamism. The modern world is a 'runaway world': not only is the *pace* of social change much faster than in any prior system, so also is its *scope*, and the *profoundness* with which it affects pre-existing social practices and modes of behavior." For Giddens, modernity is essentially a "post-traditional" order, and the resulting "integral relation between modernity and radical doubt is . . . *existentially* troubling for ordinary individuals."[1] All of this

---

1. Anthony Giddens, *Modernity and Self-Identity: Self and Society in the Late Modern Age* (Stanford, CA: Stanford University Press, 1991), 16, 21 (his emphasis). For the effects of speed on the late modern condition, see also Paul Virilio, *Speed and Politics: An Essay on Dromology,* trans. Mark Polizzotti (New York: Semiotext(e), 1986) and *The Great Accelerator,* trans. Julie Rose (Cambridge: Polity, 2012); William E. Connolly, *Neuropolitics: Thinking, Culture, Speed* (Minneapolis: University of Minnesota Press, 2002); Jonathan Crary, *24/7: Late Capitalism and*

is exacerbated further, in Giddens's view, by the fact that, whereas "in premodern settings . . . time and space were connected through the situatedness of place," in modernity, time and place have become estranged from each other, leading to a general "disembedding" of social institutions whereby social relations are "lifted out" of local contexts and rearticulated "across indefinite tracts of time-space."[2] According to Zygmunt Bauman, the fixed and normative "social standing" that supposedly defines the premodern era is replaced in modernity with "compulsive and obligatory self-determination."[3] And the end result is "a combined experience of *insecurity* (of position, entitlements and livelihood), of *uncertainty* (as to their continuation and future stability), and of *unsafety* (of one's body, one's self and their extensions: possessions, neighbourhood, community)."[4] In Bauman's scheme, late modernity literally "liquefies" the supposed solidity of the premodern past, defined primarily by "traditional loyalties," estates and classes, communal dependency, and "customary rights and obligations."[5] As a result, the late modern individual is "reshaped after the pattern of the electronic mole . . . a plug on castors, scuffling around in a desperate search for electrical sockets to plug into."[6]

For Scott Lash, another contemporary social theorist, the modern individual is a nonlinear "combinard" who "puts together networks, constructs alliances, makes deals. He must live, is forced to live in an atmosphere of risk in which self-knowledge and life-chances are precarious." Further, he is a nomad who lives in "regularizable chaos" at "the interface of the social and the technical," a place (or "place-polygamy") where the self is always fundamentally

---

the Ends of Sleep (London: Verso, 2014); Benjamin Noys, *Malign Velocities: Accelerationism and Capitalism* (Hants, UK: Zero Books, 2014); and Robin Mackay and Armen Avanessian, *#Accelerate: The Accelerationist Reader* (Falmouth, UK: Urbanomic, 2014).

2. Giddens, *Modernity and Self-Identity*, 16, 17.

3. Zygmunt Bauman, "Foreword: Individually, Together," in *Individualization: Institutionalized Individualism and its Social and Political Consequences*, ed. Ulrich Beck and Elisabeth Beck-Gernsheim, trans. Patrick Camiller (London: Sage Publications, 2002), xv [xiv–xix].

4. Idem, *Liquid Modernity* (Cambridge: Polity, 2000), 161.

5. Ibid., 23. Bauman distinguishes between an earlier, more "solid" or "heavy" modernity, in which power required "territory" in which to exercise itself (with "empire," Jeremy Bentham's Panopticon, and the Fordist-Taylorist factory standing in as arch-metaphors), and our more current "light" and "liquid" modernity, in which "power has become truly *exterritorial*, no longer bound, not even slowed down, by the resistance of space" (11). Reversing the state of the affairs in an earlier modernity, in which settled majorities ruled over nomadic minorities, in the "fluid stage of modernity, the settled majority is ruled by the nomadic and exterritorial elite," and it is now "the smaller, the lighter, the more portable that signifies improvement and 'progress.' Traveling light, rather than holding tightly to things deemed attractive for their reliability and solidity—that is, for their heavy weight, substantiality and unyielding power of resistance—is now the asset of power" (13).

6. Ibid., 14.

incomplete.⁷ Lash is careful to distinguish between what he sees as the individual of the "first" Enlightenment (or, industrial) modernity and the individual of the "second" informational modernity—the first was "institutionalized" through "property, contract, the bourgeois family and civil society" while the second is destabilized through the "retreat of the classic institutions: state, class, nuclear family, ethnic group," as well as through the general indeterminacy of knowledge, and as a result, he begins to spin in perpetual, self-reflexive motion.⁸ This individual of the later, "second" modernity, in Lash's view, never has time to reflect, only to quickly and reflexively make decisions and choices—decisions and choices, moreover, that must be continuously rethought and rechosen because knowledge is now always uncertain, "probabilistic, at best; more likely 'possibilistic.'"⁹

In Ulrich Beck's well-known "risk argument," a totalizing, globalizing economy—in conjunction with new, accelerated technologies, demystified norms of knowledge, perpetual self-reflexivity, and nontraditional social configurations—has brought about unprecedented social hazards and threats to the planet. In this scenario, individualization is to be understood as a change of biographical patterns in which private existence "becomes more and more obviously and emphatically dependent on situations and conditions that completely escape its reach."¹⁰ To be a human individual today is to live in "a state of permanent (partly overt, partly concealed) endangerment," but Beck and Elisabeth Beck-Gernsheim argue that this state of affairs also potentializes the release of individual creativity that, in turn, creates a "space for the renewal of society under the condition of radical change."¹¹ Whether or not individual creativity really has any space left for itself in an overcrowded and overdetermined (and increasingly, post/human) modernity remains an open question.¹²

---

7. Scott Lash, "Foreword: Individualization in a Non-Linear Mode," in Beck and Beck-Gernsheim, *Individualization*, ix, xi [vii–xiii].

8. Ibid., vii, ix–x.

9. Ibid., x.

10. Ulrich Beck, *Risk Society: Towards a New Modernity*, trans. Mark Ritter (London: Sage Publications, 1992), 131.

11. Beck and Beck-Gernsheim, *Individualization*, xxi, 3. Giddens has likewise argued for the positive sociopolitical implications of the situation of the disembedded individual in a posttraditional, late modernity, in which he sees the possibility of a future-oriented "utopian realism." On this point, see Anthony Giddens, *The Consequences of Modernity* (Stanford, CA: Stanford University Press, 1990), 151–78.

12. In relation to this open question, it is interesting to note the current preoccupation, in certain philosophical and other intellectual circles, with "Accelerationism," a movement that insists "the only radical response to capitalism is not to protest, disrupt, or critique, nor to await its demise at the hands of its own contradictions, but to accelerate its uprooting, alienating,

In some of the more influential discourses of contemporary sociology (cited above), the Middle Ages offers a mainly static tableau of supposedly solid traditional loyalties, communal dependencies, highly localized social systems, and settled territorial sovereignties out of which, after various processes of the "liquefaction" of traditional social forms, commitments, and support networks alongside the general "acceleration" of everything else, emerges the posttraditional, late modern individual who is socially disembedded, fundamentally incomplete, perpetually self-reflexive, always at risk, and full of radical doubt. We have had much work in medieval and other studies that offers different and valuably complex accounts of and temporal schemata for the development of modern individuality,[13] not to mention Bruno Latour's argument that there has never really been a radical break or split with the past.[14] We have also Michel de Certeau's reminder that Western historiography has worked, perhaps too mightily, on a "labor of separation" between the past and the present, tracing "the decision to become different or no longer to be such as one had been up to that time."[15] Which is not to say that the modern individual is not much different than the medieval one—this would be a gross simplification (not to mention that "*which* modern individual, situated *where?*" and "*which* medieval individual, situated *where?*" are questions that already complicate the matter of comparison). As Jeffrey Jerome Cohen has written, the choice should not necessarily be between "continuist" and

---

decoding, abstractive tendencies" (Mackay and Avanessian, "Introduction," in *#Accelerate*, 4). See also Nick Srnicek and Alex Williams, "#ACCELERATE: Manifesto for an Accelerationist Politics," May 2013: http://accelerationism.files.wordpress.com/2013/ 05/williams-and-srnicek .pdf.

13. See, for example, David Aers, *Community, Gender, and Individual Identity: English Writing, 1360–1430* (London: Routledge, 1988); Jeffrey Jerome Cohen, *Medieval Identity Machines* (Minneapolis: University of Minnesota Press, 2003); Carolyn Dinshaw, *Getting Medieval: Sexualities and Communities, Pre- and Postmodern* (Durham, NC: Duke University Press, 1999); L. O. Aranye Fradenburg, *Sacrifice Your Love: Psychoanalysis, Historicism, Chaucer* (Minneapolis: University of Minnesota Press, 2002); Robert Hanning, *The Individual in Twelfth-Century Romance* (New Haven, CT: Yale University Press, 1977); Anthony Low, *Aspects of Subjectivity: Society and Individuality from the Middle Ages to Shakespeare and Milton* (Pittsburgh, PA: Duquesne University Press, 2003); Colin Morris, *The Discovery of the Individual, 1050–1200* (New York: Harper and Row, 1972); David Gary Shaw, *Necessary Conjunctions: The Social Self in Medieval England* (New York: Palgrave Macmillan, 2005); R. W. Southern, *The Making of the Middle Ages* (New Haven, CT: Yale University Press, 1953); Paul Strohm, *Social Chaucer* (Cambridge, MA: Harvard University Press, 1989); and Charles Taylor, *Sources of the Self: The Making of the Modern Identity* (Cambridge, MA: Harvard University Press, 1989).

14. See Bruno Latour, *We Have Never Been Modern*, trans. Catherine Porter (Cambridge, MA: Harvard University Press, 1993). This is also the argument being advanced, collectively, by the authors and editors of *postmedieval: a journal of medieval cultural studies*.

15. Michel de Certeau, *The Writing of History*, trans. Tom Conley (New York: Columbia University Press, 1988), 2, 4.

"alterist" approaches to the past "when both these metanarratives contain truths about the relation of the medieval to the modern and postmodern."[16]

I would take this one step further and say that almost all of our notions of time and temporality are insufficient to their weirdness and ungraspability, and therefore most of our attempts to map and trace particular causal-linear histories fail at some level to get at the truth, or essence, of what might be called time's continual and dissonant "forking."[17] I borrow the idea of forking time from the political theorist William Connolly, who writes:

> In every moment, the pressures of the past enter into a dissonant conjunction with uncertain possibilities of the future. The fugitive present is both constituted by this dissonant conjunction between past and present and rendered uncertain in its direction by it. Often enough that uncertainty is resolved through continuity; but below the threshold of human attention indiscernible shifts and changes have accumulated, sometimes finding expression in small mutations and sometimes in large events. So occasionally time forks in new and surprising directions. . . . A rift through which at any moment a surprising fork may emerge, ushering microscopic, small, large, or world historical shifts into an open future unsusceptible to full coverage by a smooth narrative, sufficient set of rules, or tight causal explanation.[18]

Literary narratives, I would argue, can serve as ideal sites through which to explore the emergence of time's dissonant conjunctions and surprising forks, arising as they do from minds that are both transhistorical and rooted in particular times and places, and because literary texts are also objects that, as Jonathan Gil Harris has argued, are inherently polychronic and untimely, looking forward and backward and sideward simultaneously and always "out of joint" with their own "times"—more pleated accordion, or palimpsest, than smooth singularity.[19]

---

16. Jeffrey Jerome Cohen, "Introduction: Midcolonial," In *The Postcolonial Middle Ages*, ed. Cohen (New York: Palgrave Macmillan, 2001), 5 [1–17].

17. Bruce Holsinger's book *The Premodern Condition: Medievalism and the Making of Theory* (Chicago: University of Chicago Press, 2005) is worth noting here for the ways in which it critiques and disrupts the widely held idea of postwar French theory as a type of *nouvelle critique* that arises out of the historical conditions of the 1960s, when in fact the medieval archive played a huge role in the most important theoretical projects of what we now refer to as postmodern theory. See also Andrew Cole and D. Vance Smith, eds., *The Legitimacy of the Middle Ages: On the Unwritten History of Theory* (Durham, NC: Duke University Press, 2010).

18. Connolly, *Neuropolitics*, 145.

19. See Jonathan Gil Harris, *Untimely Matter in the Time of Shakespeare* (Philadelphia: University of Pennsylvania Press, 2008).

Malory's *Morte darthur*, written in the fifteenth century and arriving as it did on the heels of so many long-established Arthurian narrative traditions—traditions it labored to absorb, recompile, and also refashion—provides for us, I believe, an exemplary site for excavating the traces of a nascently (or proto-)modern human individual who is certainly bound and contained within local and national networks of chivalric tradition and centralized, sovereign authority, but who is also thrust, through *aventure*, into the "compulsive and obligatory self-determination" of a certain alienating *past*modernity. In this sense, the medieval knight of Malory's Arthurian "discography" is untimely in just the way Harris describes the handkerchief in Shakespeare's *Othello*: heterodox time is all "crumpled up" in him.[20] I am inventing here the term "*past*modernity" to evoke a special temporal zone in the so-called "medieval" past in which modernity arrives, as it were, in fits and starts ahead of itself, just as "postmodernity" names a variety of temporalities and world "conditions," whereby modernity is seen as a becoming-something-else while still remaining in "undead" traction with older social, cultural, political, psychic, and like formations. The present moment, in *any* time, is therefore partly the sum of certain movements of what Cary Howie calls "traherence," in which nothing really "gets free of what it ostensibly emerges from" and every Now is simultaneously a "not yet" and a "then."[21] Indeed, in one of the tales that occurs early on in the *Morte*, "The Tale of Balyn and Balan," we can detect a certain *traction* between a sedimentation of traditional systems for both hailing and fantasizing the medieval sovereign subject and the arrival of what Scott Lash has called the nonlinear nomad of late modernity who lives in "regularizable chaos" at the "interface of the social and the technical," a place (or "place-polygamy") where the self is always fundamentally incomplete.[22]

---

20. See chapter 6, "Crumpled Handkerchiefs: William Shakespeare's and Michel Serres's Palimpsested Time," in Harris, *Untimely Matter*, 169–87. It is worth noting here as well that Frederic Jameson's analysis of medieval romance included an appreciation of its internal contradictions and anachronisms, as well as its ability to resist easy or totalizing symbolizations: "Magical Narratives: Romance as Genre," *New Literary History* 7.1 (1975): 135–63.

21. Cary Howie, *Claustrophilia: The Erotics of Enclosure* (New York: Palgrave, 2007), 7, 112. "Traherence" is a neologism coined by Howie. In this same vein, see also Linda Charnes, "Reading for the Wormholes: Micro-periods from the Future," where she asks us to us "imagine a textual circumstance or event that we'll call a 'wormhole,' in which we can detect an idea whose time arrives in advance of its historical 'context.' . . . Future ideas must in some way be 'embedded' in the texts of the past in order for us to discern their emergence from the position of hindsight. Such ideas might appear inexplicably as odd blips on the textual radar only to recede without further ado. Or they might crash onto a textual scene, sending up clouds of smoke that demand that attention be paid. The way to read for them is by looking for what seem to be mysterious crash sites: anachronistic ideas and depictions the causality of which remain indeterminate" (*Early Modern Culture: An Electronic Seminar*, Issue 6: Timely Meditations, 2007: http://emc.eserver.org/1-6/charnes.html).

22. Lash, "Foreword," in Beck and Beck-Gernsheim, *Individualization*, xi.

Balyn is often described as one of Malory's "lesser" or "minor" knights and even as a kind of "anti-knight," and he certainly operates within his tale—comically or tragically, depending on your viewpoint—as a kind of free radical from whose hands every imaginable disaster is produced. He is often praised for the "prowess" of his hands, and he certainly is a killing machine, and a reckless one at that; everywhere he goes, heads fall off and bodies are split asunder, either by him, or by others while he is simply watching, perhaps in a state of bewilderment at the mayhem he has unwittingly caused. Indeed, Balyn pretty much never gets anything right, and no matter how many times Arthur and Merlin intervene to try and stop him and give him counsel, he simply and willfully ignores it, and therefore, he cannot be contained—in the ways knights such as Lancelot, Gareth, Galahad, and Gawain are—by what might be called the *system* or *assemblage* of Camelot, a system which nevertheless establishes the fairy world through which Balyn moves and acts and for which he claims his every bumbling action and will is directed. He springs, quite literally, from Arthur's prison, where he first distinguishes himself by being able to pull a sword out of a damsel's scabbard that no one, not even Arthur, is able to remove, and when he is cautioned not to keep the sword or else it will spell his total ruin, he cheerfully and belligerently submits to the "aventure" of *not* returning it, at which point he becomes "the knight with two swords," and then all hell breaks loose. A short summary of the tale, which has a complicated plot line, may be helpful here:

> Consider the chain of doleful events: first, he shames Arthur by decapitating the Lady of the Lake in court, in Arthur's presence; next, he slays an Irish knight, Launceor, in a joust, and allows Launceor's "damesel" to commit suicide in his presence; he assures safe conduct to Harleus de Berbeus, whom the invisible knight Garlon promptly slays in Balin's presence; another knight, Peryne de Mounte Belyarde, joins Balin's company, only to be slain in turn by Garlon; Balin finally meets Garlon visible and quickly slays him, which leads to Balin's crippling King Pellam by striking him with a "Dolorous Stroke" which not only wounds Pellam but prompts a Godly death-blow which leaves "the peple dede slayne on every side" for miles around; he next comes to the aid of the lovelorn Garynysh of the Mownte, causing Garnysh not only to slay the woman he loves, but to also commit suicide; and to cap all this Balin slays his own brother Balan.[23]

---

23. D. Thomas Hanks, Jr., "Malory's Anti-Knights: Balin and Breunys," in *The Social and Literary Contexts of Malory's Morte DArthur*, ed. D. Thomas Hanks, Jr. and Jessica Gentry Brogdon (Cambridge: D. S. Brewer, 2000), 96–97 [94–110].

What is not included in that summary is that, in killing his brother, Balyn himself is also slain. Despite this seemingly self-destructive trajectory, and because this is an enchanted world—by which I mean, a *literary-fabulist* one—we can also glimpse in Malory's text, especially in all of the accidents that punctuate Balyn's quest, a certain future-oriented "evential hermeneutics"—the phrase coined by the philosopher Claude Romano to describe the human being as an "*Advenant*" who is "constitutively open to events, insofar as humanity is the capacity to be oneself in the face of what happens to us." For Romano, there is no originary "Being" (or being-there) for the human, who instead "happens to his possibilities only from an even greater *passability* with respect to the events that punctuate his adventure and thus give him a history."[24] For Romano, passability

> arises from the origin of our self-projecting adventure lying outside ourselves (in birth), and therefore coming before any activity or passivity. It is a "being exposed beyond measure to events, in a way that cannot be expressed in terms of passivity, but precedes the distinction between active and passive." As such, it is a sort of "*pre-subjective* opening," because "a passivity that would be mine . . . is given only in the after-shock and counterblow of the event."[25]

And this definition of what I would call the *contingent* human also accords exceedingly well with what Allan Mitchell has written about Balyn in his book *Ethics and Eventfulness in Medieval English Literature*—that Balyn is "an emphatic example of . . . one who is touched by events. . . . More than most knights-errant, Balin finds himself to be particularly gifted and given over to temporality and exteriority."[26]

This being "given over" to temporality and exteriority can be seen, especially, in the fact that, although Balyn sets out for his adventures from Camelot,

---

24. Claude Romano, *Event and World*, trans. Shane Mackinlay (New York: Fordham University Press, 2009), 20. It is important to note here that Romano distinguishes between impersonal "facts," which "happen within a world, are subject to causal explanation, and are inscribed within a datable present," and the "evential" (a term he coined), which designates events that are "addressed to particular entities, reconfigure the world, cannot be explained by causes, and occur with a 'structural' delay that opens the future" (Shane Mackinlay, "Event, World, and Place," paper presentation, Australian Society for Continental Philosophy Conference, University of Tasmania, 6 December 2007, 6).

25. Mackinlay, "Event, World, and Place," 14. Passages cited within the quotation from Mackinlay are Mackinlay's translations of Claude Romano, *L'événement et le monde* (Paris: Presses Universitaires de France, 1998) and "Le possible et l'événement," in *Il y a*, Épiméthée: essais philosophiques (Paris: Presses Universitaires de France, 2003), 55–111.

26. J. Allan Mitchell, *Ethics and Eventfulness in Medieval English Literature* (New York: Palgrave, 2009), 129.

as most knights do, unlike most of the rest of them, he never returns, and while, at times, he seems completely unconscious of the possible consequences of his often furious and seemingly blind actions, at other times, he appears all too aware that he is giving himself over, almost passively, to the wild contingency of the Outside. Just before passing on to the castle where he will meet his death at his twin brother's hands, and which castle is fronted by a sign that says, "IT IS NOT FOR NO KNYGHT ALONE TO RYDE TOWARD THIS CASTEL," Balyn hears a horn blow "as it had ben the dethe of a best," and he says to himself, "That blast . . . is blowen for me, for I am the pryse—and yet I am not dede." And then, as is typical for Balyn, he goes right on in. Although he soon "repenteth" that he ever *did* go in, at the same time, he claims that, regardless of life or death, he "wille take the adventure that shalle come to me" (58, 59).[27]

In Romano's "evential" hermeneutics, which is an elaboration and up-ending of Heidegger's ontological hermeneutics (where Being precedes events and is then projected into them), we can see a beautiful conjuncture with the important trope of "adventure" in Malory's *Morte*, which literally founds the knightly individual. Although it is always in Arthur's court—wherever it is being held—that everyone gathers as a community, self-identity, however tied to that court, can never really be discovered (or uncovered) there. It is always on the Outside—the zone of *aventure* (what Jane Bennett has called a "heteroverse," as opposed to a "universe")[28]—where the social relations of the Arthurian world are "lifted out" of the superstructure of Camelot and rearticulated across indefinite tracts of space-time, represented by chains of endlessly deep and winding forests, hallucinatory tableaux, and the nonlinear "traveling life" of the knight himself. And in Balyn's story, in particular, Balyn's claim early on, that "manhode and worship [ys hyd] within a mannes person" (42)—an important claim for the medieval chivalric ideal in general, indicating that honor resides not necessarily in clothing and gear and titles, but within some sort of interior space of personhood—this claim is completely up-ended by the details of Balyn's own narrative, which seems to argue instead

---

27. All citations of "The Tale of Balyn and Balan" are from the Norton Critical Edition of Sir Thomas Malory, *Le Morte Darthur, or The Hoole Book of King Arthur and of His Noble Knyghtes of the Round Table*, ed. Stephen H. Shepherd (New York: W. W. Norton, 2004), referenced by page number.

28. "Heteroverse" is a term coined by Jane Bennett to describe how Thoreau conceives of an outside "Wildness"/world that is nonhierarchized. "Heteroverse," as opposed to "universe" (which implies a world with "rounded" wholeness), suggests "both how heterogeneous elements intersect or influence one another and how this ensemble of intersections does not form a unified or self-sufficient whole. It may also, through the idea of *verse*, convey the sublime character of this dissonant combination" (*Thoreau's Nature: Ethics, Politics, and the Wild*, rev. ed. [Lanham, MD: Rowan and Littlefield, 2002], 53).

for the idea, elaborated in Romano's philosophy of the event, that Balyn comes into existence as a person only through that which happens to him, and there is, technically speaking, no "inside" or interior personhood that could precede the events of his own story.

Despite Balyn's own intentions (such as they are minimally articulated throughout his "Tale," primarily as the somewhat self-destructive desire for, as Balyn himself puts it, the regaining of Arthur's love, regardless of the risks),[29] Balyn's story highlights the idea that "as one to whom events happen, we are neither simply active nor passive, but live out of a *possibility* that puts our very selves into play and is a capacity to appropriate our possibilities and thereby *advene* to ourselves."[30] Another way of putting this would be to consider that the world is not the place where *we take place,* but rather, the impersonal events of the world, arriving to us, open us up as *encounterable,* and thereby also open up the world itself. World and subject open together in events, the chief example of which is our very own births. In the magical zone of adventure in medieval romance, the fictional conceit is that the knight comes into chivalric being as he passes from one site to another, encountering events that supposedly reveal the worthiness he always possessed as he, again, passes through them and supposedly comes more fully into his own being, which is like a thing finally *revealed* in the world (and which also assumes an Outside, a Nature, that has no distinction until we arrive and *take place* in it). But I would ask instead, following Romano, that we reverse this ontology and say that it is the world that arrives upon the knight, who can only really *advene* to himself in the events that can never be predicted in advance. It will have to be admitted that Balyn himself is often wholly impervious and *impassable* with regard to the possibility of advening to himself through the events that literally, and without predetermined meaning, *happen* to him, at which times Balyn is a kind of pure negation who cancels in advance, through his often unwitting violence or inattention, the very *possibility* of passability, but he is also a sort of beautiful movement, a *sensation* that Deleuze might say acts as "a break within the flow of absolute consciousness,"[31] with the absolute consciousness in this case being the assemblage of Camelot.

---

29. After Balyn has killed the knight Launceor who pursues Balyn in order to avenge Balyn's decapitation of the Lady of the Lake and his resulting affront to Arthur's honor, and has also watched helplessly while Launceor's lover Colombe kills herself on Launceor's sword, Balyn tells his brother Balan, "I am right hevy that my lorde Arthure ys displeased with me, for he ys the moste worshypfullist kynge that regnith now in erthe; and hys love I woll gete—other ellis I woll putte my lyff in adventure" (46).

30. Mackinlay, "Event, World, and Place," 1 (my emphasis).

31. Gilles Deleuze, *Pure Immanence: Essays on a Life*, trans. Anne Boyman (New York: Zone Books, 2001), 25.

And Camelot is an assemblage, I would argue, in the way that Manuel DeLanda describes Deleuze's thinking on such systems: it is characterized by "relations of exteriority," which imply that "the properties of the component parts [a knight's "doughty hondes," for example, or the "fayre foreste," or the call of a distressed damsel] can never explain [on their own] the relations which constitute the whole [Camelot, or, the "machine" of Arthurian romance], that is, 'relations do not have as their causes the properties of the [component parts] between which they are established,' although they may be caused by the exercise of a component's capacities."³² A knight or lady, as a singular component, may be plugged into any number of different literary assemblages (other than Malory's Camelot). Their interactions with other components cannot be predicted in advance, but place these things in relation to each other within the spatial boundaries of a medieval romance (e.g., a knight seeking "aventure" riding through the "fayre foreste" with a lady running toward him and crying out that her lover has been wrongfully killed) and we know what happens next—or rather, that one of just a few outcomes, or further "relations," can be predicted in advance. There is a good reason, when we teach Arthurian romance, that our students struggle to keep characters, locations, and separate "adventures" straight: they are all, more or less, exactly the same, and only the names seem to change.

There is a high degree of internal homogeneity and territorialization in the world of Arthurian romance, which contains certain well-defined spatial boundaries (there is always a forest, always a castle, always a perilous bridge, always a set of tents in which Arthur can be found holding court, etc.) as well as nonspatial "sorting processes" whereby certain characters are allowed in this world, others are kept out, and face-to-face relations are predetermined to a certain extent by generic scripts that constrain possibilities, but this is not to say, of course, that each medieval romance is not utterly different from every single other medieval romance, which is why it also has to be argued that Malory's Arthurian world is an assemblage, not *only* because of its internal homogeneity and symbiosis (which, left to itself, would make that world more of a stratum, or a *stone-world*), but because it is a system of bodies, actions, passions, statements, expressions, and enunciations that, in the words of Deleuze and Guattari, "swing between a stratum state and a movement of destratification . . . between a territorial closure that tends to restratify them and a deterritorializing movement that connects them to the Cosmos."³³

---

32. Manuel DeLanda, *A New Philosophy of Society: Assemblage Theory and Social Complexity* (London: Continuum, 2006), 10, 11. The quote within the citation from DeLanda is from Gilles Deleuze, *Empiricism and Subjectivity* (New York: Columbia University Press, 1991), 98.

33. Gilles Deleuze and Félix Guattari, *A Thousand Plateaus: Capitalism and Schizophrenia*, trans. Brian Massumi (Minneapolis: University of Minnesota Press, 1987), 337.

It may be that the generic yet highly idiosyncratic Balyn is an agent, or *cutting edge*, of deterritorialization, a kind of contagion who seeks to carry the whole assemblage away with him by, in a sense, taking the rules of this world to their too-literal extreme and hurrying headlong thereby into the void of his own death—an end predicted to him with dire seriousness several times throughout his tale. During the twin brothers' penultimate battle on a little island in one of the many no-places of the Arthurian Outside, both Balyn and Balan are wearing borrowed armor and therefore do not recognize each other. And being equally matched, they are wounded and die simultaneously, possibly demonstrating—in a kind of beautiful miniature of the entire genre—that there can finally be no individual lives. There can only be expressions or enunciations of the system, which requires not just death but even the undoing of one's birth (or of the possibility of being reborn both *to* and *in* the world). Indeed, after Balyn realizes he has mortally wounded his brother Balan and falls backward from grief, Balan removes Balyn's helmet and does not "know him by the visage, it was so full hewen and bledde" (60): for the most part, this is a truly faceless world—Balyn never possessed a face even before his nonface was shredded by his brother, and therefore, the absence of Balyn's face in this scene figures a sort of sublimely terrifying slippage of faciality that reveals the black box of Arthurian nonsubjectivity (everyone is a "subject" of Camelot, and yet everyone is also no one in particular because everyone is fully exchangeable *and* expendable). The brothers' final request, made in one joined voice, is to be buried in one pit together, just as they came into the world, "bothe oute of one wombe, that is to say one moders bely" (60)—which is to say, as if they had never entered the world to begin with, or ever been *encountered* by the world.

But for me, there is also one moment in Balyn's story that signifies the spot of a kind of crash landing from the future of the richer possibilities of Romano's "evential hermeneutics"—this is the moment when, after Balyn kills the Irish knight Launceor, Launceor's lover Colombe arrives to announce to Balyn, "Two bodyes thou hast slayne in one herte, and two hertes in one body, and two soules thou has lost," and immediately after saying this and making "grete dole oute of mesure," she takes her lover's sword and after struggling for a bit with Balyn, who is trying to wrest that sword from her, she sets "the pommel to the grounde, and rove hirselff thorowoute the body" (46). This scene is not, in and of itself, extraordinary within Malory or even the larger corpus of medieval romance. Knights are often accidentally killing *someone*'s lover—male *and* female—and you can almost always count on the injured party to show up, give vent to sorrow "oute of all mesure," and then throw themselves on their lover's sword, and if enough people are there to witness it, they will also throw themselves on the ground and shed a reservoir of tears. But what *is* unique in this scene is that, immediately after Colombe's suicide, Balyn is so struck with wonder at her will to self-destruction over her love for the dead Launceor, and so ashamed of himself for causing that self-destruction, that, as Malory writes, "For sorow he myght no lenger beholde them, but turned hys horse and loked toward a fayre foreste" (46).

It is only for a moment that Balyn turns away,[34] and the sight of his brother suddenly riding out of the forest toward him quickly breaks the scene, but in that singular instance of both being struck with amazement at the power of eros—of a fierce attachment to the world, and more pointedly, to one particular body in that world, without whom this world has been drained of reason and possibility—and also in turning away from the sight of two particular loving-destroying bodies, Balyn reveals his capacity for what remains unthinkable for him in almost every other moment of his story: the ability to stop, to pause in astonishment at the sight of an event that reveals the wonder of the sudden presence of a body, a *being*, who is so saturated with herself and her lover's sword (which is also to say, his body and his *things*) that she is opting out of the system in order to go on as a lover, even without her body. Further, this scene of erotic, bodily grief and astonishment—as event, even as a *cutting through* of Balyn himself as an event—deterritorializes the strata of Balyn's world and threatens to literally carry him away. But Balyn's astonishment, which causes him to turn away from the sight of the very world that we might say he cannot *bear*, which threatens to carry him away from and back to himself in a new way, is almost immediately broken by the sight of his brother Balan riding toward him out of the "fayre forest," which, in Malory's world at least, is the classic route of escape. It is also the image of an incorruptible

---

34. It is significant, further, that this momentary act of turning away, because Balyn could "no lenger beholde them," is unique to Malory's version of the story. In the French prose *Suite de Merlin*, considered to be Malory's primary source for this narrative, Balyn does not turn away in his astonishment and the author also qualifies Balyn's astonishment as being related to Balyn's surprise that a *woman* could love so intensely (whereas in Malory, it is the sight of the *two dead bodies together* that affects Balyn so profoundly, in addition to his shame at having caused the damsel's grief): "Quant il voit ceste aventure, il ne set que dire: car il est si durement esbahis qu'il ne set s'il dort ou s'il veille. Car il ne vit onques ou siècle chose don't il s'esmervillast autant comme il fait de ceste. Si dist que loiaument amoit la damoisele et que il ne cuidoit pas que en cuer de feme peust entrer amour si vraie" ["When he saw this event, he did not know what to say: for he was so astonished that he didn't know if he were asleep or awake. He had never seen in this world a thing that amazed him as much as this one did. He said to himself that the damsel loved loyally and that he hadn't thought such true love could enter into the heart of a woman"]: cited from *Le Roman de Balain: A Prose Romance of the Thirteenth Century*, ed. M. Dominica Legge (Manchester: Manchester University Press, 1920), 20; the translation is mine.

beauty, because it is not really a beautiful forest, but an idea of one, seen at a distance: the very frame of the aesthetic (and inhuman, faceless) narrative to which Balyn must return.

And the two dead lovers, left behind, shimmer in their eventfulness, which the narrative hurries to cover over and look away from. The only way forward, then, is to Balyn's own catastrophic death—to be slain himself by his own brother whom he himself will slay, bringing him back, perhaps ironically, to this earlier scene in which two hearts in one body and two souls have been irrevocably lost *together* (and always will be)—this is the foregone conclusion of a life devoted to the idea of knighthood, to its aesthetic beauty and chaos of mistaken identities, and ultimately, its supposedly "higher" impersonality, which requires death . . .

. . . And yet, because Malory's world re-unfolds each time we return to it as readers, its events—Balyn's momentary astonishment, which is a sort of suspension of himself (as well as his and his brother's uncannily doubled death, which is also a return to their mother's womb as if they had *never been born at all*)—remain always in the future. The characters are, as it were, shut up in a narrative in which the same things happen to them over and over again with no possibility of a different ending—just as every time we read *Anna Karenina*, Anna will always jump between the cars of the oncoming train. Yet there is an apophatic element inscribed in the body of the language of Malory's (or any literary) text, which we might say is also an important function of the "event" of Colombe's suicide and Balyn's astonishment at it—an event, moreover, that, in John Caputo's words, is "inexhaustible" and "possessed of unplumbable depths, an inner restlessness and dynamic by virtue of which the event is never given a final expression in words and never reaches a final realization in things."[35] This might also be a new credo for the human individual as an *advenant* who desires, not to master the world, nor *merely* (or overly aggressively) to project herself into that world (as becoming-human), but rather, seeks opportunities to *well up* in the "diachrony of the radically burst open and non-synchronisable times"[36] of events, to take place in the *taking-place* of the world. This would be to live both within, and against the grain, of the genre itself—which is to say, the "romance," but also history.

---

35. John D. Caputo, "Bodies Still Unrisen, Events Still Unsaid," *Angelaki* 12.1 (April 2007): 83 [73–86].

36. Romano, *L'événement et le monde*, 65; quoted in Mackinlay, "Event, World, and Place," 9.

CHAPTER 3

The Book of Hours and iPods, Passionate Lyrics, and Prayers

Technologies of the Devotional Self

TIM SPENCE

PRELUDE[1]

Near the turn of the last Millennium, in their song "Styrofoam Boots / It's All Nice on Ice," Modest Mouse pointedly linked prayer with the ringing of a telephone, and ironically commented on the implications of this link: "I'll be damned."[2] These words invoke the spirit of this essay, which focuses on the relationship between communication technologies and the identity of those who use these technologies as devotional media. I argue that the devotional

---

1. This essay began as a paper to be presented to a live audience. Its original structure was lyrical, and, as it has changed media several times since its invention, that more ephemeral structure has dissolved. Many, countless thanks to the benevolence of Myra Seaman and Eileen Joy in their assistance in this transformation.

2. Modest Mouse, "Styrofoam Boots / It's All Nice on Ice," *The Lonesome Crowded West* (LP), Glacial Pace, 1997.

self in the twenty-first century is caught up in a web of electronic media, symbolized most immediately by the iPod and its smartphone descendants. Devotional practices enabled by the music these digital technologies convey seem fresh, current, real. When the world outside seems to have all gone mad, I can soothe my soul with my favorite songs, no matter where my body may be. This essay proposes, however, that this escape into such a personalized technology is not unique in the history of Western devotional practice. In fact, it is the primary goal of this essay to illuminate the strange harmony resonating between the crises of belief and identity in our twenty-first century and the crises of belief and identity that happened in the thirteenth through fifteenth centuries in England and across all of Europe. First, let me begin by turning to what I mean by a crisis of belief and identity.

Identity folded in on itself—onto its own subject—with the rise of revolutionized devotional cultures in Western Europe from the twelfth through the fifteenth centuries.[3] During this period, several communities of devotion developed pedagogical programs designed to train new practitioners in certain fundamental exegetical skills (i.e., hermeneutic and compositional) necessary to fulfill the duties of their calling: remembering the Body of Christ through prayer (*oratio*).[4] Many of these skills, such as the development of emotional memory, required a significant amount of introspection, self-reflection, and personal meditation. Out of foundational prayers of confession focused on the individual's flaws and shortcomings, the practitioner of devotion would ascend to more abstract forms of prayerful meditation, through which the individual might eventually *feel* a personal relationship with the Divine.[5] As more lay people acquired the means to practice devotion, more individuals habituated themselves to systems of private reading and private prayers.[6] In his personal

---

3. For an extended analysis of this historical moment, see Giles Constable, *The Reformation of the Twelfth Century* (New York: Cambridge University Press, 1996).

4. See Jerome Taylor, Introduction to *The Didascalicon of Hugh of St. Victor*, ed. Taylor (New York: Columbia University Press, 1991), 3–39.

5. Richard Rolle's *Emendatio vitae*, a twelve-step program of devotional practice, begins with conversion, or confession, and ends with solitary contemplation of God (*Richard Rolle: Emendatio Vitae; Orationes Ad Honorem Nominis Ihesu*, ed. Nicholas Watson [Toronto: Pontifical Institute of Mediaeval Studies, 1995]). For the mystical potential of prayer, see Barbara Newman, "What Did It Mean to Say 'I Saw'? The Clash between Theory and Practice in Medieval Visionary Culture," *Speculum: A Journal of Medieval Studies* 80.1 (2005): 1–43.

6. Cf. Anne Stanton, *The Queen Mary Psalter: A Study of Affect and Audience*, (Philadelphia: American Philosophical Society, 2001), 69. Devotional texts such as the breviary for the religious and the Psalter developed before and were the models for the book of hours (65). The book of hours interfaced with the *ars praedicandi* in Northern Europe during the thirteenth century: "In a [lay] religious environment that was increasingly congenial to images, one conditioned by the *highly imaged preaching of the friars*, the book of hours would have seemed

study, beside her favorite window, or in a garden removed, these practices of private devotion eventually folded into the reflective subject, the *cogito ergo sum* that guided us into the modern age.

Most of the various pedagogies that helped ignite this subjective implosion stemmed from a Greco-Roman rhetorical tradition that was judicial in nature and focused on three types of persuasive proof: logos (an appeal to reason), pathos (an appeal to emotion), and ethos (a charismatic appeal based on the speaker's persona).[7] Devoted practitioners of reflective, meditative, lyrical prayer—individuals such as Hugh, Adam, and the other twelfth-century Victorines—saw the mortal and divine united in emotions associated with and accessible through the composition and rehearsal of meditations and prayers on Christ's Passion.[8] Devotional culture at this time was based on interweaving highly emotional prayers of confession, praise, petition, and thanksgiving for Christ's Passion, Love, and Mercy.[9] These prayers all served one function:

---

more user-friendly, to use a modern phrase, than the Psalter" (69–70; emphasis mine). Stanton draws a conclusion with which I agree: "The implication is that the psalms are for family use and education, while the hourly readings function more clearly as private devotions" (70). Even as the rhetoric of preaching moved deep into the Parish system, the book of hours began its own ascent of influence as a devotional technology, reaching its apex by the middle of the fourteenth century and maintaining its dominance of the devotional technology market for at least two hundred years.

7. George A. Kennedy, *Classical Rhetoric and its Christian and Secular Tradition from Ancient to Modern Times* (Chapel Hill: University of North Carolina Press, 1980), 23–24. For an illuminating study of Antiquity's influence on the Latin culture throughout Western Europe, see Ernst Robert Curtius, *European Literature and the Latin Middle Ages* (Princeton, NJ: Princeton University Press, 1967).

8. For informative work on the use of emotional commonplaces in monastic spirituality, see Mary Carruthers, *The Craft of Thought: Meditation, Rhetoric, and the Making of Images, 400–1200* (New York: Cambridge University Press, 1998); and Caroline Walker Bynum, *Docere Verbo et Exemplo: An Aspect of Twelfth-Century Spirituality* (Missoula, MT: Scholars Press, 1978). For more on the transition of this spirituality from the monastery into the laity, see Barbara Newman, "What Did It Mean to Say 'I Saw'?" For more on the role of emotions and the significance of Christ's Passion in medieval devotional practices, see Caroline Walker Bynum, *Jesus as Mother: Studies in the Spirituality of the High Middle Ages* (Berkeley: University of California Press, 1982); *Fragmentation and Redemption: Essays on Gender and the Human Body in Medieval Religion* (Cambridge, MA: Zone Books, 1991); and *The Resurrection of the Body in Western Christianity, 200–1336* (New York: Columbia University Press, 1995). See also Carruthers, *Craft of Thought*, 14–16, 21, 117, and 168. For examples of twelfth-century Victorine manuals that teach these methods of meditation and prayer, see Hugh of St. Victor's *Didascalicon*, Book III, and his related *De modo orandi*, as well as the pseudo-Hugh treatise *De modo dicendi et meditandi* and the anonymous *De meditando seu meditandi artificio* (Jerome Taylor, ed. *The Didascalicon of Hugh of St. Victor*, [New York: Columbia University Press, 1991]).

9. Compare these four types of prayer to the twelfth century practice of monastic prayer as described in Rachel Fulton, "Praying with Anselm at Admont: A Meditation on Practice," *Speculum: A Journal of Medieval Studies* 81.3 (2006): 700–33. I am presently preparing a translation and commentary on three arts of prayer written at St. Victor Abbey in the late twelfth

their "coding," or "script," activated within the individual user a cluster of emotions that made the subject feel communion with Christ and his corporate Body on earth.

In the first decade of the twenty-first century, identity is folding in again, only now identity seems to be morphing out of the form into which it folded with the dawn of the printing press. In an "in through the out door" maneuver, the active voice of *cogito ergo sum* is collapsing into the passive *digeror ergo sum*.[10] Identity is collapsing in the Digital Ages into a worldwide wormhole connecting everyone to everything at any time via electronic media. Today, diverse cultures of devotion focused on myriad emotions find great pleasure in feelings generated by the digitized lyric.[11] Devotional cultures of our Digital Ages use electronic technologies to interweave highly emotional playlists as the lyrical background of practitioners' daily lives. This shared techno-devotional phenomena is the starting point of this essay: devotional practices in the Middle and Digital Ages engage portable, hand-held communication devices. Both the medieval and digital collapses of subjective identity were expedited by complex, handheld communication technologies much more adaptable to individual end users and thereby more intimate to individuals' daily lives than the printed book.

VERSE I

The book of hours was a technological motherboard that enabled the construction of a devotional self.[12] Individuals used the book of hours to activate specific emotions privately.[13] This intentional, learned process of manipulating

---

century. These texts taught the rhetorical skills necessary for devotional prayer to novitiates in a monastic setting.

10. "Sorted, therefore, I am."

11. Hate groups based on clusters of extremely powerful emotions have flourished in the Digital Ages. See, for example, Dina Temple-Raston, "Experts Aim to Explain Spike in LA Hate Crimes," *All Things Considered*, National Public Radio, 25 November 2008.

12. For example, see Carruthers's discussion of *machina memorialis* in *Craft of Thought*, 1–10, 22–4, and 92–94. Hugh of St. Victor considered knowledge itself "mechanical" (*Didascalicon* I.8) and felt the mechanical arts were "man's efforts ... to supply both the internal and external needs of his body" (see Taylor, *Didascalicon* II.xx; ibid., 191, n.59). Martin of Laon defined "mechanical art" as "any object which is clever and most delicate and which, in its making or operation, is beyond detection, so that beholders find their power of vision stolen from them when they cannot penetrate the ingenuity of the thing" (Ibid, n.64). For another recent discussion of prayers as machines, see Fulton, "Praying with Anselm."

13. Medieval notions of privacy differ greatly from our own various, ever-changing notions of privacy. Here, I consider the example of one woman reading to several members of her

a devotional book like a book of hours triggered an emotional experience that, by design, created a feeling of communion with the corporate body of Christ.[14] Devotional books, in other words, enabled individuals to experience a sense of transcendence based on learned activities of discovering the divine from within their own human, subjective, day-to-day existence. Practitioners of devotion interacted with their prayer books to discover appropriate material for their prayers and meditations, either scripted or original. This "discovery" of and participation in the Divine Word were the result of several complex technologies—some cognitive, some concrete—working together to provide the proper content, state of mind, and interpretive engines necessary to move one's emotions in a pre-scripted manner.[15] These technologies included the text; the manuscript's overall content, organization and illumination; architectural spaces of cathedrals, chapels, libraries and gardens; and temporal technologies such as the calendar and clocks, and all merged together in a process its practitioners and critics called *lectio divina*. According to St. Gregory, this complex method of reading "corresponds with the state of the student; it goes, stands, is lifted up with him, like the wheels according as he is striving after the active life, after stability and constancy of spirit, or after the flights of contemplation."[16] This type of reading, *lectio,* seems to have moved the orator

---

household (her own children, private guests, perhaps) to be a semiprivate use of this technology. Though, cf. Stanton, who points out that Psalters were used for didactic purposes in small groups, but books of hours "function more clearly as private devotions" (*Queen Mary Psalter,* 70).

14. For more on the networked physical and cognitive technologies that enabled this corporate identity, see Lara Farina, *Erotic Discourse and Early English Religious Writing* (New York: Palgrave MacMillan, 2006); Fulton, "Praying with Anselm"; John Higgitt, *The Murthly Hours: Devotion, Literacy and Luxury in Paris, England and the Gaelic West* (London: British Library and University of Toronto Press, 2000); Newman, "What Did It Mean to Say 'I Saw'?"; and Roger S. Wieck, *Time Sanctified: The Book of Hours in Medieval Art and Life* (New York: George Braziller, 1988) and *Painted Prayers: The Book of Hours in Medieval and Renaissance Art* (New York: George Braziller, 1997).

15. For more discussion on the musical techniques and technologies involved in the practice of devotion at this time, see Bruce Holsinger, *Music, Body, and Desire in Medieval Culture: Hildegard of Bingen to Chaucer* (Stanford, CA: Stanford University Press, 2001), especially part 2. Holsinger argues that the "New Song" of medieval devotional communities depended upon a conception of embodiment that fundamentally distinguished between body and flesh. "Body" in this sense is a technologically mediated form of flesh that links the practitioner of devotion to greater networks of musical potential, that is, to greater harmonies with the divine.

16. The reference here is to the vision of Ezekiel described in Ezekiel 1:21: "When those went these went, and when those stood these stood, and when those were lifted up from the earth the wheels were also lifted up together and followed them: for the spirit of life was in the wheels." This quotation from Ezekiel, as well as the description quoted in the main text above, are from Beryl Smalley, *The Study of the Bible in the Middle Ages* (Notre Dame, IN: University of Notre Dame Press, 1964), 32. For both the quote from Ezekiel and her description of

beyond his or her codex—removed from others and into an active life engaged with the world around them. Devotional reading becomes an all-inclusive mode of being active in the world, a way of fulfilling Paul's mandate to Christians in Thessalonica to pray without ceasing. Some of the cognitive technologies involved in the process of *lectio divina* included hermeneutical systems that generated rich semiotic relationships between the text and the divine.[17] These relationships were further processed by mnemonic systems of retention and contemplation, as well as other rhetorical systems of prayer composition such as *elocutio* and *dispositio*. Together, these cognitive technologies interfaced with the various technologies of the manuscript codex—to include the semiotics of marginalia, illuminations, various uses of colored script, and so on—in the practice of medieval devotion.

The mass production of books of hours for laity amplified the technological turn toward the individual person in terms of communication media.[18] For the first time in history, significant numbers of people could afford to own a book, a technology designed to expedite private religious devotion.[19] Perhaps

---

lectio divina here quoted, Smalley cites St. Gregory's *Homilia in Ezechiel* I.vii, from *Patrologia Latina*, ed. Jacques Paul Migne, vol. 176 (Paris: Parisiis, 1849), col. 847–48.

17. For more on the central role of rhetorical hermeneutics in the Middle Ages, see Rita Copeland, *Rhetoric, Hermeneutics, and Translation in the Middle Ages: Academic Traditions and Vernacular Texts* (New York: Cambridge University Press, 1991).

18. Cf. Anne Stanton's observation: "In a religious environment that was increasingly congenial to images, one conditioned by the highly imaged preaching of the friars [i.e., more lay than regular], the book of hours would have seemed more user-friendly . . . than the Psalter" (*Queen Mary Psalter*, 69–70). For more on the production of books of hours (and medieval book production) from the thirteenth through fifteenth centuries, see Paul Binski and Stella Panayotova, *The Cambridge Illuminations: Ten Centuries of Book Production in the Medieval West* (London: Harvey Miller, 2005); Linda L. Brownrigg, ed., *Medieval Book Production: Assessing the Evidence: Proceedings of the Second Conference of the Seminar in the History of the Book to 1500, Oxford, July 1988* (Los Altos Hills, CA: Anderson-Lovelace, 1990); Ralph Hanna, *Pursuing History: Middle English Manuscripts and Their Texts* (Stanford, CA: Stanford University Press, 1996); Kathryn Kerby-Fulton and Denise Louise Despres, *Iconography and the Professional Reader: The Politics of Book Production in the Douce Piers Plowman* (Minneapolis: University of Minnesota Press, 1999); Elizabeth Moore Hunt, *Illuminating the Borders of Northern French and Flemish Manuscripts, 1270–1310* (New York: Routledge, 2006); Robin Myers and Michael Harris, *A Millennium of the Book: Production, Design & Illustration in Manuscript & Print, 900–1900* (Winchester, DE: St. Paul's Bibliographies and Oak Knoll Press, 1994); Susie Nash, *Between France and Flanders: Manuscript Illumination in Amiens* (London: British Library and University of Toronto Press, 1999); and Mary A. Rouse and Richard H. Rouse, *Authentic Witnesses: Approaches to Medieval Texts and Manuscripts* (Notre Dame: University of Notre Dame Press, 1991).

19. For a detailed study on England's transition into documented culture, see Michael T. Clanchy, *From Memory to Written Record, England 1066–1307*, 2nd ed. (Oxford: Blackwell, 1993); Derek Brewer, "Medieval Literature: Chaucer and the Alliterative Tradition," in *The New Pelican Guide to English Literature*, vol. 1, ed. Boris Ford (New York: Penguin Books, 1982), 133–53.

(though far beyond the limits of this present work) it is through this inner reflection that the black hole of modern subjectivity, Mr. Cogito, emerged from the dense center of this habituated devotional practice. A befuddled Everyman conceived by the poet Zbigniew Herbert, Mr. Cogito crystallizes a late modern age now gone—though its ghosts still haunt us, and we are still lured by many of its more appealing spirits.[20] In his review of Herbert's collection of poems, *Mr. Cogito*, Stephen Dobyns described this figure as "slightly foolish, slightly flummoxed and always sincere as he confronts the problems of our age."[21] Mr. Cogito also invokes Descartes's *cogito ergo sum*, a major premise of the modern epoch equating rational thinking to being. Much like John Kennedy Toole's Ignatius Riley in *A Confederacy of Dunces*, however, part of Mr. Cogito's complexity is the ironic contrast between an individual borne aloft in an untimely manner by his inner thoughts and the chaotic circumstances in which he finds himself, a world always just outside of the thinking being's control. In terms of this present essay, I consider Mr. Cogito an allegorical archetype representing modernity's deference to subjective thought. Mr. Cogito replaced Mr. Oratio—or the medieval deference to devotional prayer—the moment introspective meditation stopped producing corporate prayers and began producing subjective analysis for the self-reflective individual's independent self. In the terror twilight of his own age, Mr. Cogito's foolish and flummoxed condition indicated the dawning of a new era, in which thinking and being are no longer linked so substantially to one another, the way they once were in some mythical premoment of the modern era.

Identities in the Digital Ages are radically rewiring the interface between thought and being. Information technology now pervades our most intimate moments at several levels. Tragically, the massacre at Virginia Tech on 16 April 2007 made all of us painfully aware of how personal rage may broadcast itself in a digital age. A sick youth about to slaughter thirty-two students and faculty members in an engineering building on campus videotaped himself giving a two-and-a-half minute manifesto. This digitized broadcast of psychotic delusions was a juvenile attempt to produce a prepackaged media event. The cell phones and cameras used during this event by many of the tragedy's victims and witnesses wove the unthinkable ever more tightly into the electronic web of instantaneous information. Even in the pastoral mountains of southwestern

---

See also the quotation in note 36. For more on the various types of interiority enabled by private reading in the Middle Ages, see Daniel Boyarin, ed., *The Ethnography of Reading* (Berkeley: University of California Press, 1993).

20. Zbigniew Herbert, *Mr. Cogito* (Hopewell, NJ: Ecco Press, 1993).

21. Quote by Stephen Dobyns from *The New York Times Book Review*, printed on back cover of Ecco Press, 1993 edition.

Virginia, life is intimately and already enveloped in a digital web of instantaneous information technology. Individuals in the first decade of the twenty-first century experience the world with and through their digital information devices.

From within this labyrinth of digital media, I form my major conceit: the collapse of identity in the Digital Ages has a structural similarity to the collapse of identity in the High Middle Ages. In both instances, a network of technologies wove together a very intimate and sensual relationship between the individual user and a larger, corporate body of being. In the Middle Ages, the codex became a standard platform for such scripted techniques of *lectio* and *meditatio*. The intimate nature of medieval devotion's *via contemplativa* compelled the individual using book-of-hours technology to withdraw from public affairs.[22] The book of hours enabled a similar implosion, or interiorization of identity, in a growing number of readers from the thirteenth through the fifteenth centuries: lay men and women interested in developing a devotional self connected to a greater corporate body of the Divine Word. This corporate body—the community of Christ—transcended the physical, material, and social communities in which the devotee might have found him- or herself.

This collapse seems to be very similar to the current collapse of identity in the Digital Ages. A variety of technologies flow into the iPod or smartphone through the music we play, the information we consume, and the images we store; each iPod or smartphone user forms an intimate relationship with this technology. The heightened level of musical intimacy enabled by the iPod tends to distance the individual from the physical, material, and social communities in which the user might find him- or herself. Often, however, what remains hidden in the immediacy of the lived moment of a song are the abstract, corporate communities into which we subsume ourselves every time we plug in. This essay sketches significant similarities between post- and premodern cultures, between the Middle and the Digital Ages, which together form a chiasmic bracket of the mythical modern age like a linked pair of parentheses. The Middle and the Digital Ages are both contiguous with a modern epoch, a time begun by the printing press and ended by the incessant twittering of digital media. This parabolic relationship between the Middle and Digital Ages emerges quite clearly if we consider concepts like

---

22. For more on the sensuality of reading, especially in the context of an Anglo-Saxon notion of communal reading, see Lara Farina, "Before Affection: *Christ I* and the Social Erotic," *Exemplaria* 13.2 (2001): 469–96. This social erotic differs from the increasingly privatized reading involved in later devotional manuscripts, immediately preceding the advent of the printing press.

the experience of time, the structure of temporality itself, and the various histories told within its framework. Together these two epochs delimit a modern temporality, a structure of time that was quite linear in essence and quite different from the flatness of pre- and postmodern ages.

In contrast to modern histories based on linear temporalities, the structure of history during the Middle Ages resembles what Walter Haug describes as "a storehouse of exempla illustrating the relationship between God and humanity."²³ Chronological order is not very important in such a database, not nearly as important as moral criteria and stylistic questions of circumstantial propriety. Beginning in the Renaissance, however, and developing with greater vitality in the Reformation,²⁴ the structure and experience of time, as well as the structure and function of history itself, all undergo dramatic ideological and cosmological changes. Departing from the medieval concept of divine temporality in which chronological order is flattened, the moderns developed a temporality based upon scientific observation, discrete systems of measurement using technologies of scientific notation, and printed books that helped broadcast groundbreaking ideas. Calendars were fixed, clocks adjusted, measurements standardized, and time pieces shrunk to fit on the wrist of a train conductor and engineer hurtling forward at a hundred miles an hour. Perceived as a series of unique events, time and its historical narratives in the modern epoch tell stories arranged chronologically as a chain of events strung together by a series of cause and effect relationships. Although the eighteenth-century rhetorician Giovanni Battista Vico saw history curve back on itself in a spiral, the modern epoch overwhelmingly shaped most of its histories into chronological lines.²⁵ At the beginning of modernity, space and time seemed abundant at both the macro- and microscopic levels, but with the advent of such communication technologies as the printing press, the novel and periodicals, the individual's experience of both time and space began to converge. We might say, for example, that because of the advancements of daily newspapers and the advent of the trans-Atlantic telegraph, Paris was not nearly as far away from Baltimore for Gertrude Stein as it was for Edgar Allan Poe. When

---

23. Walter Haug, *Vernacular Literary Theory in the Middle Ages: The German Tradition, 800–1300, in its European Context*, trans. J. M. Catling (Cambridge: Cambridge University Press, 1997), 56.

24. For a detailed analysis of the role the printing press played in the Reformation, see Brian Cummings, *The Literary Culture of the Reformation: Grammar and Grace* (New York: Oxford University Press, 2002), 16–19, and 32–42.

25. Michel Serres says of modernity's various notions of time (e.g., scientific or historicist): "Whether this time is cumulative, continuous, or interrupted, it always remains linear" (Michel Serres with Bruno Latour, *Conversations on Science, Culture, and Time*, trans. Roxanne Lapidus [Ann Arbor: University of Michigan Press, 1995], 57).

Poe wrote, Europe was exotic to the American middle class; when Stein wrote, Europe was the incubator for some of America's greatest writers and artists.

For the Digital Ages, however, quantum physics has turned cosmology and temporality inside out through its theories of deep time, patterned chaos, subatomic quarks, and fractal spaces. History in our Digital Ages is essentially flattened. In fact, for the purpose of this essay, we will say that the Digital Ages emerged when modernity's memory flatlined on the Internet with the first squelching of the dialup modem: when digital information became overwhelming, and everything to be known was already waiting in a database somewhere for someone to google. According to Paul Virilio, during the modern era, Western cultures prioritized speed over other political, social, and environmental concerns.[26] This obsession with speed and its related desire to compress time has had an extremely negative effect on the public sphere, simultaneously gutting democracies while beefing up the power of the military industrial complex.[27] According to Virilio, the proliferation of visualizing technologies is closely related to this need for speed and its subsequent forms of oppression.[28] This "pernicious industrialization of vision" disorients individuals and standardizes visual experience.[29] Individuals living in a world of industrialized vision experience picnolepsy, a period of time in which the subject loses track of real time, real place events.[30] With the smartphone, we are experiencing a pernicious industrialization of another sense, our sense of hearing. When an individual's world becomes mediated by electronic, digital devices, the subject becomes lost to what Rob Bartram describes as "a civilization of forgetting, a live (live-coverage) society that has no future and no past, since it has no extension and no duration, a society intensely present here and there at once—in other words, *telepresent to the whole world.*"[31] In stark contrast to the phenomenological "Now," this digitized telepresence generates a surrealistic absence from the real time, real place moment rooted in our body's physical extension in space. If we consider the three epochs (medieval, modern, and digital) in terms of the concepts of time, temporality, and the

---

26. For example, see Paul Virilio, *Speed and Politics: An Essay on Dromology*, trans. Mark Polizzotti (New York: Semiotext[e], 1986).

27. Rob Bartram, "Visuality, Dromology and Time Compression: Paul Virilio's New Ocularcentrism," *Time and Society* 13.2–3 (2004): 289 [285–300].

28. Virilio develops a concept of "endo-colonialism" in which urban space is colonized through the use of "vision machines" in *Information Bomb* (trans. Chris Turner [London: Verso, 2000]).

29. Paul Virilio, *Open Sky* (London: Verso, 1997), 89; quoted in Bartram, "Visuality, Dromology and Time Compression," 293.

30. Ibid., 295.

31. Ibid., 293 (emphasis in original).

function of history within each, then the modern stands out by the linear extension of its temporality, contrasted against the Middle and Digital Ages, both of which have referential structures of history and compacted conceptions of time.

VERSE II

The Middle Ages and Digital Ages are both founded upon and weave themselves together by networking certain information technologies. Central to the medieval networking of technologies was the written document, the manuscript; central to the digital network is the motherboard, with its silicon chips and electronic processor. The various cultures of each epoch use these technologies not only to produce important cultural material but also to educate the next generation of cultural participants.

More significant similarities between the Middle and Digital Ages emerge at this technological interface between cultural memory, media, and the individual user. French anthropologist Pierre Bourdieu provides a helpful comment on the social relationship between cultural tradition and individuated identity within a specific culture with his observation that "in a determinate social formation, the stabler [sic] the objective structures and the more fully they reproduce themselves in the agents' dispositions, the greater the extent of the field of doxa, of that which is taken for granted."[32] Cultures of devotion from the twelfth through the fourteenth century (via the book of hours) and cultures of musical devotion in the twenty-first century (via the iPod) all take a great deal of prescription for granted. In other words, there is a considerable amount of invisible pre-scripting involved in the mass production of these cultures of devotion.

Let me briefly explain what I mean by "invisible pre-scripting" and leave the complexities of cultures operating in these periods to another place and time. What the monks did with classical theories of rhetoric in the twelfth century is very much like what Steve Jobs and Bill Gates did with binary code not too long ago. Both groups of individuals figured out how to make information accessible in a whole new way. Medieval monks and our contemporary techies each discovered codes, grammar, and syntax—a technological language—that enabled effective communication of nearly limitless pieces of information. If you want to encode information today, you need to know how

---

32. Pierre Bourdieu, *Outline of a Theory of Practice*, trans. by Richard Nice (New York: Cambridge University Press, 1977), 165–66.

to manipulate the code, the deep "languages" enabling the effective communication of information in the Digital Ages.[33]

Classical rhetoric was the basic code or operating language for medieval institutions of Church and government. Nearly all competitors, like those who scripted oral codes in songs and folk incantations, were wiped out or converted. By the end of the eleventh century, Roman-based administrative systems of power that were based on written documents began to rule most of Europe through the extension of the parish system. Scholars such as Brian Stock,[34] Thomas Clanchy, and Emily Steiner have greatly enhanced our understanding of how literacy and textual-based methods of documentation shaped not only the legal but also the poetic imaginations of England from the eleventh through the fourteenth centuries. Meanwhile, in our nascent Digital Ages we are already enamored of sublime images of digitized identity, its euphoric grasp on our imaginations accelerated by myriad electronic media.

Of course it can be argued that electricity is the most significant element—the catalyst—of this primary infatuation of the Digital Ages, even more than the binary code enabling the electronic inscription of everything from DNA to my son's third birthday. Once combined with the vibrant vernacular traditions of blues and bluegrass music, for example, electricity sparked quite the revolutionary spirit among a wide variety of groups. Take, by way of illustration, the AM-analog revolutions of the 1960s and 1970s engendered by the combination of 45 rpm records and broadcast radio. Among the most infamous of these groups was the small band of Maoist terrorists known as the Weather Underground. When its members went into hiding from the FBI's furtive and hostile COINTELPRO, they took their operative name from their parent group, the Weathermen, which itself refers to Bob Dylan's prophetic line, "You don't have to be a weatherman to know which way the wind blows."[35] The Weather Underground's decision to wage war on common citizens exemplifies a revolutionary spirit sublimated beyond reason by electrified lyrics.

In ways much like the spurious and self-destructive Weather Underground, medieval mystics like Richard Rolle and the Beguines of Northern Europe were often moved by passionate lyrical meditations to take direct

---

33. For more on the deep language of hypertext media, see Stuart Malthrop, "So You Say You Want a Revolution? Hypertext and the Laws of Media," *Postmodern Culture* 1.3 (1991): 691–704, http://jefferson.village.virginia.edu/pmc/text-only/issue.591/moulthro.591.

34. Brian Stock, *The Implications of Literacy: Written Language and Models of Interpretation in the Eleventh and Twelfth Centuries* (Princeton, NJ: Princeton University Press, 1983); Clanchy, *From Memory to Written Record;* and Emily Steiner, *Documentary Culture and the Making of Medieval English Literature* (New York: Cambridge University Press, 2003).

35. Bob Dylan, "Subterranean Homesick Blues," *Bringing It All Back Home* (Columbia Records, 1965).

action against the dominant social, political, and ideological power. The mystics' decisions to speak outside the authorization of the Church inevitably brought them rebuke from their peers, and often times this public chastisement proved fatal. It might well be that the emotional insight of the lyric enabled the mystic to "see" the true limits of the Church's corporate matrix of power structuring their society. We know that the women of the Beguine movement, for example, who never took oaths to the Church, produced the first lyricist to write in Dutch,[36] several theological treatises,[37] as well as a host of devotees burned at the stake. Perhaps because the lyricist's sense of truth is rooted in the individual's experience of a song, only a devotee can truly understand the struggle that ultimately invoked the human *pathos* of the song itself. Nevertheless, the lyric represents the sound of an individual subject struggling against the inhuman for the sake of his or her own humanity. If you get a lyric or a song, then you feel this subjective struggle of the song's *pathos*. This feeling of having personal insight into an immediate truth provides the mystic and revolutionary alike the courage to accept the ultimate sacrifice for his or her core beliefs.

The power of scripting gives both ages what seems to be great revolutionary potential. In both eras, two sectors of society from which social unrest has stemmed have been the highly educated unemployed (i.e., university students) and the extremely poor and/or marginalized sectors of society. These sectors of society often have used lyrics rather than (though sometimes in addition to) violence and civil disobedience to articulate social unrest. In the early 1990s, for example, the explosion of both the indie rock and hip-hop music scenes were predicated on a rejection of mainstream "white" suburban American culture.[38] Take Public Enemy's *Fear of a Black Planet*,[39] featuring such titles as "911 Is a Joke," "Burn Hollywood Burn," and "Revolutionary Generation." The album's first single release to hit number one on the Hot Rap Singles chart

---

36. Hadewijch of Brabant.

37. E.g., Marguerite Porete, *The Mirror of Simple Souls*, and Mechthild of Magdeburg, *The Flowing Light of the Godhead*.

38. We must be cautious, however, in our assessment of these "revolutions." The music industry has commodified countercultures for decades: records are pressed and CDs are burned to be sold. As Stephen Malkmus pointedly remarks in one of his self-reflexive lyrics, "Songs mean a lot when songs are bought / And so are you" ("Cut Your Hair," on *Crooked Rain, Crooked Rain* [Matador Records, 1994]). For more on the false dichotomy so easily and often constructed between "mainstream" culture and "counterculture," see Thomas Frank, *The Conquest of Cool: Business Culture, Counterculture, and the Rise of Hip Consumerism* (Chicago: University of Chicago Press, 1997), and, with a few caveats, Joseph Heath and Andrew Potter, *Nation of Rebels: Why Counterculture Became Consumer Culture* (New York: Harper Business, 2004).

39. Def Jam Recordings, 1990.

was "Fight the Power," written in response to the 1989 "Greekfest Riots" in Virginia Beach, in which police and African American college students clashed during an annual Labor Day weekend festival, plagued with racial tensions. While Public Enemy's album stirred up controversy and sold over a million copies, Seattle-based Nirvana was preparing their second album, *Nevermind*.[40] This album brought the "grunge" sound international attention and catapulted indie rock from the college radio scene into the mainstream marketplace.[41]

As early as the eleventh century, social unrest was quite present and culturally embodied by the Goliards, a group of highly educated, unemployed young men. Two heaps of broken images that we moderns have of this lost *ordo vagorum* are the *Carmina Burana* and *Carmina Cantabrigiensia* [*Cambridge Songs*].[42] These young men adopted monikers such as Hugh Primas and the Archpoet, reminiscent of the names of today's hip-hop stars such as Notorious B.I.G., Tru Master, and Mos Def. Like their kindred spirits in the twentieth and twenty-first centuries, these wandering musicians believed it was better to burn out than to fade away: "Meum est propositum in taberna mori, / ubi vina proxima morientis ori" ["My plan is to die in a tavern, / where wine is near to my dying mouth"].[43] Like the modern hip-hop artist or rock and roller, these twelfth-century lyricists also imagined themselves outside of the law: "Non me tenent vincula, non me tenet clavis, / quaero mei similes et adjungor pravis" ["Chains do not hold me, the [jailor's] key does not hold me, / I seek those like me and I'm bound to the outlaws"].[44]

CHORUS

But what does this change in media really mean? How have electricity and the media it conveys changed our lives?[45] How does digitization change the way

---

40. Geffen Records, 1991.

41. *Nevermind* has sold over 30 million copies: see Lou Thomas, "Review, Nirvana's *Nevermind*," BBC, 23 April 2007, http://www.bbc.co.uk/music/release/f8dp/.

42. For more on Hugh Primas and the Archpoet, see Fleur Adcock, *Hugh Primas and the Archpoet* (New York: Cambridge University Press, 1994). Compare with the reviews of this book by Carolinne White, *Medium Aevum* 65.1 (1996): 118–19, and A. G. Rigg, *Speculum* 71.4 (1996): 925–26. See also Helen Waddell, *The Wandering Scholars* (London: Constable, 1966).

43. From Stephen Gaselee, ed., "Wine, Woman, and Song" [a.k.a. "Archpoet's Confession"] in *The Oxford Book of Medieval Latin Verse*, 3rd ed. (Oxford: Clarendon Press, 1946), 125. The translation is mine.

44. Ibid., 124. The translation is mine.

45. For more on how media technologies influence the individual's experience of reality, see Jane Avrich et al., "Forum—Grand Theft Education—Literacy in the Age of Video Games," *Harper's* (September 2006), 31–39; Donna Haraway, "A Cyborg Manifesto: Science, Technology,

we interact with and perceive the world around us? How does the digitized lyric move us, how does it habituate us to the world when we consume music electronically in a private sphere? Music in silence—that's a concept that common sense might say sounds quite impossible. A century ago, music was of necessity a shared experience. Today, however, when someone plugs into his or her iPod, that person is immediately, emotionally, and privately transported to an electric state of mysticism. What fascinates me about medieval devotion is its ability, like the music I fell in love with during the 1990s, to sweep individuals away in its lyrical emotion. For example, like David Berman of the Silver Jews, Stephen Malkmus of Pavement, and Isaac Brock of Modest Mouse, the fourteenth-century mystic Richard Rolle equated his mystical states of being to musical harmony and was made famous for his ability to create lyrics that brought others into a similar feeling of harmonic being.

We'll come back to Rolle, but I would first like to clarify my interests as a historian of devotion: I study the modes of being people occupy on a daily basis through rituals and regimens. I understand a "mode of being" here in terms of *habitus*, a medieval concept originating in Greco-Roman antiquity and popularized by Bourdieu. He defines *habitus* as "systems of durable, transposable *dispositions*, structured structures predisposed to function as structuring structures, that is, as principles of the generation and structuring of practices and representations."[46] I am interested in the rituals individuals learn to perform that increase their "inventive capacity" as agents within particular social groups. Together, these various rituals, the technologies they use, and their endemic dispositions form an individual's practice of devotion. Though the technologies and trappings have varied throughout the ages, the devotee's ability to manipulate his or her emotions through ritualistic uses of a specifically designed technology of devotion has remained strikingly consistent.

Prayer books and iPods enable individuals to "create" themselves in inventive ways in the most intimate of daily spaces. These technologies enhance

---

and Socialist-Feminism in the Late Twentieth Century," in *Simians, Cyborgs and Women: The Reinvention of Nature*, ed. Haraway (New York: Routledge, 1991), 149–81; Steven Johnson, *Interface Culture: How New Technology Transforms the Way We Create and Communicate* (San Francisco: HarperEdge, 1997); Marshall McLuhan, *Understanding Media: The Extensions of Man* (Cambridge, MA: MIT Press, 1994); and Sherryl Vint, *Bodies of Tomorrow: Technology, Subjectivity, Science Fiction* (Toronto: University of Toronto Press, 2007).

46. Bourdieu, *Outline of a Theory of Practice*, 72 (emphasis in original). Bourdieu includes the following footnote for "dispositions": "The word *disposition* seems particularly suited to express what is covered by the concept of habitus (defined as a system of dispositions). It expresses first the *result of an organizing action*, with a meaning close to that of words such as structure; it also designates a *way of being*, a habitual state (especially of the body) and, in particular, a *predisposition, tendency, propensity*, or *inclination*" (*Outline of a Theory of Practice*, 214, n.1).

the inventive capacity of agents by assisting individuals to affect their dispositions, or modes of living, in such a way that they fill their world with potential meaning. In her essay on medieval visionary culture, for example, Barbara Newman recognizes the important role books of prayer played in the privatization of devotion:

> Within the broader context of late-medieval Christianity, scripted visions can be seen as one aspect of a comprehensive and profoundly ambivalent trend toward domestication of the sacred, along with vernacular Bible translations, books of hours, indulgenced prayers, and devotions "by number" such as the rosary.[47]

In a similar, profoundly ambivalent manner, my iPod enables me to create the soundtrack to my own life. The sounds I've prescribed myself through my iPod's playlists mediate my experience of the world and my interaction with those around me. Digitized lyrics woo and soothe me and over seventy million others around the world every day.[48] When I am walking in the city and feel withdrawn as I weave among its masses, I might very well choose a melancholic melody from Leonard Cohen to nurture my conflicted feelings of being crowded and alone at the same time. Such an intentional use of this technology verifies my strange fits of passion as universal—one might even say "catholic"—even as it soothes them with its electric aura.

The personal verification and comfort that stems from the habitual use of devotional technologies is rooted in the fact that everything becomes symbolic in the *habitus* of devotion. For example, we know in particular that the *habitus* propagated at the Abbey of St. Victor during the twelfth century under Hugh and his disciples sought three levels of meaning in textual exposition.[49] Moreover, through *meditatio*, this pedagogic community sought "the cause,

---

47. Barbara Newman, "What Did It Mean to Say 'I Saw'?", 33. Newman provides the following bibliographic note to this claim: "A trend first noted by Johan Huizinga in *The Waning of the Middle Ages: A Study of the Forms of Life, Thought and Art in France and the Netherlands in the Fourteenth and Fifteenth Centuries*, trans. F. Hopman (London, 1924; repr. Garden City, NY, 1954). Cf. Eamon Duffy, *The Stripping of the Altars: Traditional Religion in England, c. 1400–1580* (New Haven, CT, 1992), 33, n.107." I would add to these Nicholas Watson, "Censorship and Cultural Change in Late-Medieval England: Vernacular Theology, the Oxford Translation Debate, and Arundel's Constitutions of 1409," *Speculum* 70.4 (1995): 822–64.

48. In the public high school where I teach, there are at least two students with emotional issues who have Individual Educational Plans (IEPs) that allow them to use their iPods or mp3 players to calm themselves when they feel stress levels rising. In these instances, at least, the Commonwealth of Virginia and healthcare providers have recognized a positive application of this technology in the effective control of human emotions.

49. Taylor, *Didascalicon* III.8, 92).

source, manner and utility of each and every thing."⁵⁰ The figurative nature of religious lyrics enabled easy encoding of vast amounts of information pertinent to the *habitus* of devotion to the Word made Flesh. Once the *orator* has encoded enough prayers and exempla, he (and later, she) would thereby be enabled to create his own playlists of prayers to manipulate himself into a *compassionate*, devoted state of being through which he is able to participate actively, that is, "to feel" the emotions involved with the idea of Christ's Passion.

The iPod and the medieval book of hours are—within appropriate cultural conditions—both able to convey lyrical content targeting specific human emotions in a very immediate and personal manner.⁵¹ If I'm feeling depressed because my loved one seems demanding, hearing Uncle Tupelo's line "rivers burn and then run backwards. / For her, that's enough" somehow makes me feel less alone in my suffering. Lyrics enable us to commune with one another over disparate places and at various times. Lyrical figures and tropes create an emotional space in which devotees might commune within the emotional geography, or *pathos*, constructed by the song. I can pick and choose songs to match almost any experience I have. If I want to feel a particular way, I choose a song that evokes that emotion in me, and I am more than half way *inside* my desired emotional mode of being. Likewise, a mystic like Rolle living in fourteenth-century Hampole found lyrics that both moved him and amplified his feeling of *pathos*. His lyrical *orationes* were so popular they were gathered together and copied separately in miscellanies⁵²—thus they might be seen as a lyrical playlist broadcasted through medieval prayer, books such as Psalters, devotional miscellanies, and books of hours.

I'm interested in prayer and prayer composition because I see prayer as an intentionally developed cognitive technology of considerable social import.

---

50. "Meditatio est frequens cogitatio modum, et causam et rationem uniuscujusque rei investigans" ["Meditation is frequent cogitation, investigating the mode, cause, and scheme of each and every thing"], incipit of *De meditando seu meditandi artificio opusculum aureum*, attributed to Hugh of Paris in Jacques Paul Migne, ed., *Patrologia Latina*, vol. 176 (Paris: Parisiis, 1849), col. 0993–98A.

51. The field of lyric studies is vast and well populated with brilliant flowers from which much more is to be gleaned than this essay's tiny cups can appropriately accommodate. For more on medieval lyrics, see Peter Dronke, *The Medieval Lyric* (Rochester, NY: D. S. Brewer, 1996); Andrew Scott Galloway, "Chaucer's Former Age and the Fourteenth-Century Anthropology of Craft: The Social Logic of a Premodernist Lyric," *ELH* 63.3 (1996): 535–54; John C. Hirsh, *Medieval Lyric: Middle English Lyrics, Ballads, and Carols* (Malden, MA: Blackwell Publishing, 2005); Emily Steiner, *Documentary Culture;* and Siegfried Wenzel, *Preachers, Poets, and the Early English Lyric* (Princeton, NJ: Princeton University Press, 1986).

52. Cf. Nicholas Watson, Introduction to *Richard Rolle: Emendatio Vitae; Orationes Ad Honorem Nominis Ihesu* (Toronto: Pontifical Institute of Mediaeval Studies, 1995), 6 [1–30].

The cognitive machinery of prayer enabled individuals to "program" their minds by a particular habituation to exist within a particular, perhaps even predetermined, world. In the fourteenth century, this *habitus* of devotion was endemic to a life of prayer.[53] Devotional prayer compositions were passionate lyrics presented in a very moving form. The book of hours and devotional miscellanies that compiled and formatted these lyrics were technological devices designed for a specific cultural purpose; in essence, they served as a multimedia platform that conducted the individual into a broadly conceived, multimedia experience of devotion in fourteenth-century England.

Hollins University's McVitty Book of Hours is a good example of how books of hours were designed to engage individuals in a multimedia experience of devotion. This impressive codex was made in France during the fifteenth century, and its finely crafted illumination cycle for the Hours of the Virgin are in their original order.[54] The illuminations have stylistic elements common to northern France. In the first full-page illumination used to indicate the beginning of the Gospel readings (f. 16r), we see St. John himself, sitting on the island of Patmos, presented in a medieval landscape, writing in a book.[55] This illumination gives this devotional technology corporeal authority: the book of hours *is* the Word of God presented in the illumination, transmitted "live," so to speak, through the Word made flesh with the ink absorbed on the manuscript's parchment leaves like a tattoo. The McVitty Book of Hours is a well-crafted example of how this devotional book strengthened its position of authority within the practitioner of devotion's worldview by engaging its user at a personal, even intimate level with its visual imagery. Like almost every book of hours, the McVitty codex was designed to guide a particular individual through the emotionally based *habitus* of oration, a perpetual life of prayer within a community that included the Virgin, her Son, and a whole host of saints, martyrs, and confessors.

The vast numbers of illuminated books of hours produced in France and the Low Countries that survive from this time period indicate that the producers of books of hours successfully packaged monastic technologies of prayer for a lay audience, who would not have been able to operate a monk's breviary in fifteenth-century France or England. The breviary's complex technology would have challenged even a literate layperson, someone who might

---

53. Compare with Hugh Kempster, "Richard Rolle, Emendatio Vitae" (PhD diss., University of Waikato, 2007) and Watson, Introduction to *Emendatio Vitae*, 11–17.

54. The codex was rebound in its original order at the University of Texas in the late 1980s.

55. See Figure 1, McVitty Book of Hours: *St. John on Patmos* (f. 16r); "In principio erat verbum;" Gospel Readings: John 1:1. Thanks to Joan Roulle and Beth Harris of Hollins University's Wyndham Robertson Library for providing me access to this Book of Hours.

perhaps be familiar with composing business letters in Latin, but not prayers. The book of hours emerged as a devotional technology that enabled literate laity of varying levels to develop a suitable *habitus* of prayer in their daily lives. One way in which the book would develop this *habitus* was to present visual images that helped the individual see and feel as if he or she were performing the duties of *habitus* correctly. The image of Mary holding a book and actively engaging in the practice of prayer throughout the cycle of images used in the McVitty Book of Hours was a prompt for its user: a woman of some material wealth living in Northern France, devoted to the Cults of Mary and Jesu Christi, who was a practitioner of daily devotional prayer enabled by a specific handheld device. As she used this manuscript to guide her through the varying cycles of daily prayers, she could visually imagine herself within the series of Marian images depicting the ideal woman using her prayer book to perform devotion. These images represent a certain ordering of code, like today's iPod playlists, which were copied and shared by devotional book users and producers throughout Northern Europe, including England and Ireland, during this period. This user-friendly technology helped create a market for devotional books that dominated manuscript production in Northern Europe from the mid-fourteenth century forward, even into the advent of the printed book industry.

Beyond the visual strategies that engage the devotional practitioner in an immediate identification with the content of the prayers she is reciting, the McVitty Book of Hours has other evidence of individuated design. One of the most striking is its organization, the ordering and selection of songs in its *orationes* playlist. Unlike most books of hours, the McVitty manuscript's Hours of the Holy Spirit (ff. 24r–31r) and Hours of the Cross (ff. 32r–42r) precede the Hours of the Virgin (ff. 43r–94v). This organization seems designed with a particular user in mind.[56] Perhaps circumstantial, though worth mentioning, is the fact that folio 24 in the McVitty codex is visibly stained along its edge from use, indicating that it was sought after most by at least one of this codex's users. We will never be able to tell whether its original user or a subsequent one stained that folio in daily repetition of its matins in praise of the Holy Spirit. It does make sense, though, that the original user would have done so, were she the one who had arranged her book of hours to list the Hours of the Holy Spirit first, before the Hours of the Virgin Mary, because she was in some way more fond of its cycle of prayers.

The addition of a litany with two other prayers in the McVitty Book of Hours makes me believe that the original user of this book of hours was

---

56. The McVitty's uncropped folia still contain catchwords used to order quires for binding, and these catchwords match throughout the manuscript.

potentially quite literate in terms of prayer composition. She knew how to do more than simply modify her playlist. One the one hand, the Marian litany indicates to me that she could, like Chaucer's Prioress, take the raw, inventional *materia* of a prayer—a catalog of Mary's attributes—and turn it into her own, spontaneous prayer of devotion.[57] Such original prayers would serve the same function as either the "Obsecro te" or "O Intermerata": they would capture the benevolence of the Virgin, prepare the reader emotionally and mentally for her office of prayer, and ask for the Virgin's pity and help in cleansing her life of sin. On the other hand, the substitution of "Sub tua protectione" and "Domine ihu xpriste rogo te" for the more common prayers also indicates that the original user of this manuscript knew how to change her playlist, substituting other pre-scripted prayers that fulfilled the same emotional and structural function as the "Obsecro te" and "O Intermerata." The selection of "Sub tua protectione" and "Domine ihu xpriste rogo te" further indicates to me that the devotee who designed the McVitty Book of Hours shared an interest in the Cult of Christ as well as the Cult of Mary. Whereas the two more common prayers focus on the Virgin herself, the McVitty Book of Hours provides one prayer in praise of the Virgin and one prayer in praise of Christ. This feeling of regulated spontaneity (improvisational composition based on a technical method) in the service of devotion must have been quite a cherished phenomenon from within a fifteenth-century *habitus* of prayer. The term used to describe this feeling was "sweetness," a concept to which we will turn later. For now, I'll tag "sweetness" by equating it to the feeling I have when I hear the opening measure of the first song on my iPod's "Favorites" menu; it is a feeling that combines the satisfaction of mastering a technology with the transient joy of rock and roll's electrified rhythm, as well as the excitement of anticipating the familiar songs I know will soon come to soothe my soul.

I mentioned above that the ability to use a Book of Hours manuscript in private devotion functioned very much as a cultural literacy for the people who practiced a life of prayer in fourteenth-century England (and across Europe). However, "literacy" is a sticky word. Michael Clanchy reminds us that "medieval assumptions about functional literacy differed from modern ones."[58] Due to the dominant cultural force of religious institutions, Clanchy continues, "the emphasis in reading (and writing) was ... put not on mass schooling for the state's and industrialists' purposes, but on prayer: collectively

---

57. I discuss the compositional method reflected in the Prioress's prologue and tale in more detail in "The Prioress's Oratio Ad Mariam and Medieval Prayer Composition," in *Medieval Rhetoric: A Casebook*, ed. Scott D. Troyan (New York: Routledge, 2004), 63–90.

58. *From Memory to Written Record*, 13.

in the church's liturgy and individually at home with a Book of Hours."⁵⁹ In fact, European literacy remained grounded in "individual prayer" until the nineteenth century.⁶⁰ It is easy to glean from Clanchy's discussion and others' the modern underestimation of the cultural power of prayer. Prayer was at least a twelfth-century gateway into full-blown literacy, if it was not literacy itself. Dante's writings provide numerous examples of prayer's important social role. For example, in *Purgatorio* 8.8–18, he describes orators engaged in prayer. In discussing this passage, Mary Carruthers observes:

> The group begins the evening hymn, Te lucis ante terminum, with such sweet notes ("dolci"), sung sweetly and devoutly ("dolcemente e devote"), that Dante exits his own mind ("che fece me a me uscir di mente") along with the rapt singers, in contemplative gaze upon the circling heavens. Sweetness here is the vehicle of harmony and of ascent to the divine. ⁶¹

"Sweetness," a learned rhetorical style, indicates the height of the group's literacy. The banality of medieval prayer books obscures the presence of the cognitive technology (i.e., prayer literacy), which depended upon the physical codex for its broadcasted transmissions. Likewise, a thousand years from now post-humans will scratch their heads at the caches of silicon chips and mountains of burned-out monitors scattered among the detritus of our nascent epoch, and they will understand very little about how these strange artifacts related to literacy at the dawn of the Digital Ages.

To learn more about the literacy of prayer in fourteenth-century England, though, let's look to what Richard Rolle told a young girl in the second quarter of that century. The girl, his initial audience, was probably no older than thirteen and preparing to take the vows of a nun. Rolle tells her: "If you are resolute in burning love for God while you live here, there can be no doubt that your seat can be allotted for you very high up and most happily, close to God's presence among his holy angels."⁶² Rolle's words would have connected this girl to a very vivid realization of his image. We might assume that the girl has seen a Psalter, since she is able to receive a written letter of instruction. Even if we can imagine her never having seen an illuminated page, she could have remembered the images commonly found throughout her region on stained glass windows, roodscreens, and frescoes. These images of light

---

59. Ibid.
60. Ibid.
61. Mary Carruthers, "Sweetness," *Speculum* 81 (2006): 1002 [999–1013].
62. From Richard Rolle, "Ego Dormio," in *Richard Rolle, the English Writings*, ed. Rosamund Allen (New York: Paulist Press, 1988), 134 [132–41].

and shadow figuratively embodied an entire field of hierarchical knowledge regarding angels and their various roles in the Divine Cosmos.[63] So the girl knew that if she could impassion herself, move herself emotionally, she would find her place in that eternity in the here and now of her prayers.[64] The book of hours brought all of this semiotic power together in the palms of its user's hands. Aren't we similarly "impassioned" by the music that flows directly into our brains along an electric wire? Being able to persuade yourself emotionally was what the rhetoric of devotional prayers was all about. Reason had very little to do with it.

VERSE III

David Bowie's youthful persona, Ziggy Stardust, embodied in an exemplary manner what I would call a form of postmodern mysticism swept up in the traditional *pathos* in ways also found in medieval devotion. Through his several musical personae of the late 1960s and 1970s, we can see Bowie playing with the image of a visionary, both in his costumes as well as in his lyrics. For example, in "Quicksand," he captures a negative dialectic that simultaneously bemoans and celebrates his postmodern condition. Though Bowie's persona tells us in the first stanza that he is not a prophet, he goes on to say he's "just a mortal with the potential of a superman," effectively translating with this lyrical juxtaposition the visionary mode of devotion from a religious past to a post-Nietzschean present.[65] The next stanza further inverts the image of religious mystic, drawing attention to the "bullshit faith" of Christian salvation. What really strikes me about these lines, however, is their deep "anti-modern" tenor. Bowie's lyrical "I" laments the fact that it is "tethered to the logic of Homo Sapien," drawing attention to the limits of *logos* that had attempted, at least since the time of Locke, to eradicate *pathos* from the rhetoric of modernity. For me, the line from which this lyric gleans its name, "I'm sinking in the quicksand of my thoughts," expresses the emotional darkness of modernity's rational gaze. This image invokes the "iron cage" of ascetic rationalism, a worldview described by Max Weber that shackles individuals to mechanized industries driven by greed and the need for speed. According to Weber, nature became a passive object following rules prescribed to it by

---

63. See Ibid., 212, n.2.
64. Cf. Watson, Introduction in *Emendatio Vitae*, 17.
65. Such a translation of mysticism from Christian to a more magical form of spirituality is further indicated by Bowie's reference to Aleister Crowley's Hermetic Order of the Golden Dawn in the lyric's opening lines.

universal laws of science, with modernity's faith placed firmly on human reason. Modern bureaucracies developed using standardized methods of scientific measurement and industrialized technologies to administer social needs fairly and impartially.[66] In other words, bureaucracies evolved as macro, corporate machines designed to manage the relationship between industrial technologies and societies that it both feeds and feeds upon. Bowie's lyrical lament is for the individual overlooked at the macro corporate level.

Today in our Digital Ages, thirty years after Bowie's mystical lamentations, rock-and-roll cults of devotion still use lyrics to move their participants emotionally. Look, for example, at John Cameron Mitchell's *Hedwig and the Angry Inch*, a brilliantly conceived dramatic monologue built around a transgendered persona. *Hedwig* tells the story of a boy named Hansel, who was born in East Berlin. He was courted and fell in love with an American soldier. Hansel undergoes a sex-change operation in order to marry the soldier and move with him to the United States. Unfortunately, the operation was a botched job, and Hedwig (the boy-now-woman) was abandoned in a trailer park by her G.I. Joe soon after moving to the United States. Later, she finds her one true love, who also abandons her, steals her music, and uses it to become an arena-rock star. Hedwig tells her life story at concerts held in Bilgewater Inn Seafood restaurants around the country. Her tour dates coincide with those of Tommy Gnosis, the lover turned superstar who broke her heart. The film ends with a lyrical description of music itself, the medium of Hedwig's intoxicated highs and tragic, drunken lows. The lyrics of "Midnight Radio" describe music and love as something that "hits you so hard, filling you up, and suddenly gone." Hedwig calls out to brothers and sisters everywhere so that they might feel the mystical power of love in a forsaken world where dreams, or songs, are "burn[ed] dry" by falling rain. It is not reason that will discover the wholeness of being for this postmodern mystic: it is the emotional force of rock and roll, and the body that feels its powerful, electrified love.

In order to assist those who participate in Hedwig's spiritual lyric by listening to it repeatedly, she also includes a litany of saints, martyrs, and heroines,

---

66. Cf. Jane Bennett's discussion of Max Weber's concept of bureaucracy in *The Enchantment of Modern Life: Attachments, Crossings, and Ethics* (Princeton, NJ: Princeton University Press, 2001), 105. Critics such as Weber, Walter Benjamin, and Paul Virilio are very somber in their conclusions about how modernity's drive for technological speed and the bureaucracies modernity has developed to manage a world dedicated to speed affect the individual subject. Bennett, however, brightens the corners a bit, seeing bureaucracy and its myriad technologies as "a cage with a seductive aura. Bureaucracy would enclose and suppress and . . . propel the urge to break out, but it would also sometimes fascinate and lure. Both sets of effects would have the same source, the complexity of the structure . . . provoking painful and pleasurable affect" (105).

such as Patti Smith, Tina Turner, Yoko Ono, Nico, and Aretha Franklin, among others. This list of exemplary individuals forms a House of Fame to which she can turn in her moments of desperation. The cinematography of the film version of *Hedwig* visually underscores the ecstasy of the lyrical moment. Throughout her narrative, an emotional *bildungsroman* in which she wanders through a wilderness of emotional beasts trying to find her true self, Hedwig has struggled with failure after failure. She is an archetype of the abject, postmodern saint looking for spiritual connection in a world void of love. When she begins her lyrical lament, however, Hedwig's entire world "whites out," as she and the entire band are transformed into black-and-white clad rock stars playing on a set emblazoned with light bleeding everywhere with its cleansing, purified, radiant beams. The strength Hedwig finds by imagining herself among her exemplars in turn gives her the strength to call out to others to "hold on to each other." Like a fourteenth-century prayer of devotion, Hedwig's invocation of rock-and-roll saints serves as a means of stabilizing devotion for both herself and any "strange rock and rollers" who might participate in her song in a digitized performance of ritualized repetition.

Both the prayer book and the iPod are technologies involved in the reproduction of devotional cultures. The *habitus* that form around the use of these technologies embody a process that uses the individual's actions, via rituals, to compose his or her individuality; yet the very use of these technologies moves each individual into participation with something in excess of the individual, a corporate body that is both omnipresent and often invisible. This everywhere but nowhere quality of an emotionally driven *habitus* brings both pleasure and pain for both mystics and rock and rollers. In Hedwig's meditation on love, she focuses on the emotional fullness of song with the double imperative equating love with life: "Breathe feel love." Hedwig's vision, like Bowie's, champions *pathos* and a somatic way of knowing that is in opposition to the rational parameters of *logos*: "You know in your soul, / Like your blood knows the way, / From your heart to your brain, / Knows that you're whole." What our body knows—the love it feels—sublimates the individual's isolated identity and broadcasts it throughout the heavens where the individual is "shining / Like the brightest star" as well as transmitting like a radio signal and "spinning / Like a 45." Let's compare those complex overtones of love's relationship to breath and the body and transcendence with Richard Rolle's fourteenth-century lament:

> My sang es in syghyng, whil I dwel in [th]is way,
> My lyfe es in langyng, [th]at byndes me, nyght and day . . .
> Langyng es in me lent, for lufe [th]at I ne kan lete.

My lufe, it hase me schent, [th]at ilk a bale may bete.⁶⁷
Sen [th]at my hert was brent in Cryste lufe sa swete,
Al wa fra me es went, and we sal never mete. ⁶⁸

My song is in sighing, while I dwell in this way;
My life is in longing, which binds me, night and day . . .
Longing lies hidden in me, for love which I can't leave,
My love, it has ruined me, the same a sorrow may relieve.
Since my heart was burned in the love of Christ so sweet,
All woe from me has turned, and we shall never meet.

The song itself is a somatic place for the body to be bound to God in love. Devotional prayer was a medieval technology of self that enabled a particular, emotionally based *habitus* that equated life with longing, devotion, and suffering for love. Rolle in particular was fond of using biblical *imitatio* to place himself within what Hugh Kempster calls "the salvation history, language and metaphor of Christian and Hebrew scripture."⁶⁹ In the lines quoted above, Rolle has created an emotional device designed to communicate a state of enchantment through its imagery and style of *pathos*. In a book focused on contemporary technology and the postmodern world, Jane Bennett describes enchantment as "a state of wonder, . . . the temporary suspension of chronological time and bodily movement. To be enchanted, then, is to participate in a momentarily immobilizing encounter; it is to be transfixed, spellbound."⁷⁰ Though from another epoch, Rolle's words indeed communicate a state of being "bound night and day," where one "cannot leave" on account of love longing. This love longing, or "bale," is a sublime mode of being in which the individual experiences strong feelings of pleasure and pain simultaneously.⁷¹ This same modality is available to the literate practitioner of private

---

67. This use of "bale" is common in the religion of love developed in the later Middle Ages. Chaucer, the *Pearl*-poet, and Malory also use "bale" to communicate love-longing.
68. From Richard Rolle, "Song of Love-Longing to Jesus," in *English Writings of Richard Rolle*, ed. H. E. Allen (Oxford: Oxford University Press, 1963), 37–40; the translation is mine.
69. Kempster, "Richard Rolle, *Emendatio Vitae*," xxii. See also John A. Alford, "Biblical Imitatio in the Writings of Richard Rolle," *ELH* 40.1 (1973): 1–23, and "The Biblical Identity of Richard Rolle," *Fourteenth-Century English Mystics Newsletter* 2.4 (1976): 21–25.
70. Bennett, *Enchantment of Modern Life*, 5.
71. Bennett later explains that "enchantment begins with the step-back immobilization of surprise but ends with a mobilizing rush as if an electric charge had coursed through space to you" (104). As such, enchantment is a sublime mode of being that entails "both painful and pleasurable affect" (105).

devotion—that is, to the individual subject—who composes him- or herself through meditation on specific patterns of words.

Rolle's writings were a major conduit through which Latin-based devotional techniques were translated into his vernacular language. This great vernacularization of devotion enabled the spread of pre-scripted personal devotion through lay communities, especially women from the emerging middle class. These devotional techniques were themselves revolutionized in the eleventh and twelfth centuries. By 1215, the Church's parish system had united all of Europe, Northern and Southern, as well as the Atlantic Islands, into a corporate body of Latin documentation. Everyone in Europe, lay and religious, was responsible for composing a prayer of confession—to document their sins—in such a way that they reacted emotionally to it. Prayers of confession were scripted to make the orator *feel* compunction, a sorrowful guilt for one's acts of transgression. The impact of this emotional rhetoric was the gateway into a *habitus* of lived prayer, a disposition honed by monks in the twelfth century. The rhetorical "code" of literacy was initially acquired by studying grammar, rhetoric, and logic.[72] It is in their research into classical arts of rhetoric that twelfth-century monks discovered a process that enabled individuals to code emotionally moving prayers at will.

Monastic prayer technicians working in the twelfth century adapted the cognitive technologies of ancient rhetoric (*inventio, dispositio, elocutio, memoria,* and *actio*) to fulfill a specific cultural need. These medieval monks were sworn to live a life of prayer. They obeyed, in a very literal sense, Paul's commandment at Thessalonica, "Pray without ceasing."[73] Prayer technicians used the principles of rhetoric conveyed by classical systems of education called *progymnasmata* to develop a culture of devotion.[74] This pedagogy, or rhetorical

---

72. It seems clear, however, that by the fourteenth century, prayer literacy could be obtained by the study of prayers themselves. Margery Kempe, for example, seems to have developed quite a high level of literacy, though scholars still debate about her knowledge of "letters," per se.

73. See the final sentence on *meditatio* in Hugh of St. Victor's *Didascalicon*: "The more a man knows how great is the admiration which all things deserve, the more intently does he give himself to *continual meditation* upon the wonders of God" (Taylor, III.10, 93).

74. For more information on the origins and development of this progymnasmata, see Werner Jaeger, *Paideia: The Ideals of Greek Culture*, vol. 2, *In Search of the Divine Centre* (New York: Oxford University Press, 1986); James J. Murphy, *A Short History of Writing Instruction from Ancient Greece to Twentieth-Century America* (Davis, CA: Hermagoras Press, 1990); and Marjorie C. Woods, "The Teaching of Writing in Medieval Europe," in *A Short History of Writing Instruction from Ancient Greece to Twentieth-Century America*, ed. James J. Murphy (Davis, CA: Hermagoras Press, 1990), 77–94. For more background on how this system of education was adapted by Hugh of St. Victor specifically for his school, see Beryl Smalley, *The Study of the Bible in the Middle Ages* (Notre Dame, IN: University of Notre Dame Press, 1964), and Taylor, Introduction to *Didascalicon*, 3–39.

method of teaching, developed the cognitive skills necessary to live a life of continuous prayer, that is, continuous mental activity. We must remember, however, that for the practitioner of devotion, this mental activity was a perpetual act of remembering the body of Christ, a process based on the ability to emotionally tag, record, and recall feelings through cognitive technologies learned under the tutelage of a master orator, a technical engineer of prayer composition.

CONCLUSION

We can make several statements regarding the function of prayer within fourteenth-century devotional communities. To begin with, prayer was of vital importance in a world imagined within a divine cosmology; prayer was an act that remembered Christ's Body. Subsequently, if you could live your life as a prayer, then you would embody Christ's Love on earth. As a tool in the embodiment process, devotional prayers were designed to fill the orator and his audience with "sweetness," an emotional state of being that was likened unto God's Love. Through a process that sublimates the individual into the corporate, learning how to pray perpetually introduced massive numbers of people to the corporate power of the Living Word accessible only through the technologies of prayer. Finally, prayer manuals, devotional practices, and rules of living were interrelated technologies developed to habituate individuals into a life of prayer. We can conclude from these statements that prayer was used as a tool to access the individual's passions.

We can make a similar set of statements regarding the function of the digital playlist within twenty-first-century devotional communities. Music is central to a world imagined within the iPod's endemic digital cosmology, which includes the flattening of space and folding of time. If you live your life like a song, then you will come to embody the emotions generated by the playlists you habitually hear. Playlists are designed to fill audiences with specific, shared emotions. Digital technologies like the iPod allow us immediate access to our private passions. Yet, I'm not quite sure we are fully aware of all that we embody when we partake of the electronic word, sample, or sound bite. Consider the images from iPod's Shadow Campaign launched in the middle part of this last decade. One iPod advertisement reads, "The new iPod" to the left of a darkly shadowed image of a thin, seemingly young individual holding an iPod up for the viewer to see. Lower, and to the individual's left, are the words, "The best just got better," in smaller font than the statement's antecedent referent. The individual holding the device is thin, and a quick glance reveals that he or she is wearing a fedora-style hat, as well as some sort of wristband on his or her right arm. Most importantly, however, and central to the entire composition, is the iPod the figure is holding up to the viewer. The figure's pose is a classic "Jazz Hands" pose, except in this image only one of the hands is flared; the other is cupped around the source of sound itself: the iPod.

On closer inspection, the slightest hint of three tiny slivers of lighter grey across the otherwise flat black surface indicates that the figure is wearing a golf-style collared shirt. But the viewer can perceive no more. The individual's flattened shape in the ad transcends racial stereotypes, fulfilled just as easily by Hispanic, white, black, or Asian images of stylish, thin, twenty-something metrosexuals. This androgynous, post-racial figure is a true Everyman of the Digital Ages. Like an amplified rosary, the thin white line leading to the iPod's earbuds stands out above the individual's flat background, tracing the flow of electricity from the corporate source to the corporatized individual. By simply using the technologies of digital devotion, you could become your own version, your own embodiment of this transcendent image that is iPod. Even your most intimate best could get better, if you only had the latest iPod.

We cannot neglect or forget the message of this electronic media: through digital technologies, individuals now (once again) have a corporate medium that can control our most intimate passions. Mastering these devotional technologies enables us to transform the individual into something more than he or she is in mortal flesh and bones. Yet, there is a significant loss that accompanies the embrace of digitized technologies. What is lost might be the last, dying glimmer of humanism itself. Our children are growing up in a world where it is okay to ignore the person you are sitting next to while you text someone who is not sharing actual physical space with you. Immediate gratification is habituated into these young minds in our point-and-click world. Anything a child would ever want to know anything at all about (for better or worse) lies just a tumble away on the Web. The patience it takes to become a slow reader shrivels away in a world of instant this and automatic that.

The mystic and the rock and roller stand as bookends opposed to modernity. Both icons extend far beyond Mr. Cogito's reason, the logos of the printed Word. Richard Rolle embodies—and tries to instruct others how to embody—a constant state of sweetness in the form of a song. Rolle's notion of embodiment has much more in common with Hedwig's angry inch than either do with *Grey's Anatomy*. The mystic rocker embodies a *habitus* of devotion based on complex and compact lyrical imagery. The images of these cultures of devotion focus on a limited number of themes, including personal suffering, particularly in love and love-longing. Unlike a *habitus* based on scientific reason, the mystic rocker embraces emotions as a viable medium for cultural memory

FIGURE 1. McVitty Book of Hours: St. John on Patmos (f. 16r); "In principio erat verbum"; John 1:1. Gospel Readings. Special Collections, Wyndham Robertson Library, Hollins University (Roanoke, Virginia).

and social communication. By habituation, the mystic rocker orders his or her myriad lives in a spiritual manner, using emotions as vehicles through which individuals might experience a particular physical sensation—oftentimes describable as "bittersweet"—whenever he or she wants. In the early fifteenth century, the most popular vehicle, or medium, for an intimate and immediate invocation of this pleasure/pain through spiritual devotion was the book of hours; in the early twenty-first century, it is the iPod/smartphone. But the intimacy of the devotional manual and the intimacy of the iPod belie their corporate function. Using a prayer book or an iPod habituates an individual into a mode of being that links human emotions to a corporate identity that is both omnipresent and invisible, and not at all human.

CHAPTER 4

What *Does* Language Speak?
Feeling the Human with Samuel Beckett and Chrétien de Troyes

DANIEL C. REMEIN and ANNA KŁOSOWSKA

> And when it comes to neglecting fundamentals, I think I have nothing to learn, and indeed I confuse them with accidentals.
> —Samuel Beckett, *Molloy*

THIS ESSAY IS BEING WRITTEN to ask what language speaks.[1] The book in which this essay is published asks, among other questions, what it means to still desire something human. As part of such a book—whether we want to save or destroy certain fragments from a vanishing humanism; whether we would catalogue or remember them; regardless of whether or not such fragments will survive or for how long, or what the stakes are of their survival—in advance of such verdicts, the authors of this essay would release a fragment of what our desires for these texts would speak: an unlikely invitation to read Chrétien de Troyes's *Perceval* and Samuel Beckett's *Molloy*—with a detour through Chrétien's *Yvain*—near to each other, face to face, as in the same

---

1. We would like to thank Nicola Masciandaro, Sarah Bagley (for conversations in 2005–10), and the editors and the Press Readers for their generous comments and helpful suggestions.

neighborhood.[2] These texts, to use phrases from Heidegger, "draw into the others' nearness,"[3] a nearness that "does not depend on space and time considered as parameters."[4] Molloy, Perceval, and Yvain address each other as questions rifting the space-time of literary and intellectual history, indeed the history of language and of the human: an extraordinary address, a call to nearness from each to each that still "does not wrest what it calls away from the remoteness."[5]

We would listen here, specifically, to two moments of naming in texts that possess a strange nearness to each other in literary history: romance in Old French octosyllabic couplets and the end of the modern novel. Even so, we will hear that Molloy is no end for the novel, but a beginning—not a nihilistically antihumanist, but an ecstatic, even erotic, undoing—exhausting every end of the human.

Why *Molloy*? Precedents for citing *Molloy* in such a discussion include, in reverse chronological order, Michel Foucault's "What Is an Author?" (1969), Roland Barthes's "The Death of the Author" (1968)—key texts of the twentieth-century obsession with whether a *who* is speaking—and, some years earlier, Maurice Blanchot's first articles on Beckett, which open with the question: "Who speaks in the void made by word in the open privacy of him who disappears there?" (1953).[6] As we see, Blanchot responds soon after the publication of *Molloy* (1951) and *Godot* (1952).

In 1969, at the Collège de France, where he will give his inaugural lecture on the "Order of Discourse" the following year, Foucault—then a professor at the experimental University Center in Vincennes, created in the wake of May 1968 (an experiment that perhaps may not have gone fully as intended, as the students called to abolish that bastion of the bourgeoisie, the going to classes)—cites Beckett's "What does it matter who speaks?" as the starting point of his invited lecture on the question "What is an Author?"[7] "Writing,"

---

2. See Martin Heidegger, "The Nature of Language," in *On the Way to Language*, trans. Peter D. Hertz (New York: Harper, 1971), 82 [57–108].

3. Ibid.

4. Ibid., 103.

5. Martin Heidegger, "Language," in *Poetry, Language, Thought*, trans. Albert Hofstader (New York: Harper, 1971), 196 [185–208].

6. Michel Foucault, "Qu'est-ce qu'un auteur?," *Bulletin de la société française de philosophie* 63:3 (1969), 73–104. Roland Barthes, "La mort de l'Auteur," *Manteia* 5:4 (1968), 12–17 (published in English in 1967); Maurice Blanchot, "Où maintenant? Qui maintenant?," *La nouvelle revue française* (10 October 1953), 678–86, reprinted in Blanchot, *Le livre à venir* (Paris: Editions de Minuit, 1959). All translations are ours, unless indicated.

7. Foucault, "Qu'est-ce qu'un auteur?" 73. We gratefully thank the anonymous Press Reader for bringing up Foucault's essay in this context. In his 1968 lecture, Foucault also mentions Jean Hyppolite, who died in October 1968, creating the vacancy at the Collège that Foucault was elected to fill the following year. The lecture was at the invitation of Jean Wahl. The

says Foucault, "is not the manifestation or exaltation of the gesture of writing; it is not the pinning down of a subject in a language; it is the opening of a space where the writing subject never ceases to disappear."[8] Foucault's lecture, along with the one by Roland Barthes—copied by students, taught by teachers—becomes an unavoidable part of the canon of poststructuralism.

In asking, *why Molloy?*, we implicitly answer the question, *why Perceval?* Building on R. Howard Bloch's readings of the text, Kłosowska earlier pointed out that in Chrétien's *Perceval*, "the quest for lineage is no longer an excuse for the narrative, rather the problematic nature of language as a pattern of all symbolic orders calls into question the status of the author and of meaning."[9] Similarly, our diachronic comparative mode is neither quite historical nor quite ahistorical, but primarily responsive to the specific temporal and ontological logics of texts. For the literary historian mindful of precedent, Beckett's most obvious medieval interlocutor is not Chrétien, but Dante, and we cite below Beckett's essay on the "the divine Florentine," with whom Beckett's characters are often familiar: *Molloy* is undoubtedly indebted to the *Purgatorio*.[10] The logic of this essay does not require that Beckett's text include a marked response to Chrétien. Rather, Beckett's and Chrétien's texts offer this resonance: a narrative, more or less, of errancy and adventure on the part of an ill-equipped and idiosyncratically formed subject who, trying to return to his mother, forgets his name, and then suddenly remembering it, names himself. These distinct points of comparison and formal allusions will only become apparent by degrees, but we assure the reader that they will be clear by the end of the essay.

---

participants of record included Wahl, Maurice de Gandillac, Lucien Goldman, Jacques Lacan, Jean d'Ormesson, and Jean Ullmo.

8. Ibid., 74; d'Ormesson, 103.

9. Anna Kłosowska, *Queer Love in the Middle Ages* (New York: Palgrave, 2005). See also R. Howard Bloch, *Etymologies and Genealogies: An Anthropology of the French Middle Ages* (Chicago: University of Chicago Press, 1983), 206–7.

10. E.g., Samuel Beckett, "Rough for Radio II," in *Samuel Beckett: The Grove Centenary Edition*, vol. 3 (New York: Grove Press, 2006), 322. Outside the walls of the city where Molloy will begin his journey, still in an antepurgatory, Molloy crouches in the shadow of a rock, "like Belacqua or Sordello, I forget." See Beckett, *Molloy*, in *Samuel Beckett: The Grove Centenary Edition*, vol. 2 (New York: Grove Press, 2006), 6–7 [1–168]. Molloy is thinking of Belacqua, who crouched or sat [*sedeva*], grasping his knees with his held face low between them [*abbracciava le ginocchia / tenendo 'l viso giù tra esse basso*] in the shadow of a big rock [*un gran petrone / a l'ombra dietro al sasso*], among the negligent—but Molloy may be forgiven his confusion, as Sordello, too, is found crouching or lying [*posa*] in antepurgatory, two cantos later, if beneath a slope [*costa*] and not a rock. See Dante Alighieri, *The Divine Comedy of Dante Alighieri Vol. 2: Purgatorio*, trans. Robert M. Durling (Oxford: Oxford University Press, 2003), Canto 4, ll. 100–105, Canto 6, ll. 68–73. See also Beckett's main character, Belacqua, in *More Pricks than Kicks*, which opens with him reading, "stuck in the first canti of the moon," in *Samuel Beckett: The Grove Centenary Edition* vol. 4 (New York: Grove Press, 2006), 77.

Chrétien is as an echo by anticipation of Beckett, an analeptic echo, so to speak. We will listen to Perceval's self-naming: an opening of an inexhaustibly human riddle of what language speaks. Heidegger famously circles around from the notion that "man speaks" to "Language speaks. What about is it speaking?"[11] As a way of thinking the capacity of literary history to intervene in the history of a vanishing humanism, we would return to the radical risk of the second question. For Heidegger, this does not deny that we speak, but asserts that we only speak by listening to what language speaks, speaking only in response: "The way in which mortals, called out of the dif-ference into the dif-ference, speak on their own part, is: by responding."[12] How does a critical moment like ours, celebratory of nonhuman ontologies and inhuman agencies, return us anew to the question of how language speaks us? If the language of humanism is left only in fragments, how and what would a fragment of a language speak? What might it speak between the vast precinct lodged in the intimate time between Molloy and Perceval, and what human or nonhuman could respond to it? If what language still speaks remains—in some fragmentary way still, or not yet, human—what does the human feel like?

A third axis of this essay would adapt certain impulses and attitudes from new materialism and related critical turns, broadly defined as approaches to a philosophy of matter that do not merely extend but rewrite, modify, depart from, and permanently alter phenomenology, systems and networks theories, the distinction between physics and metaphysics, Marxism, and so on. Our interest in such thought is not a rejection of any previous linguistic turn but a queer desire to think with—not about—matter (to paraphrase the title of a recent book by the anthropologist Eduardo Kohn, *Forest Thinking*, among innumerable other recent books that abandon *about* in favor of *with*—thinking with stone, anonymous materials, plants, animals, etc.). This essay is an attempt to think of matter not as an object of humanistic thought, but from the perspective of a nonhuman facticity.[13] The impulse of such posthumanist thought is ethical.

---

11. Heidegger, "Language," 188–91.
12. Ibid., 206.
13. Eduardo Kohn, *How Forests Think: Towards an Anthropology Beyond the Human* (Berkeley: University of California Press, 2013), and Kohn, "How Dogs Dream: Amazonian Natures and the Politics of Transspecies Engagement," *American Ethnologist* 34:1 (2007), 3–24. Kohn defines forests as "lineages or associations of organisms" that change, evolve, or adapt. An organism, he says, "constitutes a guess about what the world is like," a guess repeated by generations because it "fits that world one way or another. This fittedness is a representation, it is a thought," he says. Thinking beyond the human takes into account "forms and patterns that propagate through the forest." Kohn keeps the human thinking and beyond-the-human thinking separate because that allows an analytical advantage. On Kohn and posthumanism, see, among others, Philippe Descola, "All Too Human (Still): A Comment on Eduardo Kohn's *How Forests Think*," *HAU: Journal of Ethnographic Theory* 4.2 (2014): 267–73. A frequent critique

The focus on materials is apparent in one word of our chapter's title, "feeling": a material word for cognition. For, neither *Molloy* nor *Perceval* will allow us a version of speculative realism, object-oriented ontology, or new materialism that forgets the human or her body—sexed, idiosyncratic, and entangled in the various gravities and histories of language. Therefore, our approaches to *Molloy* and *Perceval* in this recent critical turn are routed through feminisms or queerness.[14]

Both the title-bearing characters in question, Molloy and Perceval, realize and say aloud their names at the end of—or as the result of—an episode of intense erotic fixation on and by nonhuman objects: Molloy, in what amounts to a potential incident of public inanimaphiliac intimacy with a bicycle that seems mechanically impossible—unless it echoes an early form of bicycle, the dandy horse, popular in the 1820s—and Perceval, in his sustained gaze on a train of candelabras, a bleeding lance, and of course the *graal*—a gaze that arrests all of his usually inquisitive speech. *Molloy* (1951) is a novel in two parts, the first in the voice of Molloy—an effectively homeless man with exponentially increasing health problems (notably, joint pain and bowel trouble) and a low proficiency in what the schools would call "expressive spoken language." Molloy's section chronicles his both wretched and delicately meticulous errancy that begins as a journey to find his mother and proceeds through a sexually abusive captivity, a journey to the sea, and a creaturely crawling in the wilderness. The second part of the novel is in the voice of Jacques Moran, giving the report of his failed attempt to track down Molloy on the orders of some unnamed and unknown—indeed not directly encountered, even by Moran—but seemingly nefarious administrative agency, and his precipitous transformation into a proto-Molloy. Near the beginning of his monologue, Molloy explains how he sets out on his bicycle to find his mother—an attempt that will get him arrested in a strange police action by the local state apparatus:

> It was a chainless bicycle, with a freewheel, if such a bicycle exists. Dear bicycle, I shall not call you bike, you were green, like so many of your generation, I don't know why. It is a pleasure to meet it again. To describe it at length would be a pleasure. It had a little red horn instead of the bell fashionable in your days. To blow this horn was for me a real pleasure, almost a vice. I will go further and declare that if I were obliged to record, in a roll of honour, those activities which in the course of my interminable existence have given me only

---

of Kohn that Descola also makes is that he unnecessarily restricts the scope of posthumanism to plants ("life thinks; stones don't," Kohn, *How Forests Think*, 100), while we see the benefit of expanding it to all matter (Descola, "All Too Human," 271–72).

14. E.g., Elizabeth Grosz, *Chaos, Territory, Art: Deleuze and The Framing of Earth* (New York: Columbia University Press, 2008).

a mild pain in the balls, the blowing of a rubber horn—toot!—would figure among the first. And when I had to part from bicycle I took off the horn and kept it about me. I believe I have it still, somewhere, and if I blow it no more it is because it has gone dumb. Even motor-cars have no horns nowadays, as I understand the thing, or rarely. When I see one, through the lowered window of a stationary car, I often stop and blow it. This should all be written in the pluperfect. What a rest to speak of bicycles and horns. Unfortunately it is not of them I have to speak, but of her who brought me into the world, through the hole in her arse if memory is correct. First taste of shit. So I shall only add that every hundred yards or so I stopped to rest my legs, the good one as well as the bad, and not only my legs, not only my legs. I didn't properly speaking get down off the machine, I remained astride it, my feet on the ground, my arms on the handle-bars, my head on my arms, and I waited until I felt better.[15]

Mark here, briefly before going on, a certain therapeutic bliss: the affection in the intimate address; the simple declaration that "it is a pleasure to meet again," even if only in print; the delight in the soft horn and its subsequent treatment as fragmentary relic; the effortless account of a feco-natality; and, finally, the apparent capacity of the bicycle to make Molloy feel better.

Chrétien de Troyes's *Perceval, or the Story of the Grail* is an unfinished twelfth-century French narrative poem, or romance, that is also bipartite in structure. The first part focuses on Perceval, while the second, after Perceval finally encounters the Arthurian court, recounts Gawain's adventures as much as Perceval's. The opening traces the transformation of Perceval from a provincial innocent, full of ignorant questions about the physically alluring objects of chivalry and courtly life, into a *chevalier*, newly trained by a man he will learn is his uncle. Characteristically for Chrétien, the poem has a strongly analeptic structure: events and objects only acquire crucial significance *in retrospect*.[16] In the episode where Perceval first encounters the Grail, the young knight—who is to be told the next day that his mother is dead of grief over his departure to become a knight—takes up lodging, on the recommendation of a strange fisherman, in a mysteriously appearing castle. There, he witnesses a marvelous procession with the *graal*. This witnessing of the grail and Perceval's subsequent self-naming (as we will show) happen as the culmination and

---

15. Beckett, *Molloy*, 12.

16. For a recent treatment, from another angle, of the way that the quest is defined and accrues meaning—becomes knowledge—only in *retrospect* in Chrétien's work, see Zrinka Stahuljak et al., *Thinking Through Chrétien de Troyes* (Suffolk: D. S. Brewer, 2001), 75–109, and Sarah Kay, "Commemoration, Memory and the Role of the Past in Chrétien de Troyes: Retrospection and Meaning in 'Erec and Enide,' 'Yvain,' and 'Perceval,'" in *Reading Medieval Studies* XVII (1991): 31–50.

exhaustion of his chivalric training, his pedagogical transformation from wild "Welsh" boy to Arthurian *chevalier.*

Chrétien recounts the episode in the way of Old French couplets, building it cinematically, fragment by fragment, framing the description in terms of Perceval's gaze and inviting the reader to identify with Perceval's position, looking on objects as they fill the frame:

> Un graal entre ses .II. meins
> Une damoisele tenoit,
> Qui aviau les vallez venoit,
> Et bele et gente et bien senee,
> Quant ele fu leianz antree,
> Atot lo graal qu'ele tint,
> Une si grant clartez i vint
> Qu'ausin perdirent les chandoilles
> Lor clarté comme les estoilles
> Qant li solaux luist o la lune.
> Aprés celi en revint une
> Qui tint un tailleor d'argent
> Li graaus qui aloit devant
> De fin or esmeré estoit,
> Pierres precïeuses avoit
> El graal de maintes menieres,
> De plus riches et des plus chieres
> Qui an mer ne an terre soient.
> Totes autres pierres passoient
> Celes do graal sanz dotance.

A grail between her two hands / a girl held / who came with the young men, / and (she was) beautiful and pleasant and well bred. / When she entered there / with the grail that she held, / such a great radiance came there / that the candles lost / their radiance like the stars / when the sun shines or the moon. / After this another [female] one returned / who held a carving dish of silver. / The grail which went in front / was of fine purified gold. / There were precious stones / in the grail, of many kinds / of the most magnificent and desired (stones) / that there were in the sea or on the earth. / They surpassed all other stones / (those of the grail) without doubt.[17]

---

17. *Le Conte du Graal ou Le Roman de Perceval*, ed. Charles Méla, in *Chrétien de Troyes: Romans*, ed. Michel Zink et al. (Paris: Livre de Poche, 1994), ll. 3158–77. This edition uses as its base the fourteenth-century MS Berne 354, Bibl. de la Ville, 354. We mark citations from

The group of women critics writing collectively as the "Chrétien Girls" also notice how the narration here seems to follow "the shifting gaze of the young knight";[18] yet, while Perceval's eyes may determine the direction of the gaze, the scale of what fills the frame must be determined by an apparatus other than the human eye. The poem cuts drastically from a frame filled only with the dish itself to the girl carrying the dish, to a view of the whole *cortège*, and then back to the dish again—only now we are shown less solid surfaces than glimmer and brightness itself. By the end of the passage, we are left not so much with the feeling of a gaze commanded by an observing subject as with the feeling of the commanding and fixating power of the close-up. This closeness and command is near—but not quite—pornographic desire itself, like the ominous close-up of the face of Grace Kelly just *before* the famous kiss in the opening of *Rear Window*, or like Greta Garbo's sphinx-like face that inspired Roland Barthes's famous essay in the *Mythologies*, a face capable of "plung[ing] the audience into the deepest ecstasy, when one literally lost oneself in a human image as one would in a *philtre*, when the face represented a kind of absolute state of the flesh, which could be neither reached nor renounced."[19]

THEORETICAL GROUNDS: HEIDEGGER, METAPHYSICS, SPECULATIVE REALISM, AND DELEUZE AS "PURE METAPHYSICIAN"

One question that these two passages, in their nearness, procure is: What about the "complicity with the anonymous materials,"[20] a complicity shared between the two passages, even if the materials are so different—the warm, red rubber of the first, the cosmically cold minerals of the second? How can our question about "what language speaks" address these narratives of erotic physical complicities?

---

this edition as *Perceval B*. All citations of Chrétien's romances are from this collection unless otherwise noted. All translations from Chrétien are ours, often rendered in knowingly awkward syntax in order to allow for a closer approximation of the Old French verse-lineation.

18. Stahuljak et al., *Thinking through Chrétien de Troyes*, 148. Rather than using a truncated list of authors, we refer to the author of this text throughout as "Chrétien Girls" because its preface identifies this moniker as a "*senhal* or *nom de plume*" of the authorial collaboration (which includes, in its entirety: Stahuljak, Virginie Greene, Sarah Kay, Sharon Kinoshita, and Peggy McCracken).

19. Roland Barthes, "The Face of Garbo," in Barthes, *Mythologies*, trans. John Cape (New York: Hill and Wange, 1972), 56 [56–57].

20. We borrow this expression from Reza Negarestani's book *Cyclonopedia: Complicity with Anonymous Materials* (Melbourne: re.press, 2008).

We circle around to that question by borrowing from Heidegger's essays on Language, but only to find a before-and-after place to hear him (or more simply, to "put into question"). Heidegger says: "Poetry and thinking are in virtue of their nature held apart by a delicate yet luminous difference, each held in its own darkness: two parallels, in Greek *para allelo*, by one another, against one another, transcending, surpassing one another each in its fashion . . . intersect[ing] in the infinite . . . with a section that they themselves do not make. . . . That cut assigns poetry and thinking to their nearness to one another."[21] We want to go before and after the parallel relationship between poetry and philosophy that Heidegger plots. We could oppose to Heidegger any number of philosophers writing in verse, or we can mention one case: Novalis, early German Romantic poet and philosopher of nature who saw as his goal the "progressive universal poesy." The quote from Novalis on the specificity of language as that which is only concerned with itself (and because of that unknowable, "precisely known to no one") opens and closes Heidegger's reflection in *On The Way to Language*, constituting, quite literally, Heidegger's limits: "We recall at the end, as we did in the beginning, the words of Novalis: 'The peculiar property of language, namely that language is concerned exclusively with itself—precisely that is known to no one.'"[22] For Heidegger,

> Language *is* monologue. . . . It is language *alone* which speaks authentically; and, language speaks *lonesomely*. Yet only he can be lonesome who is not alone, if "not alone" means not apart, singular, without any rapports. But it is precisely the absence in the lonesome of something in common which persists as the most binding bond *with* it. The "some" in lonesome is the Gothic *sama*, the Greek *hama*, and the English *same*. . . . Saying is in need of being voiced in the world. But man is capable of speaking only insofar as he, belonging to Saying, listens to Saying, so that in resaying it he may be able to say a word. That needed usage and this resaying lie in that absence of

---

21. Heidegger, "The Nature of Language," 90.
22. Idem, "The Way to Language," *On the Way to Language*, trans. Peter D. Hertz (New York: Harper, 1971), 133 [111–36]. Further, "Novalis understands that peculiarity in the meaning of the particularity which distinguishes language. In the experience of the nature of language, whose showing resides in Appropriation, the peculiar *property* comes close to *owning* and *appropriating*. Here the peculiar property of language receives the original charter of its destined determination. . . . We are not capable of seeing the nature of language in the round because we, who can only say something by saying it after Saying, belong ourselves within Saying. The monologue character of the nature of language finds its structure in the disclosing design of Saying. That design does not and cannot coincide with the *monologue* of which Novalis is thinking, because Novalis understands language dialectically, in terms of subjectivity, that is, within the horizon of absolute realism" (133–34).

something in common which is neither a mere defect nor indeed anything negative at all.

In order to be who we are, we human beings remain committed to and within the being of language, and can never step out of it and look at it from somewhere else.[23]

Departing from Heidegger only the better to return to him later, we think of Deleuze, whose grounded philosophy borrows thought forms from the forms and habits of materials, animals, and others. Deleuze's concepts of language and material, and therefore concepts of poetry-to-philosophy and philosophy-to-place and -to-material, can be contrasted with Heidegger. If Heidegger's Being lives in the so-called prison house of language and technology/tools, for Deleuze it is a playground, the sandbox of language—with bottle caps, forgotten toys, and other wonderful *bricolage* supplies: "For the question was not how to elude the order-word but how to elude the death sentence it envelops, how to develop its power of escape, how to prevent escape from veering into the imaginary or falling into a black hole, how to maintain or draw out the revolutionary potentiality of the order-word . . . in the order-word, life must answer the answer of death, not by fleeing, but by making flight act and create."[24] For Heidegger, language and technology progressively (as they factically develop) separate man from being in the world; for Deleuze, being-machine, being-animal, being-other are so many ways of being in the world.

Deleuze's philosophy shares one important characteristic with both the work of mystical or transcendent philosophers like Empedocles or Novalis and with contemporary materialist mystics, that is, speculative realists (for all

---

23. Ibid., 134. This ineluctability of being *in* language, what some new materialists might spurn and we might hold onto, leads to Heidegger's famous recollection that "Language has been called 'the house of being'" (ibid. 135), which in turn gives us the source of this phrasing from Heidegger's 1946 *Letter on Humanism*: "But the human being is not only a living creature who possesses language along with other capacities. Rather, language is the house of being in which the human being ek-sists by dwelling, in that he belongs to the truth of being, by guarding it" (trans. Frank A. Capuzzi, in Martin Heidegger, *Pathmarks: Texts in German philosophy*, ed. William McNeill [Cambridge: Cambridge University Press, 1998], 254).

24. Gilles Deleuze and Félix Guattari, *A Thousand Plateaus: Capitalism and Schizophrenia*, trans. Brian Massumi (Minneapolis: University of Minnesota Press, 1987), 110. Thus, in their schizoid-analytical account of linguistics and structuralism, "November 23, 1923: Postulates on Linguistics," Deleuze and Guattari reverse or invert the death-cult reverence for language as the architectonic order of a home accessed only as death-limit and instead assert the torsions by which it connects with living bodies: "For even at the moment when the two planes are most distinct, as the regime of bodies and the regime of signs in an assemblage, they are still in reciprocal presupposition. The incorporeal transformation is the expressed of order-words, but also the attribute of bodies" (108).

their essential differences): that common trait is the interest in *proliferating multiplicities*—"to transform the compositions of order into components of passage."[25] If Heidegger thinks the world-as-we-know-it ends when man lands on the moon,[26] Empedocles is always already prepared for the eventuality that this world is not the only one.[27] Empedocles would welcome moonwalking. For Empedocles, moonwalking would be the illustration of his theory that the world is going through a phase. As for Deleuze, although he removed from his official bibliography his early paper on universal mathesis, perhaps influenced by his then-associates' interests in metaphysics, mature Deleuze says of his work, in the specific context of his style—proliferating, not subtracting terms: "I feel I am a pure metaphysician."[28]

So, in the playground of language, we still hear the lonesome call of a language that is not human: still concerned only with itself, still staunchly and proudly refusing instrumentalization; but instead of a mournful plaint or an elegy for its retreating gods, it lets loose the *honk!* of a rubber horn or the awkward silence that tracks the procession of the dazzling, radiant, metallic, bejeweled grail. And yet, while the complicity may here be anonymous, the materials are not; the grail remains *the Grail*, the bicycle remains Molloy's particular idiosyncratic machine. The critical description of complicities of Bicycle and Human Pleasure, or Chevalier and Shining Grail would then require *both* that lonesome, inhuman, call of an appropriating Language *and* the moonwalk through the sandbox. As Shevek, the physicist-hero of Ursula Le Guin's science fiction novel *The Dispossessed: An Ambigious Utopia*, puts it, "We don't want purity, but complexity, the relationship of cause and effect. . . . Our model of the cosmos must be as inexhaustible as the cosmos."[29]

---

25. Ibid., 110. Compare with Graham Harman, *Tool-Being: Heidegger and the Metaphysics of Objects* (Peru, IL: Open Court Publishing, 2002).

26. "I don't know if you were frightened, but I at any rate was frightened when I saw pictures coming from the moon to the earth . . . only a god can save us" (Martin Heidegger, "'Only a God Can Save Us': *Der Spiegel*'s Interview with Martin Heidegger [1966]," trans. Maria P. Alter and John D. Caputo, in *The Heidegger Controversy: A Critical Reader*, ed. Richard Wolin [Cambridge, MA: MIT Press, 1993], 105–7).

27. See Reza Negarestani, "Memento Tabere: Reflection on Time and Putrefaction," http://blog.urbanomic.com/cyclon/archives/2009/03/memento_tabi_re.html.

28. For the discussion of Deleuze in the context of metaphysics, see *Collapse* 3 (2007), especially the introduction by Robin Mackay (4–39) and Quentin Meillassoux's "Subtraction and Contraction: Deleuze's Remarks" (63–107). For an English translation of the abovementioned paper by Deleuze, see Gilles Deleuze, "Mathesis, Science and Philosophy," *Collapse* 3 (2007): 141–55.

29. Ursula K. Le Guin, *The Disposessed: An Ambiguous Utopia* (New York: Harper, 1974, reprint, Harper Voyager, 2011), 226.

In Chrétien and Beckett, these complicities manifest in astonishingly similar ways—on at least three counts: (1) via the relationship with the ones who hold them, modeling the desire of those who behold them (Perceval, reader), inviting the reader to take on and feel their desire; (2) the fact that these materials are more precisely, at best, semianonymous: they are shaped, not exactly as tools, but somewhere in between tool and matter; (3) they are connected to pleasure in a short circuit that, looked at closely, seems vertiginous ("erotic fixation on/by non-human objects"). And yet we don't see this fixation as fetishistic; that is, the fixation on the object or other nonhuman—for example, an aspect (the shine of the grail) is not, as it is in Freud, an obstacle that prevents the realization of a masculine and/or heterosexual sexual act (for instance, recall Freud's famous example of the fixation on the shine on the nose, where Freud explains that the erotic fixation is based on homonyms). Rather, this nonhuman hybrid eroticism makes human-human sexuality boring in comparison—or more precisely, superfluous. Further, Molloy's "public inanimaphiliac intimacy with a bicycle" is not infantile, as if he were a monstrous adult arrested among "childish things"—the first bike, the fascination with shit, both equally intense around the fifth birthday, but later to be discarded in favor of that other grail: genital sex. Rather, Molloy seems old, worn out by care or pleasure, possibly the former: "my interminable existence . . . only a mild pain . . . every hundred yards or so I stopped to rest my legs . . . I waited until I felt better."[30]

THE ALLURE OF THE (LITERARY) MATTER: *LUXURIA* AND PURGATORY

The imaginative gaze of the reader and of her double in Molloy or Perceval is caught on fragments—glints or tantalizing shards, which will escape our interpretive efforts but demand our intimacy. The reader's initial transfixed glimpse of the grail procession, "Un graal entre ses .II. meins/ Une damoisele tenoit" ["a dish, between her two hands, / a damsel held"], appears as a brief *punctum* before the shining grail is visible in its entirety:

> Li grauss qui aloit devant
> De fin or esmeré estoit,
> Pierres precïeuses avoit
> El graal de maintes menieres,

---

30. Beckett, *Molloy*, 12.

De plus riches et des plus chieres
Qui an mer ne an terre soient.

The grail which went in front / was of pure refined gold. / There were precious stones / in the grail, of many kinds / of the most magnificent and desired (stones) / that there were in the sea or on the earth. (*Perceval B*, 3167–72)

The grail is first held out for us between the arms of the girl that are themselves an object of desire. Then, it appears with precious stones. But even here the words for the precious stones, *pierres precïeuses*, remain de-emphasized—not showing up in the end-rhymes. The stones—despite how they somehow command the whole scene as the adornment of the object which was to become a major trope for much of Western European literary history—the stones do not even accede to the rank of being the subject of a sentence. And yet they are so rich and dear, that even tucked into the middle of these lines, they appear quite illuminated. It is as if they had been always already appearing from the moment the arms of the girl came into view—their own rhyming couplet cradling the grail.

The radiance of the grail emits an unattributable light that washes out the other precious objects of the *cortège* and begins to absorb Perceval—and us—into the erotic field of its luminescent territory:

Une si grant clartez i vint
Qu'ausin perdirent les chandoilles
Lor clarté comme les estoilles
Qant li solaux luist o la lune.

Such a great radiance came there / that the candles lost / their radiance just as the stars / when the sun shines or the moon. (*Perceval B*, 3164–67)

The *clarté* [radiance, light] which "came there" is like that of the sun when it *luist* [shines]—a radiance outshining all other sources of light. *Luire* is an appropriate verb to illuminate a moment of conspicuous poetic brilliance—the reflex of Latin *luceo, lucere*, whose poetic usages can denote becoming light, being evident (appearing, in general), and being conspicuous (an excess of appearance), while its prose usage remains linked to the material *candelabra*, the instruments and signs of such conspicuity.[31] Shining in this sense can

---

31. Interestingly, the Guiot manuscript has "leve" (rises) instead of "luist" (shines) in line 3166. See Chrétien de Troyes, *Oeuvres complètes*, ed. Daniel Poirion, Anne Berthelot, Peter F.

mean a becoming-light or even a becoming-appearance itself—yet in a way that remains inescapably tied to mundane physicality.

Still, such brightness can also shine with the clarity of what is at once holy and erotic. The formula, "Cler luist la lune, les esteiles flamboient," appears in the context of that disturbing account of a "holy-war," the *Chanson de Roland*, while later a fourteenth-century English didactic text that claims to teach "Good French" describes a bald head that "luist come s'il eust esté enointez" ["shines as if anointed"].[32] Such attestations link the brilliance of *luire* to the saintly nimbus. And yet, a related noun from the same stem, *luisoire*, converts such saintly light-energy into bestial heat-energy—as it can describe the very nonhuman yet still-living sexual *heat* of animals (i.e., of an animal "in heat").[33] *Luisoire* is related to the Latin noun *luxuria*, in which the meaning of its stem noun, *lux* (related to the *lux* of *luceo*) undergoes both a semantic narrowing to a focus on the conspicuity resulting specifically from light and heat, and a semantic pejoration to a focus on excess that gives light such conspicuity: the result is a noun that, in its literal usage, denotes the rich excess of vegetal vibrancy, "rankness, luxuriance *of plants and trees*,"[34] and in its tropological usage, comes to mean more or less the same as its present-day English reflex, *luxury*, "riotous living, extravagance, luxury, excess."[35] What these etymologies reveal, on a much more scandalous level, is that the semantic field linking *light* and *heat* in canonical medieval, early modern, and even modern thought,

---

Dembowski, and Philippe Walter (Paris: Gallimard, 1994). This variant, we believe, only confirms our libidinous and lascivious reading of *luire* (for libidinous puns on *lever* or *se drecier* [rise], see for instance, *Yde et Olive* [ll. 6502–3] or Marie de France's *Lanval* [ll. 621–24]: "Men rise regularly at the sight of beauty in French romance, leading us to wonder what was conveyed beyond the gesture of greeting" (Kłosowska, *Queer Love in The Middle Ages* [New York: Palgrave Macmillan, 2005], 106). And see Algirdas Julien Greimas, *Dictionaire de l'ancien français* (Paris: Larousse, 1992), sv. *luisir*; Greimas glosses the term in its first sense as "Luire, briller," but also as "Faire un temps clair." From the Latin *lucere*—meaning, according to Lewis and Short, "to be light, or clear, to shine, gleam, glow glitter" as well as "to become light," as in the moment of dawn; and, tropologically, "to shine forth, to be conspicuous, apparent, clearly evident," Charleton T. Lewis and Charles Short, eds., *A Latin Dictionary* (Oxford: Oxford University Press, 1998), sv. *luceo*. Cf. *Anglo-Norman Dictionary*, sv. *luir (lure, lucer, luser, luicer, luisir),v.n*, "to be light, bright" (*Anglo-Norman Dictionary* Online edition, http://www.anglo-norman.net/D/luire[1]).

32. In *La manière de langage qui enseigne à bien parler et écrire le français. Modèles de conversations composés en Angleterre à la fin du XIVe siècle*, ed. Jean Gessler (Bruxelles: l'Édition Universelle; Paris: Droz, 1934).

33. See Greimas, sv. *luisoire*. Greimas cites the verb *luisoire* as one which describes one "Qui est en chaleur, en parlant d'une femelle d'animal [who is "in heat," in speaking of a female of the animal]."

34. Lewis and Short, *Latin Dictionary*, sv. *luxuria, ae*, I. Lit.

35. Ibid., II. Trop.

also actively links the light of reason and religion to an excessive, vibrant, and corporal heat—of worldly human bodies, vegetal erotics, and bestial sex. The same light that gives holy clarity is the light that blends the proximity of sight with the heat of the nonhuman erotic. As it concerns the articulation of Perceval and the Grail in the language of the poem, the shining grail appears in a prepositional relation to things that frustrates the intimacy of knowledge and the exegetical in favor of the intimacy of physics, of erotic heat and light in an event of partial co-becoming-*luxuria*. The Grail itself is only a fragment that emerges in this passage in fits and starts; only a dull backdrop to the intensity of the fragments of glitter in the precious stones that lend the scene the *clarté* that surpasses all others with its saintly and beastly ability to command Perceval's silence—his amnesia of the question that has evaporated, the heat and light where human and nonhuman perceptions touch.

This burning—and our own philological burning—is to be likened to Beckett's desire for a certain purgatorial burning in language and so should be taken as a portal between Perceval and Molloy—in the manner of Deleuze and Guattari's insistence that one should answer the sort of tyrannical question that is an "answer already contained in a question" with "words that pass, words that are components of passage."[36] In his essay, "Dante ... Bruno . Vico .. Joyce," Beckett writes of his wariness of a too-easy elision of philosophy and philology, warning—albeit with great admiration—against Giambattista Vico's insistence on the "complete identification between the philosophical abstraction and empirical illustration," and offering an alternative maxim: "The danger is in the neatness of identifications."[37] With both philology/philosophy and the grail, *the danger is in the neatness of identifications*. Regardless of what we are later told, the fact of the narrative is that the light of the grail does not give rise to the light that would procure knowledge and information related to the famous unasked question. For Perceval, such a fundamental relationship between language and the Grail, one of the neatness of identification, is not possible—only the intensity of *clarté* shining forth in the language of the poem.

Tradition heaps blame on Perceval for not asking any questions of his host about the grail. But, are we not too harsh on our awkward *chevalier*, who,

---

36. Deleuze and Guattari, *A Thousand Plateaus*, 110.

37. Samuel Beckett, "Dante ... Bruno . Vico .. Joyce," in *Samuel Beckett: The Grove Centenary Edition*, vol. 4 (New York: Grove Press, 2006), 495–510. The peculiar ellipses of this title are meaningful: "From Dante to Bruno is a jump of about three centuries, from Bruno to Vico about one, and from Vico to Joyce about two" (attributed to Beckett, see Richard Seaver, ed., *I Can't Go On, I'll Go On: A Selection from Samuel Beckett's Work* [New York: Grove Press, 1976], 105–6).

perhaps pleasurably, sits silent, one luxurious fragment of wonder among others? A wonder such as the grail appears, as the "Chrétien Girls" write, "at the fault line between knowledge and experience."[38] And, even if the grail scene is a kind of melancholic void, silent and unproductive in its lack of questions, it is nevertheless a "vibrant, unsettling 'unsaid'"[39]—an alternative way of being-spoken that is yet a wondrous breach of the tyranny of the question. For at the same time, the grail is a fragment of burning light that will cut a hole in the language of the whole tradition of romance and then the novel that will follow it—making everything that comes after it a footnote to the lines of Chrétien above, including (1) the later Grail-narrative continuations and amplifications of Chrétien's narrative, (2) the satirization of romance as a genre in Cervantes and others, (3) its lowering of rank in realism, (4) its ominous return in symbolism, and finally, (5) its emptying in Beckett.

As to the purgatorial burning, then, what could burn up in, or be burned up by, language? How does language itself burn, refine itself, bring itself to speak radiance—without succumbing to an Eliotic or Poundian desire for the purification of the dialect of the "tribe"? In "Dante . . . Bruno . Vico . . Joyce," Beckett compares the geometries of the purgatorial processes he finds in the work of the writers in his title; of Dante and Joyce in particular, he explains, "Dante's [purgatory] is conical and consequently implies culmination. Mr. Joyce's is spherical and excludes culmination."[40] The shape that Beckett himself would lend to purgatory remains obscure (Molloy's red rubber horn is a combined, conical and spherical option), but what he would find there would be akin to Joyce's nonculminating sphere: "No more than this; neither prize nor penalty; simply a series of stimulants to enable the kitten to catch its tail."[41] What Beckett finds is the purgatorial agent itself, "the partially purged,"[42] which is the desired motion of the circular, perhaps inane and meaningless, but certainly nonappropriative, and potentially inhumanely, autoerotic. The partially purged: Molloy on the rocks, on his bicycle; Perceval burning in the pornographic light of the Grail. Someone with only a cursory acquaintance with Beckett might squeak surprise at the discovery of such a potentially happy kitten in Beckett's cartography of literary purgatory. Such is the power of Chrétien as an alternative to Dante in the role of the great anticipator of a modernity and its literature whose human can only be medieval.

---

38. Stahuljak et al., *Thinking through Chrétien de Troyes*, 95.
39. Kłosowska, *Queer Love in the Middle Ages*, 22.
40. Beckett, "Dante . . . Bruno . Vico . . Joyce," 510.
41. Ibid.
42. Ibid.

NAMING AND THE LIMITS OF LANGUAGE

The morning after his failure to ask about the grail, Perceval encounters what *almost* amounts to a genuine literary example of a "damsel in distress," complete with a beheaded lover (ll. 3392–93). She cradles the corpse of the lover like the damsel from the night before cradled the grail. However, rather than playing the helpless and grateful damsel in distress, this damsel is openly hostile to Perceval and begins a round of punitive naming. First she explains about the owner of the castle who "Li Rois Peschierre a non" ["is named the Fisher King"] (l. 3458) and then she carries on a famous point-for-point conversation with Perceval about each object he saw and whether or not he asked questions about it, followed by the list of questions about what he saw. Finally, the dialogue culminates with the moment of naming:

> Comment avez vos non, amis?
> Et cil qui son non ne savoit
> Devine et dit que il avoit
> Percevaus li Gualois a non,
> Ne ne set s'il dit voir o non,
> Mais il dit voir, et si no sot.
> Et quant la damoisele l'ot,
> Si s'et encontre lui dreciee
> Dit comme fame correciee:
> Tes non est changiez, biax amis.
> —Commant?—Percevaus li chaitis!
> Ha! Percevaux, malaürous

> How are you named, friend? / And he who did not know his name / divines and says that he had / Perceval the Welsh as his name. / He does not know if he says the truth or not, / but he says the truth, and doesn't know it. / And when the damsel hears it, / She rose against him, / (and) says as an angry woman (would): / your name is changed, dear friend. /—how?—Perceval the wretched! / Ha! Perceval the unhappy. (*Perceval B*, ll. 3510–21)

In the wake of the grail's radiance, Perceval, not knowing whether or not he is saying the truth, speaks his name. He feels the name of that which language speaks as himself: the result of his pedagogic training *in language* as a recognizably human *chevalier*.

The self-naming is sudden; it gives one's name as a surprise to oneself, it gives availability to oneself and to relation in general in a suddenness that must feel vertiginous, lofty, and yet quirkily and eerily chthonic. From where, from what, or from whom does the name arrive? Perceval's name is divined by him but is not a product of knowledge; it is not received as information. Paradoxically, his legibility as a proper subject and a proper noun in the relational atmosphere of language is not here given to him as *information*: it wells up from that excess or luxuriance that is bestial, vegetal, and brightly mineral.

Yet for all this, his name is not a talisman of protection and in fact it leaves him vulnerable. Unlike the anonymity of becoming-luxuriant in the light of the grail the night before—for while it is *the Grail*, it is still paradoxically wrapped in anonymous mystery—Perceval, named, does not shine and astonish with an erotic *clarté* whose event horizon marks a kind of force field against all availability for instrumentalization. Even as Perceval "divines and speaks" [divine et dit] his name, his substance is exposed in a new way to a threshold of language and matter that has its pernicious side as much as it invites complicity in the erotics of bestial and vegetal luxury. His name renders him available to two potentially terrifying operations: (1) legibility and availability to be *spoken as*—such that named, his being will always be articulated *in terms of this or that* rather than as erotic availability—Perceval the *x* or Perceval the *y*, and (2) *renaming*.

As Heidegger explains in his famous discussion about the origin of a work of art:

> Language, by naming beings for the first time, first brings beings to word and to appearance. Only this naming nominates beings *to* their being *from out of* their being. Such saying is a projecting of the clearing, in which announcement is made of what it is that beings come into the Open *as*.[43]

The grail scene opens Perceval to this Open—to a kind of radical availability, realized first in Wonder and luxury, but now in grief and disciplinary blame. Finally named in language and called into the neighborhood of his own somatic substance, Perceval is, for the moment, punitively scared off from further pursuit of such Wonder by the damsel, what with her cackle or scoff and her act of renaming that will damn Perceval to literary wandering and the endless resistance-less (i.e., *non sequitur*) narrative of poetic production. Eventually, the narrative of *Le conte du graal* will abandon Perceval altogether—much as *Molloy* abandons Molloy in favor of Moran—abandon him for the adventures of a Gawain who is constantly harassed in his putative search for Perceval. The poem abandons that Perceval whose name the poem

---

43. Heidegger, "Origin of a Work of Art," in *Poetry, Language, Thought*, 71 [15–86].

itself comes to bear. Thus is Perceval the Welshman shortly renamed Perceval *li cha(i)tis*, the wretched one—the one who needs correction. It is both as if there is some terrifying threat in not asking any questions of radiant Wonder, and as if some punitive force in the world would scare off the pure swerve of the named—of the Being's response *qua* Being to language having been intimate with matter: a sort of disciplinary apparatus, imposed in response to a delightful, inappropriate gaze in the heat of those holy jewels.

VOLTE-FACE: THE TURN FROM LANGUAGE TO FACE AND AN OPTIMISTIC RENAMING

The Demoiselle's *inquiral attack* (we borrow the phrase from Michael Snediker) is no less pointedly situated than the *graal* procession or the bicycle ride. She is sitting under an oak tree, her decapitated lover in her arms.[44] She is Perceval's cousin, and the scene is the cousin of the grail procession, as well. As Nicola Masciandaro shows, the dialetheic hermeneutics of beheading (dialetheia, a figure we encounter more often nowadays, where both the statement and its negation are true: not "either/or" but "either *and* or") is no less circularly mysterious than language: as Heidegger observes, "Severing also is still joining and relating."[45] Parallel to this instantiating of extreme logic (dialetheia) and language (it, too, can be perceived as severing, joining, and relating all at the same time), severing and decapitation throw into sharper relief the interwoven (not discrete) philosophical and literary objects: life and death, vitality and inertness/inanimateness, personhood of things and thingness of persons:

> The presence-producing, deeply *factical* aesthetics of beheading, the strong sense in which seeing the severed head is seeing *that* someone is beheaded, a *that* which occupies a special phenomenal durability or ontic aura through the intimate identification between person and head, as if the severed head itself emanates the psychic immanence of the beheaded *person*, endlessly bleeding an atmosphere of what it is, beheading produces or brings into

---

44. Michael Snediker, *Queer Optimism: Lyric Personhood and Other Felicitous Persuasions* (Minneapolis: University of Minnesota Press, 2009), 106.

45. Nicola Masciandaro, "*Non potest hoc corpus decollari*: Beheading and the Impossible," in *Heads Will Roll: Decapitation in Medieval Literature and Culture*, ed. Larissa Tracy and Jeff Massey (Leiden: Brill, 2012), 15–36; the citation is from Martin Heidegger, "Logik: Heraklit's Lehre vom Logos," in *Heraklit*, 'Gesamtausgabe,' Bd. 55 (Frankfurt am Main: Vittorio Klostermann, 1970), 337.

presence the more extreme thingness of a being, the thingy presence of what is not a "thing" at all.⁴⁶

We want to bring this violent *either and or* scene into the vicinity of another, lighter moment from Chrétien's *Chevalier au lion* (*Yvain*): the anointing of Yvain (ll. 2913-3013). Two Demoiselles and their Lady discover a deranged, near-bestial, naked Yvain in the forest. After some confusion, one of the Demoiselles recognizes his *face*, wound or scar (*plaie*), and *name*—Yvain, the world's worthiest knight (ll. 2924-25), who embodies the promise of freeing the Demoiselles and their Lady from their harassers (l. 2941). The Lady asks the Demoiselle who recognizes Yvain to anoint the forehead and temples of the knight with an ointment given to her by the fairy Morgane that cures any kind of madness [*rage*], located in the head [*teste*] (ll. 2956-57), or in the brain [*cervel*] (l. 2975). The precious ointment is to be used sparingly (ll. 2967-69). "Wise Morgane's" (l. 2955) fairy ointment is magical, and it is supposed to be only magically and prudently applied: only to the temples, the seat of reason. Instead, the Damoiselle forgets herself, and erotically and with abandon applies it all over, until the substance runs out. In a cascade of irrepressible repetitions that sound like the percussion of a laugh, the Demoiselle anoints Yvain "so much that nothing was in the box at all" (l. 2994): "She covets his . . . healing so much / that she endeavors to anoint him everywhere" (ll. 2995-96); "she immediately expends it so . . . / that she cares not for the prohibition . . . / of her lady, or recalls it" (ll. 2997-99); "she puts more there than necessary / she uses it very well—so she thinks!" (ll. 2999-3000); "she rubs his temples and his forehead . . . / and his whole body, down to his toes" (ll. 3001-2); "she did mad things with the body / that he didn't need at all" (ll. 3008-9); "if she had half a gallon of it, / she would keep going" (ll. 3010-11).⁴⁷

Here, we find that object-oriented philosopher Graham Harman has a view of substance apposite to that of the Demoiselle's unstinting use of the ointment.⁴⁸ As Harman says, while analytic philosophy "takes pride in never

---

46. Masciandaro, "*Non potest hoc corpus decollari*," 22.

47. "Half a gallon" translates the text's five *setiers*, from Lat. *sextarius*, a measure that corresponds either to ca. 0.5 liter, or to 7.6 liters (i.e. roughly 1/8th of a gallon or 2 gallons).

48. Since the composition of the earliest drafts of this essay, in which OOO, SR, and New Materialism were all sets of borrowed clothes and largely unknown potentials (and at which time, such discussions could be found in print almost exclusively in the new journal *Collapse* and had certainly not yet gained the notoriety in literary criticism that lead to an issue of *New Literary History* 43 [2012]), professional and disciplinary responses to these schools of thought have of course multiplied like a good and proper hydra of controversies. The appearance of Harman's work here indicates mainly an aesthetic appositeness, not an adherence to—or, for that matter, abjuring of—any particular development in new materialist or object-oriented thought.

suggesting more than it explicitly states, this procedure does no justice to a world where objects are always more than they literally state."⁴⁹ Liberal like Harman's ways with substance, the Demoiselle's ways with ointment mark the passage, in Chrétien, from symbol, abstraction, magic, ritual, theory, to bodily dimensions. As in Emily Dickinson's phrase "Give Balm—to Giants— / And they'll wilt, like Men,"⁵⁰ Harman's take on objects may feel like a lungful of air after holding breath underwater in the death-cult caves of a Modernist Ocean; a welcome expansiveness, a "strange new realism in which entities flicker vaguely from the oceanic floor."⁵¹ In his essay "On Vicarious Causation," Harman explains:

> In the past century, the doctrine of Parmenides that being and thought are the same has been implied by Husserl, stated explicitly by Heidegger, and restated quite emphatically by Badiou. But this equation of being and thought must be rejected. . . . To revive the problem of causation means to break free of the epistemological deadlock and reawaken the metaphysical question of what relation means.⁵²

Is this not just what Molloy has done in resting on his bicycle, what Perceval has done in failing to procure knowledge from the grail's burning heat, what the Demoiselle has done in pouring out and rubbing in every last drop of ointment and multiplying its vitality and its allure—to ask the question of what relation means? For Harman, the term "allure" functions to define the difference between a sensual object and its qualities.⁵³ It is this potentially infinite manner of cutting up objects in their constitutive differences that allows objects access to other objects, offering up accidents as "tempting hooks protruding from the sensual object allowing it the chance to connect with others and thereby fuse two into one."⁵⁴ Such accidental *luxuria* is necessary for relation, so that objects are not exhausted in touching, subsumed by relation: "For

---

49. Graham Harman, "On Vicarious Causation," *Collapse* 2 (March 2007): 195 [187–221].
50. Emily Dickinson, *The Poems of Emily Dickinson*, ed. Mabel Loomis Todd and T. W. Higginson (Cambridge, MA: Harvard University Press, 1948, repr. Hayes Barton Press, 2007), 276.
51. Harman, "On Vicarious Causation," 177.
52. Ibid., 171–73.
53. Ibid., 199: "The separation between a sensual object and its quality can be termed 'allure.' This term pinpoints the bewitching emotional effect that often accompanies this event for humans, and also suggests the term 'allusion,' since allure merely alludes to the object without making its inner life directly present. In the sensual realm, we encounter objects encrusted with noisy accidents and relations."
54. Ibid., 202.

there is an excess in our pieces beyond what is needed to create us, and this excess allows new and unexpected things to happen."[55]

Like the Demoiselle's decapitated corpse, Molloy's bicycle, or the bestial shining of the grail, Yvain's mindless body is an alluring puzzle, an irresolvable opening, neither dead nor alive, calling for at least enough of the speculative spirit to allow us to circumvent the question "is it human?" altogether. Harman poetically and philosophically postulates, "The Heidegger-Blanchot death cult must be expelled from ontology, and perhaps even from metaphysics."[56] Harman's weird realism removes death from its privileged position as that which gives meaning to life by limiting it, even as he also seems to give a sort of lyric archetypal life to objects, all the while keeping in mind that they are not archetypal but transitory and vulnerable.

The allure of the *graal* is phrased as its *severed* quality. The *graal* is elliptically described as handled or offered in the Demoiselle's arms, as if anticipating the severed head the following morning. Naked and asleep in the forest, Yvain first appears unrecognizable for lack of quality and clothes—almost as if untouchable, as if surrounded by an invisible force field until the discovery of some accident. The two, quality and clothes, are in a zeugmatic relationship to that "*of which he was,*" as if his essential quality lodged therein, and not, non-elliptically, in the clothes in which he was dressed: "que rien nule sor lui veïst / qui reconuistre li feïst" ["for she saw not anything *on him* / that *made* her recognize/him recognizable"] (ll. 2897–98). She finally recognizes his scar (l. 2911), and this particular accident (the scar) then functions as the tempting hook that not only facilitates but multiplies points of touch. The Demoiselle's protracted look reaches and touches "everywhere" to find a scar on the ... face!—a face that, to boot, she knew very well. Of course, this is *Yvain,* the world's worthiest knight! This makes us laugh and prepares us for her rubbing the ointment on the temples ... and all the way down to his toes, in an erotic anamnesis;[57] that erotic anamnesis is also what Harman describes as love: "In love, the beloved entity has a certain magic hovering beneath the contours and flaws of its accessible surface."[58]

This instance of naming—the recognition of the naked *chevalier* and the recollection of the name, *Yvain*—follows these episodes of erotic anamnesis

---

55. Idem, *Circus Philosophicus* (Winchester, UK: Zero Books, 2010), 75.

56. Harman, "On Vicarious Causation," 194.

57. We borrow the term "erotic anamnesis" from Giorgio Agamben, *The Coming Community,* trans. Michael Hardt (Minneapolis: University of Minnesota Press, 1993), 2: "Erotic anamnesis ... transports the object not toward another thing or another place, but toward its own taking place—toward the Idea."

58. Harman, "On Vicarious Causation," 200.

and the subsequent experience of allure or severing of a quality—the scar—from the real object. Again, it is contact with a fragment—with an accident, a mere quality—that catalyzes the event of naming, as if mere shards of substance were responsible for speaking the being of the world's worthiest knight:

> Au reconnoistre mout tarda;
> Et nepourquant bien l'esgarda,
> Quë en la fin li fu avis,
> D'une plaie qu'il ot el vis,
> C'une tel plaie el vis avoit
> Mesire Yvains; bien le savoit,
> Qu'ele l'avoit souvant veüe.
> Por la plaie l'a coneü

> She came very slowly to the recognition; / and nevertheless she looked at him, / so that in the end she realized / of a scar that he had on his face, / that such a scar, on his face, / has my lord Yvain; she knew him well, / for she had seen it often. / By the scar she recognized him (ll. 2901–8)

As the quality or accident tempts to the point of recognition, naming, and erotic touch, the rhyme here turns on the word "face" or *vis*, homonymous with "seeing," *veoir*, whose participle/*metaxy* is *vis*. The homonym extends to another expression, which means "realizing," *li fu avis*. Apart from this expression, *avis* can mean "opinion"—but the term is formed from the past participle of the verb *aviser* (meaning "to see, to take a look," and eventually, "to consider, to be attentive"),[59] a verb related to that word for "countenance" or "face," *vis*, from the Latin *visum* (from *videre*, "to see"): it is an expression deriving from a sense of relation to the face, seeing the face, being face to face with.[60]

This facial recognition, articulated around and caught on the tempting hook of Yvain's scar, intertwines with an erotic complicity between Yvain, the damsel, and of course, the magic potion. We retranslate the lines cited above to underscore this process: "She realized [a*vis*] about the scar that he had [*avoit*] on the face [*vis*] that such a scar on his face [*vis*] had Sir Yvain,

---

59. Greimas, *Dictionaire de l'ancien français*, sv. avis. This dimension of the semantic field of Old French *avis* (in the sense of give/change/take/share/be of *avis*), is still active in Present Day English "advice," the direct reflex of a Middle English loanword from Anglo-Norman first recorded in the early fourteenth century (*Oxford English Dictionary*, sv. advise, etym., 1.)

60. See Greimas, *Dictionaire de l'ancien français*, sv. aviser, vis; *Anglo-Norman Dictionary*, sv. aviser¹.

she knew [*savoit*] him/it well, she had seen [*veü*] it/him enough, by the scar she knew [*coneü*] him" (ll. 2901–8). The verb to know, *connoître*, includes in the recesses of its semantic field—and, at the same time, in its parts so public and open that we don't think about it—the delicious recess of her person and anatomy, *le con,* about which the romance, with its PG-13 conventions, never speaks: it never speaks of the excess, *de surplus ne parle point*. Literally, the damsel *l'a coneü*, "knew him"—a distinct *double entendre* identical to the one also possible for the Latin relative of the French past participle or adjective *coneü* (from the Latin *cognosco*), while *vis* is also the homonym of the *vit* (male member).[61] We are thus taken from an unknown face to an erotic complicity between bodies and a magic potion by a series of subtle transformations of the alluring phonemic qualities of end-rhyme words, accomplished graphically in one- or two-letter increments (*avis/vis/avoit/savoit/veü/coneü*).

At the same time as being vaguely but—given the context of nakedness and anointing—insistently inappropriate for children, these lines signal a proleptically Levinasian focus on the face in the determination of knowledge and in naming—a Levinasian take without the Levinasian phobia of nonhuman substance.[62] Is not the turn to forget or to fall out of language without turning away from language the very essence of Levinas's thought? The linguistic turn was terminally inscribed (at least in French letters) at the time (of Levinas, of Beckett), by Blanchot's and Heidegger's obsession with death and negativity, on the impossibility to testify: a theory that conveniently defines reality as inaccessible through language—as Jim Creech has shown, Blanchot and Heidegger, who were Nazis, were desperate for this "impossibility" to always remain in force; testimony destroyed their character.[63] Levinas's *volte-face* cir-

---

61. Lewis and Short, *Latin Dictionary*, sv. *cognosco*, 1.A.b.

62. Our turn to Levinas (as our turn to Heidegger, or to OOO) can only be tentative and partial because Levinas's incontrovertible commitment to the Unique and the One sets his an-archic humanism of the face against "the inconsequence of denouncing the absolute of the human in the name of evidence brought forth by the social sciences [namely, structural anthropology]" (Emanuel Levinas, "Humanism and An-Archy," in *Humanism of the Other,* trans. Nidra Poller [Urbana: Illinois University Press, 2006], 47 [45–57]). It is thus pejoratively, and not without trepidation, that Levinas refers to "a nonhumnan order, suited to the name that is anonymity itself: matter" (48). For all his radical departures from Heidegger, Levinas, too, fears walking on the moon; and "to find a man in that matter and a name in that anonymity" is, for Levinas, to look, without hope, for "a being in that lunar landscape" of matter (48). These arguments were drafted with the events of May 1968 as a backdrop, and so Levinas's "moon fear" is roughly contemporary with, but a bit subsequent to, Heidegger's (1966)—perhaps a marked allusion to Heidegger's interview in *Der Spiegel.*

63. There are also echoes of the juridical and moral dimension of the Latin *visu* in Levinas. See Jim Creech's unpublished work and communications, his "La Honte dans la théorie," in *Le Coq Héron* 184, *Secret, Honte et violences: La honte à l'épreuve de la psychanalyse*

cumvents the impossibility or negativity of language through the focus on the *visage*, which simply steps around the yawning abyss by setting language—at the level of the signifying act itself—on a queer, askew, course: "The face disorients the intentionality that sights it."[64] The teleological *aim* of intentionality that would govern the model of signification in which (as the linguistic turn taught us) the signifier fails to signify (because it never arrives at its signified), is set askew before the arrow can even be drawn, much less be let loose from the bow.

In Levinas, as in *Yvain* and in *Perceval*, the turn from language to the face occasions an optimistic renaming. We say optimistic, in spite of Perceval's cousin's reproach and her renaming of him as *chaitis*, wretched. As in *Yvain*, tears follow the naming: the woman who discovers Yvain turns to her companions and tells them the story, weeping from pity at the present ruin of his exemplary knighthood (l. 2919). Perceval's cousin rises and speaks angrily of his mother's death caused by grief at his departure (l. 3580), before she too succumbs, mourning her dead lover (l. 3690). But here, we would ask for an optimistic reading of weeping. It is a mourning of a personhood that throws into relief its value. The woman in Yvain mourns his reason or *sen* (sense, ll. 2932, 2935, 2937) that she suspects he lost through mourning or *duel* (akin to modern French *deuil*, "mourning, broken heart") (ll. 2928, 2930). Perceval's cousin mourns her lover, becoming excessive and unreasonable (*se demante et se desresne*, l. 3432), an abdication of self against which Perceval warns her (*folie*, l. 3632). We want to go beyond the statement that erotic anamnesis—whether it is a grail- or bicycle-fixation, or an erotic forgetting, or forgetting-oneself in *Yvain*—leads to naming and mourning that goes on to abdication of self or *sen* (*sen*, "reason, sanity, mind, meaning") and descent into the amnesia or anamnesis of madness. Instead, we want to suggest that all three—erotic anamnesis, naming, mourning—are part of the sincere connection to the personhood of the other: an instantiation of the importance of the other, whether pleasurable (erotic) or painful (mourning). And we should also consider that all these instances of intense relation to personhood are connected, originate from, and are inscribed in the condition of the allure of real objects: in our examples here, these alluring objects are the *graal*'s jewels, the decapitated body, the senseless body of Yvain. The sensual objects with which the characters in the story connect are accidentally encrusted with the tremendously profound essence of these real objects: the *graal* has healing properties, the

---

(Winter 2006): 100–108, and "De la honte à la théorie," in *Lire, écrire la honte: Actes du colloque de Cérisy*, ed. Bruno Chaouat (Lyon: Presses Universitaires de Lyon, 2007).

64. Emanuel Levinas, "Signification and Sense," in *Humanism of the Other*, trans. Nidra Poller (Urbana: Illinois University Press, 2006), 33 [9–44].

decapitated body is that of a lover, Yvain's senseless body is that of the world's worthiest knight.

And so we return to the bicycle and the horn. What is the allure of Molloy's bicycle to a medieval romance?[65] What do we glimpse in Molloy's self-naming—in its nearness to the elegant, strange, and fragmentary limits of the human articulated by the grail, Yvain's body, or the magic potion? Molloy's self-naming comes specifically after an arrest predicated on the machinations of the police-state in which he lives and their reaction to Molloy's erotic intimacy with his bicycle. Passing through the city gates, Molloy dismounts his bicycle as required by law:

> But a little further on I heard myself hailed. I raised my head and saw a policeman. Elliptically speaking, for it was only later, but by way of induction, or deduction, I forget which, that I knew what it was. What are you doing there? he said. I'm used to that question, I understood it immediately. Resting, I said. Resting, he said. Resting, I said. Will you answer my question? he cried. So it always is when I'm reduced to confabulation, I honestly believe I have answered the question I am asked and in reality I do nothing of the kind. I won't reconstruct the conversation in all its meanderings. It ended in my understanding that my way of resting, my attitude when at rest, astride my bicycle, my arms on the handlebars, my head on my arms, was a violation of I don't know what, public order, public decency.[66]

Suffice it to say, it was indecent. Pleasures, for the homeless, are too often considered just so. The very existence of private property often renders forms of public eroticism usually prohibited by law (forms that would be, for a non-homeless person, totally voluntary) as a basic compulsory condition of sex for some homeless persons. Things only get worse when all Molloy can provide as official papers are those he uses "to wipe myself, you understand, when I have a stool" (16), introducing only more shit into the mix (a substance that seems to follow naturally, for Molloy, in both discussions of his bicycle). For

---

65. For another alluring Beckettian bicycle, see Beckett's early short story "Fingal," in *More Pricks Than Kicks, Samuel Beckett: The Grove Centenary Edition* vol. 4 (New York: Grove Press, 2006), in which the Dante-loving and Dante-alluding hero, Belacqua, comes to a place "where a bicycle was lying, half-hidden in the rank grass." The bicycle is here only half-dressed, a kind of bicycle pinup, or bicycle smut: for, "Belacqua, *who could on no account resist a bicycle*, thought what an extraordinary place to come across one" (italics ours, 92). Seen from afar, later on, we notice the machine's alluring qualities: "the nickel of the bike sparkled in the sun" (95). Belacqua slips away on the bike to find that "it was a fine light machine, with red tires and wooden rims," and that "the machine was a treat to ride" (96).

66. Beckett, *Molloy*, 16.

Molloy, the papers that should produce him as a human person before the law produce only shit, only the waste of a singularly queer creature—perhaps a natural course of his naive but still resistant response to the law.[67] And then, threatened "with a cylindrical ruler," and able to give almost no intelligible information to the police, Molloy, just like the *chevalier* of the romance before him, names himself:

> And suddenly I remembered my name, Molloy. My name is Molloy, I cried, all of a sudden, now I remember. Nothing compelled me to give this information, but I gave it, hoping to please, I suppose. They let me keep my hat on, I don't know why. Is it your mother's name? said the sergeant, it must have been a sergeant. Molloy, I cried, my name is Molloy. Is that your Mother's name? said the sergeant. What? I said, Your name is Molloy, said the sergeant. Yes, I said, now I remember. And your mother? said the sergeant. I didn't follow . . .[68]

The similarity to Chrétien's *Perceval* is, of course, striking. We would still not claim here that the allusion is certain or intentional, though Beckett was certainly capable of such a thing. We would rather consider it as Molloy asking, across time, of Perceval, what in the hell to do. As in *Perceval,* here too there is that whiff of an inevitable Oedipal narrative of an entry into language via naming in connection to an attempt to travel to the Mother. And yet, the moment is not so *determined* as in a Lacanian entry into language, nor so fixed in its proper path as a Freudian organism setting on its course from an exquisite polymorphous perversity towards heterosexual object choice. Such is the availability or cruisability of these fragments of Beckett's text, like those of Chrétien's, for queer love.[69] In both cases, what the law fails to understand is the an-epistemic and an-informational function of the preceding adventure—in which adventure is determined as inanimaphilic radiance. As the "Chrétien Girls" write of adventure in Chrétien, "To phrase wonder as a question is not

---

67. On this point of Molloy's frustration of the kind of Althusserian interpolation attempted by the police, see Calvin Thomas, "Cultural Droppings: Bersani's Beckett," *Twentieth Century Literature*, 47.2 (Summer 2001): 169–96: "Molloy's defiance here is cast in terms highly redolent of the very theoretical scene from which the Althusserian word *interpolation* derives. . . . But Molly's failure to produce on demand a clean and proper proof of identity, his refusal to establish personhood before the law, is rather a far cry from that 180-degree turn in affirmative and obedient response to a policeman's hailing" (181).

68. Beckett, *Molloy*, 19.

69. For a very differently focused reading of Beckett as part of a queer critical project, particularly one moving both in and beyond psychoanalysis, see Thomas, "Cultural Droppings."

to obtain information."[70] To name oneself in the wake of pleasure cannot be understood as giving information.

Molloy, the absurd conversationalist, both too loose (of speech) and too avaricious (of communication), mirrors a young Perceval who (when we first encounter him in Chrétien's narrative) cannot stop getting off-topic. This is, at least, what an unnamed *chevalier* ("horseman") learns when he tries, in vain, to corral this "beast," young Perceval (*beste*, ll. 244–45) into a conversation. The poem imagines that first, iconic encounter between Perceval and the Arthurian knights via a full complement of four dramatic minitableaux—comical in their cumulative, mounting absurdity. They constitute four topical "stanzas" on pieces of knightly armor (*lance, escuz, haubers, hernois*) articulated by the repeated "refrain" of the *chevalier*'s resigned and exasperated realization: as with the cop who stops Molloy, there will be no end to the conversation, but he will *not* receive answers to his questions (ll. 168–306). Such are Perceval's and Molloy's responses to language: attempts at naming, stuttering at a threshold of language and substance.

And yet, this stuttering eventually resolves into a name. In the same way that Perceval divines his name without knowing whether or not he speaks the truth, Molloy explains, upon naming himself: "Nothing compelled me to give this information, but I gave it, hoping to please." Molloy names himself aloud for the sake of pleasure, just as before he spoke about his bicycle because it "would be a pleasure."[71] After recounting his self-naming, in a move typical of the texture of his monologue, Molloy exults in *non sequitur*—recalling that "they let me keep my hat on, I don't know why"—interrupting his narration of the law's putative attempt to convert this speech about Molloy's name into something useful, or to discover his mother's name. When prompted to give his mother's name, Molloy himself literalizes the *non sequitur* [does not follow]: "And your mother? said the sergeant. *I didn't follow* . . ." (italics ours). Molloy does not give his name as a packet of information, but like Perceval, *performs the act* of *naming*. Accordingly, to give his mother's name as information would not follow. Although he will eventually guess that "her name must be Molloy too,"[72] Molloy will not go on this journey with the law, being unable or unwilling to "follow" to wherever this name might be punitively appropriated.

The relationship between language and Molloy's substance will be articulated far from the terms of fascist legal documents or police speech acts,

---

70. Stahuljak et al., *Thinking through Chrétien de Troyes*, 93.
71. Beckett, *Molloy*, 12.
72. Ibid., 19.

in an entirely different neighborhood of delights. Surprised at his swift release, Molloy proclaims: "To apply the letter of the law to a creature like me is not an easy matter."[73] The second half of the novel, in the voice of Jacques Moran (who at the very least thinks himself an agent of a shadowy and nefarious administrative agency), only confirms this assertion. Believing himself in receipt of an order to track down Molloy on grounds that are as unknown to Moran as to the reader (one can guess, however, that Molloy's creaturely off-the-grid life of intimacy with matter could constitute a threat to the state, to some punitive agency, or even simply to a bourgeois "good conscience")—but also aware that he, Moran, has "no colleagues" in his line of work and receives messages from a man named Gaber who does not understand the messages he carries, messages which in turn come from a mysterious man named Youdi that Moran has never met—Moran worries that he may have invented the whole thing, "Found him [Molloy] ready made in my head."[74] Given Molloy's assertion about the difficulty of applying the letter of the law to a creature like him, it is not insignificant that Moran's anxiety plays out in terms of a sudden and radical uncertainty as to Molloy's name—specifically, whether it be *Molloy* or *Mollose*.[75] One may rephrase the difficulty of "applying the letter of the law" to Molloy in terms of the difficulty of the law to apply any letter to him at all.

PLEASURE TO READ

Where does the allure of the self-naming of Perceval and the self-naming of Molloy lead us? Critic Calvin Thomas finds in Molloy, and in Beckett himself, a "failure to narrate" that signals a "failure to reproduce the person"—a failure in which Thomas locates a refusal of cultural redemption in artistic production that he wants to call queer.[76] We would *partially* link the radiance of which we speak (the allure of substance on the threshold of language and sex)

---

73. Ibid., 20.
74. Ibid., 106, 89–90.
75. Ibid., 107: "Of these two names, Molloy and Mollose, the second seemed to me perhaps the more correct. But barely. What I heard, in my soul I suppose, where the acoustics are so bad, was a first syllable, Mol, very clearly, followed almost at once by a second, very thick, as though gobbled by the first and which might have been oy as it might have been ose, or one, or even oc. And if I inclined towards ose, it was doubtless that my mind had a weakness for this ending, whereas the others left it cold. But since Gaber had said Molloy. . . . I was compelled to admit that I too should have said Molloy and that in saying Mollose I was at fault."
76. Thomas, "Cultural Droppings," 188.

to such a superfluity and non-productivity—but to a joyous one. It would be a pleasure, after all, to describe a purgatory of ease.

And is *this* the clearing of Being? And, in this strangely radiant place of nonhuman erotic complicities, what is the role of the *literary*? Is there still a fragment of something we might want to call human in what is besotted by, or spoken by, the allure of substantial qualities? For Heidegger, "What poetry, as illuminating projection, unfolds of unconcealedness and projects ahead into the design of the figure, is the Open which poetry lets happen, and indeed in such a way that only now, in the midst of beings, the Open brings beings to shine and ring out."[77] Reading without disdain for substance, without a fear of the moon, would this not indeed signal that it would be a *pleasure* to describe Molloy's bicycle *at length*?

What emerges here is twofold.

(1) If we listen to Heidegger's insistence that Language speaks us—but still test it—while sifting through fragments "of the human" and "of humanism" in these two nodes in the literary history of the novel (*Perceval*, from the novel's medieval protohistory in *romanz*, and *Molloy*, one of many postwar experiments in the undoing of the novel), if we listen to how Heidegger's claim echoes when sounded in the precincts where *Perceval* and *Molloy* draw near to each other, then we learn that, if Language indeed speaks us, the Language speaking in these extremes of literary history articulates beings not out of any totality, but out of the shards and fragments of language that can fleetingly operate in erotic complicity with the allure of accidents.

Heidegger has difficulty deciding "flatly whether poetry is a kind of thinking, or thinking really a kind of poetry,"[78] and perhaps this difficulty results from the nagging trouble of just how to conceptualize the moment of *poiesis* that resists appropriation as interpretation other than as a response to and in language as such. For Heidegger, this moment must be so expansive as to involve a cosmological totality—the fourfold of world and earth, gods and mortals, as in "the saying of world and earth, the saying of the arena of their conflict and thus the place of all nearness and remoteness of the gods."[79] This determination of *poiesis* as a response to the speaking of Language that lets the Open happen *yet must still involve such a totality* surely contributes to Heidegger's particularly fascist way of imagining *poiesis* as what allows language to burst again into History (determined in that terrifying way, which eases the conscience of the Nazi project, as the enactment of a people's "appointed

---

77. Heidegger, "Origin of the Work of Art," 70.
78. Heidegger, "The Nature of Language," 83.
79. Heidegger, "The Origin of the Work of Art," 71.

task").[80] Now, we would not want to contest every sense in which "whenever art happens . . . a thrust enters history," even as we must acknowledge the risk here, and never stop acknowledging it—of radical evil. However, instead of a threshold of language that must entangle cosmological totality, our readings would suggest an alternative account of the Open that "brings beings to shine and ring out"[81]: an Open that brings beings to shine in an erotic burning of intimacy and complicity between mortals and matter, that rings out in the *honk!* of a bicycle horn, that flutters between humans and the sensual objects on which they are caught. Here is *poiesis* that matters in the tiniest and most fragmentary of spaces: the Open as a measure of intensity and possibility, and not spatial expansiveness. Here, the Heideggerian clearing of Being still appears at the threshold of language and cosmos, not as magic or metaphysics, but as the moment of the erotic radiance of language caught on and besotted by fragments.

(2) In a more minor vein, concerning the details of literary history itself, Chrétien now emerges as an important node of an alternative circuit in the literary history of the novel itself, and specifically the novel we would call *Modernist*. It is as if reading about Perceval's chivalric training and learning to take pleasure in the erotic complicities spoken by Chrétien's language were the best preparation for *chevalier*-readers to take pleasure in Beckett's texts as producing something other than the dour pessimism they are almost constantly assigned.

---

80. "Whenever art happens—that is, whenever there is a beginning—a thrust enters history, history either begins or starts over again. History means here not a sequence in time of events of whatever sort, however important. History is the transporting of a people into its appointed task as entrance into that people's endowment" (Ibid., 74).

81. Ibid., 70.

PART II

Human, Inhuman, Spectacle

CHAPTER 5

Aninormality

JEFFREY JEROME COHEN

PERCEPTIBLE THINGS

To be trained as a medievalist is to learn to worship at the altar of Clio. Because the Middle Ages are so distant, history becomes a guarantor of truth in explication, the surety that a grasp of the temporally remote is not distorted by anachronism. Thus the disciplinary ardor for *historicism,* a research-intensive interpretive mode in which analysis proceeds via nuanced understanding of political events, literary traditions, law, and cultural context—emplacing a moment from the past into its synchronic totality. Rigorous yet flexible, historicism endures because it serves humanistic study well, transforming a past thick with heterogeneity and messy with unrealized possibility into an explicable expanse.[1]

---

1. Rejecting the possibility or at least the desirability of such a straightforward encounter with the past, queer theory has offered a compelling critique of historicism's hegemony.

In historicist inquiry, contemporary context is quietly granted the power to determine the limits of what a work of art can mean. Thus Robert M. Stein opens his book, *Reality Fictions: Romance, History and Governmental Authority, 1025–1180*, with some words about the relation between text and circumstance that demonstrate eloquently how historicism proceeds:

> I suggest in this book that the provocation to romance writing is the same as the provocation to history: they grow out of the same cultural need and intend to do the same cultural work.... I am writing about a political process [state formation] and its connection with literary innovation.... I intend ... to deal directly with the pressures on modes of representation that are correlative to changes in the structure of political power.[2]

Stein links romance to history through changes in governmental structures and political ambitions. To make his thesis cogent, he invokes doctrines that historicism (old and new) taught medievalists long ago to accept: art is intractably enmeshed within its originary geotemporality; art performs a definitive social function; art is enabled by zeitgeist and itself undertakes cultural work.

Yet compare Stein's point of interpretive departure to Helen Vendler's swift application of the emergency brake when critics of contemporary poems attempt politically minded readings. Beauty (which might be loosely defined as an ecstatic experience of a work's inherent vitality) seems indifferent to history, since in Vendler's rather modernist conceptualization of art dwells in a privileged, exterior space. In a review of Vendler's recent criticism, Rachel Donadio observes:

> Vendler took the critic James Fenton to task for his interpretation of Robert Frost's 1942 poem "The Gift Outright," a version of which was recited by the

---

Queer theorists often argue for a perverse or (in the words of Glenn Burger and Steven F. Kruger) *preposterous* rendezvous with history: see their introduction to *Queering the Middle Ages*, ed. Burger and Kruger (Minneapolis: University of Minnesota Press, 2001), xi–xxiii. Historicism's seemingly univocal truth, they argue, is "a retrospective selection of some facts [and narratives] over others," imbuing the chosen evidence with explanatory force; those roads not taken and stories passed over in silence, meanwhile, are assumed to be "dead ends" (xx). History assumes different contours, and takes a different position alongside the present, when supposed culs-de-sacs are followed rather than refused. Along these same lines, I would like to think of this essay's project as a *queer* one, meaning that I'd never have launched it had its course not been suggested by my reading in queer theory. There is something in the surplus of desire, value, and (as Roger Caillois will have it) *lyricism* that art possesses that is directly related to the queer: to sexuality as something more than conjugality or genitality, to ardent estrangement of the natural.

2. Robert M. Stein, *Reality Fictions: Romance, History and Governmental Authority, 1025–1180* (Notre Dame, IN: University of Notre Dame Press, 2006), 2.

aging poet at the Kennedy inauguration in 1961. Fenton, in her view, had imposed a mistaken interpretation on a poem as much "about marriage as about colonials becoming Americans," because "his politics has wrenched him into misreading it." (Some argued Vendler herself was misreading the poem by choosing to ignore its subject matter.)[3]

Most scholars who work with premodern materials will find their sympathies drawn to Robert Stein and James Fenton over Helen Vendler's idea of timeless, acontextual art. Medievalists work in a discipline that stresses context so heavily that it is difficult to be satisfied with an impassioned aesthetics that lacks anchoring in determinative history. The return to beauty, so trumpeted in the contemporary-focused humanities after the publication of Elaine Scarry's *On Beauty and Being Just* (2001), has failed to recruit many participants among scholars of the Middle Ages, who seem constitutionally incapable of detaching artistic analysis from the social and the cultural.[4] How medievalists understand the relation of a text or artwork to our present interpretive moment may differ widely: we may argue that the medieval is much like our own times (the Middle Ages as threshold of the Same), or we may hold that the period is vastly different from the present (the Middle Ages as chastely Other), or we may even stress the simultaneity or coevality of both modes. Yet in all cases, history and context, past and perhaps present, determine the meaning within the form. Art remains historically bound and rather inert.

The historicist model does not, in other words, do all that much for the work of art itself. When historicism and other socially minded forms of criticism ignore aesthetic effect, they do not leave sufficient room for what Jennifer Green-Lewis and Margaret Soltan have powerfully described as "art's thrilling intimation of an untapped plenitude within us and in the world."[5] In art, Green-Lewis and Soltan argue, inheres the ability "to move us to a condition of ecstasy as we lose ourselves in its particular forms of beauty." Unlike transports familiar from medieval religious experience, this movement

---

3. Rachel Donadio, "The Closest Reader," *New York Times Review of Books*, 10 December 2006, http://www.nytimes.com/2006/12/10/books/review/Donadio.t.html. See also Harris Feinsod, "The Tolson Exception: The Anthology in the 21st Century," *Arcade* (9 January 2012) http://arcade.stanford.edu/blogs/tolson-exception-anthology-21st-century.

4. Elaine Scarry, *On Beauty and Being Just* (Princeton, NJ: Princeton University Press, 2001).

5. Although they would not recognize themselves as fellow travelers with Leo Bersani and Ulysse Dutoit, the argument formulated by Green-Lewis and Soltan shares much with the unbinding or shattering of the self ("a renewable retreat from the seriousness of stable identities") described in *Forms of Being: Cinema, Aesthetics, Subjectivity* (London: BFI Publishing, 2004) and "Psychoanalysis and the Aesthetic Subject," *Critical Inquiry* 32 (2006): 161–74.

outside of the self offers what they call "a cheerfully secular faith," one in which "beneath the mundane life of daily consciousness lies a deep source of meaning, a motive to action, joy."[6] Conventional historicism has, admittedly, a difficult time articulating how the Middle English poem *Sir Gawain and the Green Knight*—with its green holly conjoined to crimson blood, its frisson of terror intercut with infectious exuberance—could have a rapturous, bodily effect, could possess a beauty that more mundane medieval texts do not hold. This beauty, it seems, moves the poem outside of its own history, into a realm where its meditations on Ricardian kingship or contemporary Welsh-English relations matter less than its ability to render birdsong in a winter storm as plaintive to medieval ears as to our own. Both historicism and the contemporary turn to beauty embrace a binary where none may flourish: *aesthetics*, after all, derives from the Greek word for perceptible things, an inhuman impress that can convey history as easily as the sublime. Aesthetics is a science of unlikely life, a mapping of how matter acts.

Beauty is frequently found by artists and critics in the nonhuman world: oceans, flowers, snowy mountains, celestial objects, birdsong, and the sound of words are favorite sources. Claude Monet discerned London's grandeur by painting a city devoid of inhabitants. Wisps of fog, the glimmering Thames, and stony architectures made nebulous by stains of light appear more frequently on his canvases than human figures. Yet for all the privilege the nonhuman enjoys as a trigger to aesthetic experience, beauty is ultimately a deeply human category. For Elaine Scarry, beauty's innate symmetry is intimately related to a notion of justice based upon proportion and balance: "Through its beauty, the world continually recommits us to a rigorous standard of perceptual care," a foundational principle of fairness and proportion.[7] Beauty stages an ethical relation and exists to make us better in our humanity. "There will always be those who believe," write Green-Lewis and Soltan, "the intoxicating power of art inclines us toward civic virtue by invigorating our faith in humanity, clarifying our spiritual and ethical particularity, and inspiring us to do great and good things."[8] Though this ameliorating, humanizing power of art may be true, I can't help wondering what beauty does for the animal or for

---

6. Jennifer Green-Lewis and Margaret Soltan, *Teaching Beauty in DeLillo, Woolf, and Merrill* (New York: Palgrave Macmillan, 2008), 3. For an exposition of the relation of secular faith to aesthetic experience, see xviii. My framing of the inanimate vivacity that beauty betrays owes much to Jane Bennett, *The Enchantment of Modern Life: Crossings, Energetics, and Ethics* (Princeton, NJ: Princeton University Press, 2001) and *Vibrant Matter: A Political Ecology of Things* (Durham, NC: Duke University Press, 2010).

7. Scarry, *On Beauty* 81, 94–95.

8. Green-Lewis and Soltan, *Teaching Beauty*, 3.

the rock formation that finds itself its bearer. Can stones become intoxicated, beasts invigorated by a humanity they find suddenly within themselves? Can either be moved to accomplish great and good things?[9]

Something exists in art that is inapposite, extraneous. Art is not reducible to its enmeshment in historical circumstance, even if the time and place in which it arose wholly saturates it. Nor can art inhabit some space exterior to history. Can art be imagined as an active agent in a world of human and nonhuman forces? Can art produce, intervene within, intensify, and transform the history within which it arises? As one force among many, can art call worlds into being without falling wholly back into those worlds, without ever escaping from a perpetual unfolding? Can art be something more than a human product, beauty something more than a human perception? What if rocks, animals, and texts produce art rather than serve as art's receptacle? What if art is the acting of matter in an aesthetic register? What if rocks and texts create, from their own structure or through an innate vibrancy, a posthuman kind of beauty?

CAILLOIS AMONG THE NONHUMANS

Theorizing the interface between humans and their others, especially animals, has proven an especially rich critical topic. Steve Baker, Jacques Derrida, Susan Crane, N. Katherine Hayles, Noreen Giffney and Myra J. Hird, Elizabeth Grosz, Donna Haraway, Alphonso Lingis, Karl Steel, Julian Yates, Jonathan Gil Harris, Bruno Latour, and Cary Wolfe (among many others) have stressed the tenuousness of any line that would segregate the human from the nonhuman. Just as valuable to this multidisciplinary investigation, I would argue, is the eclectic work of Roger Caillois. Connected in complicated ways to Andre Breton and French surrealism, Caillois maintained friendships that read like a *Who's Who* of francophone theory. He was introduced to Georges Bataille by Jacques Lacan. With Bataille and Michel Leiris he founded the influential College of Sociology in 1938. When Bataille determined that the secret society he had formed (*Acéphale*) needed to cement its membership around an act of human sacrifice, and when someone (possibly the perennially depressed Leiris) volunteered as victim, Bataille—it has been suggested—attempted to convince

---

9. I do realize that I am using "art" and "beauty" as synonyms here, an equivalence that many would argue against, but one found in Scarry as well as Green-Lewis and Soltan. Roger Caillois will qualify art as the work of human hands, but will then (as will be seen) find that work to be part of a cosmic or universal impulse rather than a strictly human achievement.

Caillois to be the executioner.[10] Needless to say, the sacrifice did not take place: Roger Caillois was by nature ambivalent toward any group desiring his membership. Indeed, this reticence goes a long way toward explaining why his work remains relatively neglected, while that of almost everyone who moved through his intellectual circle has proven influential in the world of theory. There is something anomalous about Caillois, both as a person and as a writer. Caillois is useful for thinking about the world from a nonanthropomorphic point of view. He devoted his life to exploring such mysteries as why stones are such accomplished artists and why animal mimicry does not actually imitate anything.[11] He never wanted to keep uncertainty in place simply out of reverence. Famously, he broke with the Surrealists when Andre Breton refused to cut open a Mexican jumping bean.[12] Caillois thought it ridiculous to argue that the bean's secret interior ought to be preserved simply to keep mystery intact. Yet Roger Caillois also insisted that a place exists within science for beauty.

Caillois's recent editor and translator, Claudine Frank, makes two statements about his early intellectual projects that well summarize his promise for posthumanism: that "he was always seeking out new monsters," and that he was engaged in composing a kind of "reverie" that could engender a "subversive, revolutionary New Science," interrogating rather than dismissing the imaginative and the fantastic.[13] These projects involved the displacement of *homo sapiens* from assumed centrality, discovering the alien within the unraveling contours of the human—and the human within insects, octopi, butterflies, agates, inhuman architectures, the workings of the cosmos. "Man is a unique case only in his own eyes," Caillois observes in his provocative essay "The Praying Mantis: From Biology to Psychoanalysis" (c. 1934).[14] Here he

---

10. See Claudine Frank's provocative reconstruction of the events from surviving references in her excellent introduction to Roger Caillois, *The Edge of Surrealism: A Roger Caillois Reader*, ed. Claudine Frank (Durham, NC: Duke University Press, 2003), 28–32.

11. I became interested in Caillois's work through the reverence shown him by the philosopher Elizabeth Grosz, a feminist reinterpreter of Lacan, Deleuze, and Darwin. See especially *Space, Time, and Perversion: Essays on the Politics of Bodies* (New York: Routledge, 1995). The essays "Animal Sex: Libido as Desire and Death" (187–206) and "Experimental Desire: Rethinking Queer Subjectivity" (207–28) have been especially helpful to me in framing this project.

12. The infamous "incident of the Mexican jumping beans" is examined by Claudine Frank in her Introduction to *Edge of Surrealism*, 10.

13. Ibid., 5, 12.

14. Marguerite Yourcenar articulates Caillos's beliefs well in her introduction to one of his last works, *The Writing of Stones*: "He advocated an inverted anthropomorphism in which man, instead of attributing his emotions, sometimes condescendingly, to all other living beings, shares humbly, yet perhaps with pride, in everything contained or innate in all three realms, animal, vegetable, and mineral" (*The Writing of Stones*, ed. Marguerite Yourcenar, trans. Barbara Bray [Charlottesville: University of Virginia Press, 1985], xii).

takes as his starting point the eternal fascination men betray with the *femme fatale* of the insect world, the mantis who beheads her partner as a prelude to mating. Caillois acknowledges that this recurring interest may derive simply from "some obscure sense of identification" elicited by the insect's "remarkably anthropomorphic form."[15] Yet he is not satisfied by a principle of simple projection, as if by detailing the function of the mantis within male fantasies, the insect's uncanniness would stand explained. There exists in the praying mantis, he writes, an innate lyricism, an irreducible superfluity.[16] Even when decapitated, the mantis is capable of walking, mating, laying eggs, feigning *rigor mortis* to escape impending danger. Attempting to describe this acephalous body having sex, living its life, and imitating a cadaver leads Caillois to observe of his own convoluted language: "I am deliberately expressing myself in a roundabout way as it is so difficult, I think, both for language to express and for the mind to grasp that the mantis, when dead, should be capable of simulating death."[17] He finds a similar impulse to lyricism (or "objective lyrical value") in almost all scientific writing about the insect, an irresistible provocation to poetry that overcomes habitual "professional dryness"[18] and swiftly carries writers out of their accustomed technical lexicons.

The mantis offers no comfortable lessons about the anthropomorphism of insects. Its lyricism (that is, its ability to unsettle human observers and trigger reverie) is not a human projection, but a fact of its being, a cosmic given that it shares across boundaries with other human and nonhuman bodies:

> Such research tends to establish that determinations caused by the social structure, however important, are not alone in influencing the content of myths. We must also take into account half-physiological, half-psychological factors. . . . We should pay more attention to certain basic emotional reactions and clusters that sometimes exist only as potentialities in human beings, but that correspond to phenomena explicitly and commonly observed throughout the rest of nature.[19]

The mantis suggests the entomonous infecting the human, as well as the human within the insect, pointing toward what is shared by both, breaching

---

15. Roger Caillois, "The Praying Mantis: From Biology to Psychoanalysis," in *The Edge of Surrealism: A Roger Caillois Reader*, ed. Claudine Frank (Durham, NC: Duke University Press, 2003), 73.
16. Ibid., 74, 78.
17. Ibid., 79.
18. Ibid., 78.
19. Ibid., 81.

the barrier between anthropocentric subject and nonhuman environment. This exorbitant similitude becomes proof of what Caillois calls "the systematic overdetermination of the universe"[20]—quite a burden for a small bug to bear. By refusing allegory, by refusing contextualization into mere human meaning, the praying mantis restores danger to the object under scientific scrutiny, allowing that the act of contemplation itself immediately trespasses the distinction between observer and observed, rendering them inextricable.

Caillois develops these themes further in "Mimicry and Legendary Psychasthenia," an essay likewise exploring the intimacy of the insectal. Caillois's work here proved instrumental for the psychoanalyst Jacques Lacan as he formed his notion of the Mirror Stage. Against those who see in every attribute of an animal an evolutionary use value, Caillois develops an antiutilitarian argument in which the spatial and the corporeal interpenetrate.[21] Mimicry, the vertiginous displacement of environment onto body, is for Caillois not a survival strategy but an unnecessary surplus, an aesthetic maneuver, and a "dangerous luxury." Hunters are seldom deceived, he observes, when their prey adopt attributes of the space they inhabit, such as when a butterfly imitates a twig or a beetle disguises itself as a pebble. Most animals hunt by smell, not sight: "Numerous remains of mimetic insects are found in the stomach of predators." Many inedible creatures imitate their environments needlessly.[22] Mimicry—whether animals becoming their worlds, or humans imitating their surroundings, magically or artistically—is a succumbing of body and subject to the "lure of space."[23] This "dispossession" of the privilege of being one's own center spells the death of the autonomous subject, as self is scattered across landscape and landscape intermixes with self. Caillois gives a literary example, Gustave Flaubert's rendition of the desert-dwelling Saint Antony. The hermit rapturously witnesses the "interpenetration of the three natural kingdoms" (vegetal, animal, geological) and "disperse[s] himself everywhere, to be within everything."[24] Elizabeth Grosz writes in summation that what Caillois has

---

20. Ibid., 76.

21. "One of the working hypotheses of modern science—that nature always worked with the greatest possible economy of means toward the most practical of ends—finally came to appear unacceptable to Caillois. 'Nature is not a miser.' He had become more aware of it as a mine of prodigality, a feast of superfluity; of the element of fantasy, where the aesthetic factor whether conscious or otherwise which is inherent in every scrap of matter and of which man's own aesthetic may be no more than one of many manifestations, and one often extorted by our own exaggerated awareness of it" (Yourcenar, Introduction to *The Writing of Stones*, xii–xiii).

22. Roger Caillois, "Mimicry and Legendary Psychasthenia," in *The Edge of Surrealism: A Roger Caillois Reader*, ed. Claudine Frank (Durham, NC: Duke University Press, 2003), 96–97 [91–103].

23. Ibid., 99.

24. Ibid., 101.

identified is "a certain structural, anatomical, or behavioral superabundance, perhaps it is the very superfluity of life over and above the survival needs of the organism."[25] This superfluity of life is, by a more expressive name, *art*.

Later in life, Caillois argued that art is not possessed only by humans or by animals. Art is a superfluous beauty fashioned by geology as easily as human hands. *The Writing of Stones* is a stunningly illustrated tour of nonhuman art: lithic sculptures offered for no particular audience to admire, the petrification of a universal impulse to produce beyond utility, geological phenomena that had seemed, until Caillois looked so intently upon them, to be inert. He finds in marble, amethyst, jaspers, limestone, and agates an aesthetic formed of "surprising resemblance" to human art, a resemblance "at once improbable and natural,"[26] a resemblance better described as a commonality. This "intrinsic, infallible, immediate beauty, answerable to no one" and possessed indestructibly by certain rocky formations, is the "promise and the foundation" of human beauty:

> Stones—and not only they but also roots, shells, wings, and every cipher and construction in nature—help to give us an idea of the proportions and laws of that general beauty about which we can only conjecture and in comparison with which human beauty must be merely one recipe among many others.... In stones the beauty common to all the kingdoms seems vague, even diffuse, to man, a being lacking in density.[27]

Humans may resist beholding in the colors, textures, and resemblances of stones the colors, textures, and resemblances of their own art, the "endless variation" of cosmic phenomena as evident in fern fronds and mollusk shells as in eruptions of quartz and Rothko canvases. Humans may resist seeing in themselves and in their works architectures of beauty that connect them to the cosmic, the microscopic, the inanimate, to "works executed by no one," to "the aesthetics of the universe."[28] Yet despite this disavowal, something exists within "imperturbable stone which neither feels nor knows" that its excess of pattern, color, harmony, and form triggers "something we might describe as the lapidary" that fills us with "wonder and desire."[29] Often we answer such

---

25. Grosz, "Animal Sex: Libido as Desire and Death," 190 [187–206].
26. Caillois, *Writing of Stones*, 1.
27. Ibid., 2–3.
28. Ibid., 13, 3. Although it is difficult to say exactly what such a universal aesthetic would comprise, Caillois clearly aligns it with the symmetry and formality of theorists of beauty like Elaine Scarry, comparing it to a kind of "total geometry" (3), or (more flexibly) to "a geometry that is both capricious and harmonious, airily combining rigor and ease" (49).
29. Ibid., 75, 3.

lapidary pull by becoming collaborators with stone—most famously, when early modern artists painted scenes from *Orlando Amoroso* or the *Divine Comedy* on pieces of marble that provided naturally occurring backgrounds of forests, ruins, and flames.[30]

Interested as he is with art within stone, Caillois does not mention the stoneworks that would seem the ultimate expression of such alliance: menhirs, dolmens, and vast lithic arrays like Avebury. Stonehenge, for example, may be in part a human version of the naturally occurring standing stones of the Preseli Mountains in Wales. Here dolerite can be found in the form of rectangular pillars, seemingly rough-hewn by some primal architect, sometimes appearing to have been positioned as an orderly line of monoliths. The stones tower over an expansive landscape of grass, lichen-encrusted boulders that appear to have been smashed by giants, and springs that according to local myths possess curative powers. These bluestones of the Preseli Mountains were the source of the oldest stones erected at Stonehenge, 250 miles away. The archeologist Geoffrey Wainwright calls the bluestones "a natural monument" of columns and pillars, and has found ample evidence that they were venerated in Neolithic times, often through the inscription of artwork on their surfaces.[31] Something about the formations so inspired their beholders that they transported eighty or so monoliths, each weighing up to four tons, through an almost inconceivable amount of effort to distant Salisbury plain. Nature's exorbitance called forth a human response that was just as excessive. The Preseli bluestones are an artwork wrought through the shifting of the landscape over vast spans of time, the expenditure of gravitational and climatic energies. Stonehenge is an artwork wrought through the release of energy in sinew and muscle, but is also something more than a simple imitation of a natural original. Both cases seem the product of ongoing and restless forces that effloresce into enduring forms; human or not, both are worlds wrought in stone.

Caillois stresses throughout his analysis that even though lithic art seems embedded within what is dead, immobile, and unchanging, what in fact fascinates is the active connection between stone and world, evident in the unbearably slow formation of its artwork, and evident as well in the participation it

---

30. Caillois describes these *paesine* at length and provides vivid illustrations in *The Writing of Stones*, 26–36. He observes: "The painter cooperates with nature.... It is as if nature not only provided a stock of models but also directly created works worthy of admiration—works capable of competing on equal terms with human achievements without having to pass through the alchemy of human art" (32–34).

31. The quotation—and much of my information about the bluestones—is taken from the excellent overview of recent archeological work on Stonehenge contained in Caroline Alexander, "If the Stones Could Speak: Searching for the Original Meaning of Stonehenge," *National Geographic* (June 2008): 53 [34–59].

demands from its environment—including the human observer. Gazing upon a sheet of scaled jasper, he writes, "Even while I am reducing things to their chemical constituents I cannot help descrying swathes of arctic light shining meagerly on inky lichens, struggling vegetation exhausted by rough winds and burned by frost."[32] Such reverie is not human projection, he insists, but a participation across kingdoms (animal, mineral) activated by the tempestuous beauty common to both. Sometimes in stone we behold lively traces: the fossilized wisps of ancient leaves, remnants of animals whose ancient bulk troubles the imagination to body forth. Sometimes we behold natural resemblances to such recurring forms. Often we witness the archive of a history that did not otherwise endure: "life's mistakes, to remind nature of its monsters, its botched jobs, its blind alleys."[33] Or perhaps in this abortive past, we behold a future that includes ourselves, observers made of more stone-stuff than we care to acknowledge:

> [These "monsters"] somehow announce the coming, in the distant future, of a species that makes mistakes. . . . They presage new powers, imperfect but creative. . . . They seem to be manifestations of what I have ventured to call a natural fantasy . . . a lasting and inalienable collusion between this series of fertile abortions and their ultimate beneficiary.[34]

Caillois has been accused of pessimism, even misanthropy: "a kind of indifference toward what is human."[35] Yet what Caillois attempted was to view the world through a less anthropocentric lens, one in which stones and artists share a common impulse toward the production of beauty, one in which humans and rocks share secret affinities and ontology-crossing vitalities. As the heir to nature's creative experiments, Caillois wrote, humans must "recognize, among the daunting mass of nature's ventures, those which, though they did not succeed, opened up for him, through their very failure, a glorious way ahead"—one in which animals, rocks, and *homo sapiens* bear in their forms and substance the imprint not of some divine maker, not of an intelligent design, but of an art-making "universal syntax"[36] that sometimes, through its conjunctions, commits artistic errors, births monsters, and sometimes, through these same recurring processes, animates an imperfect world with a beauty more than human.

---

32. Caillois, *Writing of Stones*, 64.
33. Ibid., 81.
34. Ibid., 82–84.
35. Yourcenar, *The Writing of Stones*, xii.
36. Ibid., 84, 104.

Roger Caillois is famous for his meditations on the sex life of the praying mantis, the misfires of mimicry among animals, the power of stones to pull the human observer into disruptive encounters with inhuman art—a collaboration of the animate and the inorganic propelled by beauty ("innate lyricism"). He formulates modes of analysis that move us beyond arguments based upon evolutionary, cultural, or symbolic use value. Caillois proposes an innate aesthetic trigger to mobility that might be called *aninormality*: an antiutilitarian conception of the nonhuman that propels us into a lively realm where human and nonhuman counterinfect, where all kinds of bodies lose the rigor of their boundaries and become animated, anomalous.

MEDIEVAL ANINORMALITY

Aninormality is restless and inhuman vivacity, superfluous to and intimate with that which holds and is held by it, confounding distinctions between self and other, object and milieu. This ecstatic disruption of boundary and its intermixing of what might otherwise seem discrete occurs through the opening up of sublime new worlds—or, to foreground the activity that inheres in aninormality, broaches a possibly infinite series of *worldings*. Roger Caillois found such densities, such enfolded eruptions, within animals and stones. Medieval art, however, also offers a rich site for exploring aninormality's aesthetic dispossessions and interpenetrations.

Take, for example, Geoffrey of Monmouth's *History of the Kings of Britain*, a Latin text widely known not for its artistry, but for its contributions to history: the establishing of a new historiographical tradition, the promulgation of a potent origin myth for Britain, the bestowal to the future of Arthur and his court.[37] Possibly composed to boost Welsh ethnic pride, c.1136, this rhetorically unadorned work could not be more time-bound. Its vision of ancient Britain is an antidote to English triumphalism, to what had been the dominating version of the past of the island. *The History of the Kings of Britain* was a success from the moment of its first appearance, likely because it offered a radically reconfigured insular past in which the Welsh and Bretons played a heroic role. By offering a counternarrative to the eighth-century author Bede, whose *Ecclesiastical History of the English People* was seen by the twelfth century as the truth of early English history, Geoffrey of Monmouth's *History*

---

37. Latin quotations from Geoffrey of Monmouth's *History* are from *The Historia Regum Britannie I: Bern, Bürgerbibliothek MS 568 (the 'Vulgate' Version)*, ed. Neil Wright (Cambridge, UK: D. S. Brewer, 1984); translations are from *The History of the Kings of Britain*, trans. Lewis Thorpe (London: Penguin Books, 1966).

offered the possibility of a present that did not have to culminate in lasting English glory, a present in which room existed for the conquering Normans' transformation of the country into the appendage of a transmarine empire. The popularity of Geoffrey's text can be ascribed to the cultural needs it satisfied: Welsh and Breton patriotism, the Norman desire for a present in which their presence was something more than a baffling interruption of the island's English destiny, a more pluralistic vision of the British archipelago.

Yet if the text were so wholly of its moment, we should expect the enthusiasm elicited at its appearance to dissipate as the historical exigencies it arose to address were ameliorated by its success. *The History of the Kings of Britain* should have followed the arc of all propaganda, from spectacular ascent to rapid decline in the wake of the cultural changes it embodied and brought about, to lingering existence at some margin where it could be acknowledged as the somewhat embarrassing remnant of a transcended past. Ardor for the text, however, only burgeoned over time. Copies and versions proliferated. Translations from its international Latin into the indigenous tongues of French, English, and Welsh quickly appeared. From historiography its narratives migrated into chronicle, lyric, romance, lai. Each transformation was an amplification: as the poet Wace, for example, adapted Geoffrey's unadorned Latin prose into rhymed French verse (c. 1155), he added details like King Arthur's creation of a Round Table. Through his publication of the *History*, Geoffrey created what might be called a consensual world, a time-place that may never have existed, that comes into being and is sustained only through the texts by which writers populate its envisioned landscapes, but a world which nonetheless functions as if real, inviting other authors and scholars and fans to contribute their fictions masquerading as histories, their new characters, their enlargements of the consensual world's inherent possibilities. Without Geoffrey of Monmouth's innovative narrative, the Arthurian realm would not have come into being. Stories of the Grail, Lancelot, Morgan le Fay, the Lady of the Lake, and the Green Knight are simply the additions of later writer-fans to a universe, the loose parameters and initial content of which Geoffrey of Monmouth was the primary engineer. This expansive *worlding* of Geoffrey's rather sparse textual realm originates at least in part from the powerful moments he placed in his narrative, when what Caillois called innate or objective lyricism propels the text outside of history, when the thin finitude of mundane existence is disrupted through entangling intensification, resulting in temporal density and aesthetic vitality.

Lists of kings with regnal spans, bare accomplishments, and progeny structure long expanses of Geoffrey's narrative, a chronicling that tends toward the laconic. The dullness of his lists of data give the *History of the Kings of Britain* the heft of an artifact, the substantiality of something real. Thus the brief but exciting story of a sodomy-prone king devoured in the wilds by "ravening wolves" is tempered by the dry facticity of his son's *vita*:

> After the death of Mempricius, his son Ebraucus, who was very tall and a man of remarkable strength, took over the government of Britain and held it for thirty-nine years. He was the first after Brutus to sail a fleet to the shores of Gaul. He made war upon the provinces of the Gauls, slaughtering their menfolk and sacking their cities. By the time he came back victorious he was enriched with a vast booty of gold and silver. At a later date he founded a city on the farther side of the Humber, which city he called Kaerebrauc after himself, that is to say the City of Ebraucus.
>
> At that time King David was reigning in Judea and Silvius Latinus was king in Italy. In Israel, Gad, Nathan and Asaph were the prophets.
>
> Ebraucus also founded the city of Alclud over in Albany; and the castle of Mount Agned. . . . What is more, by the twenty wives which he had, he was the father of twenty sons and of thirty daughters. For forty years he ruled over the kingdom of Britain with great firmness. The names of his sons were as follows: Brutus Greenshield, Margodud, Sisillius, Regin, Morvid, Bladud, Lagon, Bodloan, Kincar, Spaden, Gaul, Dardan, Eldad, Ivor, Cangu, Hector. . . . (78–79)

Twenty sons are listed in total, and, having finished this catalog, Geoffrey goes on to name the thirty daughters, a weighty piling up of information that imbues this catalog of British, Roman, Greek, and invented appellations with the verity of an archive. This truth effect is enhanced through reference to events happening simultaneously in Israel and Rome, giving an invented past the authority that derives from having unfolded alongside familiar biblical and classical history. Invoking Brutus, the founding father of Britain in Geoffrey's *History,* builds Ebraucus's majesty and buttresses Brutus's own tenuous reality through self-referentiality.

The inventory of countries conquered, cities founded, and children fathered does its work, answering the preceding account of a king turned too inward. The sodomitical copulations of Mempricius, Ebraucus's father, express sexually his unwillingness to think about the life of his country beyond the termination of his reign ("he did away with any who he feared might succeed him in the kingship . . . he deserted his own wife") and his inability to rouse himself from self-enclosure in Britain and to expand his domain into an empire. His lupine ingestion within a valley where he wanders alone and abandoned is a rebuke to the tyranny through which he has built pan-insular dominion. His son's reign offers contrast: a king whose vigorous imperialism is paralleled in his exuberant sexuality, whose ardor for founding cities and building castles finds biological expression in his fecundity in producing heirs. Geoffrey's rhetorical prowess is evident in how he structures the opposition between the two monarchs. His tale of father and son allows him to buttress quietly a kind of empire-loving kingship never practiced by the Britons of whom he writes, but beloved by the Normans who had annexed England to holdings that stretched to Sicily and the Holy Land. Geoffrey's *History*, in other words, advances a useful argument about contemporary kingship and thereby makes itself culturally necessary.

Because it is structured through such cleverly contrived historicality, the *History of the Kings of Britain* remains largely an unadorned chronicle, its art more evident in its deep structure than in anything that effloresces from the work itself. Yet the narrative is interrupted by moments of unexpected and superfluous beauty, smaller stories that derail the progress of the larger plot with their vibrancy and, at times, poignancy.[38] Such aesthetically charged eruptions can saturate this otherwise arid text with moments of profound emotional enlargement. Think, for example, of the princess Ignoge, forced to marry the warrior who has ruthlessly defeated her father. According to Geoffrey, Brutus, the eventual founder of Britain, was wandering in exile from vanquished Troy when he discovered some countrymen held captive by the Greek king Pandrasus. After liberating these people through force, Brutus demands that Pandrasus provide him food, gold, ships, and his eldest daughter "as a comfort." The Trojans depart for remote horizons. Like them, the history-making narrative itself pushes relentlessly onward. Yet in an unexpected moment of pause, the tearful Ignoge stares from the ship's deck as the shores of known Greece fade. In this moment when the forward movement of the *History* eddies backward, in this interlude when "history itself is forgotten," we watch with Ignoge as she stares fixedly across a widening sea toward her receding homeland.[39] We behold with her eyes everything she knows dwindling to its vanishing point, lost as an ocean she never desired to sail propels her toward a future she cannot know. We understand why, in a nicely balanced bit of Latin lyricism: "nec oculos a littore auertit dum littora oculis patuerunt" ["as long as the shore lay there before her eyes, she would not turn her gaze," 8]. We comprehend

---

38. Some of my analysis of Geoffrey of Monmouth finds a tentative first expression in my book *Hybridity, Identity and Monstrosity in Medieval Britain: On Difficult Middles* (New York: Palgrave, 2006), 69–76. What follows is, however, rethought and much expanded.

39. The quotations are from Robert Hanning's seminal treatment of Geoffrey's artistry in *The Vision of History in Early Britain: From Gildas to Geoffrey of Monmouth* (New York: Columbia University Press, 1966), 162.

why she weeps. If we are responsive to this uncharacteristically plaintive effusion ebbing through the customary sangfroid of the text, her tears become ours as well. Geoffrey can give her weeping no answer, no conclusion: enervated by sadness, Ignoge falls asleep in her new husband's arms.

The vessel speeds onward regardless ("Meanwhile the Trojans sailed on for two days and one night"), British history speeds onward regardless ("Then they touched land at a certain island called Leogatia," 64), but Ignoge's stubborn gaze upon shores from which she never wished departure stays with us. By leading our eyes back toward what has been left behind, the vision keeps returning us to stories without conclusion: the narratives of those forced onto this vehicle of relentless forward motion, this ship of history on which some unwilling passengers find no waking solace. We last behold Ignoge when, "worn out with crying," she falls into forgetful slumber. Her story literally ends with that sleep, ends with a hero's embrace, but emotionally, such closure is denied. How can we not wonder about the life toward which she is relentlessly conveyed, how can we not wonder about her future?

Other than to acknowledge that she bears Brutus three sons, Geoffrey is silent. By refusing to provide the narrative space opened by her longing with a conclusion or resolution, Geoffrey keeps Ignoge alive forever in alluring despair, like the heroine of an opera whose voice reverberates long after she has departed the stage. Meditating upon such performers, especially in operas that feature the spectacular demise of female protagonists, Carolyn Abbate writes of the "unconquerable" voice of the women seemingly silenced by opera's murderous narratives, arguing that "this undefeated voice speaks across the crushing plot."[40] Abbate observes that such a woman can be "undone by plot," yet remain "triumphant in voice" (ix). Geoffrey of Monmouth goes farther, demonstrating how a woman can be undone by plot yet triumphant in *art*—traumatic art, in which grief and death are nearer to hand than survival and life. Yet Ignoge's tears are an art of endurance that lacks neither beauty nor ethical complexity. Once voiced, her despair and her desires form a circuit of identification between reader and text-event (which is also a temporal circuit between past-as-text and the reading, imagining present) that brings the *History* out of history and historiography into a new realm,

---

40. Carolyn Abbate, *Unsung Voices: Opera and Musical Narrative in the Nineteenth Century* (Princeton, NJ: Princeton University Press, 1996), ix. Compare with Wayne Koestenbaum, *The Queen's Throat: Opera, Homosexuality, and the Mystery of Desire* (New York: Vintage Books, 1993) on Anna Moffo's voice in Madame Butterfly: "Her timbre was separate from its surroundings. . . . Gravely self-sufficient, it seemed not a copy of life, but life itself" (10). He then writes movingly of how the voice entered his body system and uprooted his world: "My drab bedroom shifted on its axis" (10).

a new world. This moment of art, moreover, is wholly in excess of any historical demands placed upon the text, wholly in excess of cultural needs. In its lyricism, its superfluity, liquid love of oceans and weeping and movement and dreams over the stability of fatherlands and promised destinations, this little work of art within the text opens a space within that narrative, one difficult to close back up or to forget even as the narrative moves relentlessly forward to Britain, one that pushes, without a backward glance, onward into history.

The eruption of art that occurs in the Ignoge episode involves an efflorescence of emotive beauty. An aesthetically moving moment caused by unanticipated estrangement from the dominant narrative of the story, Ignoge's vision transforms her ardor for a lost home into something that seems striking, new, capable of lifting us out of our solitary orbit (which so far has been tracing great men and their celebrated deeds) to encounter a multiply-enfolded, heterogeneous, and therefore more capacious world. This ecstatic effect depends upon Ignoge's human, all too human, longing. Yet Geoffrey is also capable of mixing the human and the inhuman in order to produce strange new kinds of artistic vibrancy. His book is interrupted at times with moments of lyrical mystery, sometimes through effusion of what is his text's most sublime substance, blood. Take, for example, the pluvial gore that drenches the island during the rule of the obscure king Rivallo, a soaking in crimson both awesome and gruesome to visualize: "In his time it rained blood for three days and men died from the flies which swarmed" (87). By saturating the landscape with a substance alien to it [*pluuia sanguinea*], this vivid reddening of the island estranges place from world: a medieval version of Christo's "Pont Neuf Wrapped" or "Surrounded Islands" hitched to a kind of charnel house art in which even death becomes an aesthetic element. The text offers a narrative precursor to T. Coraghessan Boyle's story "Bloodfall," in which a similar hematic rain transfigures the world into something violent, rotting, and weirdly beautiful.[41]

A rather similar moment involving blood occurs later in the text, when the *History* takes a swerve into what seems like a new generic register (though just as likely this swerve is actually the invention of a new genre, romance). On the run from his Saxon enemies, the traitorous British king Vortigern is frantically attempting to bring stability back to an island he once dominated. With the lines, "Uocatis denique magis suis" ["in the end Vortigern summoned his magicians"], the tone of the narrative is transformed: previously Geoffrey's

---

41. Images of the cited art projects can be found online at www.christojeanneclaude.net. "Bloodfall" offers an unnerving visualization of a literal rain of blood and is part of the collection *Descent of Man: Stories* (New York: Penguin, 1990).

History has been largely empty of enchantment, its wonder confined mainly to the natural or the naturally inexplicable, such as the sudden rain of blood.[42] *Enter the magicians*. These *magi*—the first in the text, and the first therefore in Arthurian myth—are charged by Vortigern with imagining a way to bring durability to a fugitive life. The magicians declare that such permanence can be found only in the creation of a work of architecture, "an immensely strong tower" (166). When a suitable site is chosen at Mount Erith, however, whatever stones the masons erect one day are swallowed back into the earth the next. The magicians declare that to lay secure foundations, the mortar must be sprinkled with the blood of "iuuenem sine patre" ["a boy without a father," 167]—with blood, that is, that carries none of the kind of history that Geoffrey's own text embodies, obsessed as it is with fathers, sons, and persistence through generations.

Such an escape from history—or at least from *story*—is impossible: the child without a father, a surly and precocious boy named Merlin, is the progeny of a nun and an incubus. "In specie pulcerrimi iuuenis" ["In the form of a very handsome youth," 169], the demon made frequent, secret love with the nun in her chamber's solitude. Eventually she bore his child. Ancient books verify, according to an authority summoned by Vortigern, that *incubos demones* exist between moon and earth ["inter lunam et terram," 72]. Possessed of a pedigree that ties them to the fallen angels of the Bible, incubi were, in the Middle Ages, monsters who incarnated the very spirit of Geoffrey's own *History*—that is, they incarnated a kind of *counterhistory*, stories at war with dominating traditions and mundane realities. *Enter the magicians*: What Vortigern's magi have unwittingly demanded is the coming into the narrative of a living embodiment of the shattered border between the quotidian (the ordinary world where people remain in the times and places history allots to them) and the extraordinary (the space of possibility where a cloistered nun can find love in the embrace of a mysterious, handsome knight). These magicians transport the *History of the Kings of Britain* into a new realm, where the rules that have so far structured its narrative's unfolding are suspended, remade anew.

Merlin, the boy in whose body the blood of a different kind of story pulses, has his own ideas of how Vortigern can construct an enduring structure. Merlin declares that the only true method to create a durable architecture is not to commit more violence in the present, but to acknowledge the unstable history that underlies that artwork's coming into being. Merlin insists that Vortigern's tower topples at each foundation because he is constructing its base

---

42. Lewis Thorpe makes this point well in his translation of the text (166 n.1). The Latin is from Geoffrey of Monmouth, *Historia Regnum Britanniae I* (Wright), 71.

upon ground inhabited by an unsettled past. Beneath Mount Erith, within an underground pool, inside two hollow rocks ["duos concauos lapides"] at the bottom of that water, twin dragons slumber ["duos dracones dormientes;" 73]. These are dragons of history: the white monster embodies the marauding Saxons, while in the red's pugnacious body resides the story of the Welsh. Once this buried past is spoken and moved beyond (after the boy's revelation, the dragons are dismissed from their subterranean enmity), Merlin is freed from the compulsion to yield his blood . . . and can endure in the story to erect on Salisbury plain the vast architecture of Stonehenge, rocks that when drenched with water heal bodily ailments. Vortigern, meanwhile, is eventually burnt to ash within his tower, his incineration a reminder of the oblivion that comes to those who reside only in history.

Stonehenge becomes Geoffrey's shorthand for art itself, a lithic yet living structure that conjoins distant pasts (the stones journey from Africa to Ireland to Britain, and conjoin the stories of their primal architects, the giants, with those of humans) and unexpected futures: transported to Salisbury through Merlin's engineering feats, Stonehenge stands for the futurity bestowed upon the House of Constantine, for not only will it last eternally as a memorial to the kings Aurelius Ambrosius and Uther Pendragon, the only great ruler from this family *not* interred there will be Arthur, whose absent body allows the possibility of a return to come. Merlin, through this calculus, becomes not so much an engineer as an author, an artist: his magical power is not the wizardry of spells, but the ability to add beauty to that which would otherwise be merely functional or historical—a beauty, moreover, that enlarges the world into which it arrives, that ensures the structure it inhabits will open worlds and guarantee that the artwork will endure. Thus the Vortigern's Tower episode concludes with some words about Merlin's transformation from bastard child to uncanny spirit of creativity and estrangement:

> [Vortigern] was more astounded [*ammirabatur,* "possessed by wonder"] by Merlin than he had ever been by anything. All those present were equally amazed [*ammirabantur*] by his knowledge, and they realized that there was something supernatural about him [*existimantes numen esse in illo*]. (169; 73)

Like a medieval Caillois, Merlin is expert in the writing of stones, in lapidary art—even when the stone in which this art has been enclosed has been sunken in a pool and placed within a mountain.[43] By discerning the colored dragons

---

43. Indeed, there immediately follows upon this declaration an interruption of the narrative in the form of the "Prophecies of Merlin," containing an explication of the meaning of

within the stones' heart or the healing powers within Stonehenge—by discerning the inherent surplus in something as seemingly cold and inert as buried rocks and ancient monoliths—Merlin speaks the inhuman, self-dispossessing, and unhistorical truth of art.

Geoffrey of Monmouth was far from the only medieval artist to discover at the boundary between body and world, history and ecstasy, human and inhuman, the lyrical yet confounding power of art. Marie de France, a contributor to the consensual Arthurian world put in place by Geoffrey, structured many of her lais around objects so dense in their significations that they open themselves to endless meditation: the talkative, bisexual hind and the ship of dreams in *Guigemar*; the woven cloth that materializes a sexuality in *La Cordre*; the clothing that maintains and yet confuses the corporal line between human and wolf in *Bisclavret*.[44] Guigemar, for example, is a knight so self-enclosed that he loves only of solitary pleasures. While hunting, he encounters a deer with antlers, a hermaphroditic creature that also possesses human speech. His arrow rebounds from this living artwork of an animal, wounding his thigh and hurling him into erotic possibility. Guigemar's world, like his body, has been penetrated, and will henceforth never be so circumscribed. He boards a boat that awaits in the harbor, a ship of dreams, perhaps the bark of Solomon that worthy knights board to seek the Holy Grail, perhaps a material metaphor for all the beauty of poetry. This ship conveys him to a distant land, where his ardor for an imprisoned lady allows her access to a more capacious worldview. Notably, the lady is not allowed to sail across the sea and find Guigemar once he departs until she makes the choice to propel *herself* out of her own, too familiar story, one in which she has long played the affection-starved young wife to a dry old man. "Ici sui nuit e jur enlose," she laments, "I'm shut in here night and day" (339; 349). Once she makes the choice to depart her enclosure, she finds unlocked the door to the tower in which she has languished for two years. The Ship of Poetry attends at the harbor. Could lyricism take a less human, more beautiful form than that lyrical vessel gliding unchartered seas, enlarging the world with every wave its unpiloted prow traverses? Marble tower, ebony ship, and desiring lover

---

the dragons along with ambivalent visions of a plethora of events. These prophecies in turn conclude with the auditors "filled with amazement"—but here by "the equivocal meaning of his words" (186), that is, by the fact that they cannot easily be absorbed into history.

44. Citations of the French are from *Les Lais de Marie de France*, ed. Karl Warnke (Paris: Livre de Poche, 1990); English translations are from *The Lais of Marie de France*, ed. and trans. Robert Hanning and Joan Ferrante (Durham, NC: The Labyrinth Press, 1978). I am indebted to the excellent reading of both these lais by Cary Howie in *Claustrophilia: The Erotics of Enclosure in Medieval Literature* (New York: Palgrave Macmillan, 2007), 123–27.

combine to form a living, triune metaphor (literally, a transport device) that conveys the lady outside of the small confines of her selfhood and enables her to discover beyond the still circumscription that had been her prison realms, turbulent with possibility.

In closing I offer a scene that, as with Rivallo and the pluvial gore, opens another milieu through blood; a scene enclosed, like Geoffrey's sleeping dragons, in stone. Just like the lady in *Guigemar*, the unnamed heroine of Marie's lai *Yonec* has been imprisoned in a tower by her jealous and elderly husband. She wastes away, her beauty daily fading in a life spent without joy. She wishes that the magical worlds of which she has read might be true, where ladies might discover lovers "so handsome, courtly, brave and valiant / that they could not be blamed, / and no one else would see them" (98–100). She wishes, in other words, that she might be like Guigemar's lady, might be like Merlin's mother, enjoying in secret the embraces denied to her in the small space into which she has been confined. *Enter the magician*: Upon its utterance, her wish takes fleshly form. A hawk flies to the ledge of the tower and enters the room as "a handsome and noble knight" (115). The bird-knight has loved her from afar for many years, but needed her to articulate her desire for a world configured otherwise before he could fly to her chamber. Not an incubus exactly, but acting very much like one, this fantasy knight who can take many forms (even the *semblance* of the lady herself) eventually impregnates the lady with a son. Her wicked husband discovers the truth of his wife's enjoyment and sets sharp spikes along the window ledge. When the hawk-knight attempts to enter again, he is torn apart, staining the bedclothes with his blood (316).

After her dying lover returns to his distant land, the lady decides upon an extraordinary course of action: she leaps from her window, leaps into activity and out of her prison of self-possession. She follows a glimmering trail of blood straight into a hillside. After a subterranean journey, an unexpected vista opens in unearthly splendor: "There was no house, no hall or tower, / that didn't seem of silver" (362–63). She enters a series of chambers, each with a slumbering knight she does not recognize: other lovers for other dream-filled ladies. On the third bed in the third room she discovers her dying knight, who speaks to her of a beautiful future yet to come. The story ends exactly where we expect: with the son taking vengeance against his wicked stepfather, the lady dying in a mixture of bliss and grief at the grave of her true love: tidy closure for this intricate little work of art. Yet to return to the lai's middle space, to its underground chamber that in no way seems beneath the earth: here we glimpse the entrance into a world where sleeping knights without names, without narrated stories, await the cloistered dreamers who will dare to envision their own rescue from the stories that imprison them. This Other

World—sealed beneath a hill but reachable after a death-embracing leap of faith, through an encounter with one's own potential obliteration—offers the possibility of infinite worlds, of spaces within the earth so strange that human imagination *almost* fails to capture their potential for disrupting the solidity of the ordinary worlds we inhabit.

Inhuman art: not in the culmination of the story of *Yonec,* an all too human tale of revenge, but in the story's dream of a hollow space within the hill, where possibilities are multiplied, where the world as we know it expands exponentially and induces the aesthetic dispossession, the ecstasy, the vertigo of ceasing to know one's place.[45]

---

45. This essay contains in an earlier form some of the material treated in my book *Stone: An Ecology of the Inhuman* (Minneapolis: University of Minnesota Press, 2015). I am grateful to Eileen Joy and Myra Seaman for their suggestions—and for enabling this project to happen.

CHAPTER 6

Humanist Waste

MICHAEL A. JOHNSON

> "Humanism," in fact, could be defined by its penchant for waste, that is, human waste.
>
> —Dominique Laporte, *History of Shit*

PART OF THE STRATEGIC CRITICAL IMPORTANCE of the Middle Ages in the BABEL Working Group's discussions around the "historically vexed terms, human, humanity, humanism, and the humanities"[1] is the challenge the medieval poses to those schemes of periodization implicitly at work in theories of the modern (e.g., Renaissance humanism as a rupture with the medieval) and of the postmodern (e.g., the posthuman as a rupture with the humanist subject of Enlightenment). As the editors of this volume suggest, the Middle Ages is both protohumanist, contesting an understanding of Renaissance humanism as radical rupture, and already posthuman, contesting the use of the term *posthuman* as an exclusively postindustrial phenomenon. The medieval is temporally both "proto" and "post"—both before and after,

---

1. Quoted from original prospectus for *Fragments* at http://www.siue.edu/babel/ProspectusFragmentsVolume.htm.

in regards to the human. But its invocation, to the end of contesting notions of historical rupture and progress at work in certain conceptions of history, also casts the Middle Ages as a kind of persistent material trace of "concepts, identities, and social forms that are always both dead and alive at once."[2]

This conception of the medieval as a persistent "material trace," a reluctant stain in the fabric of history, has a distinctly excremental ring to it. Shit is one of those concepts, and the disposal of shit one of those social forms, often associated with the Middle Ages that proves particularly resistant to historical narratives (of rupture, progress, etc.). More importantly, shit has an especially charged relationship to the human—to humanity, humanism, and the humanities—as scholars and artists such as Dominique Laporte and Wim Delvoye have shown, and which will be further detailed below. This essay imagines humanism, then, as a soiled construct, and shit or filth as a way to metaphorize the persistence of the old in the new (or the dead in the living, the ruinous in the contemporary, and so on). I look to the troubadour tradition because it has been upheld variously as protohumanist (Bec, Nelli) and antihumanist or inhuman (Lacan, Žižek). For reasons I hope this essay will make clear, the troubadour corpus is also a literary tradition in which a persistent metaphorics of excrement troubles the question of the human. Indeed, whenever we question the category of the human, the question of our shit lies never too far away, in wait.

Working, in a sense, to test out the interrelation between the excremental and the human, this chapter starts by outlining some of the forms in which shit manifests in regards to the question of the human: the essay first considers the way in which technologies of waste disposal relate to questions of civilization and history, paradoxically, as both human (tending to interiority) and inhuman (tending to exteriority); in the next section, the essay moves from waste disposal to the shit itself and asks, with Dominique Laporte and Michel de Montaigne, why human shit becomes a privileged object of humanist study, and how it is that the relationship between individual and community is haunted by animal excrement, specifically; the third section shifts from shit as object of study to the metaphorics of excrement in contemporary criticism and cultural production, wherein shit has come almost universally to signify collapse of difference, loss of meaning. The essay as a whole is unified by a more general interrogation of the concept of sublimation, which is the mediating term between the excremental and the human, and which is also, more importantly and urgently, there at the origin of artistic creation and political reimagining.[3]

---

2. Ibid.

3. Will Stockton's *Playing Dirty* (Minneapolis: University of Minnesota Press, 2011) offers a number of useful insights regarding sublimation as a mediator between human excrementality

For this reason, the second half of the essay deals more directly with the concept of sublimation by examining the role of excrement in troubadour lyric and in avant-garde plastic arts.

I begin with the simple, incontrovertible fact that our shit poses a problem for us and does so in multiple ways.

DISPOSAL

There is first the problem of how we dispose of it. As Žižek reminds us, via Lacan, a factor distinguishing the human from the animal is that the disposal of shit becomes a problem for humans, while for animals, who do not have an "interior" quite the way humans do, it—this exteriorization of the once interior—does not.[4] The shame caused by one's own shit arises from the sense of an exposed "inner self," which must be concealed from the world. Without such interiority, both shame and the human, as meaningful categories, are lost. Motivated by an all-too-human shame, then, technologies of waste disposal are associated with the distinction and elevation of the human above the animal. Beyond being a simple constitutive difference, this move, enabled by technologies of waste disposal, is viewed, in many accounts, in terms of a historical process. In the Freudian account, for example, wherein the forward movement of civilization is understood as a progressive alienation or distancing from instinctual drives, or an ever more efficient sublimation of these drives, technologies for the disposal of shit become a gauge for measuring the degree of civilization, that is, the measure of our distance from the animal.[5] Freud is explicit on this point in *Civilization and Its Discontents*:

> The incitement to cleanliness originates in an urge to get rid of the excreta, which have become disagreeable to the sense perceptions. . . . Anal erotism, therefore, succumbs in the first instance to the "organic repression" which paved the way to civilization. The existence of the social factor which is responsible for the further transformation of anal erotism is attested by the

---

and humanism, or the human, in both medieval and early modern literature. See especially his first and last chapters, "The Wondering Anus: Ben Jonson, John Harington, and Humanist Homopoetics" (1–23) and "The Pardoner's Dirty Breeches: Cynicism and Kynicism in The Canterbury Tales" (97–118).

4. Cited in Slavoj Žižek, *On Belief* (London and New York: Routledge, 2001), 59.

5. "We are not surprised by the idea of setting up the use of soap as an actual yardstick of civilization" (Sigmund Freud, *Civilization and Its Discontents*, trans. and ed. James Strachey [London: W. W. Norton, 1961], 46).

circumstance that, in spite of all man's developmental advances, he scarcely finds the smell of his own excreta repulsive, but only that of other people's.[6]

This conception of civilization—conditioned by "organic repression" and furthered by a gradual, ever-more-efficient sublimation of lower instincts into "higher" achievements and regulations (Freud cites religion, philosophy, science)—enables us to see where the constitutive elevation of the human over the animal and the more historically specific notion of "humanism" overlap, at least where technologies of waste disposal are concerned.[7] Freud would have us believe that humanist achievements are conditioned by a certain distance from the excremental, or better, that the ever-more-elaborate technologies of waste disposal might themselves constitute a certain kind of humanist endeavor. Thus, humanism, as a product and gauge of civilization, defined by its distance from the animal and from the excremental, might be aligned with "waste disposal." In this view of civilization, the horizon of humanism would be a future without excrement, wherein the apparatus of waste disposal will have reached such a level of efficiency that it would have managed to do away with excrement altogether.

But humanism, of course, although often aligned with Freud's "elevated pursuits," does not have such a straightforward relationship to civilization and would seem particularly resistant to the notion of civilization-as-progress. It is within this tension, one might in fact argue, that certain modes of speculative science fiction arise. Indeed, just such a future, free of excrement, has been imagined in various ways by science fiction. The perfect food pill is an early commonplace in the genre—this pill that delivers precisely measured nutrients rendering the activities of eating and shitting superfluous. Such projections of the future, whose degree of futuricity is often, tellingly, defined by the extent to which waste disposal is managed, are imagined not as a "humanist" liberation from animal existence but rather as the imposition of an inhuman exteriority.

One of the most emblematic visions of this inhuman, waste-managed future is George Lucas's *THX 1138*, whose characters take sedative pills to control their appetites, wear sterile white garments, and are completely shaved of body hair. Perhaps most striking in regards to the question of excrement, the eponymous protagonist inserts his wages, in the form of a colored dodecahedron, into a toilet-like device, as though to eliminate the process of

---

6. Ibid., 54–55.

7. "The word 'civilization' describes the whole sum of the achievements and the regulations which distinguish our lives from those of our animal ancestors and which serve two purposes—namely to protect men against nature and to adjust their mutual relations" (Ibid., 42).

consumption and waste altogether. When his "wages" are zapped away, the "toilet" makes a flushing sound as though a vestigial trace of its original function. This is also, significantly, a racially homogenous future in which people of color are relegated hygienically to the unreal dimension of entertainment media and are called "holograms." The excremental function of the holograms is made explicit when a robot-arm device draws sperm from the protagonist as he watches, aroused, while an oiled hologram dances naked in a manner reminiscent of Josephine Baker's filmed performances.

George Lucas likely saw the film as a response to what he saw as an increasingly dehumanized, racist society in the America of the late sixties. In other words, the film is motivated by what we must call a deeply *humanist* ethos. But if the film is, then, humanist, in a way, the only way to present "human" values in a thoroughly posthuman setting is paradoxically through the animal. In the film's final scene, as the protagonist finally succeeds in escaping the sterile, white concrete environment of the underground colony, his first encounter with the outside is a band of angry monkeys who crowd around one of their dead, mourning its death loudly and messily, in direct contrast to THX 1138 who cannot mourn the death of his mate, LUH 3417, because he does not know how. The monkeys seem to do it for him.

As THX 1138's inability to mourn suggests, Lucas's dystopic projection worries about the loss of interiority and sociality in the increasingly exteriorized spaces of (post)modernity. This projection of the future is perceived as inhuman by virtue of the vastness and exteriority of the apparatus of waste management. In a sense, the inhabitants of this future have no interior, no "private self," *because they do not shit.* By linking waste management so directly to this loss of interiority, which in turn conditions a loss of humanity, the film reflects on the inhumanity of civilization itself. Humanism, then, holds two positions in relationship to technologies of waste management. It is there where waste management seeks to elevate the human from the animal, both a response to and sign of the shame that makes the human. However, it is also there as a response to the exteriority, without shame and without humanity, toward which waste management drives. But this second "humanist" position once again requires the abject animal to distinguish the human from the technological inhuman. This second humanism, of which Lucas's film is emblematic, in fact relies on the animal to testify to the inhumanity of civilization, whose entirely "human" response to excrement has disposed with the human as it disposes with humanity's shit. The animal's excrementality, fully exterior, figures in a wonderfully paradoxical twist the human capacity for interiority. However, this other interiority can no longer be taken as an unproblematic given in Lucas's film because it is an interiority that holds exteriority within it, or better, an interiority that arises from a play of surfaces in which the human and the animal are both exterior and interior to one another.

To reiterate, then, waste management is thus a gauge of our humanity, in the sense that technologies of waste disposal may indicate our distance from the animal, while at the same time, technologies of waste management seem to tend toward the inhuman, toward an exteriority that appears frighteningly inhuman. But if humanism is, in this very particular sense, bipolar, we might return to Freud's *Civilization and Its Discontents* to ask after its relationship to history. Are we to understand the perfect food pill as the inevitable *telos* of history? *THX 1138* would suggest contrariwise. Lucas insists on the amount of force exerted to maintain such an excrement-free society (robot police, drugs, constant camera surveillance), indicating that this is anything but an inevitable, natural progression. Indeed, Dominique Laporte's *History of Shit* casts serious doubt on Freud's understanding of civilization as a "rising" out of and above the scatological. Technological progress and the evolving modes of the disposal of excrement in human society are not necessarily commensurable processes. As he writes:

> We must therefore conclude that, where its anal constituent is concerned, civilization does not follow a rhythm of linear progress. In *Civilization and Its Discontents* Freud may have asserted "the similitude which exists between the civilizing process and the evolution of the libido in the individual." But can this thesis really be sustained? It seems that civilization's primitive interest in excremental functions did not turn automatically into an appetite for cleanliness, order, and beauty. Otherwise, the nineteenth century's hygienic ideal would have irreversibly developed into an obsequious, meticulous, and parsimonious anality, of which our present civilization is hardly an example.[8]

So, as Laporte suggests, the problem of waste disposal touches on the theory of history in unexpected ways. Excrement may in fact be one of the more effective antidotes to those progress-oriented conceptions of history that tend to cast the Middle Ages as a filthy, primitive past. In other words, the persistence and nonlinearity of humanity's relationship to the disposal of shit may serve as an emblem of slow history, or "soiled" history. The persistence of what Laporte calls "primitive interest in excremental functions" even in the most technologically developed society serves paradoxically as an anchor of humanity. This is why, to take another example from science fiction, Ridley Scott's vision of the future as, in a word, filthy in *Blade Runner* would suggest

---

8. Dominique Laporte, *History of Shit* (Cambridge, MA: MIT Press, 1993), 12–13.

a reading of the film as humanist even as it thoroughly deconstructs the category of the human. The excremental in *Blade Runner* stands as a sign of the persistence of the past (institutions, objects, modes of relation) in the present, which is directly connected to the question of the human. And the paradoxical humanist deconstruction of the human that we discern in this filthy speculative future, I would suggest, is at work in the kinds of interrogations of the human undertaken by medievalists such as those included in this volume.

CONTIGUITY AND ESSENCE

After the question of its disposal, there is the problem of the shit itself. If shit is the most material manifestation of our interior, it must have something to teach us about ourselves. And yet, beyond the "truth" that shit might be able to speak, the apparent similarity of human shit and animal shit leads us to ask with some anxiety, is ours different in some essential way from that of animals? If so, what distinguishes human excrement from animal excrement? What special qualities might it possess?

The careful recording and analysis of one's own stools, a practice recovered from Greek medicine during the late Middle Ages, has long been associated with humanist endeavors. Montaigne, for example, imagined his essays, the height of humanist writing, in relationship to this practice as a collection of turds of variable consistency:

> I cannot keep a record of my life by my actions; fortune places them too low. I keep it by my thoughts. Thus I knew a gentleman who gave knowledge of his life only by the workings of his belly; you would see on display at his home a row of chamber pots, seven or eight days' worth. That was his study, his conversation; all other talk stank in his nostrils. Here you have, a little more decently, some excrements of an aged mind, now hard, now loose, and always undigested.[9]

Laporte certainly had Montaigne's chamber pots in mind when he wrote that humanism could be defined by its penchant for human waste.[10] As he explains, one outcome of the Renaissance humanists' revival of classical Roman culture was a revival of interest in the medical value of *carbon humanum* as a worthy

---

9. Michel de Montaigne, *The Complete Essays of Montaigne*, trans. Donald Frame (Stanford, CA: Stanford University Press, 1958), 721.
10. Laporte, *History of Shit*, 13–14.

object of study. "Stercorary" medicine, Laporte continues, represented one of the more intimate facets of humanism's broad project of self-inquiry and would have had as its grandiose counterpart the rediscovery of the Roman *cloaca maxima*, upheld as the "very height of civilization."[11] The stercorary humanist thus learns to check the stool for color, consistency, weight or volume, shape and odor, and most important of all, to write down these observations diligently. The study of one's own excrement is a discipline, a vocation, whose goal is the interpretation and expression of the innermost self. As Montaigne suggests, the man in his anecdote does not need to speak or write because his excrement was "all his study, all his discourse." Shit speaks an objective truth about the self that perhaps even one's own discourse about oneself cannot measure up to. Its immediate exteriority makes it possible to evaluate the internal with more objectivity. But this exteriority is also haunted by the animal whose shit, once heaped onto dung piles, becomes hard to distinguish from that of humans. Montaigne may not have minded the resemblance, judging by his musings concerning the animal-human relation in *An Apology for Raymond Sebond*:

> When I play with my cat, who knows if I am not a pastime to her more than she is to me? . . . This defect that hinders communication between them [animals] and us, why is it not just as much ours as theirs?[12]

But many of his contemporaries, such as Antoine Pierre, translator of the vast Byzantine compilation *Geoponica de re rustica selectorem Constantino quidem Caesari nuncupati*,[13] and Olivier de Serres,[14] insisted on the superiority of human shit in a number of practical and aesthetic applications. In regards to these humanists, Laporte writes:

> Shit . . . reveals the shared stuff on which humanism and philanthropy are based. The productive value of excrement is inversely proportional to the animality of its origins. . . . Shit is productive only insofar as it is human. Of all the other manures known to nature, none is equal to human fertilizer.[15]

---

11. Ibid., 14.

12. Montaigne, *Complete Essays of Montaigne*, 331.

13. Constantine Cassianus Bassus and Antoine Pierre. *Les XX. liures de Constantin César, ausquels sont traictés lesbons enseignemens d'agriculture* (Poictiers: Iehan and Enguilbert de Marnef, 1545).

14. Olivier de Serres, *Le théâtre d'agriculture et mesnage des champs* (Paris: Abr. Saugrain, 1603).

15. Laporte, *History of Shit*, 120.

Early science is continually tempted by the suspicion that human shit possesses mysterious qualities, making it superior to animal shit.[16] Thus, while one mode of humanism would claim that human shit is worthy of analysis because it comes out of us (we might call this a metonymically derived value), another humanism would assert that our shit is worthy in and of itself, distinct in essence (and this, we might call a metaphorically derived value). Laporte again:

> Whether praised or condemned, every time shit erupts in human history, rehearsing the ambivalent condition of the *Erdenrest,* it is met by a militant anthropocentricsm in which the love of the *stercus* as human is as exalted as the self-love of the *anthropos*. By hoisting himself to the top of the hierarchical scale of creation, especially with regard to his "excreta," man is revealed in his earthiness as eternally, hopelessly soiled.[17]

In these two humanist attitudes toward shit, one rooted in contiguity, the other in essence, the tension between community and individual arises with particular force. When human shit is taken to be different, in essence, from animal shit, the elevation of the "community of man" to "the top of the hierarchical scale of creation" is at stake. The temptation to see an essential difference in human shit conceals a desire for a human community built on the exclusion and subjection of animals. However, in the example of Montaigne's chamber pot, the interest in human shit as a distinct and valuable object of study does not require such a wholesale exclusion of the animal. Here the value of shit derives from its relationship of contiguity to a particular individual, a relationship predicated on temporal and corporeal contingencies that cannot be generalized.

COLLAPSE

Shit also signifies collapse. In the mouth of the defeated humanist: "The world has gone to shit." Shit is not a metaphor for loss of meaning so much as for

---

16. According to Laporte, this belief in the special properties of human feces was held all the way into the late nineteenth century in Europe. M. A. Chevallier's essay on the uses of human urine (1852) shows the extent to which the superiority of human feces was seen as mysterious, or "providential": "Human fertilizer is without equal, animal fertilizers are only effective given certain conditions; they often burn harvests. Animal fertilizer has its proper place, but through a marvelously providential law, human fertilizer has none: its place is everywhere." (Cited in ibid., 121.)

17. Ibid., 34.

the collapse of difference that is felt as a loss of meaning. Shit, as a metaphor for collapse of difference, comes out of the mouth of the depressive who can no longer locate differences that matter: "What's the difference? It's all shit anyway." In the same vein, when we refer to a person or an item as a "piece of shit," we are referring to a person or object fallen out of value. This metaphor operates, of course, strictly along an up/down axis. A "piece of shit" object has fallen out of the differential system by which value and "values," in the moral sense, are created. More than just a metaphor for the collapse of distinctions, shit-as-collapse describes most particularly the collapse of civilizations, careers, and all those humanist humanitarian endeavors that are "built upwards." This is why, in the *South Park* episode "More Crap," U2 musician and famed humanitarian Bono is revealed to be, quite literally, "a piece of crap," shat out by a Swiss scientist in 1960, because his soaring career can only be imagined in relationship to the falling of a turd. This is also why, in canto XVIII of Dante's *Inferno*, the flatterers, who "build people up" with their false flattery, are imagined as swimming up to the crowns of their heads in excrement, relegated "down" to a shit-filled moat, precisely because they have abused the differential system by which value is created in language.[18]

But how is it that shit can signify such a violent and total collapse of difference when, for the Renaissance humanists, at least, it participates in that most primary of differences, which distinguishes the self from the rest of the world? There are two, closely related but distinct, explanations for this. The first concerns shit as the product of a violent process of mastication and digestion, which turns differences among living things in the world (plants and animals) into a single dead and homogenous substance. Janine Chasseguet-Smirgel explains this in terms of object-relations in *Creativity and Perversion*. The artist, in her view, is (like) a pervert who seeks to destroy difference in the world in order to replace it with one in which all things are possible. Chasseguet-Smirgel compares one mode in which the artist destroys difference—in what is a terrifically heteronormative argument—to Freud's sadistic-anal phase of childhood sexual development. What interests me here is the way in which the excremental becomes a sign for the perverse artist's urge to destroy difference in the world: "[This] indifferentiation is inherent to the sadistic-anal phase, where all objects, erotogenic zones, ideals, etc. are pulverized by the alimentary canal and homogenized into identical particles, the faeces."[19] The second explanation, also psychoanalytic, concerns shit as the "return of

---

18. Dante Alighieri, *The Inferno of Dante*, trans. Robert Pinsky (Noonday Press: New York, 1994), 180–87.

19. Janine Chasseguet-Smirgel, *Creativity and Perversion* (London: Free Association Books, 1985), 141.

the sublimated." If, as Freud claimed, libidinal interest in money is merely the sublimated expression of a more primitive (childhood) libidinal interest in excrement, the failure or collapse of sublimation will restore the stink of shit to money and the market.

In both cases, shit results from the breakdown of important differences. In the first, the digestive system, which we can imagine as a pole running from the mouth to the anus, constitutes the mediating term, while in the second case, it is the psychic operation of sublimation that constitutes the mediating term, running between the "valued term" (money) to the "debased term" (shit). In both cases, when the mediating term is collapsed or destroyed, shit signifies the result of the breakdown. The notion of shit as signifying a collapse of difference, and especially shit as a "return of the sublimated," informs many diagnoses of late capitalism from critics such as Jean Baudrillard, who characterizes social relations in consumer culture under the sign of shit: "*Controlled, lubricated, consumed*, faecality has passed into things; it seeps everywhere into the indistinctness of things and social relations."[20] Baudrillard's consumer society suffers from a crisis of differentiation in which even our sense of day and night, of the seasons, or even sexual difference, is collapsed into fecal indistinctness. By making explicit reference to Freud's most fundamental example of sublimation, the quasi-alchemical transformation of shit to gold, he invites us to imagine this collapse of difference as the result of a breakdown in sublimation. As Baudrillard suggests, shit rises to the surface when we no longer have the space in which to create our own desires, the space, that is, wherein sublimation is at work.

Baudrillard is not the only one to imagine life lived in late Capitalism as somehow affected by a crisis of sublimation. For Alenka Zupančič, the internalization of consumer culture's imperative to enjoy has created a catastrophic crisis in sublimation. Using Lacanian terminology, she explains that this occurs when the Thing moves to the register of the superego and becomes the source of the imperative of enjoyment, leaving no space for the ego to formulate its own desires. As she suggests, Lacan's theory of sublimation offers a way to imagine possibilities for overcoming this crisis. Where Lacan differs from Freud in regards to sublimation is in the fact that, for Lacan, the mechanism of sublimation is not about renunciation of drive in order to adapt to social values (that are "out there" in culture causing us to either repress or sublimate our desires), but rather, sublimation is what enables the *creation* of *new* social values. Zupančič writes:

---

20. Jean Baudrillard, *The Consumer Society: Myths and Structures* (London: Sage Publications, 1998), 30.

What is at stake is that all great sublimations (art, science, religion) create new values, transform certain things into values. This is what Lacan is driving at with his claim that sublimation is "a certain relationship of desire that attracts our attention to the possibility of formulating... a different criterion of another, or even of the same, morality, in opposition to the reality principle."[21]

It is also important to insist on the fact that, whereas Freud's concept of sublimation limits itself to the elevation of debased objects to "socially valued" objects (and the shit to gold sublimation is really a structuring example for Freud here), for Lacan this need not be the case. For Lacan, any object, no matter how low, can in theory participate in this psychic operation: sublimation occurs when an object, *any object,* comes to occupy the place of Das Ding. One thing this means is that, for Lacan, the high/low distinction itself, along which values and social hierarchies are structured, is secondary to, or a mere residual effect of, sublimation.

And here the medieval enters in a surprising way, because it is in fact through a reading of medieval lyric, particularly Occitan lyric, in his seventh seminar that Lacan formulates sublimation in this manner. The corpus of troubadour lyric, in its indifference to high and low, for Lacan contains evidence of a literal "creation" of a new set of values in Western culture, *ex nihilo.* Although Lacan is not directly interested in the question of humanism, some of the specialists of troubadour lyric he cites, most notably René Nelli (but also surrealist writer Benjamin Péret), were indeed invested in the creation of humanist or protohumanist values in troubadour poetry.[22] How, we shall ask, might troubadour lyric be construed as protohumanist?

HUMANIST TROUBADOURS?

On what grounds were the troubadours imagined to have created an early humanist ethic? This reading appears to stem from the generally agreed upon notion that *fin'amors* is a kind of sublimation. René Nelli—whose work on the troubadours dissociated Catharism from *fin'amors*—describes *fin'amors,* using the language of sublimation, as the material grounds for what might be elevated to a generalized moral:

---

21. Alenka Zupančič, *The Shortest Shadow: Nietzsche's Philosophy of the Two* (Cambridge, MA: MIT University Press, 2003), 73–74.

22. Jacques Lacan, *Le Séminaire, livre VII: L'éthique de la psychanalyse* (Paris: Seuil, 1986), 177–78.

> Fin'Amors not only enabled the regulation of instinct, and thus aimed at the very core of amorous passion in establishing a *Dreg d'amor* (or, moral of courtship), but it also founded a more general morality, which, in certain cases, could transcend or negate narrowly amorous values in the service of more broadly universal values.... To the extent that [*Fin'Amors*] was a value, it aspired (as it sought to make love and virtue coincide with one another) to exceed itself.[23]

Although he avoids overtly psychoanalytic language, Nelli's concern with the "regulation of instinct" sets him squarely within a psychoanalytic frame. Indeed, once we start thinking psychoanalytically, the two paths to these "universal values" he offers, either to transcend or to negate "restrictedly amorous" values, begin to sound like the Freudian terms *sublimation* and *repression*. In both cases, what is at stake is the instituting of "higher" ethical values through the reorientation, somehow, of "lower" instincts. The key to understanding this mysterious transformation of low to high, that still somehow amounts to the same instinct fundamentally, is in the economic terminology Nelli uses. It is only insofar as *fin'amors* can be understood to be a value that we can imagine it as "aspiring" to something higher, that is, to be more than itself. *Fin'amors* is thus a value that aspires to "exceed" itself. In other words, the "regulation of instinct" creates surplus value that produces something new, different in kind yet participating in the same flow of desire. We are privy to a magical economy that the Freudian concept of sublimation, in which questions of "value" always determine the reaction formation, only begins to account for.

This economic conception of desire in *fin'amors* is quite mechanical, hardly human, let alone human-*ist*. What, then, about the "regulation of instinct" in troubadour love lyric would bring it close to the concept of humanism? To begin with, Nelli's conception of sublimation is shaped by the Freudian understanding of sublimation as a redirection of "low" drives to "high" aspirations such as art, religion, and politics—in other words, privileged domains of humanist production. But there are other reasons to see the term *humanist* tied to a particular reading of troubadour lyric. Pierre Bec's description of the sublimatory economy of *fin'amors* would be identical to Nelli's, except that he insists on the "human" quality of this generalized ethic that proceeds from *fin'amors*:

> Fin'amor becomes a school of ethical self-perfection, inspired by the virtue and value (*Pretz*) of its addressee (*destinataire*), and inseparable from

---

23. René Nelli, *L'érotique des troubadours, tome II* (Paris: Union Générale d'Éditions, 1974), 60. The English translation here is my own.

feminine beauty. We are thus dealing with an ideal that is simultaneously aesthetic, social and moral. What's more, [fin'amor] exceeds its own limits, and gradually becomes instituted as a universal system, as a general and human truth. This *aspiration à l'amour,* as René Nelli called it, strives to become the principal of all good deeds, human and humane. It is thus possible for us to speak of a humanist ethic founded on love and the idealization of the Lady.[24]

What enables Bec to add the language of the human (the humane, the humanist, etc.) to the language of aspiration and elevation used by Nelli and others? To begin with, elsewhere Bec insists on the "naturalistic" quality of the troubadours' expression of desire, in order to distinguish it from mystical and other types of religious expression. Bec uses the term "humanist" in the same vein, to distinguish his own understanding of courtly love from those who understand courtly love as a transposition of mysticism, or Catharism, into the domain of sexuality. This "universal system" of high values would arise not from contemplation of the inhuman, ineffable, divine, but rather from contemplation of the all-too-human, fully incarnate, Lady. In this sense, his use of the term "humanist" resonates with the properly historical understanding of humanism as a displacement of the divine, that is, of theologically centered cultural production.

But quite a bit more informs his use of the language of the human here. We find in it a few implicit assumptions: (1) that the Lady is in fact the "destinataire" of the lyric address of troubadour love poetry; (2) that there is something "personal," "intimate" (that is, "human") about the poet's encounter with the Lady; and (3) that the "intimate," "human" quality of this encounter somehow conditions the humanist ethic of *fin'amors.* In other words, Bec seems to imagine that the transformation at work in the sublimation of courtly love would proceed from the warm particular of the "human" to the cold universal of the "humanist." Nelli, without using the language of the human, insists all the same on the "personal" quality of the poet's encounter with the Lady. Although we might compare the "regulation of instinct" in courtly love to the tantric and Buddhist practices of *amor imperfectus,* Nelli argues, the "real women" in these Eastern arts of love only occupy the role of object or of symbol, "which was not at all the case for the Lady of the troubadours, quite to the contrary."[25] That is to say, the troubadour Lady is not of the inhuman order of object and symbol but rather of the intimate, incarnate order of the human. She is "really there."

But if we have learned anything from the past twenty-five years of criticism, it is that: (1) structurally speaking, the Lady is only occasionally the

---

24. Pierre Bec, *La Lyrique Occitane du Moyen Age* (Avignon: Éditions Aubanel, 1970), 17. The English translation here is my own.

25. Nelli, *L'érotique des troubadours,* 28.

addressee in troubadour lyric, given that they are much more often addressed to and transmitted between men in a heady atmosphere of homosocial bonding;[26] and (2) the Lady, even in her more "incarnate" modality, is anything but personal or human.[27] Perhaps for these reasons, the theory of a nascent *humanist* ethic in troubadour lyric has not exactly taken off—and with reason. How can we imagine a humanism built on an encounter with the inhuman, if it can even be called an encounter? How can we imagine a humanist ethic built on such misogynistic grounds, that is, built on a fundamentally "missed" encounter? Is it possible to salvage something from the notion of a humanism of troubadour lyric even after we've exposed the misguided investment in the "humanness" of the Lady, and in the intimacy of the encounter between poet and Lady, in criticism from the ilk of Nelli and Bec?

Whenever we question humanism or the category of the human, the question of our shit always seems to lurk nearby, as we've seen, and the question of the human in troubadour lyric is no exception to this. If there are nascent humanist values to be found in troubadour lyric, there is also a good deal of shit to be found there as well.

BEAK AND SPIGOT: THE TROUBADOUR INHUMAN

The libidinal relationship between the excremental and the economical is thoroughly exploited in much troubadour lyric, as in the *cobla*, "Dieus vos sal, dels petz sobeirana" ["May God save you, Sovereign Lady of farts"], which

---

26. Even when the Lady is addressed in the second person she is often, all the same, offered homosocially to the gaze of another man, as Simon Gaunt argues in his reading of Gaucelm Faidit: "And in the end—as is so often the case in with troubadour lyric—he addresses his love poem for an *amiga* he has interpolated in the second person, but nonetheless construed alternately as a monstrous and inhuman sovereign, and as a fantasmatic dream-like image with the perfect body, to another man, a male patron. The sovereign Gaucelm hopes will hear his highly codified chat-up line dressed up as a cry for mercy, and whom he hopes to seduce with his rhetoric, turns out in fact to be another man." (*Love and Death in Medieval French and Occitan Courtly Literature* [Oxford: Oxford University Press, 2006], 71).

27. Two important early feminist appraisals of the Lady include Joan Ferrante, *Woman as Image in Medieval Literature: From the 12th Century to Dante* (New York and London: Columbia University Press, 1975) and E. J. Burns, "The Man behind the Lady in Troubadour Lyric," *Romance Notes* 25.3 (1985): 254–70. For more recent work in this vein, see Simon Gaunt, "Poetry of Exclusion: A Feminist Reading of Some Troubadour Lyrics," *Modern Language Review* 85.2 (1990): 310–29; R. Howard Bloch, *Medieval Misogyny and the Invention of Western Romantic Love* (Chicago: University of Chicago Press, 1992); Sarah Kay, *Courtly Contradictions: The Emergence of the Literary Object in the Twelfth Century* (Stanford, CA: Stanford University Press, 2001), especially chapter 7, which treats the sublime object of "courtly love" through a reading of Lacan's seventh seminar; and Gaunt, *Love and Death*.

replaces the high courtly word *pretz* (value) with the rhyme word *petz* (fart) and imagines the Lady's multiplying farts as growing profit. The Ladies in scatological troubadour lyric threaten to explode with shit, urine, and menstrual blood, as in Afonso Eanes do Coton's "Marinha, en tanto folegares," ["Marinha, how you fornicate"] in which the poet marvels at the fact that his Lady does not explode although he has plugged all her orifices, or in Arnaut Daniel's famous "Pòis Raimons e'N Trucs Malècs" ["Though Raimon and Truc Malec"], in which the arbitrariness of the Lady is defined by the unpredictability of her machine-like excretions, which the poet fears may burst out at any moment. Perhaps not surprisingly then, the poet's artistry is envisioned in relationship to the activity of "plugging-up" the excremental Lady. As my reading of these poems will demonstrate, in fact, the excremental dimension of much troubadour poetry reveals a preoccupation with artistic creation. Excremental Ladies are worthy poetic subjects, these poems suggest, but only to the extent that the poet can exercise restraint by reigning in—or plugging up, as the case may be—her explosive and filthy materiality through the technological prosthetics of writing.

Are we to view these scatological troubadour poems as parodies of the high serious mode, as inversions of the high values otherwise upheld in troubadour poetry? Does the inversion of high and low, of *pretz* and *petz*, suggest we read these poems as carnivalesque inversions of lower and upper strata, *à la* Bakhtin? The only problem with this reading is that the carnivalesque, like Freudian sublimation, assumes an established set of values that are really *there*, waiting to be inverted. As Bakhtin makes clear, the carnivalesque inversion of high and low does not subvert the *status quo* but rather reinforces it by proposing that the world, once righted, is the only world possible; and for this reinforcement of social values to work, these social values need to be already in place.

Thus if it is true that the troubadours created altogether new values, then notions of parody, inversion, and carnivalesque, while still important, can only provide a limited reading of these scatological poems. Take, for example, the following *cobla*, which is demonstrably a parody:

Quan lo petz del cul venta
Dont Midònz caga e vis,
Vejaire m'es qu'eu senta
Una pudor de pis
D'una velha merdolenta
Que tot jorn m'escarnís,
Qu'es mais de petz manenta

Que de marabodís,
E caga mais en tres matís
Qu'autre non fai en trenta.²⁸
(1–10)

When the fart blows from the ass / From which My Lady shits and pisses / It seems I get a whiff / A stench of piss / From a shit-covered old hag / Who chides me each day, / Who is richer in farts / Than in gold coins, / And who shits more in three mornings / Than another would in thirty.²⁹

Unmistakably a parody of Bernard de Ventadorn's "Quan la freid'aura venta"³⁰ ["When the cool breeze flows"], this *cobla* uses the characteristic honorific from the high register of courtly language, *Midònz* ("My Lady"), even as it describes the Lady shitting and farting. As a parody, we might expect the poem to put forth an inverted representation of the Lady. In place of the vaguely inhuman, sublime object of Bernard's poems, we should see an earthy, sexually available, and embodied woman. In other words, we might expect to see one of the naughty bourgeoises from the fabliaux in the place of the ice queen from Bernard's poem. Indeed, readers have tended to interpret the scatological troubadour poems in this vein as featuring more embodied women. Typically, readers posit two types of women in these lyrics: the idealized woman and the debased or available woman, or as Jean-Charles Huchet does, using the language of psychoanalysis, the "femme de désir" (the desired woman) and the "femme de jouissance" (the woman with whom pleasure is taken).³¹ But these readings, perhaps motivated by a desire to define *fin'amors* in structural terms, miss what is so singular about these scatological poems:

---

28. Pierre Bec, *Burlesque et obscénité chez les troubadours: pour une approche du contretexte médiéval* (Paris: Stock, 1984), 163–64.
29. The English translation here is my own.
30. Quan la freid' aura venta
    Devès vòstre païs,
    Vejaire m'es qu'eu senta
    Un vent de paradís
    Per amor de la genta
    Vas cui eu sui aclís
    On ai mesa m'ententa
    E mon coratge assís,
    Car de totas partís
    Per leis, tant ma'talenta?

Les Troubadours: anthologie bilingue, ed. Jacques Roubaud (Paris: Seghers, 1971), 116.
   31. Jean-Charles Huchet, *L'Amour discourtois: la "Fin'Amors" chez les premiers troubadours* (Toulouse: Privat, 1987), 46–50.

the excremental Lady is no more available or intimate here than the idealized Lady is elsewhere. What's more, although she shits, she is neither embodied nor human in any clear sense.

Rather than a body or a human, the poem spits out a series of metonymic links and foregrounds its articulations without giving any impression of a whole, or even a wholeness-on-the-horizon. If we isolate the *cobla*'s metonyms, we are left with an odorous chain of associations: *the fart that is from the ass from which the woman shits and pees, the smell of which reminds the poet of the lady who chides the poet, and so on.* The Lady only appears as a tertiary, and hardly originary or causal, fragment in the series. A machine-like productivity, not a willing subject, presides over the activities of shitting and farting. Structurally, we might say, the Lady is shat out of her own ass. Indeed, the ass, not the Lady, sits at the empty center of the poem.

A similar dynamic governs Arnaud Daniel's more well-known scatological *canso*, "Pòis Raimons e'N Trucs Malècs" ["Though Raimon and Truc Malec"], Arnaud's contribution to the poetic debate known as the *Cornilh affaire*.[32] The debate, or *gap*, from which a few poems survive, centers on Bernart of Cornilh and his beloved, who stipulates that Bernart must "cornar lo corn" ["blow her horn"] as a condition for her love. Bernart, it seems, recoils in horror at Lady Ena's request. So then, the question, should Bernart have obliged her or not, is framed as an ethical question of the utmost gravity. A number of poets probably weighed in on the debate, although only four of the poems survive. Truc Malec and Raimon de Durfort both take Ena's side, singing the delights of a woman's "corn," as long as it has been cleaned up and made presentable ("l'ai fach lavar e forbir"). Arnaud weighs in on Bernart's side. As with "Quan lo petz del cul venta" ["When the fart blows from the asshole"], the Lady's ass occupies the gravitational center of the poem:

Qu'al cornar l'agra mestiers bècs
Ab que'lh traissé del còrn los grècs;
E pòis pògra ben issir cècs
Qu'el fums es fòrz qu'ieis dins dels plecs.

Ben l'agra òps que fos becutz
E'l bècs fos loncs et agutz

---

32. The whole *gap* is edited and presented together in Bec, *Burlesque et obscénité*, 139–53. For a good contextualization of the so-called "Cornilh Affair," see Caroline Jewers, "The Cornilh Affair: Obscenity and the Counter-Text in the Occitan Troubadours, or, the Gift of the Gap," *Mediterranean Studies* 11 (2002): 29–43.

Que'l corns es fèrs, laitz e pelutz
E nul jorn non estai essutz,
Et es prion dins la palutz
Per que relent' ensús lo glutz
Qu'adès per si cor ne rendutz;
E non vòlh que mais sia drutz,
Cel que sa boch' al còrn condutz.

Pro i agra d'autres assais,
De plus bèls que valgron mais,
E si En Bernartz se n'estrai,
Per Crist, anc-no'i fetz que savais,
Car l'en prs paors et esglais.
Car si'l vengués d'amont lo rais
Tot l'escaldèra'l còl e'l cais;
E no'is coven que dòmna bais
Aquel qui cornèes còr putnais.
. . . .
Dòmna, ges Bernartz non s'estrilh
Del còrn cornar ses gran dozilh
Ab que seire'l trauc del penilh,
Puois poirà cornar ses perilh.

For in order to "blow that horn" he would need a beak / with which to pluck out the "pearls" from the ass. / And even then, he might come out blind, / as the smoke from those folds is strong. / He would need a beak / and a long, sharp one, / for the ass is rough, ugly and hairy, / and it is never dry, / and the swamp within is deep. / That is why pitch ferments upward / as it continually escapes, continually overflows. / And I wouldn't like for him who brings his mouth to that pipe / ever to be a lover. / There will be plenty of other tests, / finer ones that are worth far more, / and if Lord Bernart withdrew from that one, / he did not, by Christ, behave like a coward / if he was taken with fear and fright. / For if the stream of water had landed on him from above, / it would have scalded his whole cheek and neck, / and it is not fitting also that a lady embrace / a man who has blown a stinking trumpet... Lady, Bernard should not fret / about blowing that horn if he can acquire a large spigot / with which to close that pee-hole, / after which he will be able to blow the horn with no peril.[33]

---

33. The English translation here is my own.

In Arnaud's poem, the topology of the Lady's lower regions is so elaborate we almost forget that the swampy region belongs to a Lady, who is named and later addressed. Here, no will governs the overflowing of shit, compared rather to a vast swamp, and the stream of urine is, likewise, disconnected from any governing subject. As with "Quan lo petz del cul venta" ["When the fart blows from the asshole"], there is a machine-like quality to these excretions, which can burst out arbitrarily at any moment. While certainly excremental, Lady Ena is anything but embodied and far from human. She is exteriorized to the point of becoming a vast and perilous landscape.

What is perhaps most salient about this poem is its ambivalent rhetorical and modal structure. Reduced to a bare argument, the poem would read as follows: "Although it is fitting that Bernart should flee from Ena's outlandish request, for all the following reasons (insert: elaboration of the perils of the Lady's lower region), if he *were* to decide to satisfy her request he would need to grow a beak with which to pluck those pearls and to find a large spigot with which to plug her up. Only then might he be able to enjoy her." The poem is thus concerned with the conditions and constraints necessary to the elevation of objects to the status of "art," imagined both in relationship to the animal and the technological (or prosthetic). Bernart becomes a figure for the artist, while Truc Malec and Raimon de Durfort become Arnaud's students, tutored in the ethics of artistic production. If scatological troubadour poetry, like its "cleaner" counterpart, participates in the creation of a protohumanist ethic, it would do so in a decidedly homosocial mode.

In both poems, the figure of the excremental Lady occasions dialogue among men. "Quan lo petz del cul venta" ["When the fart blows from the asshole"], for example, mirrors the metrical scheme and rhyme of Bernart of Ventadorn's poem so perfectly that we might read it as, in a sense, addressed to Bernart. Indeed, the farts in the parodic *cobla* are also a reference to the poet's name, as Ventadorn can easily be transposed as "ventador" ("the farter"), further indicating the connection between Bernart and the author of this parodic *cobla*. Farting is, incidentally, also a reference to lyric voice— a sounding wind from a low place, farts participate in both the material and the spiritual. Arnaud's poem, structured as a response, is even more explicitly homosocial. He addresses Raimon Dufort obliquely through Bernart of Cornilh, another proper name with scatological overtones,[34] and then he makes another oblique address to Bernard via Lady Ena,[35] while another oblique

---

34. Bernartz, ges eu non m'acòrt / Al dich Raimon de Dufòrt / Que vos anc mais n'aguessetz tort [Bernart, I do not agree at all with Raimon's assertions when he claims that you are in error].

35. Dòmna, ges Bernartz non s'estrilh [Lady, may Bernart not fret].

address to Truc Malec along with Raimon is made in the very first line of the poem.[36] Although the two poems ask different questions, they are both concerned with the conditions for the production of art, which are articulated through the figure of the excremental Lady.

The anonymous parody of Bernart of Ventadorn's *cobla* asks, with ironic intelligence, how much of art depends on form and context? If I can write a *cobla* that perfectly mirrors the meter and rhyme of Bernart's beautiful and "successful" *cobla*, but fill its content with (formless and homogenous) shit, will it still count as a poem? Is this art? Arnaud's poem offers something in the way of a response to this question by imagining, on the one hand, the insertion of a spigot in the excremental Lady's lower parts, and on the other, Bernart the poet-figure with a beak. Arnaud responds with a cautious affirmative. Yes, shit can be art, but one should exercise restraint, whence the need for a spigot, and one must approach the "matter" of the poem with delicacy and selectivity, whence the need for a beak. The cyborg-like image of a spigot (*dozilh*) installed on a woman, produced by Arnaud's cautioning, sets the poem squarely in the realm of the inhuman. As Arnaud would have it, art participates in the prosthetic, technological inhuman. Likewise, the image of a poet-figure growing a beak (*bècs*) in order to pluck the pearls compels us to imagine the poet as a human-animal hybrid. And of all animals, the bird is, of course, the most central and ambivalent figure of the troubadour imaginary. For Jaufre Rudel, "M'es bels douz chans d'auzels de loing" ["I am pleased by the sweet song of birds from afar"], or for Raimbaut d'Aurenga, "Brais chans quilz critz / aug dels auzels pels plaissaditz" ["I hear the tweets, songs, twitterings and cries of the birds in the hedge"], the bird song both inspires and torments the poet, taunting him with the completeness of its song, reminding him of his delayed entry into language and the symbolic, of his own incompleteness and the incompleteness of his art. The function of the troubadour bird is crystallized most movingly in Arnaud's own *canso*, "Doutz brais e critz" ["Sweet clamor and cries"] in which he hears birds singing their Latin prayers, "Aug des auzels q'en lur latin fant precs / qecs abs a par atressi cum nos fam" ["I hear the birds sing their Latin prayers, / each to the other, in pairs, like we do"]. Arnaud's birds—who pray in Latin, the language of the patriarchal symbolic, and couple up in heteronormative pairs "cum nos fam" ["as we do"]—could not provide a better encapsulation of the function of the troubadour bird. An ambivalent expression of joy and anxiety in relationship to the always-already of the symbolic (of Latin, of melody, of Christianity, of heterosexual dyadism, etc.), these birds also speak to the inhuman dimension of

---

36. Pòis Raimons e'N Trucs Malècs [Though Raimon and Truc Malec].

art production. While in the one *canso,* Arnaud imagines birds doing human things (spiritual expression), and in the other, he imagines a human doing bird-like things (plucking pearls, or seeds, out of shit with his beak), the same inhuman aspiration motivates both images. This desire is not to become animal so much as to aspire to the animal to the extent that animals already know their Latin prayers. Thus the animal, in this context, figures the inhuman in a totally counterintuitive way as another version of the prosthetic, technological inhuman.

The excremental dimension of these poems, as well as the animal dimension, does not therefore make them any more earthy or human than their more "serious" counterparts. Arnaud's uncanny image of a poet bird-man plucking pearls out of the perilous landscape of the inhuman Lady's nether regions literalizes in visual terms the troubadour aspiration to the inhuman. Shit, we might argue, brings to the fore the paradoxical dynamic of the "humanist" (i.e., aspirational) inhuman in troubadour lyric. Appearing in a deeply homosocial and cannily misogynist dialogue, the function of shit in these excremental troubadour poems recalls the use of shit in the avant-garde plastic arts. In both the excremental troubadour and the excremental avant-garde, the presence of shit has the capacity to lay bare certain structures, to mirror and perhaps even to make a critical intervention through the means of serious play. Piero Manzoni's *Merda d'Artista* (1961), in which the artist canned his own shit and sold it by weight at the value of gold, only acquires meaning in dialogue with the art market, with the masculine community of art makers and art buyers, all interested in the market's alchemical capacity to transform shit into gold.

But the fecal playfulness of the avant-garde (medieval or modern) is not necessarily harnessed to the end of dismantling the structures it reveals, or even of revealing these structures to be immoral. This is critical to point out, especially in regards to the powerful misogyny in troubadour culture. Although we might see the misogyny of troubadour writing even more blatantly in the excremental reprises, in which the excremental function of the idealized Lady is simply literalized, it does not necessarily follow that the goal of the parodist was to expose patriarchal structures at work. But conversely, it does not follow either that the excremental poet is necessarily more misogynist, or more homosocially exclusive, than those poets who wrote in the idealizing mode. For this reason, I think an anachronistic comparison between the medieval and avant-garde excremental might be useful. While the use of shit in avant-garde art is part of a consciously post- or even antihumanist project, we might ask in similar terms, what new values does this art create or make possible?

AVANT-GARDE MEDIEVAL

> Avant tout, les artistes sont des hommes qui veulent devenir inhumains.
>
> Artists are men who want, above all, to become inhuman.
> —Guillaume Apollinaire, *Les peintre cubistes*

In response to the defeated humanist's lament that the "world has gone to shit," we might put forth the jubilant avant-garde claim that even shit can be made into art. From Marcel Duchamp, André Breton, and Piero Manzoni, to Wim Delvoye, Paul McCarthy, and Andres Serrano, human shit has been a constant object of avant-garde artistic production. As long as it is framed, canned, photographed, or placed on a pedestal—that is, "conferred the status of art"—shit can acquire artistic value. But the fact that shit can acquire artistic value does not mean, "It's all the same shit." While Piero Manzoni's canned "merda d'artista" reflects on the art market and on Freudian sublimation, Andres Serrano's photographs of shit (with such punning titles as *Good Shit, Bull Shit, Deep Shit,* and even, *Medieval Shit*) reflect on the function of titles and, more generally, on the drifting of the signifier *shit* in the English language, which, Serrano reminds us, has strayed far from its primary signified. Wim Delvoye, in creating the cloaca maxima, a machine that produces "human" shit, and which, like humans, can get indigestion or constipation, and even farts when fed the wrong types of food (too much spicy food, too much alcohol, etc.), reflects on the limits of the human.[37] Isn't our excrementality—this *Erdenrest* that preoccupied Goethe and Freud—what separates us from machines? Where do we anchor our humanity once machines are able to shit like us?

Following in this vein, Delvoye's most recent project, according to sketches on his website, is to create a convertible cloaca machine, which can switch between human, rabbit, and cat shit, questioning even more intensively the iterability of human shit.[38] Delvoye's is not a project of destroying or collapsing difference into "fecal indistinctness" but rather one of studying, taking note of, and thereby *creating* important differences. Like a cyborg version of Montaigne's chamber pots, the cloaca requires a "light touch," sensitive to the

---

37. For a good overview of the excremental avant-garde in the plastic arts and a strong counterargument to my own, see Donald Kuspit, "The Triumph of Shit," http://www.artnet.com/magazineus/features/kuspit/kuspit9-11-08.asp. His argument—reliant on normative developmental narratives such as those Chasseguet-Smirgel uses—views excremental artists as childlike intellectual masturbators.

38. http://www.cloaca.be/drawings.htm.

contingency of the day-to-day, to the capriciousness of mood and temperature. The artist approaches his machine with a delicate mixture of curiosity (what happens if I feed it curry?), diligence (it must be fed at least twice a day), attentiveness (he takes note of all changes and developments within the cloaca), and so on. So while the avant-garde artist might assert playfully, "It is all shit after all," there is nothing of the depressive's understanding of shit as a sign of collapsed difference here. Rather the invitation to see all things, and especially art, as shit, requires us to be attentive to differences at a more systemic level: how is this shit contextualized, what ideologies determine the way I experience this shit? As much as shit can signify undifferentiatedness (Chasseguet-Smirgel) and indistinctness (Baudrillard), it can also, potentially, serve to signify foundational differences, the *sine qua non* of creativity and distinction. Just such a use of shit is at work in the troubadour excremental tradition, crystallized most perfectly in Arnaud Daniel's poem with the image of the man-bird-poet-figure endowed with a long beak with which to select those brown "pearls."

Thus in the end, with respect to the question of the human, or of humanism, shit is a powerfully ambivalent object. At times infused with anxiety of the animal and of the inhuman, at times elevated to the status of privileged humanist object, shit irritates the question of the human without easily falling on one side or the other. Troubadour poetry, which might be construed as a protohumanism, or as the creation of a new set of humanist values *en voie de devenir*, operates in a decidedly inhuman linguistic economy. This goes as well for the troubadour excremental tradition, which highlights with astounding clarity the aspirational *inhuman* dimension of troubadour poetry in general. But it is paradoxically this "inhuman aspiration" to know one's Latin prayers like the birds that spurs the creation of those values that later get construed as "humanist" by scholars such as Pierre Bec and René Nelli. While Bec and Nelli are mistaken in their reading of the Lady as figuring an intimate, human encounter, their shared emphasis on the aspirational or sublimatory nature of troubadour poetry suggests that *out of the inhuman comes something new.* Of course, new is not necessarily better, higher, or more or less "human." Just consider the intense misogyny created by, and not simply reflected in, troubadour culture. However, to echo Zupančič, such an engagement with the excremental inhuman represents a necessary risk; the troubadour excremental offers a desperately needed avenue for thinking our way out of the crisis in sublimation that Zupančič, Baudrillard, and others have diagnosed.

CHAPTER 7

How Delicious We Must Be / Folcuin's Horse and the Dog's Gowther, Beyond Care

KARL STEEL

> "Frank fed us human meat, and we got the hunger. That's how you become a cannibal, Dee. You get one taste of delicious, delicious human meat, none of this stuff ever satisfies you ever again for the rest of your life."
>
> —*It's Always Sunny in Philadelphia*[1]

NEARLY TWO THOUSAND YEARS AGO, during Titus's siege of Jerusalem, robbers emptied a rich woman's house of all she had, including her remaining food. According to the *Golden Legend,* the woman, in her despair, "strangled her son, had him cooked, ate half of his body, and hid the other half. But when robbers smelled the odor of the cooked meat, they burst in and threatened the woman with death if she did not give up her store of meat."[2] When she

---

1. Fred Savage, "Mac and Dennis: Manhunters," season 1, episode 4, *It's Always Sunny in Philadelphia* [Television], 2008. I thank Mike Smith for introducing me to this program.

2. Jacobus de Voragine, *The Golden Legend: Readings on the Saints,* trans. William Granger Ryan, 2 vols. (Princeton, NJ: Princeton University Press, 1993), vol. 1:276, in the life of the apostle James. Translations are my own unless, as here, otherwise indicated. The story originates in Josephus or, just as well, in Leviticus 26:27-29, Deuteronomy 28:53-57, Lamentations 4:10, or 2 Kings 6:28-29. For the narrative afterlife of this woman, Mary or Maria of Jerusalem, see Merrall Llewelyn Price, *Consuming Passions: The Uses of Cannibalism in Late Medieval and Early Modern Europe* (New York: Routledge, 2003), 65-81.

175

produced her son's half-eaten body, the robbers froze in horror, repulsed as much by the infanticide as by their deceitful appetites, which had confused meat and human flesh.

Human flesh smells like meat because it is meat. According to some medieval natural science, the difference between human and animal flesh is one of degree, not of kind: human flesh differs from other fleshes only in its relative coldness or dryness.[3] When a father who had killed and eaten his own daughter begged Innocent III for a suitable penance, the pope enjoined him "nunquam de *caetero* carnibus pro quacunque necessitate vesceretur"[4] ["never again to eat any other meat for whatever necessity"; my emphasis]. But while human flesh can be regarded as meat, it tends to be considered particularly choice. In Geoffrey of Monmouth's *History of the Kings of Britain,* King Cadwallo, driven into exile by his brother Edwin, lands on the Isle of Guernsey and, in his grief, refuses to eat until someone can provide him with venison. When Cadwallo's beloved nephew, Brian, fails in his hunt, Brian slices off and roasts a piece of his own thigh and serves it to his uncle, who "tantum dulcedinem in aliis carnibus non reperisset" ["had never found such sweetness in other flesh"].[5] The singular deliciousness of the flesh attests to the special relationship between Brian and Cadwallo and to the nobility of Brian's corporeal sacrifice; perhaps more fundamentally, the deliciousness evidences the inferiority of animal to human flesh. The savor of human flesh in this narrative is consistent with the other, rare medieval descriptions of the taste of human flesh, which always characterize it as the best of meats, the most restorative, and most delicious. In the Middle English romance *Richard Coer de Lyon,* Richard's men trick an ailing Richard, who yearns for pork, into

---

3. Phyllis Pray Bober, *Art, Culture, and Cuisine: Ancient and Medieval Gastronomy* (Chicago: University of Chicago Press, 1999), 245. Jeffrey Jerome Cohen's *Medieval Identity Machines,* Medieval Cultures 35 (Minneapolis: University of Minnesota Press, 2003), 75, makes the same point: "Whereas Augustine saw the line between animal and human as inviolable, as far as this Galenic body is concerned there is no difference between human and animal flesh." Note that 1 Corinthians 15:39 ("All flesh is not the same flesh: but one is the flesh of men, another of beasts, other of birds, another of fishes") might have prompted a discussion of the differences between human and animal flesh, but the usual exegesis remarks only on distinctions among resurrected humans, which will be like the differences in brightness among celestial bodies (see, for example, Peter Lombard's commentary on 1 Corinthians [in J. P. Migne, ed., *Patrilogiae cursus completus: series latina* (Paris, 1841), vol. 191:1685D–86C. Hereafter *PL*]). Haymo of Auxerre's commentary (*PL* 117:600B, mistakenly ascribed to Haymo of Halberstadt) is rare in discussing a material difference between kinds of flesh: he explains that although all flesh is one, birds were made from air, humans from earth, and fish from flowing water.

4. Epistola LXXX, *PL* 214:1063D–64B.

5. Geoffrey of Monmouth, *Historia Regum Britanniae,* ed. Acton Griscom (New York: Longmans, Green, and Co., 1929), 518.

eating the spiced body of a "yonge and fat" Saracen (l. 3088). While "hys folk hem turnyd away and lowgh" (l. 3114), Richard eats and regains his health and vigor.⁶ In the *Chanson d'Antioche*, the starving rabble among the crusaders discover human flesh to be a delicacy: "Mius vaut que cars de porc ne cars de cerf lardés. / Nule cars de porcel ne poroit ester tés"⁷ ["It is better than pork or fat venison. No piglet's flesh could be as good as this"; ll. 4985–86]. Marco Polo reports that the Japanese think human flesh "the choicest of all foods,"⁸ and John Mandeville that the people of Lamore "wele gladly etyn manys flesch more than ony othir flesch," despite their wealth and the ready availability of other kinds of meat.⁹ In one of Poggio Bracciolini's tales, a teenage serial killer, when caught, "fassus est se plures alios comedisse, idque se agere, quoniam sapidiores reliquis carnibus viderentur"¹⁰ ["confessed that he had eaten many other (children), and that he had done this because they seemed tastier to him than any other flesh"]. The fifteenth-century hunting manual of Edward of York follows Albert the Great in observing that "man's flesh is so savory and so pleasant that when [wolves] have taken to man's flesh they will never eat the flesh of other beasts, though they should die of hunger."¹¹

Why should human flesh be thought to taste so good? Maybe because it did taste good. Postmedieval records of anthropophagy describe it as tasting like pork, beef, tuna, veal, cheese, or, according to Guy de Maupassant, who ate a piece of human flesh during a dissection, as having no flavor at all.¹²

---

6. Peter Larkin, ed., *Richard Coer de Lyon* (Kalamazoo: Medieval Institute Publications, 2015).

7. Jan A. Nelson, ed., *La Chanson d'Antioche* (Tuscaloosa: University of Alabama Press, 2003). For more texts like this, see Jill Tattersall, "Anthropophagi and Eaters of Raw Flesh in French Literature of the Crusade Period: Myth, Tradition, and Reality," *Medium Aevum* 57 (1988): 240–53.

8. Marco Polo, *The Travels of Marco Polo*, trans. Ronald Latham (New York: Penguin, 1958), 248.

9. M. D. Seymour, ed., *The Bodley Version of Mandeville's Travels*, EETS o.s. 253 (London: Oxford University Press, 1963), 97.

10. Poggio Bracciolini, *Facezie*, ed. Eugenio Garin, trans. (into Italian) Marcello Ciccuto (Milan: Biblioteca Universale Rizzoli, 1994), CLXXI: "Horribile de puero qui infantulos comedebat." Anders Thomas Jensen, *The Green Butchers: De Grønne Slagtere* (Newmarket Films, 2003) is one of several modern versions of such stories.

11. Edward of Norwich, *The Master of Game*, ed. William A. Baillie-Grohman and Florence Baillie-Grohman (London: Ballantyne, Hanson and Co., 1904), 60; Albert the Great, *De animalibus libri XXVI*, ed. Hermann Stadler, 2 vols. (Munich: Aschendorff, 1916), 2:1410.

12. For Guy de Maupassant, see Wilhelm Stekel, "Cannibalism, Necrophilism, and Vampirism," in *Sadism and Masochism*, trans. Louise Brink (New York: Grove, 1965), 305 [238–330]. Stekel's analysis exemplifies the common conviction that anthropophagy in "modern" societies represents a return of the primitive repressed. Issei Sagawa, a graduate student in literature at the Sorbonne who in 1981 murdered his classmate Renée Hartevelt, described her flesh as

But, so far as I know, no medieval witness to the flavor of human flesh spoke either from personal experience or from interviews with anthropophages; as is usual in records of anthropophagy, what the tellers claim to know they know only by hearsay.¹³ The many psychoanalytic critical readings of anthropophagy provide a ready approach for explaining the purported deliciousness of human flesh. Freud's myth of the origins of the superego in anthropophagy would explain that whatever is most prohibited—total freedom and dominion, incest, anthropophagy—must be imagined to be most pleasurable;¹⁴ or, readings inspired by Klein rather than by Freud would see the pleasure as one of eradicating troubling distinctions between self and other.¹⁵ Political readings, inspired by the medieval troping of tyranny as anthropophagy, would

---

tasting like tuna. For beef, see Gananath Obeyesekere, *Cannibal Talk: The Man-Eating Myth and Human Sacrifice in the South Seas* (Berkeley: University of California Press, 2005), 139, and pork, in the same book, 28. For veal, see William Seabrook, *Jungle Ways* (New York: Harcourt, Brace and Co., 1931), 173, and for cheese and beef, see Piers Paul Read, *Alive: The Story of the Andes Survivors* (Philadelphia: Lippincott, 1974), 199 and 98. I use the words "anthropophagy/anthropophage" instead of "cannibalism/cannibal" because of the roots of the word "cannibal" in colonialism and genocide.

13. This point appears as early as Herman Melville, *Typee*, in *The Writings of Herman Melville*, ed. Harrison Hayford, Hershel Parker, and G. Thomas Tanselle, 9 vols. (Evanston, IL: Northwestern University Press, 1968), whose narrator observes, "It is a singular fact, that in all our accounts of cannibal tribes we have seldom received the testimony of an eye-witness to the revolting practice. The horrible conclusion has always been derived either from the second-hand evidence of Europeans, or else from the admissions of the savages themselves, after they have in some degree become civilized" (1:234). For the foundational critique of reports of cultural anthropophagy, see William Arens, *The Man-Eating Myth: Anthropology and Anthropophagy* (New York: Oxford University Press, 1979). See also the restatements and refinements of his position in William Arens, "Cooking the Cannibals," in *Consuming Passions: Food in the Age of Anxiety*, ed. Jennifer Wallace and Sian Griffiths (Manchester, UK: Mandolin, 1998), 156–66, and "Rethinking Anthropophagy," in *Cannibalism and the Colonial World*, eds. Francis Barker, Peter Hulme, and Margaret Iversen (New York: Cambridge University Press, 1998), 39–62. For a survey of the cannibalism debates, see Lawrence Osborne, "Does Man Eat Man? Inside the Great Cannibalism Controversy," *Lingua Franca* (April/May 1997): 28–38, and Peter Hulme, "Introduction: The Cannibal Scene," in *Cannibalism and the Colonial World*, 1–38, who corrects Arens's frequently intemperate critics. Most recently, see the first chapter, "Anthropophagy and the Man-Eating Myth," in Obeyesekere, *Cannibal Talk*.

14. See the myth of the origin of the superego in Sigmund Freud, *Totem and Taboo: Some Points of Agreement between the Mental Lives of Savages and Neurotics*, trans. James Strachey (New York: Routledge, 2001), 164–69, repeated in *Moses and Monotheism*, trans. Katherine Jones (Letchworth, UK: Hogarth Press, 1939), 130–33.

15. The most ambitious use of Melanie Klein's theories of the anthropophagic imagination is Maggie Kilgour, *From Communion to Cannibalism: An Anatomy of Metaphors of Consumption* (Princeton, NJ: Princeton University Press, 1990). Also see Alex Blumstein, "Masochism and Fantasies of Preparing to Be Incorporated," *Journal of the American Psychoanalytic Association* 7 (1959), 292–98

explain its pleasure as a pleasure of power, or, using the Kristevan dynamic of abjection, they would see the intense pleasure of anthropophagy as representing the disgusting, disordered pleasures that must be put off for normative subjects to fix the boundaries of their identities.[16] These and other readings understand anthropophagy as a concretized metaphor for dynamics of interiority, exteriority, and incorporation; or as a metaphor for ethnic, political, or familial fantasies; none, however, deals with anthropophagy in relation to carnivorousness in general.[17] Slaughter and meat-eating take place all the time, without inspiring any horror or obsessional desires. Few narratives and fewer still medieval narratives consider carnivorousness in general as worth recording.[18] Symbolic analyses of anthropophagy that make little or no reference to carnivorousness in general may therefore be justly accused of parochialism, or what Richard Ryder in 1970 termed "speciesism," since they attend, without justification or without good justification, only to the subset of carnivorousness that most directly injures humans.[19] Most tellingly, such analyses simply assume anthropophagy is a special kind of horror, and, in so doing, uncritically perpetuate the distinction of humans from nonhuman animals: they fail

---

16. For anthropophagy in *Richard Coer de Lyon* as "Christian military-gustatory aggression," and thus as a pleasure of power, see Geraldine Heng, *Empire of Magic: Medieval Romance and the Politics of Cultural Fantasy* (New York: Columbia University Press, 2003), 73. For tyranny troped as anthropophagy, see Philippe Buc,"Manducation et domination: Analyse du Métaphore" in *L'Ambiguïté du Livre: Prince, pouvoir, et peuple dans les commentaires de la Bible au Moyen Âge* (Paris: Beauchesne, 1994), 206–31, and Nicola McDonald, "Eating People and the Alimentary Logic of *Richard Coeur de Lion*," in *Pulp Fictions of Medieval England: Essays in Popular Romance*, ed. McDonald (Manchester, UK: Manchester University Press, 2004), who observes that, "Like sex and commerce, medieval politics, in particular the politics of national expansion, is fraught with the anthropophagic urge: lords 'eteþ' their underlings and 'deuouren' the poor; knights 'swolwe' one another and so too kingdoms; enemies are 'glotons'; and victors 'feste' on hard-won land" (126) [124–50]. For further political readings of anthropophagy, see Heather Blurton, *Cannibalism in High Medieval English Literature* (New York: Palgrave Macmillan, 2007). For the dynamics of abjection, see Julia Kristeva, *Powers of Horror: An Essay on Abjection*, trans. Leon S. Roudiez (New York: Columbia University Press, 1982).

17. Other metaphorical approaches to anthropophagy are available: for example, for sacrifice, see Alec Irwin, "Devoured by God: Cannibalism, Mysticism, and Ethics in Simone Weil," *Cross Currents* 51 (2001): 257–72; but see C. Richard King, "The (Mis)uses of Cannibalism in Contemporary Cultural Critique," *Diacritics* 30 (2000): 106–23, and Rob Latham, "Cannibals and Kitchen Sinks [Review of Priscilla Walton, *Our Cannibals, Ourselves*]," *Contemporary Literature* 47 (2006): 502–4.

18. A few medieval examples survive, although they seem to be meant as parodies; for example, see the poem "Flevit lepus parvulus" ["The Little Hare Wept"], in which a hare laments being hunted by dogs: see Giuseppe Scalia, "Il *Testamentum Asini* e il *Lamento della lepre*," *Studi Medievali*, series 3 (1962): 129–51, at 143–44.

19. The well-known systematic development of the implications of Ryder's coinage is Peter Singer, *Animal Liberation* (New York: Random House, 1975).

to investigate how the human differentiates itself from other life, how, to put it simply, the human is made, not born.[20]

Any explanation of the purported deliciousness of human flesh in anthropophagy must therefore begin by explaining why anthropophagy itself should be considered so remarkable, or, more precisely, what function is performed by its being considered remarkable. It should examine what humans lose as humans when they suffer anthropophagy. Humans are animals, too. Like humans, other animals are animate creatures of flesh, subject to growth, injury, and disease, creatures who communicate and love; most problematically, animals, whether nonhuman or human, all die, rot, and turn to dust. If one acknowledges no significant differences between humans and nonhuman animals, and if meat-eating is regarded as an acceptable practice, there is no particular reason not to turn humans into meat. The standard objection, through the Middle Ages and to the present day, is that humans uniquely have language, reason, and immortal souls, and therefore humans should not be eaten, and that animals, because they lack these things, are their inferiors, given over to humans for their just use. This objection precisely reverses cause and effect. Augustine explains that humans possess a capacity that allows them to subdue animals and that keeps humans from being subdued in turn, and adds "what better name for that [capacity] than 'reason.'" When this maxim is read in conjunction with Augustine's proof that the irrationality of animals subjects them "to us to kill or keep alive for our own uses," the tautology through which the human *constitutes itself* as human becomes obvious. Since rational creatures would not allow themselves to suffer as animals do, the very fact that animals are kept alive or killed for the sake of humans proves that animals lack reason and therefore deserve to suffer fates that no human ever should.[21] *Human* is therefore not just a species name; it is a structural position. This logic distinguishing human from animal traverses the whole of the Middle Ages, and indeed, as Derrida argued, "the whole history of humanity."[22] The human killing of animals—or, more precisely, what humans call animals—as Derrida argued, is a "denegation of murder. The putting to

---

20. Josephine Donovan and Carol J. Adams, eds., *The Feminist Care Tradition in Animal Ethics* (New York: Columbia University Press, 2007) well illustrates the indebtedness of critical animal theory to feminist thought.

21. The Augustine comes, respectively, from *On Free Choice of the Will,* trans. Thomas Williams (Indianapolis, IN: Hackett Pub. Co., 1993), 13, and *The City of God,* trans. Marcus Dods (New York: Modern Library, 1950), 26.

22. Jacques Derrida, *The Animal that Therefore I Am,* ed. Marie-Louise Mallet, trans. David Wills (New York: Fordham University Press, 2008), 14. For surveys of Derrida's engagement with the animal, see Matthew Chrulew, "Feline Divinanimality: Derrida and the Discourse of Species in Genesis," *The Bible and Critical Theory* 2.2 (2006): 18.1–18.22, and Matthew Calarco,

death of the animal, says this denegation, is not a murder. I would link this denegation to the violent institution of the 'who' as subject," because through this ongoing denegation, the human subject exclusively claims "speech or reason, the logos, history, laughing, mourning, burial, the gift, and so on."[23] The punning title—*L'animal que donc je suis* [The Animal that Therefore I Am/Follow]—of a posthumous collection devoted to the animal question presents his argument in miniature. Revising Descartes's cogito, Derrida argues that the human discovers itself not in isolation before a world it apprehends through (or doubts in) its private thoughts, but in the operations of "carnophallogocentrism,"[24] a relationship of repeatedly enacting domination through which this living thing retroactively claims the category of the human for itself and consigns all other species to animality. In short, because "power over the animal is . . . the essence of the human,"[25] both the human and animal must therefore be understood not as essential identities but as ongoing events.[26] Since these events determine who lives and who dies, and, more specifically, who will be mourned and who will simply be killed, in the "natural order of things," these distinctions are anything but innocent.

Recognizing the violent, inessential relationality of human and animal means recognizing that the special horror of anthropophagy derives primarily from its violation of codes, not of polity or faith, but of privilege. Anthropophagy confounds the distinction between human and nonhuman animal life, between what can be murdered and what can only be slaughtered, by feeding to the stomach what the regime of the human demands be honored with a

---

Zoographies: The Question of the Animal from Heidegger to Derrida (Columbia University Press, 2008), 103–49.

23. Jacques Derrida, "'Eating Well,' or The Calculation of the Subject," in *Points: Interviews, 1974–1994*, ed. Elisabeth Weber, trans. Peggy Kamuf (Stanford: Stanford University Press, 1995), 283, and *The Animal That Therefore I Am*, 5. Further thought and quantitative analysis on the "who" can be found in Gaëtanelle Gilquin and George M. Jacobs, "Elephants Who Marry Mice are Very Unusual: The Use of the Relative Pronoun Who with Nonhuman Animals," *Society and Animals* 14 (2006): 79–105, who conclude that "changes in language . . . are not enough, because—as we have seen—the use of (who) with nonhuman animals does not necessarily reflect a positive attitude toward them" (99).

24. For "carnophallogocentrism," see *The Animal that Therefore I Am*, 104.

25. Ibid., 93.

26. My debt to Judith Butler, *Gender Trouble: Feminism and the Subversion of Identity* (New York: Routledge, 1990) should be obvious: "Gender is always a doing, though not a doing by a subject who might be said to preexist the deed" (25). I am also guided by Donna Haraway, *When Species Meet* (Minneapolis: University of Minnesota Press, 2008), where she writes that "relationships are the smallest possible patterns for analysis" (25–26). For an early appraisal of the role of "othering" animals in human self-definition, see Esther Cohen, "Animals in Medieval Perceptions: The Image of the Ubiquitous Other," in *Animals in Human Society: Changing Perspectives*, ed. Aubrey Manning and James Serpell (London: Routledge, 1994), 76 [59–80].

grave. The special horror of anthropophagy is therefore its impossibility, for a human who has been slaughtered and eaten, by losing the exemption from routine violence through which it defines itself as not animal, is no longer recognizable as an *anthropos*.[27] However, the mere act of telling stories about anthropophagy, while not telling stories that evince any special horror for the consumption of animals, counteracts anthropophagy's dehumanizing confusion. Narratives of anthropophagy acknowledge human vulnerability; they decry the violence humans have suffered; they mourn lost human life while also memorializing it; and, in the process, they silently exclude animals from consideration. Communities, as Judith Butler points out, are as much constituted "by those [they] do grieve for as by those whose deaths [they] disavow," and that therefore obituaries—which, for example, record the individual deaths of American soldiers while recording the deaths of Afganistanis or Iraqis, if at all, only en masse—should be understood as acts of community formation.[28] Observing that no casualty list ever records the deaths of beasts, Chloë Taylor reformulates Butler by adding that the obituary should also be understood as an act by which animals' lives are forgotten.[29] Narratives of anthropophagy should be understood, in Taylor's sense, as obituaries, as simultaneously acknowledging the special vulnerability of human lives while obliterating the lives of animals. The narratives thus exclude animals from the community of what Butler terms "grievable lives" and prevent what they suffer from being recognized as violence. Tellingly, in medieval narrative and social practices, virtually the only beings marked as injured by carnivorousness, apart from the humans consumed by anthropophages, are the ascetics who lose control over their appetites, bodies, and vows by eating meat.[30] Humans are buried

---

27. My ideas accord with those expressed in a roundtable discussion that concludes the anthology by The Animal Studies Group, ed., *Killing Animals* (Chicago: University of Chicago Press, 2006), where Erica Fudge suggests that "to eat a human is not just eating flesh and bones," but rather a kind of destruction of the human itself ("Conclusion: A Conversation," 196 [188–210]); Steve Baker responds that anthropophagous animals, because they have reversed the structure of subjugation, might no longer properly be called "animal," in "'You Kill Things to Look at Them': Animal Death in Contemporary Art," in *Killing Animals*, ed. The Animal Studies Group (Chicago: University of Chicago Press, 2006), 69–98.

28. Judith Butler, *Precarious Life: The Powers of Mourning and Violence* (New York: Verso, 2004), 46; for her insights on obituaries, see 34–37.

29. Chloë Taylor, "The Precarious Lives of Animals: Butler, Coetzee, and Animal Ethics," *Philosophy Today* 52 (2008): 60–72. For allied insights, see Erica Fudge's comments in *Pets* (Stocksfield, UK: Acumen, 2008) on omissions in John Berger's work: "Even as Berger reminds us how significant the concept of home is to our sense of self he, like so many others, remains silent about the presence and role of pets in that home. . . . We might regard the silence itself as an object of analysis" (14).

30. An emblematic medievalist exclusion of animals from consideration is Albrecht Classen, ed., *Violence in Medieval Courtly Literature: A Casebook*, Routledge Medieval Casebooks

and prayed for, their deaths memorialized, the violence they suffer an object of obsessive horror or singular caution; animals are slaughtered—sometimes after suffering harassment by dogs, not for entertainment, but to tenderize their meat—and their useless remains are, for example, dumped into the Thames, washed away, forgotten.[31]

Like anthropophagy narratives, the purported deliciousness of human flesh also serves to preserve human superiority at a crisis point. Although the eaten human loses their human privilege, the anthropophage's desire for human flesh itself preserves human supremacy. Questions of the "actual" flavor of human flesh, at least in this context, are irrelevant. The violence of the human being eaten resembles that suffered by martyrs in hagiography, where every torment inflicted on them by some insatiable compulsive tyrant bears witness not to the tyrant's power but to the power of Christianity, incarnated by the martyr's mutilated and holy flesh. It is therefore to the *advantage* of humans that the taste of their flesh encourages anthropophagy. The belief is akin to the self-satisfaction felt in imagining other people's grief at one's own funeral, a fantasy of power over others even after death. Here, the human imagines itself dead, apparently powerless, while nonetheless sustaining itself as human through the obsessions of others for its uniquely human deliciousness. This false but intense belief sustains the human sense of superiority interpassively, to use Slavoj Žižek's locution, as humans preserve their human particularity by "believing or enjoying through the other."[32] In "Je sais bien, mais quand même ... ," Octave Mannoni reappraised Freud's work on disavowal and fetishism to argue that the subject does not need to believe in the fetish directly; the subject can sustain the potency of its fetish by believing that certain, unsophisticated others truly believe in that which it knows to be false.[33] Developing this point, Žižek has written about the "subject supposed to believe,"[34] someone—or even something—external that believes sincerely

---

(New York: Routledge, 2004). Its introduction explains that "our focus will rest on the manifestation of mostly physical violence as understood by the modern (and medieval) sense of the word, that is, as violence that leads to the harm or even death of another person, to the destruction of an object, an institution, or a political entity" (15). Classen neither justifies his exclusion of living non-persons from this list nor defines what counts as a person.

31. Ernest Sabine, "Butchering in Mediaeval London," *Speculum* 8 (1933): 350 [335–53]. For tenderizing flesh through baiting, see Oscar Brownstein, "The Popularity of Baiting in England before 1600: A Study in Social and Theatrical History," *Educational Theatre Journal* 21 (1969): 237–50.

32. Slavoj Žižek, *The Plague of Fantasies* (NY: Verso, 1997), 113.

33. Octave Mannoni, "Je sais bien, mais quand même... ," *Clefs pour l'imaginaire ou l'autre scène* (Paris: Editions du Seuil, 1969).

34. Slavoj Žižek, *How to Read Lacan* (NY: W. W. Norton and Co., 2007).

in that which we know to be false in some fundamental sense: true belief is out there, somewhere. In anthropophagy narratives, in fantasies of the superb taste of human flesh, humans preserve their sense of themselves, whatever their doubts, by believing that the anthropophage stupidly, directly "believes" in the human subject's importance. Held aloft passively by desiring others, whether these are animal, monstrous humans, or God Himself, who sacrifices Himself in His pure and direct love for the sake of human subjects who know themselves not to be worth the trouble, the human subject comports itself as if it were desirable, as if it especially mattered.

The fifteenth-century moral treatise *Dives and Pauper* argues that the verb "occidit" of the sixth commandment does not apply "boþyn to man & of beste,"[35] but it still places limitations on the slaughter of animals: anyone who butchers an animal "for cruelte & vanite," that is, anyone who enjoys killing the animal, has sinned. Demanding that humans pity animals as God's creatures, the only causes for killing it legitimizes are those that work past or use up the animal's life on the way to satisfying some human need: food, clothing, self-defense. No animal, it commands, should be killed "withoutyn cause." Yet depraved killers of animals also kill with causes, however secret they may be. These killers sin not by being indifferent but rather by paying too much attention to animal suffering; they sin by treating nonlife as life. Proper killers look past animal life; depraved killers acknowledge that this life has value in itself, in excess of what could be used up in the creation of some product. The obverse of this sin would be to slaughter humans without "cruelte & vanite," without some glimmer of inassimilable excess, whether of grief or mourning or sadistic delight. Slaughtering humans must therefore not be simply a job, but a sin, a horror, a drive, or a pleasure that coerces, a pleasure that infects eaters with "the hunger."

·

Presenting medieval thinking about humans and animals in this way has the advantage of shaking loose human smugness by turning human privilege into a question. But the focus on *medieval* examples has the potential to reaffirm a modern smugness at the expense of the medieval archive: the danger might be of assuming that the medieval—being so doctrinally obsessed with human privilege, being so violent—would have had more occasion to think about anthropophagy than modern writers. This would be the flip side of the

---

35. Priscilla Heath Barnum, ed., *Dives and Pauper,* 2 vols., EETS o.s. 275, 280 (London: Oxford University Press, 1976), 2:33.

presumption that medieval people lived more closely with animals than people did after the wide-scale use of mechanized labor and transport (from roughly the twentieth century to the present, in other words): both are ways of presuming that the medieval is somehow more bestial than the present, whenever that is. Of course, the importance of anthropophagy in dystopian science fiction like *Make Room! Make Room!*, *The Road,* and *Cloud Atlas* gives the lie to this presumption: here we have either the return of "medieval degradation" in the so-called era of late capitalism, the stubborn persistence of an old worry, or a new formulation of the recognition of mutual fleshiness of humans and animals in an era of massive overproduction and impending collapse. The first part of this chapter should be understood, therefore, as at once saying something about medieval culture and also pointing at the transhistorical presence of these cultural elements anywhere that the human jealously guards its carnivorous privilege; this should be read, then, as an invitation to scholars of postmedieval culture to collect their own period's anthropophagy texts to further consider how the fantasy of the "hungry other" (as in classic cartoons of the missionary stewing in a cannibal pot) sustain some subject's persecuted sense of itself.

Then as now, however, medieval people could imagine other relations to the animal, less concerned with violence and saving human privilege. I have selected two such occasions here, deliberately choosing examples from difficult cases, the first from a religious chronicle, the second from a chivalric narrative; the one from a genre typically concerned only with human events and professionally trained in the intellectual protection of human supremacy, the latter eager to celebrate violence, concerned with animals primarily as monstrous enemies, as mounts, or as food. Readers are invited to seek out still more difficult cases in, especially, medieval philosophy and religious doctrine, or to play with the material of Breton lais, like the famous collection of Marie de France, so often indifferent to human privilege. My ultimate goal will be to explore a possible ground for ethics outside of anthropophagic interpassive fantasies.

Folcuin of Lobbes's *Deeds of the Abbots of Saint Bertin* tells the story of the horse of a ninth-century bishop of Thérouanne, also named Folcuin. The horse loved Folcuin so much that "ante eius feretrum preisse"[36] ["it went before his bier"] at its master's funeral procession, and "omnem deinceps hominem ferre recusasse, nec passus est post menbra [*sic*] tanti pontificis voluptatibus

---

36. O. Holder-Egger, ed., "Gesta abbatum S. Bertini Sithiensium," in G. Waitz, ed., *Monumenta Germaniae Historica SS 13* (Hanover: Impensis Bibliopolii Hahniani, 1881), 619, for this and subsequent quotations from the story. For directing me to it, I thank Rob Meens, "Eating Animals in the Early Middle Ages: Classifying the Animal World and Building Group Identities," in *The Animal/Human Boundary: Historical Perspectives*, eds. William Chester Jordan and Angela N. H. Creager (Rochester, NY: University of Rochester Press, 2002), 7 [3–28].

deservire alicuius hominis" ["afterwards it refused to carry all men, nor, because of its great delight in the bishop, would it suffer the limb of any other man"]. It would be simplistic to identify the relationship between horse and bishop as just another instance of animal subjugation. Certainly, the horse is the bishop's, but once the bishop has gone, the horse stays loyal, unwilling to give itself up to anyone else; or it simply becomes free. After the horse's death, the humans try to put the horse back in its place. But according to the *Deeds*,

> Et merito cadaver eius canes non poterant lacerare, super quem ymnidica cantica Christo decantata erant sepissime. Quod videntes cives, eum humano more sepelierunt, quem nec bestiae nec volucres tangere presumpserunt.

> Because of the merit of its corpse upon which hymns to Christ were so often chanted, the dogs could not mangle it. When the citizens saw this, they gave a human burial to what neither beasts nor birds had presumed to touch.

This is a corpse, no mere carcass. It has more than instrumental value, more than just fleshy existence. The honor the horse receives may derive only from the sanctity of Folcuin and the hymns he sang while riding; it may derive only from the logic of the pet, which protects the one, cherished horse while excluding all other animals, "bestiae et volucres," which, implicitly, will never be buried "humano more."[37] The story may be understood even as a historical curiosity, since Thérouanne is located in a region where horse burial was once not uncommon.[38] Folcuin does not, however, conclude the story with a pronouncement on the power of God, or on the sanctity of his namesake, or with a condemnation of the relics of an equine cult. Furthermore, Folcuin refrains from either humanizing or animalizing the horse. He does not speak of the love of the human for the horse; he makes no claims for the horse's rationality; nor does he claim that the horse will be resurrected into immortal life. Although the horse is buried "humano more," it is not presented as if it were, in some fundamental sense, human, or as if it were privileged to be protected because of human love for it; but neither is it presented like a mere beast. Nor is the horse the only one affected by its death: all creatures who

---

37. The concept and term come from Jonathan Elmer and Cary Wolfe's 1995 "Subject to Sacrifice: Ideology, Psychoanalysis, and the Discourse of Species in Jonathan Demme's *The Silence of the Lambs*," reprinted in Wolfe's *Animal Rites: American Culture, the Discourse of Species, and Posthumanist Theory* (Chicago: University of Chicago Press, 2003), 97–120.

38. Sébastian Lepetz, "Sacrifices et inhumations de chevaux et de chiens en France du nord au IIIe siècle après J.-C.," in *Ces animaux que l'homme choisit d'inhumer: Contribution á l'étude de la place et du rôle de l'animal dans les rites funéraires; Journée d'étude Université Liège, 20 mars 1999*, ed. Liliane Bodson (Liege, Belgium: Liege University Press, 2000), 93–125.

contact it have perhaps undergone—as Judith Butler characterizes the possibilities of mourning—"a transformation . . . the full result of which one cannot know in advance."[39] The dogs and birds do not "presume" to eat the horse; it is not that they *could not* (non potuerunt) touch the body, but that they *would not* dishonor the horse by eating it. And it is their behavior that leads the humans to bury and to memorialize the horse. What has happened to the humans as humans and animals as animals when humans allow themselves to be instructed by the *cultural behavior* of animals?

The fourteenth-century Middle English chivalric narrative *Sir Gowther* offers a similar suspension of human privilege. *Sir Gowther* tells the story of a half-human, half-demon knight driven by his infernal heritage to rape and immolate nuns, force friars off cliffs, and hang parsons from hooks. When he discovers his demonic paternity, Gowther immediately seeks out the Pope, who demands that the knight do penance by eating only food that he "revus of howndus mothe" ["snatches from a hound's mouth," 296] and by not speaking a word. The penance works *as* penance only because we are meant to understand this as a humiliation. During his penance, Gowther gradually rebuilds himself as a good Christian and good human, learning to have proper regard for the flesh of his fellow Christians and contempt for the Saracens, whom he sneaks away, in disguise, to massacre on three successive occasions. At the story's end, he marries and then dies a saint, although notably without progeny. Yet before he begins his violent humiliation, a dog *gives* Gowther food as a gift:

> He went owt of that ceté
> Into anodur far cuntré,
> Tho testamentys thus thei sey;
> He seyt hym down undur a hyll,
> A greyhownde broght hym meyt untyll
> Or evon yche a dey.
> Thre neythtys ther he ley:
> Tho grwhownd ylke a dey
> A whyte lofe he hym broghht;
> On tho fort day come hym non,
> Up he start and forthe con gon,
> And lovyd God in his thoght.[40]
> (307–18)

---

39. Butler, *Precarious Life*, 21.
40. Anne Laskaya and Eve Salisbury, eds., *The Middle English Breton Lays* (Kalamazoo: Medieval Institute Publications, 1995).

He went out from that city and into another far country, as the records say; he sat down at the base of a hill, and a greyhound brought him food every day. Three nights he lay there: and the greyhound each day brought him a white loaf of bread, and on the fourth day did not come to him. Gowther got up and went forth and loved God.

Below the hill, in a moment of astonishing tenderness, Gowther pauses between violence and struggle. For a time, Gowther lives out of doors, out of all civilized organization of space; for three days, he receives a dog's charity, not snatching it, but accepting what the dog offers. This is far from the penance he was meant to seek out. Unlike St. Roch, similarly fed by a dog, he can offer nothing in return: there is no blessing, no approval, no protection, nothing he can give; nor do we see that the dog expects anything. In this hillside idyll, between the violences of demonic and divine *teloi,* Gowther inhabits, with this dog, an open space without economy,[41] indifferent to human superiority or Gowther's need to labor on civilizing his soul. The dog is never identified, never explained, and Gowther, encountering it, allows himself to receive without asking, without ever behaving as if he were quite human or the dog were quite canine. This is a moment of relaxation where something new might have happened had the narrative not been so tightly bound to rushing the knight along to a proper, holy conclusion.

The temptation would be to praise the stories of Folcuin's horse and Gowther and the dog as examples of a more fluid, conjoined selfhood, indifferent to rigid binaries, firm boundaries, and hierarchies, all of which serve as the opponents—or strawmen—for critical animal studies, ecocriticism, and a host of other well-meaning modes of critique. Certainly, all of these have the advantage of eliminating any naturalized foundation for a decision. The "deterritorialized" wasp of Deleuze and Guattari, whose "molecular" becoming cannot be distinguished from the orchid it pollinates, nor finally from the "animals, plants, microorganisms, mad particles, a whole galaxy" with which we are all dependently enmeshed;[42] Haraway's dog, whose cotraining with her is a "naturalcultural practice" that redoes them both "molecule by molecule," allows "something unexpected" to come into being, "something new and

---

41. See Jacques Derrida, *Given Time: I. Counterfeit Money,* trans. Peggy Kamuf (Chicago: University of Chicago Press, 1992), 7: "But is not the gift, if there is any, also that which interrupts economy? That which, in suspending economic calculation, no longer gives rise to exchange? That which opens the circle so as to defy reciprocity or symmetry, the common measure, and so as to turn aside the return in view of the no-return?"

42. Gilles Deleuze and Félix Guattari, *A Thousand Plateaus: Capitalism and Schizophrenia,* trans. Brian Massumi (Minneapolis: University of Minnesota Press, 1987), 262, 293, and 250.

free, something outside the rules of function and calculation, something not ruled by the logic of the reproduction of the same"[43]; or, a less frequently cited example, Ralph Acampora's *Corporal Compassion,* whose phenomenological notion of "symphysis" recalls us to our fundamental participation with other bodied beings—notably, not *em*bodied, not minds in bodies—which is a matter of "becoming sensitive to an already constituted 'inter-zone' of some aesthetic conviviality"[44]: all of these ontologies describe the actual, mobile, intraactive productivity of things in which the self-other relations that make ethics necessary must be continually renegotiated. However, the danger is in thinking that this recognition is in itself sufficient, as if fluid metaphors were enough to save us, and everything else, from human supremacy. But, as Nicole Shukin reminds us, capitalism loves rhizomes too; it loves to blur boundaries; it loves motion, stirring up trouble, multiplying desire, and giving us new things to cherish.[45]

The key is to know all this and still make a decision, and still know that we will have always made a decision, however inadequate it will always be. The trope of the "blurred boundary" should be understood as just a call to be aware of decision-making. The key to any minimally decent "postdisenchanted"[46] approach to the human and animal is to recognize, for example, the rhizomatic ontologies of Deleuze and Guattari, while still remembering "the very real torment of suffering individuals,"[47] that in an assemblage of human and animal, only one is protected by laws forbidding murder, and that therefore nonhuman animals may have to be minimally singled out in assemblages as objects of care.[48] At the same time, we must also remember, with Donna Haraway's account of training with her dog, that animals are not only passive victims that need to be rescued or let alone, and that our engagement with animals changes us as it changes them. Inspired by Haraway, we will throw open the doors of the philosopher's study. In the case of Derrida and his now

---

43. Haraway, *When Species Meet,* 228 and 223.

44. Ralph R. Acampora, *Corporal Compassion: Animal Ethics and Philosophy of Body* (Pittsburgh, PA: University of Pittsburgh Press, 2006), 84.

45. Nicole Shukin, *Animal Capital: Rendering Life in Biopolitical Times* (Minneapolis: Minnesota, 2011), 31–32.

46. I borrow this term from Carolyn Dinshaw, who used it in a roundtable discussion led and edited by Elizabeth Freeman, "Theorizing Queer Temporalities," *GLQ* 13 (2007): 185.

47. I quote from the appraisal of Deleuze and Guattari in Elizabeth A. Grosz, *Volatile Bodies: Toward a Corporeal Feminism* (Bloomington: Indiana University Press, 1994), 163, whose work in imagining a "psychical corporeality" (and whose cautious use of Deleuze and Guattari) I have found inspiring.

48. For a rich elaboration of this idea, to which I am much indebted, see Leonard Lawlor, *This Is Not Sufficient: An Essay on Animality in Derrida* (New York: Columbia University Press, 2007), 71–114. See also Cary Wolfe, *Before the Law: Humans and Other Animals in a Biopolitical Frame* (Chicago: University of Chicago Press, 2012), 84–86.

famous encounter with the fathomless, singular mystery of his cat, we should account for the individual and species history that placed this cat in this particular house fed some particular meat by this particular world-class philosopher. One of the advantages of Haraway over Derrida is just this attention to the more-than-philosophical, material history of domesticated animals, especially in her *Companion Species Manifesto*.[49]

In the case of *Gowther*, for example, we should also recognize that while the particular encounter between knight and dog may break open the circle of penitential exchange "so as to defy reciprocity or symmetry, the common measure, and so as to turn aside the return in view of the no-return,"[50] violence still makes this encounter possible. In this brief, beautiful moment, Gowther and the dog are literal companions (*with bread*). The gift of bread is the gift of food; it is nourishment, life, and an invitation to this demonic nonhuman to seek out a companionship outside a lonely human conviviality. And this mundane, material attention to Gowther's hunger interrupts his journey to satisfy his spiritual needs, with their hope of a final, celestial escape from responsibility for himself and for vulnerable others. Still, the exchanged object is *bread*. Jared Diamond famously observed that grains are the particular foodstuff of settled, urban, highly stratified civilizations, like those of Western Europe.[51] The gift of bread—and even more so for a gift of meat—should remind us of a system that bound most people to the land, as farmers, as slaves, as overseers, as owners, and as children made to tie one landowning family to another, and of the cultivation of larger and larger oxen and horses for labor, and of the elimination of competing animals and humans as "pests." The dog bestows a gift on Gowther; the dog steals from others, reminding us, with this gift, that the dog's victims are bound to a life of laboring for others. There is no way to get it perfectly right.

At a sufficiently large or sufficiently small scale, what Gowther and the dog experience does not matter. Nothing does. There is no possible perspective at which everything can matter. The scale at which Gowther and dog are both recognizable is nonetheless the scale where their existence matters, where they need to be fed, protected, and acculturated; it is the scale we might notice, if we slow down the poem's push toward its saintly conclusion. However, everything else is also significant, including the fields of "background"

---

49. Donna Haraway, *Companion Species Manifesto: Dogs, People, and Significant Otherness* (Chicago: Prickly Paradigm Press, 2003).

50. See Jacques Derrida, *Given Time: I. Counterfeit Money*, trans. Peggy Kamuf (Chicago: University of Chicago Press, 1992), 7.

51. Jared Diamond, "The Worst Mistake in the History of the Human Race," *Discover Magazine* (May 1987): 64–66.

violence that temporarily fulfill the needs of dog and knight. Ultimately, amid the always shifting field of stuff, oriented toward the preservation of a self that this very orientation is always transforming, decisions have to be made about who or what to cherish.

Joanna Zylinska's *Minimal Ethics for the Anthropocene* is a recent, good attempt to deal with this nearly impossible demand. Synthesizing work on ontology and ethics by Henri Bergson, Emmanuel Levinas, Karen Barad, and Rosi Braidotti, Zylinska calls for a nonsystemic ethics, without fixed answers, without stable goals, in which these singular beings we call humans do what they can do responsibly, engaging in "pragmatic temporary stabilizations of time and matter,"[52] while also aware of the scales of the very large and very small, the very slow and very fast, that will always escape our notice. She requires local decision-making that disturbs an always lurking universality, whose irrepressible presence undoes our satisfaction and smugness at believing ourselves to have done things right. Zylinska does not give us a posthumanism: she challenges human supremacy, as any ecological thinker must, but her attention to particularity means she abandons neither human *singularity* nor her own human position. Others may have agency; others may be subject to responsibility; others may come after us who do what we love best better than we do, if only we were to get out of the way. All of this may be true, but none of this saves us from the requirement for "the human to take responsibility for the differentiating cuts into the flow of life s/he is herself making with his/her tongue, language, or tools,"[53] without knowing in advance whether others are doing it better, or what we should protect, or why or if we are doing it wrong.

I will conclude by returning to Derrida's naked encounter with his cat, surely an ur-moment for critical animal studies.[54] The cat comes across Derrida just as he's emerged from the shower. From here, we get Derrida feeling ashamed, and a bit ashamed of his shame; we get a sketch of philosophical distinctions between self-aware nudity and unwitting nakedness, and from there, of course, another of Derrida's dismantlings of the pretensions of the humanist tradition. To suspend or refuse human domination, Derrida lets himself be "seen seen" by his cat. He allows himself the uneasiness of being caught in his own cat's eyes; he lets himself stay uncertain; and he opposes those who take "no account of the fact that what they call 'animal' can look

---

52. Joanna Zylinska, *Minimal Ethics for the Anthropocene* (Ann Arbor, MI: Open Humanities Press, 2014), 31.
53. Ibid., 87.
54. But also see Susan Fraiman, "Pussy Panic versus Liking Animals: Tracking Gender in Animal Studies," *Critical Inquiry* 39.1 (2012): 89–115.

at them, and address them from down there."⁵⁵ Derrida's insistence that his cat is this particular being removes or preserves her from the undifferentiated, humiliated mass of creatures shunted into animality. This is a moment of wonder, of uncertainty, of an insistence on the individual, but even a bit of a threat, since the cat, with its fangs, looks curiously at Derrida's penis. Though Derrida's cat is a female cat, he often refers to her in the masculine as *chat*: had he consistently called it a *chatte,* it might have been more obviously a vagina dentata, since *une chatte* can be, as in English, a "pussy." But that is a point to be explored elsewhere, with more attention to the ways that gender intrudes upon a masculine philosophy that would prefer to forget about it: needless to say, this little mix up at least multiplies the singular cat into a growing and happily disreputable crowd.⁵⁶

Derrida moves on from here, infesting the category of the "animal" until it bursts apart. Had he stayed longer with the cat and longer in his study, he might have further undomesticated both, opening both to the larger—or smaller—world and to other animal possibilities. What if the cat were a worm or a hoard of worms? What possibility for an ethics of the singular could there be were Derrida faced with a faceless hoard, hungry and existing for all that? What if the cat were larger and could actually have eaten the philosopher? Finally, what if the cat could have done this, and simply didn't care to or didn't realize it might have? This possibility of the philosopher not being "seen seen" but being *ignored by* an indifferent animal offers another model for the groundless ground for our necessary decisions. We must suspend ourselves between two impossibilities: the unjustifiable need to defend ourselves from the appetite of others, and the dizzying fact of temporary mattering, our own and others, within a near universal indifference, where we must make cuts to care, even if what we protect takes no notice of us at all. Knowing all that we know, knowing what little good it might do, what harm it might do, and just how little it will do on any scale, we still have to care.

---

55. Derrida, *The Animal that Therefore I Am,* 31.

56. For the French, compare, for example, Jacques Derrida, *L'animal autobiographique: Autour de Jacques Derrida,* ed. Marie-Louise Mallet (Paris: Galilée, 1999), 253, "devant un chat qui vous regarde sans bouger" [before a male cat who looks as you without moving], 255–56, "le chat qui me regarde nu . . . ce chat dont je parle, qui est aussi une chatte" [the male cat who looks at me naked, the male cat about whom I speak, who is also a female cat], and 257, "la chatte qui me regarde nu, celle-là et nulle autre, celle *dont je parle ici*" [the female cat who looks at me naked, that female one there and no other, the female one about whom I am speaking here; original emphasis]. For recent good appreciations of gender and Derrida, with special attention to cats, see Carla Freccero, "Chercher la chatte: Derrida's Queer Feminine Animality," in *French Thinking about Animals,* ed. Louisa Mackenzie and Stephanie Posthumus (Ann Arbor: Michigan State University Press, 2015), 105–20, and Jessica Polish, "After Alice after Cats in Derrida's *L'animal que donc je suis,*" *Derrida Today* 7.2 (2014): 180–96.

CHAPTER 8

Excusing Laius

*Freud's Oedipus, Sophocles' Oedipus Rex,
and Lydgate's Edippus*

DANIEL T. KLINE

THE TWENTIETH CENTURY has been called "the century of the child," a term drawn from Ellen Key's 1900 meditation of the same name, but no one bears more responsibility for placing children and childhood in the spotlight than Freud.[1] In a letter dated 21 September 1897 to his confidante and collaborator Wilhelm Fleiss, Freud announced a turning point in his understanding of child sexuality and human development: "I no longer believe in my neurotica."[2] This letter marks Freud's move from the so-called "seduction theory" and toward the Oedipal complex, a view he gestures toward in another letter to Fleiss less than a month later, dated 15 October 1897: "I have found, in my own case too, falling in love with the mother and jealousy of the father, and I now

---

1. Ellen Key, *The Century of the Child* (New York: G. P. Putnam's Sons, 1909).
2. Jeffrey M. Masson, ed. and trans., *The Complete Letters of Sigmund Freud to Wilhelm Fliess, 1887–1904* (Cambridge, MA: Belknap Press, 1985), 264.

regard it as a universal event of early childhood. . . . If that is so, we can understand the riveting power of *Oedipus Rex*."³ As is well known, Freud abandoned the seduction theory in favor of exploring the nature of infantile sexuality and childhood fantasy.⁴ By placing the origins of psychic disorder in earliest childhood, Freud made the child a subject of investigation based upon adult symptomatology, establishing a developmental and ultimately teleological system for understanding psychic development: the Oedipal complex.

Rather than being physically victimized as in the seduction theory, children aggressively act out against the adults who both model and thwart their infantile desires. In a sense, then, Freud abandoned the opening act of the Oedipal narrative—the father's sexual violence and the victimized child as well—for the conclusion, wherein the adult becomes the object of the child's violence. Although the violence is both necessary but unconscious to the child, Freud's Oedipal complex isolates aggression in the child and obfuscates parental responsibility for that violence in much the same way *Oedipus Rex* seems to condemn Oedipus. Thus, the father's violence against the child and the necessity of that violence in constituting the patriarchal family is relocated from age to youth, from external world to internal fantasies, and from the social realm to the intrapsychic. Although critics have interrogated the gendered assumptions behind Freud's reading of Oedipus, few have taken into account the representation of age and life course in a story of gender, sexuality, and family violence, for the Sphinx's riddle inheres in the paradox of aging and of retaining identity or sameness within temporal difference.⁵ The answer to

---

3. Masson, *Complete Letters*, 272.

4. For a nuanced understanding of the development of Freud's *neurotica*, see Douglas A. Davis, "A Theory for the 90s: Freud's Theory of Traumatic Seduction in Historical Context," *Psychoanalytic Review* 81 (1994), 627–39. Zvi Lothane has provided the best analysis of Freud's "abandonment" of the seduction theory, including Jeffrey Masson's notorious *Assault on the Truth: Freud's Suppression of the Seduction Theory* (New York: Farrar Straus and Giroux, 1984) in "Freud's Alleged Repudiation of the Seduction Theory Revisited: Facts and Fallacies," *Psychoanalytic Review* 88.5 (October 2001): 673–723. The absolute repudiation of the seduction theory is due more to Anna Freud, Kurt Eissler, and those who perpetuated the "Freud myth" in contradistinction to Freud's own writings. Rather, "Freud clearly allows for the coexistence of seduction and infantile sexuality in his *Three Essays*" and throughout his writings, according to Lothane (693).

5. The field is vast. Jane Gallop's still relevant *The Daughter's Seduction: Feminism and Psychoanalysis* (Ithaca, NY: Cornell University Press, 1982) is a good starting point; Judith Butler's *Gender Trouble: Feminism and the Subversion of Identity* (New York: Routledge, 1990) has influenced the discussion since its appearance; Mary Jo Buhle's *Feminism and Its Discontents: A Century of Struggle with Psychoanalysis* (Cambridge, MA: Harvard University Press, 2000) examines the interrelationship of feminism and psychoanalytic theory in the American context; and Kelly Oliver and Lisa Walsh's *Contemporary French Feminism* (Oxford: Oxford University Press, 2004) takes up the question of "post-feminism."

the Sphinx's riddle—a human being—remains, but the puzzle finds its coherence in the aging human subject's ever-changing bodily form rather than any static, abstracted, atemporal human ideal. My analysis starts with the observation that the Oedipus narrative begins not with the child's violence against the parents, but with attempted infanticide. The father's violence scars the child and returns to the father to destroy the family and ultimately the state.

While the fate he suffers is tragic, Oedipus serves as a figure of humanistic enlightenment, the necessary triumph of the sovereign individual over ancient superstition. As Bernard Knox writes, when Oedipus answers the Sphinx's riddle with the single word, *anthropos* or *man*, "What is at stake in *Oedipus* . . . is Western humanism at large."[6] Oedipus stands as a figure of philosophy itself, for he is "the one who challenges sacred enigmas in order to establish the perspective of man and self," according to Jean-Joseph Goux.[7] Goux continues "that Oedipus is defined according to a new mode, one that could provisionally be called 'autological.' . . . Oedipus embodies an existence that defines itself self-referentially in an autoreflective, autoreferential, auto-ontological manner."[8] Oedipus stands as the paradigm of the isolated, rational subject, complete within himself.

For Freud as well, Oedipus illustrates a universal human impulse, and Freud, like Oedipus, has solved the riddle of the Sphinx—whose answer, *man* himself, indicates what it means to be fully human. In contrast, Emmanuel Levinas calls psychoanalysis "the end result of rationalism" and a discipline responsible for "fables" like the Oedipal complex that are unable to translate "a reality more profound than themselves."[9] For Levinas, Laius and Oedipus illustrate the inadequacy of traditional philosophical foundations, demonstrating "we are responsible beyond our intentions."[10] In Levinas's formulation,

---

6. Bernard Knox, "Sophocles' Oedipus," in *Tragic Themes in Western Literature*, ed. Cleanth Brooks (New Haven, CT: Yale University Press, 1955), 21.

7. Jean-Joseph Goux, *Oedipus, Philosopher*, trans. Catherine Porter (Stanford, CA: Stanford University Press, 1993), 3. For Sophocles in the humanistic tradition, see also, for example, C. H. Whitman, *Sophocles: A Study of Heroic Humanism* (Cambridge, MA: Harvard University Press, 1951). Walter Kaufmann's *Tragedy and Philosophy* helpfully distinguishes the uniqueness of *Oedipus Rex* among ancient accounts and notes Freud's inconsistent view of the play but still writes that "Freud is surely right on his main point; we are moved because Oedipus represents man, and his tragedy, the human condition" (Princeton, NJ: Princeton University Press, 1968), 108. Lowell Edmunds's introduction to his *Oedipus: The Ancient Legend and Later Analogues* (Baltimore: Johns Hopkins University Press, 1985), 1–46, surveys Oedipus in literature, philosophy, and the social sciences since the eighteenth century.

8. Goux, *Oedipus*, 134–35.

9. Emmanuel Levinas, "The *I* and the Totality," *Entre Nous: Thinking-of-the-Other*, trans. Michael B. Smith and Barbara Harshav (New York: Columbia University Press, 1998), 31 [13–38].

10. Levinas, "Is Ontology Fundamental?," *Entre Nous*, in *Entre Nous: Thinking-of-the-Other*, trans. Michael B. Smith and Barbara Harshav (New York: Columbia University Press, 1998), 3 [1–12].

"Laius, in attempting to thwart the fatal predictions, undertakes precisely what is necessary to fulfill them. Oedipus, in succeeding, works toward his own misfortune."[11] For Levinas, intentionality, epistemology, and ontology are inadequate bases for philosophy in light of the Holocaust, and rationality cannot in itself account for the fullness and diversity of human experience. In contrast to the egocentric tradition of Western humanism, Levinas proposes an "ethics as first philosophy" that regards our infinite responsibility to, and irreducible responsibility for, the other as antecedent to any philosophy: "The natural *conatus essendi* of a sovereign Self is questioned in the presence of the face of the other, in ethical vigilance."[12] According to Levinas's critique of the philosophical tradition, Freud's rationalistic "egology" qualifies as a form of humanism,[13] and in *Otherwise Than Being, Or Beyond Essence*, Levinas writes, "Humanism has to be denounced only because it is not sufficiently human."[14] Humanism and its compatriot, rationalism, yielded the Holocaust, so Levinas sought a foundation for philosophy outside the clutches of being. He found it in an ethics prior to epistemology or ontology, an an-archic and asymmetrical relationship to the other who calls us to responsibility through the nudity of the face.

Although a non-Oedipal reading of Oedipus seems nearly impossible in our post-Freudian world, fifteenth-century poet John Lydgate's *Siege of Thebes* depicts Edippus's full history, beginning with Layus's prayer for an heir, the patricidal prophecy, the riddle of the Sphinx, and Edippus's downfall through the internecine struggle between Edippus's sons that finally destroys Thebes. This essay reads John Lydgate's *Siege of Thebes* with Levinas against Freud's composite Oedipal narrative, for Lydgate's alternative Edippus provides a premodern lens with which to reexamine Freud's rationalistic thought. Lydgate's rendition in *Siege*, unlike Freud's, tells the whole story of Edippus, including his violent origin, the proliferation of this original violence in other forms, and its final familial, social, and political effects. The key is to read back into Freud Oedipus's prehistory, a childhood marked by violent displacement.[15] I maintain

---

11. Ibid.

12. Idem, "From the One to the Other: Transcendence and Time," in *Entre Nous: Thinking-of-the-Other*, trans. Michael B. Smith and Barbara Harshav (New York: Columbia University Press, 1998), 150 [133–54].

13. Peter Brook and Alex Woloch, eds., *Whose Freud? The Place of Psychoanalysis in Contemporary Culture* (New Haven, CT: Yale University Press, 2000), takes on this and similar questions.

14. Emmanuel Levinas, *Otherwise Than Being, Or Beyond Essence*, trans. Alphonso Lingis (Pittsburgh, PA: Duquesne University Press, 1998), 128.

15. It could be argued that violence names the single most important point of conceptual contrast between liberal humanistic and poststructuralist thought, such that we might say that, whereas humanism accepts the possibility of controlling or even eliminating violence through

that understanding the protagonist of *Oedipus Rex* as an enlightened though tragic hero is itself a pervasive humanistic myth, or more importantly, a misinterpretation, as is Freud's understanding, and these flaws become more readily visible in comparison with Lydgate's *Siege*. Crucially, the riddle of the Sphinx does not appear in Sophocles' play and, despite more than two millennia of commentary that finds with Aristotle that *Oedipus Rex* is a tragedy of fate, the play itself is ambiguous as to Laius's murderer(s). Instead, as Sandor Goodhart concludes, "Sophocles undertakes an examination of the logic that assumes Oedipus is the unique culprit.... Oedipus discovers he is guilty of parricide and incest... by voluntarily appropriating an oracular logic which assumes he has always already been guilty."[16] The logic that moves Oedipus to accept his guilt in *Oedipus Rex* parallels the Freudian move that finds adult symptomatology—as well as the ubiquity of the Oedipal complex—behind the veils of immemorial childhood. My reading of Lydgate's *Siege* begins with a brief consideration of Freud's strangely composite Oedipus, a figure only partially related to Sophocles' play, before turning to examine Lydgate's depiction of Edippus's infancy and youth, something missing in both Freud and Sophocles.[17] At the heart of this essay is my examination of the riddle of the Sphinx in the *Siege*, which is assumed but never explicitly rendered in Freud and Sophocles. Finally, I contrast Lydgate's final understanding of Edippus's crime with Freud's and Levinas's. Throughout the essay, I read the figure of the child Edippus in a Levinasian sense as a figure of ethical demand whose presence in Lydgate's *Siege* invites a reconsideration of Freud's Oedipal Everyman.

---

mediating, substitutionary, epistemic, and salvific mechanisms (contract, treaty, censorship, nation, reason, science), poststructuralism radically suggests that there is no "outside" to violence. It simply changes forms but is never eliminated. Thus, liberal humanism attempts to solve the problem of violence at its origin or stem it when it physically appears (a dually *originary* and *teleological* focus), while poststructuralism avers that violence is latent prior to its material expression and remains systemic after its seeming repression (an *an-archic* and *etiological* emphasis). Thus, Levinas's ethical phenomenology addresses the problem of intrinsic violence prior even to conceptualization. See, however, Jacques Derrida's famous rejoinder, "Violence and Metaphysics: An Essay on the Thought of Emmanuel Levinas," in *Writing and Difference*, trans. Alan Bass (Chicago: University of Chicago Press, 1978), 79–153.

16. Sandor Goodhart, "Lestas Ephaske: Oedipus and Laius' Many Murderers," in *Sacrificing Commentary: Reading the End of Literature* (Baltimore: Johns Hopkins University Press, 1996), 35 [13–42]. Frederick Ahl pursues related lines of inquiry in *Sophocles' Oedipus: Evidence and Self-Conviction* (Ithaca, NY: Cornell University Press, 1991). Girard's essays on Oedipus are collected in *Oedipus Unbound: Selected Writings on Rivalry and Desire*, ed. Girard and Mark R. Anspach (Stanford, CA: Stanford University Press, 2004).

17. A note on terminology: I will use the term "Oedipus" and "Oedipal" to refer to the modern, psychoanalytically informed theoretical construct but "Edippus" to refer to the protagonist of Lydgate's *Siege* (likewise Lauis/Layus, Jocasta/Iocasta). I will refer to Sophocles' *Oedipus* when discussing his play.

FREUD'S COMPOSITE OEDIPUS

Oedipus is guilty of incest and patricide, which become for Freud universal desires shaping the human psyche. In a famous passage, Freud writes:

> And there actually is a motive in the story of King Oedipus that explains the verdict of this inner voice. His fate moves us only because it might have been our own, because the oracle laid upon us before our birth the very curse which rested upon him. It may be that we were all destined to direct our first sexual impulses toward our mothers, and our first impulses of hatred and violence toward our fathers; our dreams convince us that we were. King Oedipus, who slew his father Laius and wedded his mother Jocasta, is nothing more or less than a wish-fulfillment—the fulfillment of the wish of our childhood.[18]

Freud's humanistic reading of *Oedipus Rex* is itself a self-fulfilling prophecy: The myth confirms the truth of his formulation, his formulation is confirmed in his observations, and his observations confirm and are confirmed by his understanding of the myth. But it is only because he selectively redacts the myth to confirm his theory, and he conforms to the humanistic tradition that has for millennia accepted the mythic violence that Sophocles' play seeks to interrogate.

In an analysis of Freud's library in London, Robin Mitchell-Boyask shows that Freud was fully familiar with the Oedipus myth in all its manifestations, not simply the Sophoclean version.[19] During the gestation of *The Interpretation of Dreams*, Freud carefully read a number of texts related to Oedipus, Greek culture, and the relationship of dreams to myth. Although Freud's primary Greek texts have disappeared from the library, depriving us the benefit of any notes he might have taken in the texts themselves, Freud cited J. C. Donner's German translation of Sophocles (1863) in *The Interpretation of Dreams*. Mitchell-Boyask notes that only one passage is marked in Donner, but it is vital—"Jocasta's assurances to Oedipus that all *men* dream of bedding their mothers (ll. 981–83 in Greek, 955–57 in Donner)":[20]

---

18. Sigmund Freud, *The Interpretation of Dreams*, vol. 4 of *The Standard Edition of the Complete Psychological Works of Sigmund Freud*, trans. James Strachey (London: Hogarth Press, 1958 [1900]), 262.

19. Robin Mitchell-Boyask, "Freud's Reading of Classical Literature and Classical Philology," in *Reading Freud's Reading*, ed. Sander L. Gilman, Jutta Birmele, and Jay Geller (New York: New York University Press, 1995), 23–46.

20. Ibid., 26 (emphasis mine).

> For many men have already seen also in dreams
> Themselves mated with mother: But who holds all this as
> Nothing, bears the burden lightly.[21]

Donner's translation significantly departs from the Greek in two important ways, according to Mitchell-Boyask. First, Donner "preserves the Greek's plural 'men' who dream about a singular 'mother,' thus increasing the effect of the universality of the paradigm." Second, Donner writes of "men *seeing themselves in dreams* doing such," rather than simply dreaming about it, adding "a level of mediating representation to the repressed wish for incest."[22] Mitchell-Boyask notes that the Oedipal desire for the (singular) mother in the dream-life of all men and the dream mechanism presented in Donner's German translation may have influenced *The Interpretation of Dreams*.[23] Ludwig Laistner likewise argued the connection between myths and dreams, particularly nightmares, in a well-read volume in Freud's library, *The Riddle of the Sphinx* (*Dai Ratsel der Sphinx*, 1889). For Laistner, as for Freud, the story of Oedipus and the Sphinx provides a model for all myth and myth's relationship to dreams.[24]

In addition to reading Donner and Laistner, Freud carefully examined Leopold Constans's *La Légende d'Oedipe: Étudiee dans l'antiquité, au moyen âge et dans les temps moderne en particuleir dans le Roman de Thébes, texte français du Xiie siècle* (1881). Mitchell-Boyask notes that Freud "underlined passages on almost every page" of Constans, who provided him with detailed readings of Oedipal traditions from ancient, medieval, and contemporary culture, including "Oedipus's name, Jocasta's age and Lauis's sexuality."[25] Constans also detailed the precursor to the Oedipal story proper, Laius's sexual violence against Pelops's son, Chrysippus, noting that Pelops curses Laius and suggests

---

21. "There is an unmistakable indication in the text of Sophocles' tragedy itself that the legend of Oedipus sprang from some primaeval dream-material which had as its content the distressing disturbance of a child's relation to his parents owing to the first stirrings of sexuality." See Freud, *Interpretation of Dreams*, 4:262. See also Freud's letter to Jung dated 11 November 1909 (Letter 160F) in William McGuire, ed., *The Freud/Jung Letters: The Correspondence between Sigmund Freud and C. C. Jung*, trans. Ralph Manheum and R.F.C. Hull (Princeton, NJ: Princeton University Press, 1974), 261.

22. Mitchell-Boyask, "Freud's Reading," 26 (emphasis in Mitchell-Boyask).

23. Ibid., 27.

24. Mitchell-Boyask cites Freud's 4 July 1901 letter to Fleiss, in which Freud notes that Laistner's "*The Riddle of the Sphinx* . . . very forcefully maintains that myths go back to dreams. . . . I see that he knows nothing of what is *behind* dreams; on the other hand, he appropriately seems to focus on the *anxiety* dream" (qtd. in ibid., 34, emphasis in Freud). Mitchell-Boyask notes that Freud seems to have minimized his real attention to Laistner since the letter comes after Fleiss and Freud's relationship had effectively collapsed.

25. Ibid., 32.

with the ancient sources that Juno sent the Sphinx to punish Laius's crime and cause his death.[26] Mitchell-Boyask suggests that Freud dropped the Laius prequel to emphasize the paradox of the individual freely choosing a divinely predetermined end and that Freud ignored the later effects of Laius's crimes because "the idea of the sins of the father being visited on the son would have violated Freud's focus on the fantasy life of the son."[27] Mitchell-Boyask concludes that Freud's Oedipus "was the result of long and careful deliberation . . . [allowing him to focus] on the experiences of the specifically Sophoclean hero and their implications for all individual men."[28] As a theorist, humanist, and heir of nineteenth-century scientific methods, Freud sought a universal paradigm, though his selective Oedipus is not strictly Sophoclean, and he reduced these multiple accounts simply to a paradigm of the same.

What Freud eliminated in his composite Oedipus is as significant as what he included, and these elisions have the character of unconscious, systematic repression. Freud knew of Laius's violence against Chrysippus and Oedipus, but they are both absent in his account of the myth. Freud thereby avoids a number of theoretical problems. Recognizing Laius's violence against Chrysippus and Oedipus would draw Freud back into the grasp of the seduction theory, for Oedipus's predicament could then be attributed to his father's physical violence. To maintain his theory, Freud therefore insulates Laius as an adult from Oedipus the infant, but allows the mature Oedipus freely to act upon Laius. Freud must narrow the social field of Oedipal interaction and denude it of its physical violence against the child to maintain the authority of the father. Freud thus minimizes an economy of paternal violence that begins with Laius's attack on Chrysippus, continues with his violence against Oedipus, and ultimately returns to a single moment of the violent and unknowing violence of a child against his father.

In describing childish enmity toward parents of the opposite sex in *The Interpretation of Dreams,* Freud writes, "In my opinion the sanctity with which we have endorsed the injunctions of the Decalogue dulls our perception of the reality [of childish rivalry and incestuous desire]. Perhaps we hardly dare permit ourselves to perceive that the greater part of humanity neglects to obey the fifth commandment [to honor thy father and thy mother]."[29] By casually invoking contemporary disregard for parents, Freud summons the violation of the fifth commandment as an analogue supporting his argument for

---

26. Ibid., 33.
27. Ibid.
28. Ibid.
29. Freud, *Interpretation of Dreams,* 4:256.

infantile aggression. At the same time, Freud ignores the second commandment and its assertion that children bear the consequences of their parents' behavior much in the same way he ignores Laius's violence against Chrysippus and its consequences for Oedipus. In both cases, Freud isolates the parents' actions from any violent impact upon their children while imputing to the children the violent desire to supplant their parents. In the same way he could not personally abide challenges to his authority from acolytes like Jung and Adler, Freud's theory cannot abide, even tacitly, "the iniquity of the fathers [visiting] upon the children, and upon the children's children, unto the third and to the fourth generation" (Exodus 34:7; see also Exodus 20:5, Deuteronomy 5:9).[30] Such an implication would place Freud's work within a theological discourse and undermine his claim for psychoanalysis's objective, scientific status. Simultaneously, Freud's ignoring the second commandment isolates the individual from sociopolitical causality. The individual remains isolated and free to act without censure or stricture, an autonomous and reasoning being. Paternal power and authority are benevolent for Freud, bestowed upon rebellious children for their own good, while violence is unidirectional from children to parents. Attributing to Oedipus the fallout from Laius's originary sexual violence would only lessen Oedipus's paradoxical triumph; attaching Oedipus's downfall to anyone but himself would alleviate him of responsibility for his own fate. Freud's figure of the father is powerful but detached, not violent but authoritative, not responsible for the consequences of his brutality but the recipient of murderous rivalry. Laius and Jocasta are Oedipus's victims. Freud invokes elements of the Decalogue and ignores others as suits his purposes.[31]

That Freud studied *La Légende d'Oedipe* is significant for the purposes of this essay because Constans's study attends significantly to the twelfth-century medieval French *Roman de Thèbes*. Likely written at the court of Henry II and Eleanor of Aquitaine, *Le Roman de Thebès* (c. 1150) expands Statius's classical *Thebiad* by adding a prequel, the story of Oedipus. John Lydgate, Chaucer's fifteenth-century heir, seems to have worked from two later prose redactions of *Le Roman de Thebès*, the *Roman de Edipus* and the *Hystoire de Thebes*, in his

---

30. The best reading of Freud's personal relationships in light of their Oedipal dimensions is Peter L. Rudnytsky, *Freud and Oedipus* (New York: Columbia University Press, 1987).

31. Freud's vexed relationship to Judaism is, of course, the subject of intense discussion. For a recent theoretically informed examination, see Jay Geller, *On Freud's Jewish Body: Mitigating Circumcisions* (New York: Fordham University Press, 2007). Sander L. Gilman's *Freud, Race, and Gender* (Princeton, NJ: Princeton University Press, 1995) is an important starting point for understanding Freud's Judaism in the context of Western anti-Semitism. See also Peter Gay's *A Godless Jew: Freud, Atheism, and the Making of Psychoanalysis* (New Haven, CT: Yale University Press, 1989).

Siege of Thebes (c. 1421–22).³² Although Lydgate's *Siege* does not extend as far back as Lauis, Pelops, and Chrysippus, Lydgate incorporates Edippus's history and reaches back to the vexed founding of Thebes.³³ Imagined as the first tale on the return trip from Canterbury and as a companion to Chaucer's *Knight's Tale*, Lydgate's *Siege* consists of four parts: In the Prologue(ll. 1–176) Lydgate joins the Canterbury pilgrimage; part 1 (ll. 177–1046) depicts the story of Edippus, and parts 2 (ll. 1047–2552) and 3 (ll. 2553–4716) detail the rivalry of Edippus's sons, Eteocles and Polynieces, for the throne, a conflict which ultimately leads to the destruction of Thebes. For the purposes of this essay, I want to focus on part 1, the story of Edippus.

EDIPPUS IN LYDGATE'S *SIEGE OF THEBES*

The son's violence against the father and his desire for the mother form the core of Freud's Oedipal complex, but Lydgate's story of Edippus in *Siege of Thebes* demonstrates how Lauis's own death and the eventual destruction of Thebes begins with a father's willful and intentional violence against his infant son. More precisely, the *Siege* opens with a threatened lineage, a divinely aided conception, and a botched attempt at child murder.³⁴ With a barren queen, Iocasta,

---

32. See Robert R. Edwards's introduction to *John Lydgate: The Siege of Thebes* (Kalamazoo, MI: Medieval Institute Publications, 2001), available online at <http://www.lib.rochester.edu/camelot/teams/thebint.htm>. John M. Bowers's electronic edition of *The Prologue to the Siege of Thebes* (from BL Arundel 119, fols. 1a–4a), fascinating for its reimagining of Chaucer's Canterbury pilgrimage, is available online at <http://www.lib.rochester.edu/camelot/teams/lydgtint.htm>. See *John Lydgate's Prologue to the* Siege of Thebes, *The Canterbury Tales: Fifteenth-Century Continuations and Additions*, ed. John M. Bowers (Kalamazoo, MI: Medieval Institute Publications, 1992).

33. With renewed interest in fifteenth-century English literature, Lydgate is enjoying a renaissance. Recent examples include Robert J. Meyer-Lee, *Poets and Power from Chaucer to Wyatt* (Cambridge: Cambridge University Press, 2007); Nigel Mortimer, *John Lydgate's "Fall of Princes": Narrative Tragedy in Its Literary and Political Contexts* (Oxford: Clarendon Press, 2005); and Maura Nolan, *John Lydgate and the Making of Public Culture* (Cambridge: Cambridge University Press, 2005). These extend considerably the standard studies of Walter F. Schirmer, *John Lydgate: A Study in the Culture of the Fifteenth Century* (Berkeley: University of California Press, 1961); Alain Renoir, *The Poetry of John Lydgate* (Cambridge, MA: Harvard University Press, 1967); and Derek Pearsall, *John Lydgate* (Charlottesville: University Press of Virginia, 1970). An important study of Lydgate's *Siege* is Dominique Battles's *The Medieval Tradition of Thebes: History and Narrative in the OF Roman de Thebes, Boccaccio, Chaucer, and Lydgate* (New York: Routledge, 2004), 144–74.

34. Lydgate also touches briefly upon the Oedipus story in his *Fall of Princes* (1430–38) (part 1, ll. 3130–843), composed after the *Siege* (1420–22). Following his source, Boccaccio's *De casibus virorum illustrium* (1355–60), Lydgate embeds Oedipus within the story of Queen Iocasta: "Off all princessis which euer stood in staat, / She was hirselff the moste infortunat" (ll. 3170–71) because she lost her son, unknowingly married him, and then lost her two

and lacking an heir, Layus, king of Thebes, offers a sacrifice and implores the gods that "he be not defrauded of His bone" (353).[35] After the gods answer Layus's prayers and Iocasta conceives a son, Layus summons advisors from across the kingdom to learn the "Chyldes fate and disposicioun" (368), and the king hears the prophecy that the child eventually will slay his father (398). He then commands Iocasta to kill the boy at birth "With-oute Mercy or moderly pyte" (405).[36] Unable to kill the child herself, Iocasta, "with wooful herte and pitous loke / And face pale" (409–10), sends the neonate away and charges servants to ensure his death. Seeing the child's "excellent beaute" (421), the servants instead abandon the infant in the forest, hanging him from a tree by pierced feet (428) and leaving his fate to "fortune" (434). "Seeing" brings the potential murderers face to face with a newborn child, and according to Levinas, the nakedness of the face issues the injunction "thou shalt not kill," calling forth responsibility for the other.[37] As Levinas writes in "Diachrony and Representation," "The commandment [against murder] here does not proceed from a force. It comes—in the guise of the face of the other—as the renunciation of coercion, as a renunciation of its force and of all omnipotence."[38] The nakedness of the face is multiplied in the visage of a helpless infant Edippus, and the hardened henchmen "beholden the fairnesse / Of the Chyld" (420–21), agreeing without "stryfe / That the child shulde han his life" (423–24). Seeing the traumatized child, the henchmen spare his life and take responsibility for Edippus.

Not only do those ordered to kill the newly born Edippus spare his life, they provide for his well being, at least marginally. As opposed to killing a child purposefully (infanticide), those who exposed or abandoned a child in ancient and medieval culture allowed for—and often expected—the child's rescue. Placing

---

grandsons. However, even here, Lydgate does not dwell on the consequences of incest. Elizabeth Archibald notes that "it is the political consequences of his story rather than the personal ones that seem to have fascinated medieval writers, Statius' version rather than that of the tragedians" (*Incest and the Medieval Imagination* [Oxford: Clarendon Press, 2001], 73).

35. All citations to the *Siege of Thebes* are from John Lydgate, *Lydgate's Siege of Thebes*, ed. Axel Erdmann and Eilert Ekwall, EETS e.s. 108 and 125 (London: Oxford University Press, 1911 and 1920). Line numbers are indicated parenthetically in the text.

36. Some ancient sources attribute the curse on Laius to Pelops, Chrysippus's father, who declaims, "May you never have a son, and if you do, may he kill you" (Edmunds, *Oedipus*, 7).

37. *The face* organizes a core thematic throughout Levinas's work. See, for example, "The face to face situation is thus an impossibility of denying, a negation of a negation. The double articulation of this formula means concretely: the 'thou shalt not murder' is inscribed on the face and constitutes its very otherness" ("The *I* and the Totality," *Entre Nous*, 34–35). See also his *Totality and Infinity: An Essay on Exteriority*, trans. Alphonso Lingis (Pittsburgh, PA: Duquesne University Press, 1969), 187–220.

38. Levinas, "Diachrony and Representation," *Entre Nous*, in *Entre Nous: Thinking-of-the-Other*, trans. Michael B. Smith and Barbara Harshav (New York: Columbia University Press, 1998), 172 [159–78].

a child in a tree protected against animal attacks, while leaving an infant at a crossroads increased the opportunities that it might be found.[39] A hunting party from a neighboring kingdom hears Edippus crying, finds him, and presents him to Polyboun, the king of Archadye, who immediately assigns the infant a wet nurse and commands physicians to care for his injuries. Facing an heirless kingdom himself, Polyboun adopts the foundling as his own (462) and provides for Edippus's needs. There is perhaps no more simple an illustration of the "asymmetrical relationship to the other" than an infant who is, to use another Levinasian trope, "hostage."[40] Layus holds the power of life and death over the child, yet the infant Edippus also draws Polyboun to responsibility and relationship. Polyboun calls the unnamed child "Edippus," Lydgate explains, because the term means "Bored the feete as in that langage" (454). Edippus's name, scar, and identity—his embodied subjectivity—bear the trace of his father's violence. In the *Siege*, the king's minions see Edippus and spare his life (420-21), while Polyboun has pity on Edippus "whan that he first þe child gan See, / Of his woundes" (449-50). The orphan, the widow, and the stranger epitomize for Levinas those others for whom openness and hospitality must be extended, and there is perhaps no orphan in history more renowned than Oedipus.

By eliminating Laius's transgression and its subsequent effects, Freud isolates Oedipus from his social and historical context. In a sense, Freud's Oedipus seems never to be physically born. He appears *ex nihilo* as in Sophocles, and we (and he) only hear his history. Freud's Oedipal infant is also strangely disembodied, a child who exists only in his violent desire and infantile fantasies. In contrast, Lydgate's Edippus experiences dual births. He is first physically born into the royal family and then "born" a second time in violence in the forest, and the *Siege* shows ethics and violence to be inversely related in Edippus's dual natalities. Violence begins with Layus, in the upper social strata, proceeds through Iocasta, and indelibly marks Edippus, with Layus's responsibility neither avoided nor rationalized away as in Freud. Iocasta is not an inert object of incestuous desire but defies her husband, the king, for the benefit of the child. Edippus himself is not a passive object but elicits sympathy from his mother and the henchmen, calling them into ethical relation. Finally, this chain of social deferrals descends from the royal family down the Theban class structure until the socially lowest character, a shepherd, accepts responsibility for the mysterious foundling and conveys the child to the adjacent kingdom. In Levinasian terms, the fate of the helpless orphan resides in

---

39. See John Eastburn Boswell, *The Kindness of Strangers: The Abandonment of Children in Western Europe from Late Antiquity to the Renaissance* (New York: Pantheon, 1988), 24–26, for a concise differentiation of the terms "exposure" and "abandonment."

40. See, for example, Levinas, "Diachrony and Representation," *Entre Nous*, 168.

the third party: initially the queen, then the henchmen who disobey the royal commands, the shepherd who intervenes, and then the neighbor who takes responsibility for the Theban royal family's abdication of responsibility.[41]

In the same way that Edippus's personal origins are doubled, so too the double founding of Thebes is fraught with violence and ambiguity in Lydgate's *Siege*, intimately joining the power of the state with the constitution of childhood and revealing the relationship of language and violence. Uniquely in medieval accounts, Lydgate incorporates two separate Theban origin stories. In the first, King Amphioun sings Thebes into existence with "his wordes swete" (229), and in the second, Cadmus plots the boundary of Thebes "With thong out-korve of a boolys hyde" (299). Stretched to their limit, the parchment-like strips enclose "a ful large space / Wher-vp-on to byld a dwellyng place" (301–2). If Amphioun represents the monarch who raises a kingdom through personal integrity and prudent rhetoric through the help of Mercury, "god of Eloquence" (215), then Cadmus indicates the ruler who dominates his territory through conquest and physical violence. Amphioun represents culture and refinement, but Cadmus embodies the savagery of humanity's dominance over nature. In recording both origin stories, Lydgate gives the impression that Amphioun's ascendancy through language motivates Thebes's greatness, but he submerges the story of Cadmus, which is recorded only in a few old sources. However, this contrast between Amphioun's "eloquence" and Cadmus's "savagery" hides a deeper etiological violence, for Lydgate then reveals that these two seemingly independent accounts actually depict a conflict over succession and control of young Thebes. Amphioun the rhetor ultimately exiles Cadmus (306–10) the warrior, much in the same way Layus casts out Edippus, his young rival to the throne. Theban history is from the outset a narrative of rivalry, aggression, and expulsion where eloquence masks an underlying brutality and political violence masquerades as rhetoric. Layus tries to avoid the inevitable succession of monarchy—that his son, as his heir, ultimately will replace him—and the "natural" consequence of patriarchal kingship, while violating the "natural" bonds of fatherhood.

Edippus's personal origin mirrors the fraught, conflictual stories of Thebes's founding, and the beautiful though scarred child grows up to be a haughty, temperamental youth. Lydgate, unlike Sophocles and Freud, narrates

---

41. In Levinas's articulation, "the second" is the other who draws me into responsibility and ethical subjectivity and to whom I am asymmetrically obligated, but "the order of justice of individuals responsible for one another does not arise in order to restore that reciprocity between the *I* and its other; it arises from the fact of the third who, next to the one who is an other to me, is 'another another' to me" ("The Other, Utopia, and Justice," *Entre Nous*, in *Entre Nous: Thinking-of-the-Other*, trans. Michael B. Smith and Barbara Harshav (New York: Columbia University Press, 1998), 229 [223–33]).

Edippus's youth, and unlike the Sophoclean Oedipus, who hears at a drunken banquet that he was a foundling, a playmate confronts Lydgate's Edippus about his ignoble, unknown past. The playmate declares that Edippus acts

> As thow were lord of vs everichon,
> And presumest fully in wyrchyng [your deeds],
> Lik as [as if] thow were sone vnto the kyng,
> And descended of His Royal blood?
> But wher so be thow wroth [angry] or wood [mad],
> Thow art no thing, and thow list [wish] take hede,
> Appartenyng [belonging] vnto his kynrede [kindred],
> But in a Forest founded and vnknowne,
> whan thow were ȝonge. thefore [sic] bere the low [humble yourself]!
> And vtterly remembre, ȝif the lyst,
> Thy byrth and blood ar bothe two vnwist [unknown].
> (488–94)

This playground taunt, a surprisingly realistic detail unknown in Sophocles, reveals that everyone but Edippus knows of his lowly origin, and the playmate warns Edippus: "You boss us around like you were the son of the king, but you're an orphan, a foundling, a nothing. So quit acting above your station and remember that your birth and bloodline are unknown and, therefore, you yourself are suspect." Putative heir to the throne, though not the throne of his birth, the youthful Edippus finds he has misrecognized his own identity and is radically severed from his origins. Unlike the autonomous hero of Freud and Sophocles' account—the rational man who knows himself fully and marks the inauguration of the humanistic subject—Lydgate's Edippus is "vnwist." His peers know more about his identity than he does himself, and they see him as an interloper. Lydgate's Edippus is nothing more than a foundling, and his natal abandonment has left him, in effect, a nonsubject: "Thow art no thing" (489). In the eyes of his peers, he is a cipher whose regal bearing belies his violent origin. The playmate's insult articulates the insoluble paradox of Edippus's ever-displaced identity. Edippus must *remember* that his birth and heritage are both "vnwist" or *unknown* (494). His subjectivity is marked by absence, not plenitude, and shifting social ties, not autonomy.

It is at the blurred intersection of memory, origin, and lineage that Edippus's subjectivity unfolds as the haunting term "unwist" rises to the surface of the narrative. The aporia of memory sends Edippus upon his quest for identity. Shaken by his playmates' accusation, Edippus implores Polyboun for the truth, and though the king attempts to lie, he "ceriously [in order]" (526) tells

Edippus the story of his discovery in the forest. Edippus then implores Appollo to reveal "of what kynrede that he was discendyd" (550), and in a Christianizing twist appropriate to Lydgate, an invisible fiend (553) sends Edippus to Thebes for the truth. Edippus's search for his heritage is simultaneously a search for subjectivity, and as Lydgate puts it, "a name" (571). The Sophoclean drama, like Freud's Oedipal theory, is teleologically determined. For Freud, Oedipus is always already guilty in the same way that all individuals must navigate the Oedipal complex. The Sophoclean Oedipus gradually recognizes the path he has already taken, but only in hindsight, and the audience experiences his horror as the play moves forward narratively while the truth moves rearward from an established telos. In contrast, the *Siege* depicts Edippus's active pursuit of a subjectivity that he can only know through approaching others who have been responsible for him.

In his abjection after leaving Arcady for Thebes, Edippus sits at the nexus of two competing social formations through which he might be subjected: birth and prowess. Traditionally in the Middle Ages, cultural position and social advancement—indeed, even personal identity—were obtained through birth into family, but by the end of the fourteenth and beginning of the fifteenth century, traditional forms of cultural affiliation were being replaced by associational alliances based upon common vocation, burgeoning new economic affiliation, or other nontenure forms of coalition. In other words, "prowess"—whether at court, guildhall, or market—competes with "birth" to shape personal identity and establish social relationships. Unlike the Sophoclean Oedipus, who ultimately believes he kills Laius after a chance meeting at a crossroads, exactly the kind of place that a foundling might be exposed to the mercy of a passing traveler, Lydgate's Edippus enters a "tornement" (566) at Castle Pylotes on the road to Thebes where many a youthful, courageous knight might "preue [prove] hem-silf . . . / by force" (569–70) or "gete a name thorgh his hegh prouesse [prowess]" (571). Here the medieval setting of Lydgate's *Siege* asserts itself, but productively so in relation to the Freudian Oedipus. Arising in the twelfth and thirteenth centuries, the tournament provided military training and inculcated a chivalric ethos, and though they "were very rough occasions, only just distinguishable from real battle," according to Maurice Keen, tournaments were also organized, legally sanctioned, and often spectacular public affairs "of individual prowess in which prizes and renown could be won."[42] Unlike the chaotic encounter at the Phocial crossroads in

---

42. Maurice Keen, *Chivalry* (New Haven, CT: Yale University Press, 1984), 85, 100. See also Keen's *Nobles, Knights, and Men-at-Arms in the Middle Ages* (London: Hambledon, 1996) and Richard W. Kaueper, *Chivalry and Violence in Medieval Europe* (Oxford: Oxford University Press, 1999). For the English context, see especially Juliet Barker, *The Tournament in England 1100–1400*

Freud and Sophocles, medieval tournaments were official events that served important social, political, and cultural functions. Edippus was no highwayman reacting violently to a roadside affront, as in Sophocles or as understood by Freud. Lydgate's Edippus was playing by the chivalric rules when, in the heat of battle and "in the pres of aventure he mette / Kyng layvus and cruelly him slogh" (580–81). Edippus secures by superior ability what he already, and unknowingly, holds by descent, and his martial abilities accord with his political potential. Edippus kills Layus not at a crossroads, in a public and open place of symbolic passage, but in a regulated and regulating, enclosed and circumscribed space. Edippus and Iocasta then marry not simply because of his heroism before the Sphinx or his intelligence in answering the riddle, but because the "lordes" of the town "set a parlement" (763–64) to ask Iocasta "to condescende be way of Mariage, / She to be Ioyned to this manly knight" (768–69). In Lydgate's *Siege*, their union is politically sanctioned—socially constrained and not individually chosen—although in Freud the marriage is taboo from the beginning because Freud supplies even what the text of *Oedipus Rex* leaves ambiguous.

What is fascinating here is that despite the centrality of the Sphinx to Freud's Oedipal schema and the importance of the Sphinx to *Oedipus Rex*, Sophocles makes only oblique reference to the monster and never narrates the Sphinx's riddle. Oedipus narrates his victory over the Sphinx to the Chorus, but the substance of the riddle remains unspoken, unlike Freud, who imports the Sphinx's riddle to the Sophoclean account. Of the three, only Lydgate's *Siege* narrates the encounter with the Sphinx in full.[43]

EDIPPUS ANSWERS THE SPHINX

Lydgate's *Siege*, like its source texts, anticipates the centrality of the riddle to Oedipus's story and narrates it in full, unlike Freud and Sophocles. The persistent series of oppositions between nature and culture in the *Siege* culminates in this crucial moment, for the Sphinx's challenge presents the

---

(Woodbridge, Suffolk: Boydell and Brewer, 2003) and Sheila Lindenbaum, "The Smithfield Tournament of 1390," *Journal of Medieval and Renaissance Studies* 20:1 (1990), 1–20.

43. For Freud, the Sphinx becomes a signifier of ambivalent (infantile) sexuality in general. In letters to Jung, Freud writes on 14 April 1907 of a patient, "He is a highly gifted individual, an Oedipus type, loves his mother, hates his father (the original Oedipus was himself a case of obsessional neurosis—the riddle of the Sphinx), has been ill since his eleventh year when the facts of sexuality were revealed to him" (Letter 20F), and on 21 November 1909 Freud writes of the Sphinx in relation to "the castration complex": "Oedipus, I believe I have told you means swollen foot, i.e., erected penis" (Letter 163F). See McGuire, *Freud-Jung Letters*, 33 and 265–66.

relationship between language and violence, figured as a separation between nature (physical brutality) and culture (narrative interpretation). In the same way that Cadmus's savagery and Amphioun's poetry are not two competing etiologies but intimately intertwined in a struggle for succession, so too the Sphinx's riddle, while attempting to separate language and violence, reveals their intimate complicity. Language is not a substitute for violence, but an extension of it. The Sphinx slays

> all that diden fayle
> To expowne his mysty dyvynaile [mysterious saying/riddle],
> His problem ek in wordes pleyn and bare
> With-oute avys [consultation] opynly to declare,
> Or with the life he myghte not eskape.
> (629–33)

There is no neutral language in Edippus's encounter with the *Siege*'s masculine Sphinx, another difference from Freud and *Oedipus Rex*, where the Sphinx's femininity contributes to its otherness. The word is either "mysty" or "pleyn," and both are deadly. If Edippus fails to meet the Sphinx's discursive challenge, he will be killed; if Edippus correctly interprets the riddle, the Sphinx will be slain. In an eruption of linguistic hubris, Edippus declares:

> But truste wel for al they sleghty [sly] wit,
> Thy false fraude shal anon be qwyt [answered/repaid]
> Me list [wish] not nowe whisper neither rowne [speak softly],
> But thy problem [riddle] I shal anon expowne [explain]
> So openly thouw shal not go ther-fro.
> (693–97)

Familiar to readers of *The Canterbury Tales*, "quiting" organizes the First Fragment and disrupts the social order of the tale-telling contest as the Miller quits the Knight, the Reeve quits the Miller, and the Cook concludes the opening series of *Canterbury Tales*.[44] Edippus's quit is as aggressive as any in *The Canterbury Tales*, but unlike the Sophoclean Oedipus who decisively answers the Sphinx with a single word (*anthropos*, or man), Lydgate's Edippus "expounds"

---

44. Lydgate uses the Middle English verb "quiten" to describe Edippus's battle of wits with the Sphinx, which indicates answering, requiting, or getting even with, though its general senses also include (1) to pay or pay for, (2) to reward, or (3) to take revenge on or overmatch. Chaucer uses the term in the First Fragment of the *Canterbury Tales* (the Knight's, Miller's, Reeve's, and Cook's tales) where "quiting" identifies a mode of social disruption and personal antagonism.

(696) and provides a "preef" (649) of his interpretation, thereby overcoming the monster interpretively before he does so physically by giving a "cleer exposicioun" (635).⁴⁵ In the *Siege*, Edippus's hermeneutic demands go beyond solving the riddle with a single word, as in the ancient sources. Lydgate's Edippus is very much a textual interpreter rather than conceptual philosopher, and his explanation is descriptive, experiential, and phenomenological rather than conceptually abstract and generalized.

In the *Siege's* version of the well-known puzzle, the Sphinx describes "a beest merveilous to se" (659) that at its birth cannot "sustene" itself on its feet (662). As the beast develops, it "makeþ his passage" (666) on four feet, and then three feet, until it is finally upright upon two. After "many sondry ʒeeres / Naturely" (670) in the course of time, "he goth aʒeyn on thre, / And sith on four" (671–72) until "he retourneth kyndely [returns naturally] ageyn / To the matere which that he kam fro" (675–76). Edippus's answer is more than just "man," an abstract and universal construct. It is the developing human being in all her temporal complexity, biological heterogeneity, social immediacy, and bodily fragility, and Edippus's interpretation ranges across the life span from birth until death:

Thilke best thouw spak of herto-forn,
Is euery man in this world yborn,
Which may not gon his lymes be so softe,
Bot as his moder bereth him alofte
In her armes, whan he doth crye and wepe.
(699–703)

Simply put, a human being is never simply one thing, divorced from individual history and social reality. The key link in each aspect of human development is the fact of locomotion or movement—rather than the mind or being—and what feet can and cannot do. Dasein arises in movement, in *falling* or *throwness,* so Heidegger considers "the problem of motion is grounded on the question about the essence of beings as such."⁴⁶ In his critique of Heidegger, however, Levinas stresses that the an-archic relation to the other antecedes

---

45. The *Middle English Dictionary* lists several references to Lydgate's works under "preve," all from *The Fall of Princes*. For example (3.155): "Wherfore Bochas heeroff to make a preeff sheweth. A cleer exauple" [(2[a]) "demonstration of the truth of a proposition, belief, or statement by logical reasoning, evidence"] and (6.1384): "His owne kyn.With venymous drynk set on hym espies. Of ther fell poisoun for to make a preeff. Hym to moordre" [(4[a]) "test of the quality or effectiveness of a substance, the veracity of a statement"].

46. From Heidegger's 1930 lectures in *Vom Wesen der menschlichen Freieit. Einleitung in die Philosophie,* ed. H. Tietjen (Frankfurt: Klosterman, 1982), 31:31, cited in Michael Inwood, *A Heidegger Dictionary* (London: Blackwell, 1999), 134.

being or essence, and Edippus's description of the infant here demonstrates that the self is irreducibly social and locomotive; the self arises only in relationship to the other to whom we are indebted. Unable to carry themselves, infants are borne up in their mothers' arms and comforted when they cry. Infants are not able to survive alone; they are dependent upon their others. This is the typical pattern, and Sophocles' Oedipus, like Freud's, understands himself to be the answer and physical embodiment of the Sphinx's riddle. Crucially here, in contrast to the humanistic reading of the Oedipal tradition, Lydgate's Edippus *cannot* himself stand in for the universal human, the sovereign isolated subject, because his own experience in the *Siege* fails to measure up to the ideal set by the riddle. Edippus was *not* hefted lovingly and comforted in his mother's arms because he was condemned by his father, expelled by his mother, abandoned as a newborn, and left immobile—turned into a thing—and exposed to die, or by chance to live. Edippus, the one who ultimately searches for his origins, begins life crippled and disabled, his gait clumsy. As Peter Stallybrass writes, "For him [Oedipus], walking does not come naturally. It remains a problem. Oedipus, not having perfect balance, stages the strangeness and difficulty of the balancing act that walking presupposes. For him, walking is haunted by loss of balance, by slips, falls, lameness, the stiffening of joints. In fact, the riddle of the Sphinx simplifies the difficulty of walking."[47] Most pointedly, then, Lydgate's Edippus brings to the Sphinx's riddle the difference that reality makes and the scars the history produces in an individual life rather than in the generalized experience of all humanity.

Edippus continues his explication of the riddle and of human development:

He gynneth forto crepe
On foure feet in his tendre ʒouth,
B'experience [According to experience] as it is ofte kouth [known],
Aforn yrekned his hondes bothe two.
(704–7)

From an abstracted point of view, it could be said that young children first become mobile by crawling on four feet. However, Edippus demonstrates that infants actually go on two feet and two hands. The Sphinx's riddle is clever, to a point, but it distorts the developmental process and fails to account for the

---

47. See Peter Stallybrass, "The Mystery of Walking," *Journal of Medieval and Early Modern Studies* 32.3 (2002), 571 [571–80]. Kalliopi Kikolopoulou notes, "Feet and fate seem to be curiously related in the ancient Greek tradition," for "Oedipus's fate is inscribed bodily in the injury of his feet, an injury that in turn is inscribed in his very name . . . 'swollen foot,'" in "Feet, Fate, and Finitude: On Standing and Inertia in the *Iliad*," *College Literature* 34.2 (2007), 175 [174–93].

subtleties of locomotion. The riddle has a conceptual relationship to human experience, but it is devoid of any embodied reality. It is, like the Sphinx itself, monstrous.

Edippus's interpretation indicates the riddle's inherent inadequacy and demonstrates that the Sphinx, though clever and vicious, does not speak from a position of understanding or accurate knowledge about human beings. (He is, after all, a monstrous Sphinx.) Edippus's explication continues inexorably as he *schools* the Sphinx about the constantly shifting temporal embeddedness and biological heterogeneity of human development. A pedagogical *tour-de-force,* Edippus's tone here is mocking and condescending, and the language insistent and accusatory:

> And by processe [in time], *thow* mayst consider also
> With his two fete, for al thy felle tene [hatred],
> He hath a staf hym-seluen to sustene,
> And than he goth shortly upon thre.
> And alther-last [at last], as it most nedes be,
> Voyding his staf, he walketh upon tweyn,
> Til it so he thorgh age he atteyn,
> That lust [vigor] of ȝouthe wasted be and spent;
> Than in his hond he taketh a potent [staff],
> And on thre feet thus he goth ageyn.
> (698–717, emphasis mine)

Resituating the Sphinx in history, in temporality, "by process," here has a wonderfully productive ambiguity, and both possibilities indict the Sphinx's philosophical presumptiveness and attack his knowledge. On one hand, as time passes infants may use walking sticks to steady their steps and then outgrow them until the infirmities of age call again for assistance. On the other, the Sphinx may have to take the time to reassess himself and his puzzle despite his hatred for humanity. Edippus here reverses the order of precedence and power, for now the Sphinx must reconsider his own formulation of the violent riddle and, by extension, himself. "By processe," or according to progression in time and narrative explication, Edippus has interpretively weighed the Sphinx and found him wanting. Even the seeming repetitions are actually distinctions, for a young person goes on three legs (or uses a staff) for very different reasons and manners than an older person. Against the diversity that marks individual human development, Edippus shows the Sphinx and his riddle to be fatally flawed because it is the Sphinx who rationalizes all human development into a single universal paradigm, reducing the many to the one.

Why the Sphinx would kill itself (or allow itself to be killed) is opaque in Sophocles and the ancient sources, and goes unmentioned in Freud, but Lydgate's Edippus offers a tenable reason: shame. Edippus's exposition of the riddle condemns the Sphinx like a *magister* might instruct an arrogant student and reduce him to powerlessness. Not only has Edippus solved the riddle, but he has also revealed the Sphinx's inadequacy, shamed its lack of understanding, and revealed its insipid self-delusion. Edippus finally drives the lesson home, emphasizing "*I* dar afferme *thow* maist it not withseyn [contradict]" (my emphasis), and repeating "B'experience as euery man may knowe" (721). The inhuman Sphinx has no social bonds or family relations, nor does he possess a developmental and temporal history. He is, traditionally, a pastiche of different species. He is no man. He has observed humanity only from the outside, so he cannot truly understand even his own riddle. When the "problem fully is expowned" (736) by Edippus, the Sphinx stands "awapyd and amaat" [amazed and overwhelmed] (741) and "disamayed and dysconsolaat" (742). In the wake of the Sphinx's discursive defeat, Edippus easily dispatches the monster. Edippus unites Amphioun's eloquence and Cadmus's violence.

Edippus's description of human aging is enfolded within an interpretation of the Sphinx's riddle that is *allegorized* rather than *universalized*.[48] In contrast to the ancient Oedipus's epiphany so important for Sophocles, Freud, and the humanist tradition, Edippus's "qwyt" serves a *pedagogical* function as it shames the Sphinx, and also performs an *allegorical* function as it interprets the riddle. Gordon Teskey writes, "The very word *allegory* evokes a schism in consciousness—between a life and a mystery, between the real and the ideal, between a literal tale and its moral—which is repaired, or at least concealed, by imagining a hierarchy which ascends toward truth."[49] The Sphinx's riddle

---

48. Because the Greek *agora* could refer to either the public marketplace or an exclusive assembly, allegory itself contains the contradictory impulses of guarded private speech within the public sphere, often the province of marginalized groups, or elitist speech apart from the commons, often the product of powerful factions. See Ann W. Astell's *Political Allegory in Late Medieval England* (Ithaca, NY: Cornell University Press, 1999), 8.

49. Gordon Teskey, *Allegory and Violence* (Ithaca, NY: Cornell University Press, 1996), 2 (emphasis in Teskey). Allegory is a vexed category with as many definitions as expositors, ranging from Northrop Frye's claim that all interpretation is allegorical (*Anatomy of Criticism: Four Essays* [Princeton, NJ: Princeton University Press, 1957], 89) to the common medieval understanding of the four-fold senses of Christian scripture (the literal, allegorical, moral, and anagogical senses). Allegory is generally seen as a two-level phenomenon in which the aspects "within" the text reference details "outside" of the text. At the same time, the dual senses of allegory that seem to expand the text's interpretive possibilities simultaneously expose features that work against these allegorical readings. Jon Whitman's anthology *Interpretation and Allegory: Antiquity to the Modern Period* (Leiden: Brill, 2000) provides an excellent overview of recent thinking, especially A. J. Minnis's contribution, "*Quadruplex Sensus, Multiplex Modus:*

stands as a figure of the developing human being, the temporal subject in its constantly changing physical constitution and social affinities, but not of Edippus's own life. Simultaneously, the temporal heterogeneity of the physical subject, those differing bodily manifestations that occur "be process of age" in Lydgate's terms (665), is ameliorated not because of its universality but by its nonidentical relation to itself and to others in the natural world, relationships that cannot be transcended. Unlike the Sophoclean Oedipus, Lydgate's Edippus describes not a sovereign subject, transcending history and immune to the ravages of nature, but an *exemplary* one in the best medieval sense: one whose experience merits imitation or avoidance, moral approbation or censure. By following the narrative of human development from birth through death, from nature to nature, Edippus has "expowned" the Sphinx's riddle (735), his elegant interpretation putting the Sphinx to shame. If there is castration in the *Siege*'s account of Edippus, it names the inadequacy of disembodied knowledge unhinged from temporal human experience. It calls such abstracted comprehension monstrous. Unlike Freud, who contends that these universal, Oedipal "wishes, repugnant to morality, . . . have been forced upon us by Nature,"[50] Lydgate's *Siege* presents diversity, disability, and dissimilarity—in other words, *otherness*—in relation to the same in ethical tension.[51]

EDIPPUS: UNKYNDE AND UNWIST

Freud's elimination of Laius's transgression and its concrete effects also isolates Oedipus from his history and severs him from his immediate social context. It makes of him a sovereign subject who heroically and single-handedly

---

Scriptural Sense and Mode in Medieval Scholastic Exegesis," 229–54. Astell's *Political Allegory* is an important study of English materials.

50. Freud, *Interpretation of Dreams*, 4:263.

51. Perhaps Freud's strongest articulation of the universality of his theory comes from a note added in 1920 to *Three Essays on Sexuality*:

> It has justly been said that the Oedipus complex is the nuclear complex of neuroses, and constitutes the essential part of their content. It represents the peak of infantile sexuality, which, through its after effects, exercises a decisive influence on the sexuality of adults. Every new arrival on this planet is faced by the task of mastering the Oedipus complex; anyone who fails to do so falls a victim to neurosis. With the progress of psychoanalytic studies the importance of the Oedipus complex has become more and more clearly evident; its recognition has become the shibboleth that distinguishes the adherents of psychoanalysis from its opponents. (*Three Essays on Sexuality*, vol. 7 of *The Standard Edition of the Complete Psychological Works of Sigmund Freud*, trans. James Strachey [London: Hogarth Press, 1953 (1905)], note to 226)

struggles against the forces of divine determinism, according to Freud: "The *Oedipus Rex* is a tragedy of destiny. Its tragic effect is said to lie in the contrast between the supreme will of the gods and the vain attempts of mankind to escape the evil that threatens them. The lesson which, it is said, the deeply moved spectator should learn from the tragedy is submission to the divine will and realization of his own impotence."[52] Freud has replaced the inviolable will of the gods with the inevitability of the Oedipal complex, yet unlike even Sophocles, who through dialogue allows Oedipus to reconstruct his life course, Lydgate's narrative allows the reader to follow Edippus's development from birth until death and to evaluate the mechanisms that drive his choices, restrict his opportunities, create his difficulties, and shape his destiny. The *Siege* ultimately ameliorates Edippus's guilt by demonstrating that others were also responsible for his destiny. Edippus is not the sole determinant of his own ends. Primary for Lydgate is that Edippus acted unknowingly ("vnwist," 811) and innocently: "Al be þat he wroght of ignoraunce, / Ful derk and blynde of his woful chaunce" (809–10). Lydgate even records Edippus's long reign in Thebes, his happy marriage to Iocasta, and his four children, particularly his two beautiful and "goodly" daughters, Antygone and Ymeyne (875–84). Minimizing Edippus's relationship to Iocasta, Lydgate's final moralization focuses upon the sons' treatment of their father. Etiocles and Polynieces deny their father a proper burial, tossing his body into a pit and treating him "wers than [a] serpent or eny tigre wood [mad]" (1013)—the same animalistic terms used to describe the Sphinx (625). Lydgate recognizes the generational reverberations of "unkyndeness": "Of cursied stok cometh vnkynde blood" (1014). "Unkynde" here takes on its full resonance—unnatural and unkind, and against kin and category. Lydgate writes:

> For which shortly to man and child I rede
> To be wel war and to taken hede
> Of kyndely riȝt and of conscience.
> (1019–21)

The opposite of "unkynde," the provocative phrase "kyndely riȝt" indicates Lydgate's double-edged solution to his Edippal problem, unlike Freud's selective mobility of the Ten Commandments. Children should respect the natural claim of parental authority and heed the moral claim of natural law that they respect their parents, no matter their social position. "Conscience" rather than "consciousness" marks the obedient child, but Lydgate calls only Ethiocles and

---

52. Freud, *Interpretation of Dreams*, 4:262.

Polynieces "unkynde," not Edippus.[53] Etiocles and Polynieces do not represent the corrupting power of political ambition as much as they typify irreverence for the fifth commandment, echoing Freud's criticism for the disrespect contemporary youth have for their parents and returning political disruption and social dislocation to the problem of parents and children:

> To do honur and due reuerence,
> To fader and moder of what estat thei be,
> Or certyn ellis they shul neuer the.
> (1022–24)

Ultimately, Lydgate's message is socially conservative, but unlike Freud, Lydgate also recognizes the parent's (and caregiver's) responsibility for their actions toward their children. Lydgate proclaims that social and political stability comes from obedience to the hierarchy of parent over child and age over youth.

Lydgate was no libertine, yet his consideration for Edippus in the *Siege* is unexpectedly generous and humane—quite the opposite of what we might expect from a medieval cleric. At the climax of Edippus's story, Lydgate shows that when Iocasta recognizes Edippus's scarred heels in private, "vpon a certeyn nyght" (895), she tells him the violent story of the child hated by his father and disowned by his mother. The key difference between the *Siege* and Sophocles is that Iocasta herself tells Edippus that the executioners defied the king and queen upon "peyne of Iugemente" (927) and that hunters in the forest saved him:

> Which lad hym forth and his feet vnbounde;
> But to what coost they coude not declare.
> Which parcel is of myn evel fare,
> Grounde and cause of myn hevy chere.
> (940–43)

Iocasta here accepts responsibility for putting her child out and for her own misfortune and state of mind ("evel fare"). At the same time, Iocasta understands the physical origin and psychological effects of her adversity ("which parcel"). In effect, she turned her newborn child into a parcel, which has returned and generated her misfortune. Edippus understands "by process" that his journey back to Thebes to find his identity and "kynrede" (984) has

---

53. Battles, *Medieval Tradition*, 161.

brought him closer to his biological origins. Having retraced his life, Edippus understands the truth of his situation. He killed his father and married his mother, but he also understands that his birth father wanted him dead, and his mother did not intercede for him. Both sides of the equation are equally devastating, though in Freud we hear only of the father's anxiety. If Edippus symbolizes a common infantile experience, it is in the unavoidable suffering that besets children when they are born.

All of these details lead to perhaps the most surprising aspect of Lydgate's depiction of Edippus: his treatment of incest and his consequent moral generosity toward Edippus.[54] Dominique Battles has identified specific adaptations Lydgate introduces into the *Siege* that minimize or even eliminate Edippus's guilt.[55] At its harshest, Lydgate's condemnation is indirect, focusing on Edippus's intention, the consequences of his action for Thebes, and his exemplary value for the audience. First and most importantly, Lydgate does not condemn Edippus's actions because he married his mother unknowingly: "Vnwist of bothe he was of her blode, / And Ignoraunt" that he had murdered his father (784–85), a definite change from Lydgate's source.[56] Lydgate makes Edippus the descendent of Amphion rather than Cadmus, linking him to the founder who raised Thebes by his eloquence, rather than the brutal king who reigned through violence. In contrast to the prose *Thèbes*, Lydgate also ameliorates Edippus's responsibility for marrying Iocasta by attributing the marriage to malevolent astrological and allegorical influences (853–66). This further "relativizes Edippus's guilt when he points blame at the on-going practice in his own day of marrying blood relations" (811–17), making Edippus's transgression a general one rather than a monstrous exception.[57] Lydgate likewise attributes Layus's death not to Edippus's intrinsic wickedness but to the circumstances of the tournament. Lydgate minimizes Edippus's guilt by "making him the victim of two irreverent sons."[58] Finally, Lydgate also uses Edippus as a negative exemplum of the fickle habits of fortune, "ensample in al manere thyng / Of Edyppus" (807–8). In a distinctly medieval turn, when Edippus was "shon most riche in his renoun, / From her wheel [Fortune] she plönged hym

---

54. See Ibid., 158–62. Archibald also notes that medieval writers generally did not develop the story of Oedipus perhaps because "the classical setting and tragic ending of the Oedipus story would have emphasized the antiquity of the problem [incest], and the remoteness of the story from the Christian world" (*Incest*, 106). Instead, "when mother-son incest does occur, the story becomes an exemplum not about the inevitability of faith but rather about the sinfulness of mankind, the value of contrition, and the possibility of divine forgiveness" (Ibid., 107).
55. Battles, *Medieval Tradition*, 158–62.
56. Ibid., 158.
57. Ibid., 159.
58. Ibid., 160.

a-doun" (889–90). Taking a Boethian position, Lydgate cautions that we must not place our trust in earthly mutability.

Both Sophocles and Lydgate's *Siege* explore the unsettling and inevitably conflictual interplay of lineage and identity, asking: Who is truly (a) father? Who truly is (a) son? What is the proper relationship between father and son? In Freud, the identifications are firmly settled: the father is the object of infantile aggression. However, the traditional humanistic, even philosophical, reading of Oedipus, also shared by Freud, becomes more difficult to accept if we recognize the separation the *Siege* articulates between Edippus's "first" and "second" births, the same division between (natural) biological birth and loving (cultural) adoption that appears in Sophocles. Both the *Siege* and Sophocles question whether nature (birth) or nurture (culture) bonds parents and children together. In the *Siege,* Polyboun nurtures, loves, and raises the orphaned, abused, discarded Edippus as his heir, while Layus is no more than the biological progenitor. The same is true in *Oedipus Rex.* In Sophocles, Oedipus himself knows only the king and queen of Corinth, who raised him from infancy, as his parents. "My father was Polybus of Corinth, [and] my mother, the Dorian Meropè," Oedipus states.[59] When the messenger arrives with news that Polybus has died of old age, Oedipus concludes that he could not have killed his father—the only father he has ever known and the one to whom he is affectively bound—"Unless, perchance, he [Polybous] was killed by longing for me."[60] In both Sophocles and the *Siege,* Lauis is no father; he is no more than a sire. Oedipus's only concern in Sophocles then is not to stray into his home territory and perchance encounter his mother Meropè. In believing he has killed his birth father and married his birth mother, even Lydgate's Edippus accepts the mantle of incest and patricide. At the same time, it is equally clear in Sophocles and Lydgate that the affective ties between father and adopted son hold more meaning than the naked biological fact of paternity, whose authority Freud preserves at all costs.[61]

---

59. *The Oedipus Tyrannus of Sophocles,* ed. Richard Jebb (Cambridge: Cambridge University Press, 1887), l. 774–75. Subsequent citations to the play will be indicated by line from this pre-Freudian, and hence pre-Oedipal, translation (if you will).

60. *Oedipus Tyrannus,* 969–70. Oedipus concludes, then, that he only need avoid Corinth (and contact with his mother) to completely invalidate the incestuous component of the prophecy.

61. Unfortunately, the myth that medieval (and even ancient) parents were not lovingly attached and emotionally invested in their children continues to persist even though data to the contrary is widespread. Barbara Hanawalt's *Ties That Bound: Peasant Families in Medieval England* (London: Oxford University Press, 1986) and her *Growing Up in Medieval London: The Experience of Childhood in History* (London: Oxford University Press, 1993) examine the English evidence, while Ronald C. Finucane, *The Rescue of the Innocents: Endangered Children in Medieval Miracles* (New York: St. Martin's Press, 1997) looks at English and Italian evidence.

FREEING OEDIPUS/EDIPPUS

The continued Oedipalization of Oedipus depends upon two moments of interpretive blindness suggested elliptically in Lydgate but generally ignored in Sophocles. The first requires overlooking the empirical contradiction concerning the number of Laius's murderers, and the second requires following without question the suspect reasoning that leads to Oedipus's claim that he himself is the guilty party.[62] Between the two branches of this crux lies a crucial and telling shift in logic. Although cited as the epitome of tragedy in the *Poetics*, Aristotle *twice* refers to the "irrationality" of *Oedipus Rex*, specifically Oedipus's ignorance concerning the number of Laius's murderers.[63] Creon assures Oedipus that the sole fact to which the massacre's survivor could attest was that a *group* of robbers, not a *single* man, fell upon Laius and his party,[64] something Jocasta later confirms.[65] Oedipus remembers only striking back at an old man and killing his attendants at the intersection of three roads. Here the logic of *Oedipus Rex* takes a revealing turn. At the moment Oedipus tries to ascertain the number of Lauis's killers, and thus confirm or repudiate his complicity in the murder, the Corinthian messenger enters, and the dialogue shifts into an inquiry after Oedipus's origins. The investigation into Laius's death remains suspended, and "when 'the one who was present [at Laius's death]' appears, the full story remains hidden. It is never even requested," as Goodhart notes.[66] The old Corinthian messenger does bring news that Polybus is dead and that Oedipus was a foundling whom he received from the Herdsman. It is when the Corinthian messenger, who as a servant also received Oedipus into Polybus's home, opines, "For if thou art what this man [the Herdsman] saith, know that thou wast born to misery" that Oedipus finally exclaims, "Oh, oh! All brought to pass—all true!"[67] He then rushes off to blind himself, sealing physically what he has accepted, or rather adopted, as truth, even though the Herdsman's account is never revealed.[68]

---

62. My argument in the following paragraphs is indebted to Goodhart, "*Lestas Ephaske.*"

63. Aristotle, *The Poetics of Aristotle*, ed. S. H. Butcher, 4th ed. (London: Macmillan, 1907), 95–97. The full quotation reads: "The tragic plot must not be composed of irrational parts. Everything irrational should, if possible, be excluded; or, at all events, it should lie outside the action of the play (as, in the *Oedipus*, the hero's ignorance as to the manner of Laius' death)." See also *Poetics*, 57: "If the irrational cannot be excluded, it should be outside the scope of the tragedy. Such is the irrational element in the Oedipus of Sophocles."

64. *Oedipus Tyrannus*, 138.

65. Ibid., 715–16.

66. Goodhart, "*Lastes Ephastes*," 18. The internal quotation is from *Oedipus Rex*, 835.

67. *Oedipus Tyrannus*, 1181–82.

68. Even at the crucial moment when the Herdsman *seems* to identify Oedipus as the child he rescued from the wilderness, the Greek itself is ambiguous, according to Jebb. The

Oedipus's self-identification as the murderer reinstantiates the very tie of blood kinship that Lauis denied with the attempted infanticide. It is a paradigmatic sacrificial gesture that Freud's interpretation, like most of the humanistic tradition, relies upon. Oedipus places himself within the narrative lacunae left open in the play, "voluntarily appropriating an oracular logic that assumes he has always been guilty."[69] In contradistinction to the long history of interpretation that finds in Sophocles' Oedipus the humanistic ideal, the lone human struggles against fate and searches single-mindedly for the truth no matter the personal cost, Oedipus in fact acquiesces to the patricidal prophecy even in the face of contrary evidence. Goodhart advocates that "rather than participate in the play's crisis . . . we might instead follow Sophocles' investigation of the enabling conditions of any Oedipal reading."[70] It is this persistent *méconnaisance* that keeps Oedipus Oedipal in the humanistic tradition.

In an interesting circumlocution, Lydgate likewise notes that, according to his source, *no one* knew how the king was killed or by whom:

Thow the story writ not the maner howh,
Ne no wight [man] can of all the companye
Be no signe verrely espye
By whos hond that the kyng was slawe.
(580–85)

In other words, the son's guilt for the father's death remains ambiguous and textually suspended even in Lydgate, but at the very moment the mystery could be revealed, a narrative of origins intervenes not so much to explain the current situation as to justify it in terms of guilt or innocence, blindness or insight, suffering or release, and by accepting these terms, Oedipus reads himself into the position of being the guilty party. This is exactly the Freudian logic. On one hand, a situation of current distress, a symptom, is explained via a detour into our origins, in which as children we internalize the affective dynamics of our families of origin. On the other hand, we adopt, at first unquestioningly, those narratives of parental fear and anxiety as if from an oracle who has determined our fates before our very births. By attributing violence to the child and alleviating the responsibility of the parent for initiating that violence, Freud requires Oedipus to adhere to the "natural" and necessary

---

Herdsman's identification of Oedipus, generally translated, "It was a child, then, of the house of Laius" (1167), "could mean either: (1) 'he was one of the children of Laius'; or (2) 'he was one of the children of the household of Laius'" (*Oedipus Tyrannus*, note to 1167).

69. Goodhart, "*Lastes Ephastes,*" 35.
70. Ibid.

obeisance a son should hold toward his father while excusing the father of any natural bonds to his child. Rather than freeing humanity from the forces of determinism, Freud's Oedipus reinforces the "natural" authority of the father. Freud's Oedipus thus remains, like Freud himself in this case, firmly in the humanistic tradition while Levinas embraces an antihumanism—figured as a deconstruction of the traditional understanding of the human—ultimately to reinstitute humanism upon a different grounding: his ethics as first philosophy and the humanism of the other person.[71]

In the end, Freud never accounts for the infant Oedipus but sees Oedipus's destiny in the early life of all humanity.[72] In contrast, Levinas's meditations on fecundity and paternity identify children as ethical subjects and childhood as a privileged category because of the child's inherent sociality, dependence upon others, and vulnerability.[73] Levinas ultimately dismantles the hierarchy of father over son, of parent over child, by observing that the father's exteriority, most clearly present in the other who calls the father to responsibility, is found in, but is not reducible to, the child. Rather than separated beings, theirs is a *pluralist existing*. The parent-child relationship subsists not in some transcendental, unchanging ideal but continually reconfigures itself in freedom toward

---

71. Levinas's relationship to humanism is complicated, involved as he was in the humanism/antihumanism debates of the 1960s. References to humanism occur throughout his writings but particularly in *Humanism of the Other*, trans. Nidra Poller (Champaign: University of Illinois Press, 2005) and in the essays on education in *Difficult Freedom: Essays on Judaism*, trans. Sean Hand (Baltimore: Johns Hopkins University Press, 1990). Two recent studies that address the question of Levinas's humanism are Claire Elise Katz, *Levinas and the Crisis of Humanism* (Bloomington: Indiana University Press, 2012) and Carl Cederberg, *Resaying the Human: Levinas beyond Humanism and Antihumanism*, Södertörn Doctoral Dissertations 52 (Stockholm: Södertörns högskola, 2010). Andrew Galloway has recently argued that Lydgate "may be nominated as [the] English founder" of "vernacular humanism" ("John Lydgate and the Origins of Vernacular Humanism," *Journal of English and Germanic Philology* 107.4 (2008), 471 [445–71].

72. Eventually, Freud was pressed to consider an Oedipal "prehistory" to his theory, which caused him enormous conceptual difficulties and ultimately splintered Freud's inner circle. Melanie Klein both extended and qualified the implications of Freudian thinking for the pre-Oedipal psyche. Lacan's first major psychoanalytic publication addresses exactly this prehistory and integrates "the Oedipal problem" into its immediate social context: the family. In his 1938 essay *Les complexes familiaux dans la formation de l'individu. Essai d'analyse d'une fonction en psychologie* (*The Family Complexes in the Formation of the Individual*), Lacan writes that "This subversive and critical movement through which man actualizes himself has its most powerful source in . . . the conjugal family" (Jacques Lacan, *The Family Complexes*, trans. Carolyn Asp, *Critical Texts* 5.3 [1988], 22 [12–29]). Asp's is a partial translation. A complete official translation has not yet appeared in English.

73. Feminist criticism has found fault in Levinas's characterization of paternity to the seeming exclusion of maternity. Simone de Beauvoir, *The Second Sex* (New York: Bantam, 1970), xvi, and particularly Luce Irigaray's "The Fecundity of the Caress," in *Face to Face with Levinas*, ed. Richard A. Cohen (Albany: State University of New York Press, 1986), 231–56.

an ever opening, nonteleological, even *messianic*, future. Levinas declares that "I am" is not an ontological essence but a consociation in constant temporal openness and proximal reorientation. Levinas does not denote "I am my son's father" or "I am my father's daughter" as shared essences, but renders their affinity in terms of multiple individual freedoms within and not outside or at the end of time.[74] This is the gift of natality. The plurality of "I am" is found in continual openness to the future with the self-same other, independent of a suffocating, isolating, overdetermined *telos*.[75] If Freud sees Oedipus as the universal human subject, the autonomous individual who acts in history, Lydgate's Edippus is the exemplary individual who is tethered to a developmental history for good and for ill. The individual is marked by change, not stasis; is embedded in culture, not isolated; adapts to the vagaries of age and change; and remains firmly wedded to the warp and woof of history.

---

74. "Time and the Other," *The Levinas Reader*, ed. Seán Hand (Oxford: Blackwell Publishing), 52 and 53 [37–58].

75. In Kelly Oliver's excellent formulation, "For Levinas, the promise of paternity is a promise not of recognition but of nonrecognition, of strangeness, of an open future, of infinity, of singularity." Oliver continues, "It is not a promise from the past, a promise that returns to itself. Rather, the promise of paternity, as Levinas describes it, is a promise of an open future, the promise that the son is to his father" ("Fatherhood and the Promise of Ethics," *Diacritics* 27.1 [1997], 47 [45–57]).

CODA

The Trick of Singularity

Twelfth Night, *Stewards of the Posthuman*,
and the Problem of Aesthetics

CRAIG DIONNE

> And yet what precisely is this "greatness?" Just where does it lie? ... This whole question is very akin to the question that has caused much debate in our profession over the years: what is a "great" butler? ... But you will no doubt also understand what I mean when I say it is not at all easy to define just what this quality is.
>
> —Stevens, in Kazuo Ishiguro, *The Remains of the Day*

> "Cast thy humble slough," says she; ...
> "put thyself into the trick of singularity."
>
> —Malvolio, from *Twelfth Night* (3.4.73-75)

DEFINING A *HUMANIST* POSTHUMAN?

Robert Scholes argues in his 2004 MLA presidential address, "The Humanities in a Posthumanist World," that it is not enough for literary humanists to serve as stewards of the "techno-bureaucratic culture or to enter the ranks of the solemn fundamentalists."[1] Further, "we humanists cannot simply embrace the past and say we stand for that.... We must show that our heritage and our disciplines can help out society through the difficult present and into the unfathomable future." And finally, in our teaching, we must "generate new human standards that reject the fundamentalist leap to absolute truth and the pragmatic denial that such standards are possible."[2]

---

1. Scholes, "The Humanities in a Posthumanist World," *PMLA* 120 (2005): 724 [724–33]. Special thanks to Christine Neufeld and Melissa Jones for advice on this paper.
2. Ibid., 731.

These are the key goals of the humanities in the era of the *posthuman*: to generate new human standards in relation to the neoconservative political and economic ideologies, a goal that becomes more challenging in the wake of high theory when it appears any attempt to address the "human" replays an endless return of romantic essentialist categories. "Human experience," "man," "nation," "ennobling culture" can no longer be innocently invoked to persuade students of the relevance of art. How can we be stewards of a literary tradition, our heritage, even though it seems that tradition is, at best, a construct, a myth, an assemblage of things, or at worst, a colonial ideology? How can we preserve and manage the transmission of a literary heritage that does not seem to directly speak to the complexity of the modern world? To address the larger issue of helping students understand the neoconservative control of discourse in the public sphere, Scholes urges us to use different texts in the classroom—"religious and political texts"—and "not to retreat into a belletrism."[3] But even Scholes seems too comfortable quoting from Yeats's "Second Coming" to help his students think of the current political context (the "war on terror," for example), in a way challenging us to stick to our (canonical) guns: "The blood-dimmed tide is loosed." Scholes continues,

> Those words . . . come to me because I am humanist, and poetry is one of the tools that the humanities have given me for coping with the world. I draw strength and insight from those words and from the other texts that are part of my cultural equipment. I would like to pass this heritage to future generations.[4]

There is an apologetic tone here, even a defensiveness. Scholes's own example relies on the metaphor of cultural stewardship: an image of a steadfast butler complete with a trunk of "cultural equipment" that helps future masters cope with their surroundings, something of a world-wise Jeeves whose profound grasp of art and culture provides an ethical ballast to the young Bertie Woosters closed to Yeats's apocalyptic vision. By his own admission, Scholes's is a humanist response to the crisis of representation in the humanities, more of an official recognition of the naming of the category of the posthuman—a term that defines a constellation of theorists and social critics working on the same problem but from positions within different critical discourses: cyborg theory, informatics, systems theory, queer studies, the turn to the body and to animal rights, as well as critical theory as recently coalesced in the BABEL Working

---

3. Ibid.
4. Ibid.

Group and in the literary and philosophical work of scholars such as Cary Wolfe, Katherine Hayles, Julian Yates, Ian Hacking, Jeffrey Cohen, Judith Butler, and Donna Haraway, among others. All of these discourses respond to the disappearance of the liberal humanist subject and the problem of social agency in the current political scene. The newly emergent discourse of the posthuman is focused on revitalizing the social and political urgency of literary studies as an ethical window into the pressing concerns of our time while keeping its eye on how to justify "literature" as a distinct discipline in the humanities.[5]

It is my argument in this essay that the posthuman turn has yet to fully discuss the new relationship between *theory* and *text* that is suggested in its applications of seemingly anachronistic pairings of digital-aged semiotics with illuminated manuscripts. The danger is that one makes the past a kind of dressing room for what Catherine Belsey has described as "history as costume drama, the reconstruction of the past as the present in fancy dress. The project is to explain away the surface strangeness of another century in order to release its profound continuity with the present."[6] As it reaches over (or through?) the gulf that separates these periods, posthumanism applies critical theories that developed in response to commodified modes of reproduction, alienation from urban space, the forced anomie of mass culture, and the violence of corporate imperialism, using them to understand a time period when such modern themes seem a jarring overlay, but not entirely anachronistic, as if when looking at Lady Fortune, we see Duchamp's *Nude Descending the Staircase*, or when lifting Tristan's visor we discover Munch's homunculus staring back. How do we make the past speak to the concerns of the posthuman without appropriating its alterity, making it a reflection of our own interests? If any text can be used to discuss embodied subjectivity, "things" or "networks," say, then why start with texts from the early modern— or, for that matter, premodern—past at all?

In the following, I want to think through the problem of the new aesthetics, following Derek Attridge's influential book, *The Singularity of Literature*, as it attempts to reconstruct a vocabulary to envision the text as a unique

---

5. A more elaborate synthesis of computer tech discourse can be found in Bruce Clarke's ambitious *Posthuman Metamorphosis: Narrative and Systems*, which folds sociological "systems theory" into narratology (New York: Fordham University Press, 2008). See also Cary Wolfe's *Animal Rites* for a critique of humanism from the position of animal rights discourse (Chicago: University of Chicago Press, 2003). The clearest description of how these various posthuman accounts relate to new trends in literary studies can be found in Eileen A. Joy and Christine Neufeld's "A Confession of Faith: Notes Toward a New Humanism," *JNT: Journal of Narrative Theory* 37.2 (2007): 161–90.

6. Catherine Belsey, *Subject of Tragedy: Identity and Difference in Renaissance Drama* (New York: Methuen, 1985), 2.

"singular event" that, in a nearly visionary manner, provides an encounter with the other. I will be reading Shakespeare's *Twelfth Night* as presenting a fable about the dangers of aesthetic delight. Reading Attridge through *Twelfth Night*—or more appropriately, *in* Shakespeare's comedy—also allows me to explore the limits of the posthuman interpretive gesture I mentioned above, where the act of reading the past becomes a moment of projecting the present into the text. Attridge's new revision of the literary invites us to consider the text as a moment of profound self-awareness; his vision of the newly charged affective text reasserts literature as a "singular" discourse needed to teach ethics to students living in a posthuman age. I will return to Attridge below, but for now, I want to pause and tease out further the theme hinted at in Scholes's conception of posthumanism's practice of institutional stewardship. The metaphor of the butler is a fruitful one, I think, because it calls attention to the idea of preserving the culture *for someone else*. Though the role of the butler as attendant of the manor house goes back centuries, it was P. G. Wodehouse's Jeeves series that invented the myth of the wise and prescient steward to the blithely obtuse ruling class. One could argue that so strong and pervasive is the pull of the popular myth of the Edwardian butler that it is hard these days not to see a production of *Twelfth Night* that is not unconsciously read through this temporal landscape, a period that serves to mediate English historical self-awareness as much as the 1950s do in American mass culture.

A more contemporary rendering of the butler as a figure of alienation can be found in Kazuo Ishiguro's *The Remains of the Day*.[7] The protagonist narrator of this novel, the unflappable Stevens, dutifully performs his tasks as head butler to an English country gentleman who, as readers slowly learn, supports the alliance of the British crown with the Nazis. Stoic, reserved, closed off to those around him, the narrator's inchoate awareness of his master's involvement in fascism becomes a resonant allegory of a modern identity closed off to the world, lost in its own peculiar obsessions or manor house customs. Stevens reflects on what makes a steward *great*; he thinks through the unsettling problem of defining perfection through a policing of the social norms that dictate manorial rule. For Stevens, this involves defining "dignity" in a butler, as it occurs to the reader that Ishiguro's narrative is a parable of aesthetics:

> Mr. Graham and I had some of our most interesting debates. Mr. Graham would always take the view that this "dignity" was something like a woman's beauty and it was thus pointless to attempt to analyze it. I, on the other hand, held the opinion that to draw such a parallel tended to demean the "dignity" of

---

7. Kazuo Ishiguro, *The Remains of the Day* (New York: Vintage, 1988).

the like of Mr. Marshall. Moreover, my main objection to Mr. Graham's analogy was the implication that this "dignity" was something one possessed or did not by a fluke of nature; and if one did not self-evidently have it, to strive after it would be as futile as an ugly woman trying to make herself beautiful. Now while I would accept that the majority of butlers may well discover ultimately that they do not have the capacity for it, I believe strongly that this "dignity" is something one can meaningfully strive for throughout one's career.[8]

Ishiguro's novel provides a starting point for us to think about aesthetic reflection as another form of self-blindness in the context of stewardship. Stevens's musings on dignity work to repress consciously the horrors of the growing fascist storm in Western culture. Stevens's unreliability—not seeing and connecting with his family and colleagues—is a function of his profession. If he seems less than human, it is because he is doing what he is trained to do. If there is a passion to his profession, it seems like a stoic rigor that ultimately leads to a *disconnection* to the others they serve, if not a profound self-alienation. We are but a short step from thinking about Malvolio's stewardship and the uses of allegory in thinking about the idea of aesthetic singularity in our profession. Ishiguro's reflections on the power of aesthetics to direct our attention inward, away from the world around us, can be seen as a harrowing tale about the problem of establishing an aesthetics of difference during a time of great economic, political, and ecological instability—a strangely familiar reminder for humanists that our own professional longing to return to aesthetics might replay something of a return of the repressed.

ALONE HIGH FANTASTICAL?

> If the historical, the social, and the political could have once been said to be the Repressed of the New Criticism (to return with a vengeance in the new theories), might not now the aesthetic be the Repressed of Cultural Theory?
> —Heinz Ickstadt, "Toward a Pluralist Aesthetic"[9]

> Let me make it clear once more that the "otherness" I am positing as central to the experience of the literary is neither a mystical ideality nor an inviolable materiality, neither a Platonic Form nor a Kantian Ding an sich. The other can

---

8. Ibid., 33.
9. Heinz Ickstadt, "Toward a Pluralist Aesthetic," in *Aesthetics in a Multicultural Age*, eds. Emory Elliot, Louis Caton, and Jeffrey Rhyne (New York: Oxford University Press, 2002), 263–78.

> emerge only as a version of the familiar, strangely lit, refracted, self-distanced. It arises from the intimate recesses of the cultural web that constitutes subjectivity, which is to say, it arises as from within the subject as outside it—and in so doing blurs the distinction between that which is "inside" and that which is "outside" the self.
>
> —Derek Attridge, *The Singularity of Literature*[10]

I want to turn now to *Twelfth Night* to think through how it speaks to the problems associated with the latest turn to ethics in the field of literary studies, particularly the problem of articulating a new theory of aesthetic autonomy as it appears in the use of this word, singularity. The play's history on stage and in criticism plays out in funny ways one of its central themes: how we see ourselves in others, how we fall in love with the other that is our self. William Shakespeare's Malvolio, perhaps the most notorious steward in English literary culture, is the target of much criticism focusing on the peculiar problem of thinking of a scripted identity: the scapegoat of the play's anxious expressions about class mobility, he is often made a surrogate of our own critical inventions, written as a symbol of the audience, or the author's own ambivalent notions of class ascendance.[11] It may seem odd to make *Twelfth Night* a story about its butler, but even from its legendary first performance at the Middle Temple Hall, its riotous subplot of gulling the vain servant has proven its comic center. Shakespeare's comedy suggests itself for a study on the limits of artistic reflection because, of all his plays, it is thinking out loud about the overpowering nature of aesthetic experience and the narcissistic quality of art's power to touch us, to move us, to make us withdraw into ourselves the very minute it allows us to see the world anew. The dominant aesthetic in the play can be found in its exposition on desire, to which the play reads like an exercise on Renaissance melancholy or self-consuming love.

When thinking about how some characters in the play reflect the quality of narcissism in their love for (an)other, it is easy to make the play an allegory of the trap of aesthetics, as the play chronicles the dangers of appropriating alterity to distinguish our own selves in the world. Suggested in the following lines from the song sung by Feste, the image of an unrequited love is rendered:

> I am slain by a fair cruel maid.
> My shroud of white, stuck all with yew,

---

10. Derek Attridge, *The Singularity of Literature* (New York: Routledge, 2004), 76.

11. For example, Stephen Booth's "Twelfth Night 1.1: The Audience as Malvolio," *Shakespeare's Rough Magic: Essays in Honor of C. L. Barber*, ed. Peter Erikson and Coppelia Kahn (Newark: University of Delaware Press, 1985), 149–67.

O prepare it
My part of death no one so true
Did share it.
Not a flower, not a flower sweet.
On my black coffin let there be strewn;
Not a friend, not a friend greet
My poor corpse, where my bones shall be thrown.
(2.4.53–61)[12]

Feste sings the song to Orsino, the patron of this art. The song is meant to mirror Orsino's own narcissistic view of love as a negating energy complete only in its ultimate deferral (both symbolically through sexual climax and in death). Orsino returns again and again to a song that seems at first glance strangely suited to his self-obsessions. The power of love is that it can diminish the virility of the lover not just through sexual climax, but in its all-consuming influence:

O spirit of love! how quick and fresh art thou,
That, notwithstanding thy capacity
Receiveth as the sea, naught enters there,
Of what validity and pitch so e'er,
But falls into abatement and low price,
Even in a minute.
(1.1. 9–14)

Ironically, love is also a catalyst for sullen reflection on this dialectic of desire: that absence is the condition of desire, an absence that leads to suffering and the exhaustion of "love's flame," or death. The play's celebratory tone of love's

---

12. All citations of *Twelfth Night* are from *The Norton Shakespeare*, eds. Stephen Greenblatt, Walter Cohen, Jean E. Howard, and Katherine Eisaman Maus, 2nd ed. (New York: Norton, 2005), 1793–1846. Shakespeare may have put words to an older tune or borrowed a folk song. John Long argues that the "metrical construction of the song strongly suggests an ayre although its subject has a traditional flavor, and the Duke describes it as a folk song," though some of the short lines "prevent the lyrics from being set to any of the traditional tunes of the period" (*Shakespeare's Use of Music: A Study of the Music and Its Performance in the Original Productions of Seven Comedies* [Gainesville: University of Florida Press, 1955], 178). Ross Duffin and Stephen Orgel suggest "Come Away Death" matches closely the versification of the "King Solomon" tune: "The first ballad set to the 'King Solomon' tune was entitled 'The Pangs of Love.' The tune appears in two sixteenth-century English manuscripts: among the cittern pieces in the Mulliner Book (ca. 1558–64) and in the slightly later *Dublin Virginal Manuscript*, which is part of the *Dallis Lute Book* (ca. 1570)" (Ross Duffin and Stephen Orgel, *Shakespeare Songbook* [New York: Norton, 2004], 98).

power and as a game for youth is overshadowed always by this shroud of mortality: "kiss me.... Youth's a stuff will not endure" (2.3.47–48).

Orsino's supine position as unrequited lover in the play embodies this love-as-death aesthetic, and it can easily be argued it is the controlling vision of the entire play. As a cosmology this view of desire functions to order the characters in its frame of reference—in terms of age, gender, and even status— to its guiding patriarchal image of love's energy "spent" in the consumption (or use) of feminine virginity. As the Duke and Cesario discuss the difference between male and female libido, we delight in the fact that the Duke puts his foot in his mouth, exposes his chauvinism to a young woman. What is surprising is the odd gender reversal, as he characterizes men as fickle beasts, explaining that men have "fancies ... more giddy and unfirm, / More longing, wavering, sooner lost and worn / Than women's are." (2.4.32–34). Speaking as Cesario, Viola finishes Orsino's thoughts on gender difference in this theory of love:

VIOLA: I think it well, my lord.
ORSINO: Then let thy love be younger than thyself,
   Or thy affection cannot hold the bent;
   For women are as roses, whose fair flower
   Being once displayed, doth fall that very hour.
VIOLA: And so they are: alas, that they are so;
   To die, even when they to perfection grow.
(2.4.34–40)

Earlier Orsino confirms the autonomy of the imagination: "So full of shapes is fancy / That it alone is high fantastical" (1.1.14–15). Yet in this dialogue above with Viola, we see how "fancy's" dynamic of desire implies a Platonic hierarchy. Though "alone" it is "high fantastical," women are objects of this imaginative power, while men, "more giddy and unfirm / More longing, wavering," are its subjects. Functioning as it does as an ideology, this aesthetic rationalizes domestic power relations picturing women as vehicles for the progress of the man's soul to perfection, with an implied rationality for the "use" of young women to satiate male appetite.

How might this aesthetic function as a parable of literary interpretation and critical practice? The play's synthesis of the humanist theme of love's narcissistic predilection, complete with its contrary perception that desire is unpredictable, can figure as the traditional model of formalist interpretation, whereby the richness of life's paradoxes obtained in the form of the text allows for readers to discover an inner life that is, somehow, closed off to them outside of books. It may be hard to picture Orsino as a literary humanist, but if you squint you can see in his self-enclosure something of the effect of the humanist close reading. Anything he stumbles upon outside his manor reminds him of his own abiding infatuations, the ambivalences of the text somehow materializing in their concrete form the inner truth that throws the newly found content into relief:

> ORSINO: O, when mine eyes did see Olivia first
> Methought she purged the air of pestilence;
> That instant was I turned into a hart,
> And my desires, like fell and cruel hounds,
> E'er since pursue me.
> (1.1.18–22)

Orsino's discovery is not so much a radical transformation of consciousness as a return to the presupposed point of the reflexive subject, who sees itself in its object. In this sense, we can read Orsino's metonymic replacement of Olivia with himself—"my desires . . . pursue me"—as an act congruent with the formalist practice of making the constituent parts of the text coherent to the larger whole. This is also a fitting metaphor for the way the humanist aesthetic closes off the world beyond its doubling mirror, its "business . . . everything, . . . [its] intent everywhere" (2.4.75), making difference appear only in the taffeta of its own choosing.

Now we can see the characters that stand in relative positions outside this model but still as servants to it in some sense—Viola and Malvolio—in relation to two practices that challenge, if not revise, the closed nature of this aesthetic grounding: deconstruction and the new posthumanism, respectively. Both Viola and Malvolio are outsiders to the patristic class they serve: their desires to climb the social ladder define just one of the play's many cultural oppositions. Viola's desire to "follow" Orsino is coded as a form of courtly service and hence her final acceptance into the ruling class seems, within the ideological grammar of the play, a natural, just reward. By comparison, Malvolio's dream to marry Olivia—the object of Maria's gulling trick—appears a perverted form of cultural and political aspiration. For me, both can be read as interesting doublings of aesthetic response within the narrative of humanism in the academy: Viola's wish to distinguish herself by playing out her master's wish, as it were, embodies the restless professionalism of poststructuralism's echo to formalism, while Malvolio's dream to shape a world outside the insulated world of the aristocratic manor only, in the end, to reproduce it ideally in the very "dream" of correcting it, embodies something of the plaguing dialectic of the new aesthetic turn in the profession today. In the case of Viola, her double form of representing herself as both Cesario and Viola—what feminist scholars have addressed as her "erasure of sexual determinacy" through cross-dressing—could be read as a fitting parable of the daring opposition deconstruction made to American formalism.[13] But we are allowed to ask, as Linda Bamber has, just how threatening Viola's presence is to the play's forced resolutions. Does Orsino have to change to accommodate her? Bamber is clear on this: "Orsino learns to allow the intruder into his world," she explains, but "he does not seem to discover himself in the process. He discovers that Viola/Cesario is really a woman and forthwith admits her into *his* world."[14] If Viola's "difference" is akin to the volatile energy of Derridean theory, it *also* suggests that Orsino's aesthetic is pliant enough to account for its potential contradictions. "The feminine Other," Bamber concludes, "is spared the necessity of change even as she is spared the necessity of choice."[15] She's allowed into the dance, but not on her terms. To follow the parable, what for poststructuralism is a radical instability in language is for formalism another instance of life's founding paradox: the former is merely absorbed as an instance of the latter.

From its outset, the structuralist moment has in various ways been accommodated to fit within a universalist framework of life's unchanging opposites, where in this instance the irreducible fact that the sign's value is conditioned by a binary of fixed opposites gets recuperated into a perdurable irony of life itself: life in death, marriage in isolation, innocence of youth "struck with yew." In our parable, Viola is, after all, working for Orsino, and her liminal status inside and outside the game of courtly love and patronage—frequenting Olivia's manor, then Orsino's, at once inside and outside the fourth wall of this game—plays out something of the strange position of the American poststructuralist critic, working within the humanities while trying to unhinge its claims to universal truth, all the way up the promotional ladder, as it were.

---

13. Viola's very discourse embodies the instability of language as an open form, as she signals in the ironic wordplay both Cesario and her own identity in her clever responses to other characters. The lack of a clear referent—is she speaking as Viola? Cesario?—attests to Derrida's understanding of language as an open process of deferral. As Cesario, she signals the difference of men and women at the heart of the aesthetic—a woman's value diminishes through sex while by implication a man's "wavering" appetite requires constant kindling. But as Viola she throws the difference into ironic erasure. Isn't she allowing us to laugh at Orsino while seemingly rearticulating his perspective? As such, Viola's presence enforces the deconstructive skepticism toward the Platonic absolutes that work in Orsino's essentialism, where the audience hears the performance of the aesthetic as myth, as an unstable system whose timeworn truths about the inconstancy of love feel archaic, the afterthoughts of a bygone idealism.

14. Linda Bamber, *Comic Women, Tragic Men* (Stanford, CA: Stanford University Press, 1982), 133, emphasis mine.

15. Ibid.

"From the closeness of deconstruction's affirmative 'free play,'" writes Herbert Grabes, "to the free play of the imagination in traditional aesthetics ... postmodernism and anti-foundationalism has, wittingly or unwittingly, come extremely close to the sphere that traditionally bears its foundation within itself: the aesthetic."[16]

THINKING AESTHETICS AND DIFFERENCE

Now we are in a position to consider Malvolio's "trick of singularity" as one of the play's alternative perspectives, a truly *counter*perspective, to what I am calling its dominant aesthetic mode of naturalizing will and desire within the social hierarchy. Malvolio is asked to elevate himself above others, to distinguish himself, to cast off his "humble slough," a kind of metaphor for aesthetic distancing. Malvolio is known for his use of language, and it is the "trick" of his singularity that he symbolizes a particular perspective on the materiality of language. The irony with Malvolio is that he distinguishes himself by attempting to internalize the language of his superiors. As a character who has learned through rote memory to affect the proper mannerisms of the landed class, to "con state without book and utter it by great swarths" (2.3.131–34), as Maria describes him, Malvolio represents one feature of Renaissance humanism that is muted in its deliberations on melancholic love, what social historians have recognized as the mnemonic aspect of Tudor humanist self-development through social mimicry of established discursive patterns.[17] "Affectioned ass," he is called by Maria (2.3.132). He has memorized "state without book"—that is, verbatim—and "utters it by great swarths." Maria continues that he is "crammed" with these "excellencies," a plebian image of being literally stuffed with commonplaced maxims useful for courtly interaction (2.3.133). Olivia defines his "self-love," ironically, as a lack of appropriate aristocratic indifference to others. He lets others get under his skin by exaggerating their slights,

---

16. Herbert Grabes, "Introduction to New Developments in Literary Aesthetics," in *Anglisteng, 1994 Graz*, ed. Wolfgang Riehle and Hugo Keiper (Tübingen: Niemeyer, 1995), 297–98. In my parable, Viola is both her own agent and also the servant of her lord, furthering her interest at the same time that she "finds" Orsino a lover (that turns out to be the wrong target, but the right person). The generations of scholars that mobilized deconstruction to unfound the logocentrism haunting the literary seem to accept their newly installed positions as Chairs and Deans with an equal sense of wonder that fortune has favored their pursuits.

17. Keith Thomas, "The Meaning of Literacy in Early Modern England," *The Written Word: Literacy in Transition*, ed. Gerd Baumann (Oxford: Clarendon Press, 1986), 97–131; and Frank Whigham, *Ambition and Privilege: The Social Tropes of Elizabethan Courtesy Theory* (Berkeley: University of California Press, 1984).

their "bird-bolts" (1.5.79). The current critical take reads Malvolio as assuaging Shakespeare's own internalized class ambitions, his father's petition to bear arms whose motto *Non Sans Droit* ("not without right") signals an inner pretension.[18] This displacement of class ambition is worked out in the way the narrative licenses one form of class ascension through marriage and patronage (Viola and Sebastian, and Maria, arguably), and scapegoats Malvolio's "dream" as madness. But we are also asked to measure the difference of these leaps in status. Malvolio's forced rhetorical display functions as a crude parody of Tudor humanist learning that was meant to bolster traditional venues of social ascension through courtly service. Malvolio's class pretensions are worn differently than Viola's, though they are essentially two sides of the same coin. Viola as much as begins the play expressing her interest in advancement, eerily similar to Malvolio's stewardship: "I'll serve this Duke . . . for I can sing, / And speak to him in many sorts of music / That will allow me very worth his service" (1.1.57–59). Both characters mirror Renaissance humanism's dream to provide service to the Prince, in the form of young courtiers whose assistance to the state relied as much on their memorization of Latin and Greek as it did on their commonplace books crammed with useful passages from the libraries of antiquity. The underbelly of the play's Ovidian fantasies of organic mutability through love is the fact that no one, the Prince included, actually internalizes the ablative singular masculine with sprezzatura. Grace and substance are learned, and Malvolio's emphasis on the materiality of language pulls the veil on the myth of instinctive civility.

As a result, Malvolio stands for a new way of thinking about language and place outside the play's paradigm of desire as the ruling force of "will." Malvolio's "ill will" is a counter to this organic view of identity as a natural expression of the system. There is, in his perspective, a different self-world relation that places him at odds with the aesthetic direction of the narrative. His rebuff to Sir Toby Belch, Olivia's infamous drunk uncle, is typically seen as condescending presumption, but I would suggest that his ability to see the difference between place and person is significant, to the extent that one's self is identified as a rational being free to choose its place in the social ladder:

---

18. Stephen Greenblatt claims, "What is ridiculed in Malvolio, then, is . . . the dream of acting the part of a gentleman. And the ridicule comes very close to describing the process by which any actor, including Shakespeare himself, must have learned his trade. . . . One of the greatest comic plots in all of Shakespeare, it draws deeply on the playwright's inner life, including a strong current of ironic laughter at the whole project—his own and that of his parents—of laying claim to a higher status" (*Will in the World: How Shakespeare Became Shakespeare* [New York: Norton, 2004], 83–84).

MALVOLIO: Sir Toby, I must be round with you. My lady bade me tell you that though she harbours you as her kinsman she's nothing allied to your disorders. If you can separate yourself and your misdemeanors, you are welcome to the house. If not, an it would please you to take leave of her she is very willing to bid you farewell. (2.3.85–90)

Malvolio's material view of language is, I would urge, equivalent to the posthuman urge to rethink aesthetic autonomy while remaining true to the seemingly contrary ideal of materialism's theory of contingency.

It is here I would like to return in more detail to Derek Attridge's *The Singularity of Literature*, as it attempts to rethink the theoretical underpinnings of aesthetics in this context. Attridge is trying to bridge the gap between materialism's view of language as an instance of discourse mediated by specific institutional aims and directives, while carving out a space to see literary language (singularity) as removed from the objectives of ideological control.[19] Like Malvolio's contradictory motives as steward to tradition, Attridge attempts to find a social use for aesthetic effect that responds to the charge of the New University to teach global awareness, the ethics of difference, and social commitment. But I wonder if in our search for a new language to articulate the heightened awareness that comes from reading a literary text, we do not fall into the trap Maria sets for Malvolio, appealing to a certain inner dream of returning to one's repressed desires that turn out, in the end, to be a part of an orchestrated cony-catching trick. Malvolio is caught dreaming of marrying Olivia. "On that vice in him," Maria explains, "will my revenge find notable cause to work" (2.3.135–6). The condition of Malvolio's dream is his penchant for seeing "love" in the eyes of others, of assuming that the world sees him as he sees himself. Moreover, the fake love letter Maria sets in his path, "obscure epistles," works because it is ambiguous—both a part of the world and not—usefully playful and open-ended, analogous to the poetic discourse embodied in Attridge's sense of singularity.

Trying to avoid the pitfalls of romantic metaphysical categories of sublimity and transcendence (the target of materialist literary criticism), critics like Attridge attempt to reinvent a critical language to reveal how the social importance of a piece of work resides in its ability to represent the object world with a distinct vision, to capture "otherness" and replay for the reader an

---

19. It's an ambitious balancing act, as it attempts to work within the established critical frameworks that have been seen to work in opposite directions, if not posed against each other as "ends" of the historicism-formalism spectrum. Like posthumanism itself, Malvolio straddles the fence of service to the court as steward while maintaining a view of language that places him at odds with the institution's founding ideology.

uncommon experience that exercises the mind's ability to live in accord with social difference. Attridge begins his argument by equating "the literary" with the encounter with the other: "This other in this situation is therefore not, strictly speaking, a person as conventionally understood in ethics or psychology; it is once again a relation—or a relating—between me, as the same, and that which, in its uniqueness, is heterogeneous to me and interrupts my sameness."[20] More of an event than a thing, the other in this definition is "a wholly new existent that cannot be apprehended by the old modes of understanding, and could not have been predicted by means of them; its singularity," he continues, "even if it is produced by nothing more than a slight recasting of the familiar and thus of the general, is irreducible."[21] Attridge wants to term this state of conditional bracketing "the other." At stake is the relative autonomy of the work of art—how it stands apart from its world. What saves Attridge's aesthetic theory from your run-of-the-mill romantic theories of art, though, is that he wants to account for the inventiveness of the literary text as a function of its place in a larger social continuum.

If the reader is meant to reflect on the alterity of the other through the literary, it is an other that bears the material traces of this greater social horizon. Again, a parallel is suggested in the play if we compare Malvolio's inward fantasy of love with that of Orsino's. We could read this autonomy as a symptom of Orsino's social position. If he is self-absorbed, it is because he has acquired the "generous" aristocratic trait of possessing a "free disposition," as Olivia has explained, to not care what others think. Malvolio, on the other hand, expresses the opposite in this regard: his retreat signals a heightened concern for the particulars of social protocol, fashion, taste. He is, in a word, lost in his regard for others: "Having been three months married to her," he begins to fantasize about Olivia as others listen from the other side of the stage. "Sitting in my state . . . Calling my officers about me, in my branched velvet gown; having come from a day-bed" (2.5.42–44).

> MALVOLIO: And then to have the humour of state and—after a demure travel of regard, telling them I know my place as I would they should do theirs—to ask for my kinsman Toby. . . . Seven of my people, with an obedient start, make out for him. I frown the while, and perchance wind up watch, or play with my—[*touching his chain*] some rich jewel. Toby approaches; courtesies there to me.
> SIR TOBY: Shall this fellow live?

---

20. Attridge, *Singularity of Literature*, 33.
21. Ibid., 29.

FABIAN: Though our silence be drawn from us with cars, yet peace.
MALVOLIO: I extend my hand to him thus, quenching my familiar
   smile with an austere regard of control.
(2.5.47–60)

Malvolio's dream here is marked by a concrete locality of courtly society; it includes cues from etiquette culture—"to have the humour of state," "after a demure travel of regard," "my smile with an austere regard of control"—as if speaking out loud the stage directions to his fantasies of becoming a self-reflective subject. He is performing the rules of decorum, displaying his regard of the conventions of signifying prestige: "I extend my hand to him thus." Importantly, these cues reflect his fascination with being accepted as authentic by others. It is this world of "being seen" that defines Malvolio's view of otherness as a process of self-reflection.[22]

We must ask, finally, if the return to aesthetics we get in this theory is not a staged return to another type of narcissism, a closed loop of self-identity where what starts as a materialist critique of the metaphysical status of humanism and mimesis ends up using the outer shell of this earlier practice by reading everything as an allegory of the self-reflective individual. As much as we have moved away from the static categories of existence presupposed in the humanist notions of universal experience, with Attridge we are still working with a model that wants to see literature as the catalyst and staging ground of the self's renewal as a thoroughly self-aware creature now told through the text as an allegory of this process. Likewise, as much as Malvolio's views of language and self challenge the traditional aesthetic categories that define his dominant culture, his project is itself limited by the dimensions of his conception of difference. Attridge wants to hold onto the structuralist conception of language as motivated from within, where "the other can emerge only as a version of the familiar" and "arises as from within the subject as outside it."[23] We might ask then how this reframes questions of difference and political notions of identity.[24]

---

22. Not only are we given his lines, but also how they will be delivered. Obsessing about how he will be seen by others, Malvolio's aesthetic of self-display is overly involved in the pragmatics of art's "effect" on its audience.

23. Attridge, *Singularity of Literature*, 76.

24. My argument would be considered a "cynical" definition of love by Alain Badiou, who rightly points out that the experience of falling in love is an aesthetic one and challenges the basic premise of subjective autonomy: "What is universal is that all love suggests a new experience of truth about what it is to be two and not one. That we can encounter and experience the world other than through a solitary consciousness" (*In Praise of Love* [Paris: Flammarion, SA, 2009], 39).

If for Attridge the contingency of the art form is recognized as a function of accommodating an alterity, it is not an alterity that threatens to change the subject as much as it helps him or her to develop a state of self-awareness. Terry Eagleton describes the self-development of the reader engaged in the phenomenology of identifying difference as a contradictory process of moving back to one's original position, an "enriched self-knowledge which springs from an encounter with the unfamiliar" that doesn't change or "upbraid" the reader as much "as simply return to himself or herself as a more thoroughly liberal subject."[25] Further, Eagleton writes that "the plurality and open-endedness of the process of reading are permissible because they presuppose a certain kind of closed unity which always remains in place: the unity of the reading subject, which is violated and transgressed only to be returned more fully to itself."[26] In Attridge, then, we find a too cautious attempt to frame the focus on the creative agent(s) involved in looking at the other—the other as "relation," the other as "process," the other as "creativity," or "imaginative speculation." Attridge imagines difference as an anomaly of self-identity, making alterity a rupture from within the cultural web that structures perception. But in this model, we are not allowed to consider how the text is involved in a social process of producing the other, how it is linked to institutions that have a stake in managing the representation of alterity, how the text functions as *discourse*.

FESTE'S SONG: FIGURING CHEVERAL CONSCIOUSNESS AND THE NEW MATERIAL TURN

> To see this age!—A sentence is but a cheverel glove to a good wit, how quickly the wrong side may be turned outward.
>
> —Feste, in *Twelfth Night* (3.1.10–12)

If the careful aesthetic refashioning risks returning to a closed world, where we read all political and real-material others as functions of aesthetic play (pondering glaciers, ocean tides, sheep, etc.), we might begin to imagine that this retreat responds to a similar global crisis. Our interest in aesthetics may be a way of appropriating the bare life of the existence of the other into a courtly melancholy of another tune. We can think of Feste in *Twelfth Night* as the joker in this stacked deck to a degree, since his difference within my parable still begs to be accounted for. I am not thinking specifically of the way

---

25. Terry Eagleton, *Literary Theory* (Minneapolis: University of Minnesota Press, 1996), 69.
26. Ibid.

his wit tends to "turn outward" the staged gender differences, nor how his fooling mocks the pretension behind stylized courtly discourse and humanist leaning: "Pigrogromitus, of the Vapians passing the equinoctial of Queubus" (2.3.23–24). Critics have discussed Feste's language as destabilizing, and to this extent, his role in the play could be equated to Viola's in that it deconstructs the hierarchies of status and outward identity. Feste can symbolize that displaced other of a new global economy in the anthropocene. Like Viola, Feste assumes the position of the vagrant subject, roaming from court to court, but also from high to low and back again in ways that reproduce what Patricia Fumerton terms "low subjectivity": a "multiply displaced identity formation" representative of itinerant laborers through the songs and ballads of the period. "The unsettled subject," she explains, shifts "from place to place, relationship to relationship, and job to job," and is "'apprenticed' in a range of different identities or roles without ever attaining the 'freedom' of formulating an integrated and singular subjectivity."[27]

In this context, Feste imports another type of perspective into the play that cannot easily be located in the various negotiations of aesthetic play. He brings with him a form of entertainment that is appropriated into the courtly system of service, but in the songs themselves, we hear fragments of experience that cannot be fully "seen" by the controlling aesthetic fashioning. His wit works on the words of others like the leather of a cheverel glove turned inside out. The vocabulary of this image is resonant of Shakespeare's father's trade. It evokes a rustic world where fine luxury goods are made out of the remainder of butchered animals. Here the endless energy of wit to make double meaning of "wanton" words is embodied in the conceit of turning inside out a napa leather glove. By implication, rhetorical wordplay not only turns outward the thin-skinned, pliable associations of language, but also exposes the soft, felt-like underbelly of language to the harsh elements of exchange, enacting what Michel Serres might identify as the dark energy of "abuse value" of the parasite, who makes analogies between incommensurate things.[28] For me, Feste embodies the placelessness of the low, unsettled subject. According to Fumerton, the "multividual unsettled subject in the early modern period

---

27. Patricia Fumerton, *Unsettled: The Culture of Mobility and the Working Poor in Early Modern England* (Chicago: University of Chicago Press, 2006), 51.

28. How not to see Feste in Serres's parasite? "Every parasite that is a bit gifted, at the table of a somewhat sumptuous host, soon transforms the table into a theater. Thus comedy is first of all a feast. One eats, speaks, speaks of eating, stops eating to speak, all amid the noise. Thus the passage from the material to the logical occurs. The court-jester, in a representation, well-fed with a full meal, starts, rather unwisely, to tell the truth, to precipitate crises, withdraws at the moment of rupture, and tries to save his neck when the global balance is being drawn up" (Michel Serres, *The Parasite* [Minneapolis: University of Minnesota Press, 2013], 11–30).

who occupied the most extreme form of unsettledness (extensive physical displacement) can ... be seen as being composed of dispersed, serial 'selves'—variously defined occupationally, relationally, or spatially—that could be taken up, adjusted, and cast off as occasion demanded." Further, this "unlocalized social experience, which extended to other urban and country spaces as well, was also for such unsettled subjects a psychological experience, a state of consciousness that existed from place to place and was thus everywhere and nowhere at once."[29] We can think of Orsino's manic love as an attempt to "perform" this unsettled subjectivity, a miming of the itinerant identity that appropriates its oscillating emotional states and shifting standpoints as a form of courtly pastime. His is the waywardness of the new materialism. We have come full circle if we remember that it was Feste's song, "Come away death," that I invoked at the beginning of the essay to chart the dynamics of Orsino's aesthetic, but now we must read it as a response to the Duke's melancholy, a mockery of his solipsistic gravity. Importantly, the "place" of the song is signaled as coming from another cultural orientation free from the court:

ORSINO: Mark it, Cesario, it is old and plain.
   The spinsters, and the knitters in the sun
   And the free maids that weave their thread with bones
   Do use to chant it.
(2.4.42–45).

As critics have noted, the song can be read as a critique of Orsino's abject position through its bombastic references to unrequited love as an absolute death.[30] But the song's bending of gender—sung by working women but in the voice of a man slain by a cruel maid—and its frame as a folk idiom "old and plain" troubles the simple appropriation of the song as a critique of Orsino's love. One can hear in its simple resignation a profoundly disturbing truth of the bare life. Here the devastating burden of living in the anthropocene, a bare life in the postsustainable present, an existence not too easily written off through the redeeming lens of the pastoral: "Not a friend, not a friend greet / My poor corpse" (2.4.61–62). There is a dialectic overturning of this disempowered position in the double voice, a kind of abusive repurposing of Orsino's aesthetic narcissism. As a song sung during the practice of "knitting

---

   29. Fumerton, *Unsettled*, 51, 55.
   30. Richard Noble makes the case the song works as a critique of Malvolio's condition, adding that "Feste hints that a beneficial medicine for such constancy might be found in employment" (*Shakespeare's Use of Song with the Text of The Principal Songs* [London: Oxford, 1966], 83).

in the sun," it is a tune that can be located within what Fumerton describes as a crucial space of itinerant existence that defined the transitory nature of piecemeal domestic labor: "In many cases, it was a poor woman's involvement in such various patchwork labor that formed the ragged, thin line separating her family from destitution."[31] The song conjures this patchwork labor and its thin line: merry entertainment to while away the time of toil, but also an expression of the deepest anxieties about the frailty of life and crushing solitude of transient labor. Feste shares in this bare existence—"for the rain it raineth everyday"—constantly begging "gratility" for his services from different characters in the play. Viola recognizes Feste's astute eye to his patron's social position as a predator-like regard: "He must observe their mood on whom he jests, / The quality of persons, and the time," she explains. "And, like the haggard"—a female hawk—"cheque at every feather / That comes before his eye" (3.1.10–13). It's an attentiveness for the other that is motivated by economic survival. His is a placeless mentality and waywardness, a shifting of conceptual parameters that recognizes the unseen truth of identity as an unfixed category contingent upon status and location. "Dost thou live by thy tabour?" Viola asks. "No, sir," he responds, "I live by the church."

> VIOLA: Art thou a churchman?
> FESTE: No such matter, sir: I do live by the church for
>   I do live at my house, and my house doth stand by
>   the church.
> VIOLA: So thou mayst say, the king lies by a beggar, if a
>   beggar dwell near him, or the church stands by thy
>   tabour, if thy tabour stand by the church.
> (3.1.4–9)

This odd exchange is frequently quoted to highlight Feste's wordplay. The simple observation about slippages in language—prepositional phrases that imply profession and status—can also represent the fact that Feste is hiding his trade. This exchange should also be read in the context of the complicated history of Poor Laws that defined the Reformation state and its response to displaced labor; the laws attempted to bring all able-bodied men to work by identifying "sturdy beggars" from the mix of roving laborers and entertainers, some of whom reportedly hid their status by feigning disability.[32] These Poor

---

31. Fumerton, *Unsettled*, 23.

32. For a description of the way Tudor England criminalized the poor, see Craig Dionne and Steve Mentz, eds., *Rogues and Early Modern Culture* (Ann Arbor: University of Michigan Press, 2004). For an historical accounting of the Poor Laws, see chapter 2, "Legislation in

Laws, especially the notorious 1572 Act of Vagabonds, made a host of itinerant practices illegal: "players in interludes, and minstrels . . . jugglers, peddlers, tinkers, and petty chapmen." Feste's allusion to playing a tabour for/next to the church seems like a cunning strategy to mask his status as a sturdy beggar.

But we can also see Feste evoking this world in his exchanges with Orisino. Feste's comment to the Duke that he should wear a "doublet of changeable taffeta"—the rich, dark velvet that, like Orsino's own narcissism, reflects the light that is caught in its folds—alludes to the textile labor hidden behind the song. Feste is symbolically dressing the Duke in the woven material of domestic labor, wrapping him with the shifting reflections of the unsettled life of the working poor, as if inverting the practice of patronage by giving the Duke a livery of his itinerant class. Feste playfully draws attention to the Duke's misidentification of alienation as melancholy, as the transient identities of spinsters and knitters in the sun are forced subject positions, not freely chosen affairs of the heart. Feste's sly response to Orsino that he would have such men "put to sea, that their business might be everything, and their intent everywhere" (2.4.76–77) can now be read as a vengeful solution to the Duke's problem: conscript him in the navy, where all vagabonds are sent, and perhaps this will cure him of his melancholy. Feste's language translates Orsino's subject position from within his own vagrant perspective, making sense of love's madness as an expression of a deeper social problem of poverty and homelessness in the late sixteenth century. Feste's retreat is also an inverted mirror image of Orsino's, an allegory of a grounded reinvestment in the ecomaterial referent hidden by our (in)attention to literary closure all along. Do not the characters in this play approach Feste like many old historicists might approach object-oriented materialists or the new ecomaterialists whose work seems to "play" at the edges of reading literature and/or sheep, rocks, oceans, objects? From Orsino's perspective anyway, Feste might seem dissociative, if not sociopathological, in his concern for the everyday "things" of his environment, or perhaps outright misanthropic in his dismissing of the Duke's concern for issues of the self and its language of the "politics of representation." Feste is mad in another key, seemingly "off the map," a tabour/chevril-obsessed vagabond, whose perspective is grounded in the malaise of what Julian Yates has termed *thing madness*.[33] In response, Feste might say, if you mean to dance on the

---

England," in Paola Pugliatti, *Beggary and Theater in Early Modern England* (Burlington, VT: Ashgate, 2003). Fumerton's chapter 3, "Disguising the Working Poor," in *Unsettled*, makes the case that migrant laborers are misperceived as vagabonds and beggars in the laws and pamphlets of the age.

33. Where the footsteps of the critic become "the remnants/traces of their putting to use, to manifest, dislocating conventional histories, to constitute their story," which in turn is read

earth, look down and pay attention to it. If you mean to wrap yourself in fibers, at least pay attention to where they come from and who makes them and the shanties they live in. Rethinking otherness in your great house will not help us think beyond the anthropocene.

To conclude, it is possible that such a vision of the world—itinerant subjects free but trapped in the destitute existence outside the manor house—can be appropriated by the humanist aesthetic that wants to reproduce the bare life as a reflection of a more ideal "houseless condition" of the liberal subject. But Feste's very language attests to the lived context outside the courtly discourse of love's madness. The "grain" of this itinerant ideology, to use one of our own rustic metaphors, resists the closure of the humanist appropriation. Within our parable, the danger for some of us who may consider ourselves "stewards" of liberal culture wanting to return to aesthetics is that we can potentially shut our ear to alterity in our very efforts to hear it, to understand it. I might point to the mode of my own analysis here as an example of the limits of this form of reflection, where the various subtleties of *Twelfth Night* are made to fit the example of my parable, where the authenticity of my argument looks to the canonical text for grounding, as if looking out the manor windows to make sense of the storm but seeing only the dim reflection of the interior in the drying drops on the glass. Like Orsino we can misread the alienating experience of the other as an instance of our own vision. I think of it as a problem posed quite elegantly in the final scene of Trevor Nunn's film production of *Twelfth Night*, where we see in the last images Feste leaving the manor to return to his homeless existence and live with the sheep. Before we return to the "comic dance" in the manor, we are asked to ponder how Feste will be affected by the winds of modernity and the respective forces of Western capitalism his new life symbolizes: surplus labor and the free proletariat, but also life as other and surviving in a postsustainable future. We must not turn our backs to the subaltern stories outside the manor, but we must be mindful not to aestheticize the bare life, either. Listening with a keen ear to the other, we should be careful we do not turn Feste's story into another plaintive tune of our own courtly melancholy.

---

by old materialists and historicists as going "'thing mad' [by] enchanting the 'everyday' with a plentitude [the critic] otherwise fail[s] to find in the real world" (Julian Yates, "Accidental Shakespeare," *Shakespeare Studies* 34 [2006]: 98 [90–122]).

BIBLIOGRAPHY

Abbate, Carolyn. *Unsung Voices: Opera and Musical Narrative in the Nineteenth Century.* Princeton, NJ: Princeton University Press, 1996.
Acampora, Ralph R. *Corporal Compassion: Animal Ethics and Philosophy of Body.* Pittsburgh, PA: University of Pittsburgh Press, 2006.
Adcock, Fleur. *Hugh Primas and the Archpoet.* New York: Cambridge University Press, 1994.
Aers, David. *Community, Gender, and Individual Identity: English Writing, 1360–1430.* London: Routledge, 1988.
Agamben, Giorgio. *The Coming Community.* Translated by Michael Hardt. Minneapolis: University of Minnesota Press, 1993.
———. *Homo Sacer: Sovereign Power and Bare Life.* Translated by Daniel Heller-Roazen. Stanford: Stanford University Press, 1998.
Ahl, Frederick. *Sophocles' Oedipus: Evidence and Self-Conviction.* Ithaca, NY: Cornell University Press, 1991.
Alaimo, Stacy. *Bodily Natures: Science, Environment, and the Material Self.* Bloomington: Indiana University Press, 2010.
Albert the Great. *De animalibus libri XXVI.* Edited by Hermann Stadler. 2 vols. Munich: Aschendorff, 1916.
Alexander, Caroline. "If the Stones Could Speak: Searching for the Original Meaning of Stonehenge." *National Geographic* (June 2008): 34–59.
Alford, John A. "The Biblical Identity of Richard Rolle." *Fourteenth-Century English Mystics Newsletter* 2.4 (1976): 21–25.
———. "Biblical *Imitatio* in the Writings of Richard Rolle." *ELH* 40.1 (1973): 1–23.
Alighieri, Dante. *The Divine Comedy of Dante Alighieri.* Vol. 2: *Purgatorio.* Translated by Robert M. Durling. Oxford: Oxford University Press, 2003.
———. *The Inferno of Dante.* Translated by Robert Pinsky. New York: Noonday Press, 1994.
The Animal Studies Group, ed. "Conclusion: A Conversation." *Killing Animals.* Chicago: University of Chicago Press, 2006. 188–210.
Ankersmit, F. R. *Historical Representation.* Stanford, CA: Stanford University Press, 2002.
Archibald, Elizabeth. *Incest and the Medieval Imagination.* Oxford: Clarendon Press, 2001.
Arens, William. "Cooking the Cannibals." In *Consuming Passions: Food in the Age of Anxiety,* edited by Jennifer Wallace and Sian Griffiths. Manchester, UK: Mandolin, 1998. 156–66.
———. *The Man-Eating Myth: Anthropology and Anthropophagy.* New York: Oxford University Press, 1979.
———. "Rethinking Anthropophagy." In *Cannibalism and the Colonial World,* edited by Francis Barker, Peter Hulme, and Margaret Iversen. New York: Cambridge University Press, 1998. 39–62.
Aristotle. *The Poetics of Aristotle.* Edited by S. H. Butcher. 4th ed. London: Macmillan, 1907.

Astell, Ann W. *Political Allegory in Late Medieval England*. Ithaca, NY: Cornell University Press, 1999.

Attridge, Derek. *The Singularity of Literature*. New York: Routledge, 2004.

Augustine. *The City of God*. Translated by Marcus Dods. New York: Modern Library, 1950.

———. *On Free Choice of the Will*. Translated by Thomas Williams. Indianapolis, IN: Hackett Pub. Co., 1993.

Avrich, Jane, Steven Johnson, Raph Koster, Thomas de Zengotita, and Bill Wasich. "Forum— Grand Theft Education—Literacy in the Age of Video Games." *Harper's* (September 2006): 31–39.

Badiou, Alain. *In Praise of Love*. Paris: Flammarion, SA, 2009.

Bahn, Paul G. *The Cambridge Illustrated History of Prehistoric Art*. Cambridge: Cambridge University Press, 1998.

Bahn, Paul, and Jean Vertut. *Journey through the Ice Age*. Berkeley: University of California Press, 1997.

Baker, Steve. "'You Kill Things to Look at Them': Animal Death in Contemporary Art." In *Killing Animals*, edited by The Animal Studies Group. Chicago: University of Chicago Press, 2006. 69–98.

Bamber, Linda. *Comic Women, Tragic Men*. Stanford, CA: Stanford University Press, 1982.

Barker, Juliet. *The Tournament in England 1100–1400*. Woodbridge, Suffolk: Boydell and Brewer, 2003.

Barnum, Priscilla Heath, ed. *Dives and Pauper*. 2 vols. EETS o.s. 275, 280. London: Oxford University Press, 1976.

Barthes, Roland. "The Face of Garbo." *Mythologies*. Translated by John Cape. New York: Hill and Wange, 1972. 56–57.

———. "La mort de l'Auteur." *Manteia* 5.4 (1968): 12–17.

Bartram, Rob. "Visuality, Dromology and Time Compression: Paul Virilio's New Ocularcentrism." *Time and Society* 13.2–3 (2004): 285–300.

Bataille, Georges. *Death and Sensuality: A Study of Eroticism and the Taboo*. Translated by Mary Dalwood. New York: Walker and Company, 1962.

Battles, Dominique. *The Medieval Tradition of Thebes: History and Narrative in the OF Roman de Thebes, Boccaccio, Chaucer, and Lydgate*. New York: Routledge, 2004.

Baudrillard, Jean. *The Consumer Society: Myths and Structures*. London: Sage Publications, 1998.

———. *The Ecstasy of Communication*. Translated by Bernard and Caroline Schultze. New York: Semiotext(e), 1988.

Bauman, Zygmunt. "Foreword: Individually, Together." In *Individualization: Institutionalized Individualism and its Social and Political Consequences,* edited by Ulrich Beck and Elisabeth Beck-Gernsheim. Translated by Patrick Camiller. London: Sage Publications, 2002. xiv–xix.

———. *Liquid Modernity*. Cambridge: Polity, 2000.

Bec, Pierre. *Burlesque et obscénité chez les troubadours: pour une approche du contre-texte médiéval*. Paris: Stock, 1984.

———. *La Lyrique Occitane du Moyen Age*. Avignon: Éditions Aubanel, 1970.

Beck, Ulrich. *Risk Society: Towards a New Modernity*. Translated by Mark Ritter. London: Sage Publications, 1992.

Beck, Ulrich, and Elisabeth Beck-Gernsheim, eds. *Individualization: Institutionalized Individualism and its Social and Political Consequences*. Translated by Patrick Camiller. London: Sage Publications, 2002.

Beckett, Samuel. "Dante . . . Bruno. Vico . . Joyce." In *Samuel Beckett: The Grove Centenary Edition*, vol. 4. New York: Grove Press, 2006. 495–510.

———. "Fingal." *More Pricks than Kicks. Samuel Beckett: The Grove Centenary Edition.* Vol. 4. New York: Grove Press, 2006.

———. *I Can't Go On, I'll Go On: A Selection from Samuel Beckett's Work.* Edited by Richard Seaver. New York: Grove Press, 1976.

———. *Molloy.* In *Samuel Beckett: The Grove Centenary Edition,* vol. 2. New York: Grove Press, 2006. 1–168.

———. *More Pricks than Kicks. Samuel Beckett: The Grove Centenary Edition.* Vol. 4. New York: Grove Press, 2006.

———. "Rough for Radio II." *Samuel Beckett: The Grove Centenary Edition.* Vol. 3. New York: Grove Press, 2006.

Belsey, Catherine. *Subject of Tragedy: Identity and Difference in Renaissance Drama.* New York: Methuen, 1985.

Bennett, Jane. *The Enchantment of Modern Life: Attachments, Crossings, and Ethics.* Princeton, NJ: Princeton University Press, 2001.

———. *Thoreau's Nature: Ethics, Politics, and the Wild.* Rev. ed. Lanham, MD: Rowan and Littlefield, 2002.

———. *Vibrant Matter: A Political Ecology of Things.* Durham, NC: Duke University Press, 2010.

Bersani, Leo. "Psychoanalysis and the Aesthetic Subject." *Critical Inquiry* 32 (2006): 161–74.

Bersani, Leo, and Ulysse Dutoit. *Forms of Being: Cinema, Aesthetics, Subjectivity.* London: BFI Publishing, 2004.

Biddick, Kathleen. *The Shock of Medievalism.* Durham, NC: Duke University Press, 1998.

Binski, Paul, and Stella Panayotova. *The Cambridge Illuminations: Ten Centuries of Book Production in the Medieval West.* London: Harvey Miller, 2005.

Blanchot, Maurice. "Où maintenant? Qui maintenant?" *La nouvelle revue française* (10 October 1953), 678–86. Reprinted in Blanchot, *Le livre à venir.* Paris: Editions de Minuit, 1959.

Bloch, R. Howard. *Etymologies and Genealogies: An Anthropology of the French Middle Ages.* Chicago: University of Chicago Press, 1983.

———. *Medieval Misogyny and the Invention of Western Romantic Love.* Chicago: University of Chicago Press, 1992.

Blumstein, Alex. "Masochism and Fantasies of Preparing to Be Incorporated," *Journal of the American Psychoanalytic Association* 7 (1959): 292–98.

Blurton, Heather. *Cannibalism in High Medieval English Literature.* New York: Palgrave Macmillan, 2007.

Bober, Phyllis Pray. *Art, Culture, and Cuisine: Ancient and Medieval Gastronomy.* Chicago: University of Chicago Press, 1999.

Bogost, Ian. *Alien Phenomenology, or What It's Like to Be a Thing.* Minneapolis: University of Minnesota Press, 2012.

Booth, Stephen. "Twelfth Night 1.1: The Audience as Malvolio." *Shakespeare's Rough Magic: Essays in Honor of C. L. Barber,* edited by Peter Erikson and Coppelia Kahn. Newark: University of Delaware Press, 1985. 149–67.

Bostrom, Nick. *Superintelligence: Paths, Dangers, Strategies.* Oxford: Oxford University Press, 2014.

———. "Why I Want to Be a Posthuman When I Grow Up." In *Medical Enhancement and Posthumanity,* edited by Bert Gordijn and Ruth Chadwick. Dordrecht: Springer, 2008. 107–37. http://nickbostrom.com.

Boswell, John Eastburn. *The Kindness of Strangers: The Abandonment of Children in Western Europe from Late Antiquity to the Renaissance.* New York: Pantheon, 1988.

Bourdieu, Pierre. *Outline of a Theory of Practice.* Translated by Richard Nice. New York: Cambridge University Press, 1977.

Boyarin, Daniel, ed. *The Ethnography of Reading.* Berkeley: University of California Press, 1993.
Boyle, T. Coraghessan. "Bloodfall." *Descent of Man: Stories.* New York: Penguin, 1990.
Bowers, John M. *The Prologue to the Siege of Thebes.* From BL Arundel 119. Folios. 1a–4a. http://www.lib.rochester.edu/camelot/teams/lydgtint.htm.
Bracciolini, Poggio. *Facezie.* Edited by Eugenio Garin. Translated (into Italian) by Marcello Ciccuto. Milan: Bibliotecha Universale Rizzoli, 1994.
Braidotti, Rosi. *Metamorphoses: Towards a Materialist Theory of Becoming.* Cambridge: Polity Press, 2002.
———. *The Posthuman.* Cambridge: Polity Press, 2013.
Bratton, Benjamin. *The Stack: On Software and Sovereignty.* Cambridge, MA: MIT Press, 2015.
Braudel, Fernand. "Histoire et sciences sociale: La longue durée." Translated by Sarah Matthews. In *Histories: French Constructions of the Past,* edited by Jacques Revel and Lynn Hunt. New York: The New Press, 1995. 115–45.
Brewer, Derek. "Medieval Literature: Chaucer and the Alliterative Tradition." In *The New Pelican Guide to English Literature.* Vol. 1. Edited by Boris Ford. New York: Penguin Books, 1982. 133–53.
Brook, Peter, and Alex Woloch, eds. *Whose Freud? The Place of Psychoanalysis in Contemporary Culture.* New Haven, CT: Yale University Press, 2000.
Brownrigg, Linda L., ed., *Medieval Book Production: Assessing the Evidence: Proceedings of the Second Conference of the Seminar in the History of the Book to 1500, Oxford, July 1988.* Los Altos Hills, CA: Anderson-Lovelace, 1990.
Brownstein, Oscar. "The Popularity of Baiting in England before 1600: A Study in Social and Theatrical History." *Educational Theatre Journal* 21 (1969): 237–50.
Brunner, Karl, ed. *Der mittelenglische Versroman über Richard Löwenherz: kritische Ausgabe nach allen Handschriften mit Einleitung, Anmerkungen und deutscher Übersetzung.* Wien: W. Braumüller, 1913.
Bryant, Levi. *The Democracy of Objects.* Ann Arbor, MI: Open Humanities Press, 2011.
Bryant, Levi, Nick Srnicek, and Graham Harman, eds. *The Speculative Turn: Continental Materialism and Realism.* Melbourne: re.press, 2011.
Buc, Philippe. "Manducation et domination: Analyse du Métaphore." In *L'Ambiguïté du Livre: prince, pouvoir, et peuple dans les commentaires de la Bible au Moyen Âge.* Paris: Beauchesne, 1994. 206–31.
Buhle, Mary Jo. *Feminism and Its Discontents: A Century of Struggle with Psychoanalysis.* Cambridge, MA: Harvard University Press, 2000.
Burger, Glenn and Stephen F. Kruger, eds. *Queering the Middle Ages.* Minneapolis: University of Minnesota Press, 2001.
Burns, E. J. "The Man behind the Lady in Troubadour Lyric." *Romance Notes* 25.3 (1985): 254–70.
Butler, Judith. "Changing the Subject: Judith Butler's Politics of Radical Resignification." Interview with G. A. Olson and L. Worsham. In *The Judith Butler Reader,* edited by Sarah Salih. Oxford: Blackwell, 2004. 325–56.
———. *Gender Trouble: Feminism and the Subversion of Identity.* New York: Routledge, 1990.
———. *Precarious Life: The Powers of Mourning and Violence.* New York: Verso, 2004.
Bynum, Caroline Walker. *Docere Verbo et Exemplo: An Aspect of Twelfth-Century Spirituality.* Missoula, MT: Scholars Press, 1978.
———. *Fragmentation and Redemption: Essays on Gender and the Human Body in Medieval Religion.* Cambridge, MA: Zone Books, 1991.
———. *Jesus as Mother: Studies in the Spirituality of the High Middle Ages.* Berkeley: University of California Press, 1982.
———. *The Resurrection of the Body in Western Christianity, 200–1336.* New York: Columbia University Press, 1995.

Caillois, Roger. *The Edge of Surrealism: A Roger Caillois Reader.* Edited by Claudine Frank. Durham, NC: Duke University Press, 2003.
——. "Mimicry and Legendary Psychasthenia." In *The Edge of Surrealism: A Roger Caillois Reader.* Durham, NC: Duke University Press, 2003. 91–103.
——. "The Praying Mantis: From Biology to Psychoanalysis." In *The Edge of Surrealism: A Roger Caillois Reader.* Durham, NC: Duke University Press, 2003. 66–81.
——. *The Writing of Stones.* Edited by Marguerite Yourcenar. Translated by Barbara Bray. Charlottesville: University of Virginia Press, 1985.
Calarco, Matthew. *Zoographies: The Question of the Animal from Heidegger to Derrida.* New York: Columbia University Press, 2008.
Caputo, John D. *Against Ethics: Contributions to a Poetics of Obligation with Constant Reference to Deconstruction.* Bloomington: Indiana University Press, 1993.
——. "Bodies Still Unrisen, Events Still Unsaid." *Angelaki* 12.1 (April 2007): 73–86.
Carruthers, Mary. *The Craft of Thought: Meditation, Rhetoric, and the Making of Images, 400–1200.* New York: Cambridge University Press, 1998.
——. "Sweetness." *Speculum* 81 (2006): 999–1013.
Cassianus Bassus, Constantine, and Antoine Pierre. *Les XX. liures de Constantin César, ausquels sont traictés lesbons enseignemens d'agriculture.* Poictiers: Iehan and Enguilbert de Marnef, 1545.
Cederberg, Carl. *Resaying the Human: Levinas beyond Humanism and Antihumanism.* Södertörn Doctoral Dissertations 52. Stockholm: Södertörns högskola, 2010.
Chambers, Iain. *Culture after Humanism: History, Culture, Subjectivity.* London: Routledge, 2001.
Charnes, Linda. "Reading for the Wormholes: Micro-periods from the Future." *Early Modern Culture: An Electronic Seminar.* Issue 6: Timely Meditations. 2007. http://emc.eserver.org/1-6/charnes.html.
Chartier, Roger. *On the Edge of a Cliff: History, Language, Practices.* Translated by Lydia G. Cochrane. Baltimore: Johns Hopkins University, 1996.
Chasseguet-Smirgel, Janine. *Creativity and Perversion.* London: Free Association Books, 1985.
Chaucer, Geoffrey. *Legend of Good Women.* In *The Works of Geoffrey Chaucer*, edited by F. N. Robinson. 2nd ed. Cambridge: Riverside Press, 1957.
Chrulew, Matthew. "Feline Divinanimality: Derrida and the Discourse of Species in Genesis." *The Bible and Critical Theory* 2.2 (2006): 18.1–18.22.
Clanchy, Michael T. *From Memory to Written Record, England 1066–1307.* 2nd ed. Oxford: Blackwell, 1993.
Clarke, Bruce. *Posthuman Metamorphosis: Narrative and Systems.* New York: Fordham University Press, 2008.
Classen, Albrecht, ed. *Violence in Medieval Courtly Literature: A Casebook.* Routledge Medieval Casebooks. New York: Routledge, 2004.
Clottes, Jean. *Chauvet Cave: The Art of Earliest Times.* Translated by Paul Bahn. Salt Lake City: University of Utah Press, 2003.
Cohen, Esther. "Animals in Medieval Perceptions: The Image of the Ubiquitous Other." In *Animals in Human Society: Changing Perspectives*, edited by Aubrey Manning and James Serpell. London: Routledge, 1994. 59–80.
Cohen, Jeffrey Jerome. "Afterword: An Unfinished Conversation about Glowing Green Bunnies." In *Queering the Non/human*, edited by Giffney and Hird, 363–75.
Cohen, Jeffrey Jerome. *Hybridity, Identity and Monstrosity in Medieval Britain: On Difficult Middles.* New York: Palgrave, 2006.
——. "Introduction: Midcolonial." In *The Postcolonial Middle Ages*, edited by Cohen. New York: Palgrave Macmillan, 2000. 1–17.

———. *Medieval Identity Machines*. Medieval Cultures 35. Minneapolis: University of Minnesota Press, 2003.

———. *Stone: An Ecology of the Inhuman*. Minneapolis: University of Minnesota Press, 2015.

———, ed. *Animal, Vegetable, Mineral: Ethics and Objects*. Brooklyn, NY: punctum books, 2012.

———, ed. *Ecologies of the Inhuman*. Brooklyn, NY: punctum books, 2014.

———, ed. *Inhuman Nature*. Brooklyn, NY: punctum books, 2014.

———, ed. *Prismatic Ecology: Ecotheory beyond Green*. Minneapolis: University of Minnesota Press, 2013.

Cohen, Jeffrey Jerome, and Lowell Duckert, eds. "Ecomaterialism." Special issue, *postmedieval: a journal of medieval cultural studies* 4.1 (2013).

Cole, Andrew, and D. Vance Smith, eds. *The Legitimacy of the Middle Ages: On the Unwritten History of Theory*. Durham, NC: Duke University Press, 2010.

Colebrook, Claire. *Death of the Posthuman: Essays on Extinction, Vol. 1*. Ann Arbor, MI: Open Humanities Press/MPublishing, 2014.

Connolly, William E. *The Fragility of Things: Self-Organizing Processes, Neoliberal Fantasies, and Democratic Activism*. Durham, NC: Duke University Press, 2013.

———. *Neuropolitics: Thinking, Culture, Speed*. Minneapolis: University of Minnesota Press, 2002.

Constable, Giles. *The Reformation of the Twelfth Century*. New York: Cambridge University Press, 1996.

Coole, Diana, and Samantha Frost, eds. *New Materialisms: Ontology, Agency, and Politics*. Durham, NC: Duke University Press, 2010.

Copeland, Rita. *Rhetoric, Hermeneutics, and Translation in the Middle Ages: Academic Traditions and Vernacular Texts*. New York: Cambridge University Press, 1991.

Crary, Jonathan. *24/7: Late Capitalism and the Ends of Sleep*. London: Verso, 2014.

Creech, Jim. "De la honte à la théorie." In *Lire, écrire la honte: Actes du colloque de Cérisy*, edited by Bruno Chaouat. Lyon: Presses Universitaires de Lyon, 2007.

———. unpublished work and communications, and his "La Honte dans la théorie." In *Le Coq Héron* 184. Secret, Honte et violences: La honte à l'épreuve de la psychanalyse (Winter 2006): 100–108.

Cummings, Brian. *The Literary Culture of the Reformation: Grammar and Grace*. New York: Oxford University Press, 2002.

Curtius, Ernst Robert. *European Literature and the Latin Middle Ages*. Princeton, NJ: Princeton University Press, 1967.

Davis, Douglas A. "A Theory for the 90s: Freud's Theory of Traumatic Seduction in Historical Context." *Psychoanalytic Review* 81 (1994): 627–39.

Davis, Kathleen. *Periodization and Sovereignty: How Ideas of Feudalism and Secularization Govern the Politics of Time*. Philadelphia: University of Pennsylvania Press, 2008.

Davis, Kathleen, and Nadia Altschul, eds. *Medievalisms in the Postcolonial World: The Idea of the "Middle Ages" Outside Europe*. Baltimore: Johns Hopkins University Press, 2009.

de Beauvoir, Simone. *The Second Sex*. New York: Bantam, 1970.

de Bergerac, Cyrano. *Histoire comique des Etats et Empire de la Lune*. In *Oeuvres*, vol. 2. Amsterdam: Jacques Desbordes, 1709. 83–85.

de Certeau, Michel. *The Writing of History*. Translated by Tom Conley. New York: Columbia University Press, 1988.

de France, Marie. *Les Lais de Marie de France*. Edited by Karl Warnke. Paris: Livre de Poche, 1990.

DeLanda, Manuel. *A New Philosophy of Society: Assemblage Theory and Social Complexity*. London: Continuum, 2006.

Deleuze, Gilles. "Mathesis, Science and Philosophy." *Collapse* 3 (2007): 141–55.

———. *Pure Immanence: Essays on a Life*. Translated by Anne Boyman. New York: Zone Books, 2001.

Deleuze, Gilles, and Félix Guattari. *A Thousand Plateaus: Capitalism and Schizophrenia*. Translated by Brian Massumi. Minneapolis: University of Minnesota Press, 1987.

Derrida, Jacques. *The Animal that Therefore I Am*. Edited by Marie-Louise Mallet. Translated by David Wills. New York: Fordham University Press, 2008.

———. "'Eating Well,' or The Calculation of the Subject." In *Points: Interviews, 1974–1994*, edited by Elisabeth Weber. Translated by Peggy Kamuf. Stanford, CA: Stanford University Press, 1995. 255–87.

———. *Given Time: I. Counterfeit Money*. Translated by Peggy Kamuf. Chicago: University of Chicago Press, 1992.

———. "Hospitality." In *Acts of Religion*, edited by Gil Anidjar. New York: Routledge, 2002. 356–420.

———. *L'animal autobiographique: Autour de Jacques Derrida*, ed. Marie-Louise Mallet. Paris: Galilée, 1999.

———. "The University without Condition." In Derrida, *Without Alibi*, edited and translated by Peggy Kamuf. Stanford, CA: Stanford University Press, 2002. 202–237.

———. "Violence and Metaphysics: An Essay on the Thought of Emmanuel Levinas." In *Writing and Difference*, translated by Alan Bass. Chicago: University of Chicago Press, 1978. 79–153.

Descola, Philippe. "All Too Human (Still): A Comment on Eduardo Kohn's *How Forests Think*." *HAU: Journal of Ethnographic Theory* 4.2 (2014): 267–73.

de Troyes, Chrétien. *Le Conte du Graal ou Le Roman de Perceval*. Edited by Charles Méla. In *Chrétien de Troyes: Romans*, edited by Michel Zink. Paris: Livre de Poche, 1994. 937–1211.

———. *Oeuvres completes*. Edited by Daniel Poirion. Translated by Daniel Poirion, Anne Berthelot, Peter F. Dembowski, and Philippe Walter. Paris: Gallimard, 1994.

Diamond, Jared. "The Worst Mistake in the History of the Human Race." *Discover Magazine* (May 1987): 64–66.

Dickinson, Emily. *The Poems of Emily Dickinson*. Edited by Mabel Loomis Todd and T. W. Higginson. Cambridge, MA: Harvard University Press, 1948. Reprint, Hayes Barton Press, 2007.

Dinshaw, Carolyn. *Getting Medieval: Sexualities and Communities, Pre- and Postmodern*. Durham, NC: Duke University Press, 1999.

———. *How Soon Is Now? Amateur Readers, Medieval Texts, and the Queerness of Time*. Durham, NC: Duke University Press, 2012.

———. "Queer Relations." *Essays in Medieval Studies* 16 (1999): 79–94.

———. "Theorizing Queer Temporalities." Edited by Elizabeth Freeman. *GLQ* 13 (2007): 177–95.

Dionne, Craig, and Steve Mentz, eds. *Rogues and Early Modern Culture*. Ann Arbor, MI: University of Michigan Press, 2004.

Donadio, Rachel. "The Closest Reader." *New York Times Review of Books*, 10 December 2006, http://www.nytimes.com/2006/12/10/books/review/Donadio.t.html.

Donovan, Josephine, and Carol J. Adams, eds. *The Feminist Care Tradition in Animal Ethics*. New York: Columbia University Press, 2007.

Dronke, Peter. *The Medieval Lyric*. Rochester, NY: D. S. Brewer, 1996.

Duffin, Ross, and Stephen Orgel. *Shakespeare Songbook*. New York: Norton, 2004.

Dylan, Bob. "Subterranean Homesick Blues." *Bringing It All Back Home*. Columbia Records, 1965.

Eagleton, Terry. *Literary Theory*. Minneapolis: University of Minnesota Press, 1996.

Edmunds, Lowell. *Oedipus: The Ancient Legend and Later Analogues*. Baltimore: Johns Hopkins University Press, 1985.

Edward of Norwich. *The Master of Game*. Edited by William A. Baillie-Grohman and Florence Baillie-Grohman. London: Ballantyne, Hanson and Co., 1904.

Edwards, Robert R. Introduction. *John Lydgate: The Siege of Thebes.* Kalamazoo, MI: Medieval Institute Publications, 2001. http://www.lib.rochester.edu/camelot/teams/thebint.htm.

Elmer, Jonathan, and Cary Wolfe. "Subject to Sacrifice: Ideology, Psychoanalysis, and the Discourse of Species in Jonathan Demme's *The Silence of the Lambs.*" 1995. Reprinted in *Animal Rites: American Culture, the Discourse of Species, and Posthumanist Theory,* edited by Cary Wolfe. Chicago: University of Chicago Press, 2003. 97–120.

Eshleman, Clayton. *Juniper Fuse: Upper Paleolithic Imagination and the Construction of the Underworld.* Middletown, CT: Wesleyan University Press, 2003.

Farina, Lara. "Before Affection: *Christ I* and the Social Erotic." *Exemplaria* 13.2 (2001): 469–96.

———. *Erotic Discourse and Early English Religious Writing.* New York: Palgrave MacMillan, 2006.

Feerick, Jean E., and Vin Nardizzi, eds. *The Indistinct Human in Renaissance Literature.* New York: Palgrave Macmillan, 2012.

Feher, Michel, Ramona Naddaff, and Nadia Tazied, eds. *Fragments for a History of the Human Body.* 3 vols. Cambridge, MA: Zone Books, 1989.

Feinsod, Harris. "The Tolson Exception: The Anthology in the 21st Century." *Arcade,* 9 January 2012. http://arcade.stanford.edu/blogs/tolson-exception-anthology-21st-century.

Ferrante, Joan. *Woman as Image in Medieval Literature: From the 12th Century to Dante.* New York and London: Columbia University Press, 1975.

Finucane, Ronald C. *The Rescue of the Innocents: Endangered Children in Medieval Miracles.* New York: St. Martin's Press, 1997.

de la Fontaine, Jean. "Preface," *Amours de Psiché et de Cupidon.* Paris: Claude Barbin, 1669. n.p.

Foucault, Michel. "Qu'est-ce qu'un auteur?" *Bulletin de la société française de philosophie* 63.3 (1969): 73–104.

———. *The Order of Things: An Archaeology of the Human Sciences.* London: Tavistock, 1966.

Foucault, Michel, with Jean Wahl, Maurice de Gandillac, Lucien Goldman, Jacques Lacan, Jean d'Ormesson, and Jean Ullmo. "Qu'est-ce qu'un auteur?" *Bulletin de la société française de philosophie* 63.3 (1969): 73–104. *Dits et écrits* 1:69.

Fradenburg, L. O. Aranye. *Sacrifice Your Love: Psychoanalysis, Historicism, Chaucer.* Minneapolis: University of Minnesota Press, 2002.

———. *Staying Alive: A Survival Manual for the Liberal Arts.* Brooklyn, NY: punctum books, 2013.

Fraiman, Susan. "Pussy Panic versus Liking Animals: Tracking Gender in Animal Studies." *Critical Inquiry* 39.1 (2012): 89–115.

Frank, Thomas. *The Conquest of Cool: Business Culture, Counterculture, and the Rise of Hip Consumerism.* Chicago: University of Chicago Press, 1997.

Freccero, Carla. "Chercher la chatte: Derrida's Queer Feminine Animality." In *French Thinking about Animales,* edited by Louisa Mackenzie and Stephanie Posthumus. Ann Arbor: Michigan State University Press, 2015. 105–20.

Freud, Sigmund. *Civilization and Its Discontents.* Translated and edited by James Strachey. London: W. W. Norton, 1961.

———. *The Interpretation of Dreams.* Vol. 4 of *The Standard Edition of the Complete Psychological Works of Sigmund Freud.* Translated by James Strachey. London: Hogarth Press, 1958 [1900].

———. *Moses and Monotheism.* Translated by Katherine Jones. Letchworth, UK: Hogarth Press, 1939.

———. *Three Essays on Sexuality.* Vol. 7 of *The Standard Edition of the Complete Psychological Works of Sigmund Freud.* Translated by James Strachey. London: Hogarth Press, 1953 [1905].

———. *Totem and Taboo: Some Points of Agreement between the Mental Lives of Savages and Neurotics.* Translated by James Strachey. New York: Routledge, 2001.

Frye, Northrop. *Anatomy of Criticism: Four Essays.* Princeton, NJ: Princeton University Press, 1957.

Fudge, Erica. *Pets*. Stocksfield, UK: Acumen, 2008.
Fukuyama, Francis. *Our Posthuman Future: Consequences of the Biotechnology Revolution*. New York: Farar, Straus, and Giroux, 2002.
Fulton, Rachel. "Praying with Anselm at Admont: A Meditation on Practice." *Speculum: A Journal of Medieval Studies* 81.3 (2006): 700–33.
Fumerton, Patricia. *Unsettled: The Culture of Mobility and the Working Poor in Early Modern England*. Chicago: University of Chicago Press, 2006.
Gallop, Jane. *The Daughter's Seduction: Feminism and Psychoanalysis*. Ithaca, NY: Cornell University Press, 1982.
Galloway, Andrew Scott. "Chaucer's Former Age and the Fourteenth-Century Anthropology of Craft: The Social Logic of a Premodernist Lyric." *ELH* 63.3 (1996): 535–54.
———. "John Lydgate and the Origins of Vernacular Humanism." *Journal of English and Germanic Philology* 107.4 (2008): 445–71.
Gamble, Clive. *Origins and Revolutions: Human Identity in Earliest Prehistory*. Cambridge: Cambridge University Press, 2007.
Gaselee, Stephen, ed. *The Oxford Book of Medieval Latin Verse*. 3rd ed. Oxford: Clarendon Press, 1946.
Gaunt, Simon. *Love and Death in Medieval French and Occitan Courtly Literature*. Oxford: Oxford University Press, 2006.
———. "Poetry of Exclusion: A Feminist Reading of Some Troubadour Lyrics." *Modern Language Review* 85.2 (1990): 310–29.
Gay, Peter. *A Godless Jew: Freud, Atheism, and the Making of Psychoanalysis*. New Haven, CT: Yale University Press, 1989.
Geller, Jay. *On Freud's Jewish Body: Mitigating Circumcisions*. New York: Fordham University Press, 2007.
Geoffrey of Monmouth. *Historia Regum Britanniae*. Edited by Acton Griscom. New York: Longmans, Green, and Co., 1929.
———. *Historia Regum Britanniae I: Bern, Bürgerbibliothek MS 568. 'Vulgate' Version*. Edited by Neil Wright. Cambridge, UK: D. S. Brewer, 1984.
———. *The History of the Kings of Britain*. Translated by Lewis Thorpe. London: Penguin Books, 1966.
Gergen, Kenneth. *The Saturated Self: Dilemmas of Identity in Contemporary Life*. New York: Basic Books, 1991.
Giddens, Anthony. *The Consequences of Modernity*. Stanford, CA: Stanford University Press, 1990.
———. *Modernity and Self-Identity: Self and Society in the Late Modern Age*. Stanford, CA: Stanford University Press, 1991.
Giffney, Noreen, and Myra J. Hird, eds. *Queering the Non/human*. Hampshire, UK: Ashgate, 2008.
Gilman, Sander L. *Freud, Race, and Gender*. Princeton, NJ: Princeton University Press, 1995.
Gilquin, Gaëtanelle, and George M. Jacobs, "Elephants Who Marry Mice are Very Unusual: The Use of the Relative Pronoun Who with Nonhuman Animals." *Society and Animals* 14 (2006): 79–105.
Girard, Rene, and Mark R. Anspach, eds. *Oedipus Unbound: Selected Writings on Rivalry and Desire*. Stanford, CA: Stanford University Press, 2004.
Goodhart, Sandor. "Lestas Ephaske: Oedipus and Laius' Many Murderers." In *Sacrificing Commentary: Reading the End of Literature*. Baltimore: Johns Hopkins University Press, 1996. 13–42.
Görlach, Manfred. *The Textual Tradition of the South English Legendary*. Leeds, UK: University of Leeds School of English, 1974.
Goux, Jean-Joseph. *Oedipus, Philosopher*. Translated by Catherine Porter. Stanford, CA: Stanford University Press, 1993.

Grabes, Herbert. "Introduction to New Developments in Literary Aesthetics." In *Anglisteng, 1994 Graz*, edited by Wolfgang Riehle and Hugo Keiper. Tübingen: Niemeyer, 1995. 297-98.

Green-Lewis, Jennifer, and Margaret Soltan. *Teaching Beauty in DeLillo, Woolf, and Merrill*. New York: Palgrave Macmillan, 2008.

Greenblatt, Stephen. *Will in the World: How Shakespeare Became Shakespeare*. New York: Norton, 2004.

Grosz, Elizabeth. "Animal Sex: Libido as Desire and Death." In *Space, Time, and Perversion: Essays on the Politics of Bodies*. New York: Routledge, 1995. 187-206.

———. *Chaos, Territory, Art: Deleuze and the Framing of Earth*. New York: Columbia University Press, 2008.

———. "Experimental Desire: Rethinking Queer Subjectivity." In *Space, Time, and Perversion: Essays on the Politics of Bodies*. New York: Routledge, 1995. 207-28.

———. *Space, Time, and Perversion: Essays on the Politics of Bodies*. New York: Routledge, 1995.

———. *Volatile Bodies: Toward a Corporeal Feminism*. Bloomington: Indiana University Press, 1994.

Grusin, Richard, ed. *The Nonhuman Turn*. Minneapolis: University of Minnesota Press, 2015.

Halberstam, Judith, and Ira Livingston. "Introduction: Posthuman Bodies." In *Posthuman Bodies*, edited by Halberstam and Livingston. Bloomington: Indiana University Press, 1995. 1-19.

Halliwell, Martin, and Andy Mousley. *Critical Humanisms: Humanist/Anti-Humanist Dialogues*. Edinburgh: Edinburgh University Press, 2003.

Hanawalt, Barbara. *Growing Up in Medieval London: The Experience of Childhood in History*. London: Oxford University Press, 1993.

———. *Ties That Bound: Peasant Families in Medieval England*. London: Oxford University Press, 1986.

Hanks, D. Thomas, Jr. "Malory's Anti-Knights: Balin and Breunys." In *The Social and Literary Contexts of Malory's Morte DArthur*, edited by D. Thomas Hanks, Jr., and Jessica Gentry Brogdon. Cambridge: D. S. Brewer, 2000. 94-110.

Hanna, Ralph. *Pursuing History: Middle English Manuscripts and Their Texts*. Stanford, CA: Stanford University Press, 1996.

Hanning, Robert. *The Individual in Twelfth-Century Romance*. New Haven, CT: Yale University Press, 1977.

———. *The Vision of History in Early Britain: From Gildas to Geoffrey of Monmouth*. New York: Columbia University Press, 1966.

Haraway, Donna. *The Companion Species Manifesto: Dogs, People, and Significant Otherness*. Chicago: Prickly Paradigm Press, 2003.

———. "A Cyborg Manifesto: Science, Technology, and Socialist-Feminism in the Late Twentieth Century." In *Simians, Cyborgs, and Women: The Reinvention of Nature*, edited by Haraway. New York: Routledge, 1991. 149-81.

———. *When Species Meet*. Minneapolis: University of Minnesota Press, 2008.

Harman, Graham. *Circus Philosophicus*. Winchester, UK: Zero Books, 2010.

———. "On Vicarious Causation." *Collapse* 2 (March 2007): 187-221.

———. *Prince of Networks: Bruno Latour and Metaphysics*. Melbourne: re.press, 2009.

———. *The Quadruple Object*. Hants, UK: Zero Books, 2011.

———. *Tool-Being: Heidegger and the Metaphysics of Objects*. Peru, IL: Open Court Publishing, 2002.

Harris, Jonathan Gil. *Untimely Matter in the Time of Shakespeare*. Philadelphia: University of Pennsylvania Press, 2008.

Haug, Walter. *Vernacular Literary Theory in the Middle Ages: The German Tradition, 800-1300, in its European Context*. Translated by J. M. Catling. Cambridge: Cambridge University Press, 1997.

Hayles, N. Katherine. *How We Became Posthuman: Virtual Bodies in Cybernetics, Literature, and Informatics*. Chicago: University of Chicago Press, 1999.
———. *My Mother Was a Computer: Digital Subjects and Literary Texts*. Chicago: University of Chicago Press, 2005.
Heath, Joseph, and Andrew Potter. *Nation of Rebels: Why Counterculture Became Consumer Culture*. New York: Harper Business, 2004.
The Hedgehog Review. "Introduction: Human Dignity and Justice." *Hedgehog Review* 9.3 (2007): 5–6.
Heidegger, Martin. "Language." In *Poetry, Language, Thought*, translated by Albert Hofstader. New York: Harper, 1971. 185–208.
———. [1946] *Letter on Humanism*. Translated by Frank A. Capuzzi. In Martin Heidegger, *Pathmarks: Texts in German philosophy*, edited by William McNeill. Cambridge: Cambridge University Press, 1998. 254.
———. "Logik: Heraklit's Lehre vom Logos." *Heraklit*, 'Gesamtausgabe,' Bd. 55. Frankfurt am Main: Vittorio Klosterman, 1970.
———. "The Nature of Language." In *On The Way to Language*, translated by Peter D. Hertz. New York: Harper, 1971. 57–110.
———. *On the Way to Language*. Translated by Peter D. Hertz. New York: Harper, 1971.
———. "'Only a God Can Save Us': *Der Spiegel*'s Interview with Martin Heidegger [1966]." Translated by Maria P. Alter and John D. Caputo. In *The Heidegger Controversy: A Critical Reader*, edited by Richard Wolin. Cambridge, MA: MIT Press, 1993. 105–7.
———. "Origin of a Work of Art." In *Poetry, Language, Thought*. Translated by Albert Hofstader. New York: Harper, 1971. 15–86.
———. *Poetry, Language, Thought*. Translated by Albert Hofstader. New York: Harper, 1971.
Heng, Geraldine. *Empire of Magic: Medieval Romance and the Politics of Cultural Fantasy*. New York: Columbia University Press, 2003.
Herbert, Zbigniew. *Mr. Cogito*. Hopewell, NJ: Ecco Press, 1993.
Herbrechter, Stefan, and Ivan Callas. *Posthumanist Shakespeares*. New York: Palgrave Macmillan, 2012.
Higgitt, John. *The Murthly Hours: Devotion, Literacy and Luxury in Paris, England and the Gaelic West*. London: British Library and University of Toronto Press, 2000.
Hirsh, John C. *Medieval Lyric: Middle English Lyrics, Ballads, and Carols*. Malden, MA: Blackwell Publishing, 2005.
Holder-Egger, O., ed. "Gesta abbatum S. Bertini Sithiensium." In *Monumenta Germaniae Historica SS 13*, edited by G. Waitz. Hanover: Impensis Bibliopolii Hahniani, 1881.
Hollywood, Amy. *Sensible Ecstasy: Mysticism, Sexual Difference, and the Demands of History*. Chicago: University of Chicago Press, 2001.
Holsinger, Bruce. *Music, Body, and Desire in Medieval Culture: Hildegard of Bingen to Chaucer*. Stanford, CA: Stanford University Press, 2001.
———. *The Premodern Condition: Medievalism and the Making of Theory*. Chicago: University of Chicago Press, 2005.
Holsinger, Bruce, and Ethan Knapp. "The Marxist Premodern." *Journal of Medieval and Early Modern Studies* 34.3 (2004): 463–71.
Howie, Cary. *Claustrophilia: The Erotics of Enclosure in Medieval Literature*. New York: Palgrave, 2007.
Huchet, Jean-Charles. *L'Amour discourtois: la "Fin'Amors" chez les premiers troubadours*. Toulouse: Privat, 1987.
Hulme, Peter. "Introduction: The Cannibal Scene." In *Cannibalism and the Colonial World*, edited by Francis Barker, Peter Hulme, and Margaret Iversen. New York: Cambridge University Press, 1998. 1–38.

Hunt, Elizabeth Moore. *Illuminating the Borders of Northern French and Flemish Manuscripts, 1270–1310.* New York: Routledge, 2006.

Huyssens, Andreas. *Present Pasts: Urban Palimpsests and the Politics of Memory.* Stanford, CA: Stanford University Press, 2003.

———. *Twilight Memories: Marking Time in a Culture of Amnesia.* New York: Routledge, 1995.

Ickstadt, Heinz. "Toward a Pluralist Aesthetic." In *Aesthetics in a Multicultural Age*, edited by Emory Elliot, Louis Caton, and Jeffrey Rhyne. New York: Oxford University Press, 2002. 263–78.

Inwood, Michael. *A Heidegger Dictionary.* London: Blackwell, 1999.

Irigaray, Luce. "The Fecundity of the Caress." In *Face to Face with Levinas*, edited by Richard A. Cohen. Albany: State University of New York Press, 1986. 231–56.

Irwin, Alec. "Devoured by God: Cannibalism, Mysticism, and Ethics in Simone Weil." *Cross Currents* 51 (2001): 257–72.

Ishiguro, Kazuo. *The Remains of the Day.* New York: Vintage, 1988.

Jacobus de Voragine. *The Golden Legend: Readings on the Saints.* Translated by William Granger Ryan. 2 vols. Princeton, NJ: Princeton University Press, 1993.

Jaeger, Werner. *Paideia: The Ideals of Greek Culture.* Vol. 2. *In Search of the Divine Centre.* New York: Oxford University Press, 1986.

Jameson, Fredric. "Magical Narratives: Romance as Genre." *New Literary History* 7.1 (1975): 135–63.

Jewers, Caroline. "The Cornilh Affair: Obscenity and the Counter-Text in the Occitan Troubadours, or, the Gift of the Gap." *Mediterranean Studies* 11 (2002): 29–43.

Johnson, Steven. *Interface Culture: How New Technology Transforms the Way We Create and Communicate.* San Francisco: HarperEdge, 1997.

Joy, Eileen A. "Like Two Autistic Moonbeams Entering the Window of My Asylum: Chaucer's Griselda and Lars von Trier's Bess McNeill." *postmedieval: a journal of medieval cultural studies* 2.3 (2011): 316–28.

Joy, Eileen A., and Craig Dionne, eds. "*When Did We Become Post/human?*" Special issue, *postmedieval: a journal of medieval cultural studies* 1.1/2 (2010).

Joy, Eileen A., and Christine Neufeld. "A Confession of Faith: Notes Toward a New Humanism." *JNT: Journal of Narrative Theory* 37.2 (2007): 161–90.

———, eds. "Premodern to Modern Humanisms: The BABEL Project." Special issue, *Journal of Narrative Theory* 37.2 (2007).

Joy, Eileen A., Myra J. Seaman, Kimberly Bell, and Mary Ramsey, eds. *Cultural Studies of the Modern Middle Ages.* New York: Palgrave Macmillan, 2007.

Kac, Eduardo. *Signs of Life: Bio Art and Beyond.* Cambridge, MA: MIT Press, 2007.

Kato, Kazumitsu. "Some Notes on *Mono no Aware*." *Journal of the American Oriental Society* 82.4 (1962): 558–59.

Katz, Claire Elise. *Levinas and the Crisis of Humanism.* Bloomington: Indiana University Press, 2012.

Kaufmann, Walter. *Tragedy and Philosophy.* Princeton, NJ: Princeton University Press, 1968.

Kaueper, Richard W. *Chivalry and Violence in Medieval Europe.* Oxford: Oxford University Press, 1999.

Kay, Sarah. "Commemoration, Memory and the Role of the Past in Chrétien de Troyes: Retrospection and Meaning in 'Erec and Enide,' 'Yvain,' and 'Perceval.'" *Reading Medieval Studies* XVII (1991): 31–50.

———. *Courtly Contradictions: The Emergence of the Literary Object in the Twelfth Century.* Stanford, CA: Stanford University Press, 2001.

Keen, Maurice. *Chivalry.* New Haven, CT: Yale University Press, 1984.

———. *Nobles, Knights, and Men-at-Arms in the Middle Ages.* London: Hambledon, 1996.

Keith, Arthur L. "A Virgilian Line." *Classical Journal* 17.7 (1922): 398–402.
Kempster, Hugh. "Richard Rolle, *Emendatio Vitae*." PhD diss., University of Waikato, 2007.
Kennedy, George A. *Classical Rhetoric and its Christian and Secular Tradition from Ancient to Modern Times.* Chapel Hill: University of North Carolina Press, 1980.
Kerby-Fulton, Kathryn, and Denise Louise Despres. *Iconography and the Professional Reader: The Politics of Book Production in the Douce Piers Plowman.* Minneapolis: University of Minnesota Press, 1999.
Key, Ellen. *The Century of the Child.* New York: G. P. Putnam's Sons, 1909.
Kikolopoulou, Kalliopi. "Feet, Fate, and Finitude: On Standing and Inertia in the *Iliad*." *College Literature* 34.2 (2007): 174–93.
Kilgour, Maggie. *From Communion to Cannibalism: An Anatomy of Metaphors of Consumption.* Princeton, NJ: Princeton University Press, 1990.
King, C. Richard. "The (Mis)uses of Cannibalism in Contemporary Cultural Critique." *Diacritics* 30 (2000): 106–23.
Kłosowska, Anna. *Queer Love in The Middle Ages.* New York: Palgrave Macmillan, 2005.
Knox, Bernard. "Sophocles' Oedipus." In *Tragic Themes in Western Literature*, edited by Cleanth Brooks. New Haven, CT: Yale University Press, 1955.
Koestenbaum, Wayne. *The Queen's Throat: Opera, Homosexuality, and the Mystery of Desire.* New York: Vintage Books, 1993.
Kohn, Eduardo. "How Dogs Dream: Amazonian Natures and the Politics of Transspecies Engagement." *American Ethnologist* 34.1 (2007): 3–24.
———. *How Forests Think: Towards an Anthropology Beyond the Human.* Berkeley: University of California Press, 2013.
Kristeva, Julia. *Powers of Horror: An Essay on Abjection.* Translated by Leon S. Roudiez. New York: Columbia University Press, 1982.
Kurzweil, Ray. *The Age of Spiritual Machines: When Computers Exceed Human Intelligence.* New York: Viking, 1999.
———. *The Singularity Is Near: When Humans Transcend Biology.* New York: Viking, 2005.
Kuspit, Donald. "The Triumph of Shit." http://www.artnet.com/magazineus/features/kuspit/kuspit9-11-08.asp.
Lacan, Jacques. *The Family Complexes.* Translated by Carolyn Asp. *Critical Texts* 5.3 (1988): 12–29.
———. *Le Séminaire, livre VII: L'éthique de la psychanalyse.* Paris: Seuil, 1986.
LaCapra, Dominick. *History and Memory after Auschwitz.* Ithaca, NY: Cornell University Press, 1998.
———. *Writing History, Writing Trauma.* Baltimore: Johns Hopkins University Press, 2001.
La manière de langage qui enseigne à bien parler et écrire le français. Modèles de conversations composés en Angleterre à la fin du XIVe siècle. Edited by Jean Gessler. Bruxelles: l'Édition Universelle; Paris: Droz, 1934.
Laporte, Dominique. *History of Shit.* Cambridge, MA: MIT Press, 1993.
Lash, Scott. "Foreword: Individualization in a Non-Linear Mode." In *Individualization: Institutionalized Individualism and its Social and Political Consequences*, edited by Ulrich Beck and Elisabeth Beck-Gernsheim and translated by Patrick Camiller. London: Sage Publications, 2002. vii–xiii.
Laskaya, Anne, and Eve Salisbury, eds. *The Middle English Breton Lays.* Kalamazoo, MI: Medieval Institute Publications, 1995.
Latham, Rob. "Cannibals and Kitchen Sinks [Review of Priscilla Walton, *Our Cannibals, Ourselves*]." *Contemporary Literature* 47 (2006): 502–4.
Latour, Bruno. *We Have Never Been Modern.* Translated by Catherine Porter. Cambridge, MA: Harvard University Press, 1993.

Lawlor, Leonard. *This Is Not Sufficient: An Essay on Animality in Derrida.* New York: Columbia University Press, 2007.

Le Guin, Ursula K. *The Disposessed: An Ambiguous Utopia.* New York: Harper, 1974. Reprint, Harper Voyager, 2011.

Lepetz, Sébastian. "Sacrifices et inhumations de chevaux et de chiens en France du nord au IIIe siècle après J.-C." In *Ces animaux que l'homme choisit d'inhumer: Contribution á l'étude de la place et du rôle de l'animal dans les rites funéraires; Journée d'étude Université Liège, 20 mars 1999,* edited by Liliane Bodson. Liege, Belgium: Liege University Press, 2000. 93–125.

Leroi-Gourhan, André. *Treasures of Prehistoric Art.* New York: Abrams, 1966.

———. *Les religions de la Prèhistoire.* Paris: Presses Universitaires de France, 1964.

Le Roman de Balain: A Prose Romance of the Thirteenth Century. Edited by M. Dominica Legge. Manchester, UK: Manchester University Press, 1920.

Les Troubadours: anthologie bilingue. Edited by Jacques Roubaud. Paris: Seghers, 1971.

Levinas, Emmanuel. "Diachrony and Representation." *Entre Nous: Thinking-of-the-Other.* Translated by Michael B. Smith and Barbara Harshav. New York: Columbia University Press, 1998. 159–78.

———. *Difficult Freedom: Essays on Judaism.* Translated by Sean Hand. Baltimore: Johns Hopkins University Press, 1990.

———. *Entre Nous: Thinking-of-the-Other.* Translated by Michael B. Smith and Barbara Harshav. New York: Columbia University Press, 1998.

———. "From the One to the Other." *Entre Nous: Thinking-of-the-Other.* Translated by Michael B. Smith and Barbara Harshav. New York: Columbia University Press, 1998. 133–54.

———. "Humanism and An-Archy." In *Humanism of the Other,* translated by Nidra Poller. Urbana: Illinois University Press, 2006. 45–57.

———. *Humanism of the Other.* Translated by Nidra Poller. Champaign: University of Illinois Press, 2003.

———. "The I and the Totality." *Entre Nous: Thinking-of-the-Other.* Translated by Michael B. Smith and Barbara Harshav. New York: Columbia University Press, 1998. 13–38.

———. "Is Ontology Fundamental?" *Entre Nous: Thinking-of-the-Other.* Translated by Michael B. Smith and Barbara Harshav. New York: Columbia University Press, 1998. 1–12.

———. "The Other, Utopia, and Justice." *Entre Nous: Thinking-of-the-Other.* Translated by Michael B. Smith and Barbara Harshav. New York: Columbia University Press, 1998. 223–33.

———. *Otherwise Than Being, Or Beyond Essence.* Translated by Alphonso Lingis. Pittsburgh, PA: Duquesne University Press, 1998.

———. "Signification and Sense." In *Humanism of the Other,* translated by Nidra Poller. Urbana: Illinois University Press, 2006. 9–44.

———. "Time and the Other." *The Levinas Reader.* Edited by Sean Hand. Oxford and Malden, MA: Blackwell Publishing, 1989. 37–58.

———. *Totality and Infinity: An Essay on Exteriority.* Translated by Alphonso Lingis. Pittsburgh, PA: Duquesne University Press, 1969.

Lindenbaum, Sheila. "The *Smithfield* Tournament of 1390." *Journal of Medieval and Renaissance Studies* 20.1 (1990), 1–20.

Lingis, Alphonso. "Animal Body, Inhuman Face." *Zoontologies: The Question of the Animal,* edited by Cary Wolfe. Minneapolis: University of Minnesota Press, 2003. 165–82.

Long, John. *Shakespeare's Use of Music: A Study of the Music and Its Performance in the Original Productions of Seven Comedies.* Gainesville: University of Florida Press, 1955.

Lothane, Zvi. "Freud's Alleged Repudiation of the Seduction Theory Revisited: Facts and Fallacies." *Psychoanalytic Review* 88.5 (October 2001): 673–723.

Low, Anthony. *Aspects of Subjectivity: Society and Individuality from the Middle Ages to Shakespeare and Milton.* Pittsburgh, PA: Duquesne University Press, 2003.

Lydgate, John. *John Lydgate's Prologue to the* Siege of Thebes, *The Canterbury Tales: Fifteenth-Century Continuations and Additions*. Edited by John M. Bowers. Kalamazoo, MI: Medieval Institute Publications, 1992.

———. *Lydgate's* Siege of Thebes. Edited by Axel Erdmann and Eilert Ekwall, EETS e.s. 108 and 125. London: Oxford University Press, 1911 and 1920.

Mackay, Robin. Introduction. *Collapse* 3 (2007): 4–39.

MacCormack, Patricia, ed. *The Animal Catalyst: Toward a Human Theory*. London: Bloomsbury, 2014.

Mackay, Robin, and Armen Avanessian. *#Accelerate: The Accelerationist Reader*. Falmouth, UK: Urbanomic, 2014.

Mackinlay, Shane. "Event, World, and Place." Paper presentation. Australian Society for Continental Philosophy Conference, University of Tasmania, 6 December 2007.

Malkmus, Stephen. "Cut Your Hair." *Crooked Rain, Crooked Rain*. Matador Records, 1994.

Malory, Thomas. "The Tale of Balyn and Balan." In *Le Morte Darthur, or The Hoole Book of King Arthur and of His Noble Knyghtes of the Round Table*, edited by Stephen H. Shepherd. New York: W. W. Norton, 2004. 40–61.

Malthrop, Stuart. "So You Say You Want a Revolution? Hypertext and the Laws of Media." *Postmodern Culture* 1.3 (1991): 691–704, http://jefferson.village.virginia.edu/pmc/text-only/issue.591/moulthro.591.

Mannoni, Octave. "Je sais bien, mais quand même. . . ." *Clefs pour l'imaginaire ou l'autre scène*. Paris: Editions du Seuil, 1969.

Marco Polo. *The Travels of Marco Polo*. Translated by Ronald Latham. New York: Penguin, 1958.

Marie de France. *The Lais of Marie de France*. Edited and translated by Robert Hanning and Joan Ferrante. Durham, NC: The Labyrinth Press, 1978.

Masciandaro, Nicola. "*Non potest hoc corpus decollari*: Beheading and the Impossible." In *Heads Will Roll: Decapitation in Medieval Literature and Culture*, edited by Larissa Tracy and Jeff Massey. Gainesville: University of Florida Press, 2010. 15–36.

Masson, Jeffrey. *Assault on the Truth: Freud's Suppression of the Seduction Theory*. New York: Farrar Straus and Giroux, 1984.

———, ed. and trans. *The Complete Letters of Sigmund Freud to Wilhelm Fliess, 1887–1904*. Cambridge, MA: Belknap Press, 1985.

McDonald, Nicola. "Eating People and the Alimentary Logic of *Richard Coeur de Lion*." In *Pulp Fictions of Medieval England: Essays in Popular Romance*, edited by McDonald. Manchester, UK: Manchester University Press, 2004. 124–50.

McGuire, William, ed. *The Freud/Jung Letters: The Correspondence between Sigmund Freud and C. C. Jung*. Translated by Ralph Manheum and R.F.C. Hull. Princeton, NJ: Princeton University Press, 1974.

McLuhan, Marshall. *Understanding Media: The Extensions of Man*. Cambridge, MA: MIT Press, 1994.

Meens, Rob. "Eating Animals in the Early Middle Ages: Classifying the Animal World and Building Group Identities." In *The Animal/Human Boundary: Historical Perspectives*, edited by William Chester Jordan and Angela N. H. Creager. Rochester, NY: University of Rochester Press, 2002. 3–28.

Meillassoux, Quentin. *After Finitude: An Essay on the Necessity of Contingency*. Translated by Ray Brassier. London: Bloomsbury, 2010.

———. "Subtraction and Contraction: Deleuze's Remarks." *Collapse* 3 (2007): 63–107.

Meli, Mark. "'Aware' as a Critical Term in Japanese Poetics." *Japan Review* 13 (2001): 67–91.

Melville, Herman. *Typee*. In *The Writings of Herman Melville*, edited by Harrison Hayford, Hershel Parker, and G. Thomas Tanselle. 9 vols. Evanston, IL: Northwestern University Press, 1968.

Meyer-Lee, Robert J. *Poets and Power from Chaucer to Wyatt.* Cambridge: Cambridge University Press, 2007.

Migne, J. P., ed. *Patrologia Latina.* Vol. 176. Paris: Parisiis, 1849.

Minnis, A. J. "*Quadruplex Sensus, Multiplex Modus:* Scriptural Sense and Mode in Medieval Scholastic Exegesis." In *Interpretation and Allegory: Antiquity to the Modern Period,* edited by Jon Whitman. Leiden: Brill, 2000. 229–54.

Mitchell, J. Allan. *Becoming Human: The Matter of the Medieval Child.* Minneapolis: University of Minnesota Press, 2014.

———. *Ethics and Eventfulness in Medieval English Literature.* New York: Palgrave, 2009.

Mitchell-Boyask, Robin. "Freud's Reading of Classical Literature and Classical Philology." In *Reading Freud's Reading,* edited by Sander L. Gilman, Jutta Birmele, and Jay Geller. New York: New York University Press, 1995. 23–46.

Modest Mouse. "Styrofoam Boots / It's All Nice on Ice." *The Lonesome Crowded West* (LP). Glacial Pace, 1997.

Mohen, Jean-Pierre. *Prehistoric Art: The Mythical Birth of Humanity.* Translated by John Tittensor. Paris: Pierre Terrail, 2002.

Montaigne, Michel de. *The Complete Essays of Montaigne.* Translated by Donald Frame. Stanford, CA: Stanford University Press, 1958.

Moravec, Hans. *Mind Children: The Future of Robot and Human Intelligence.* Cambridge, MA: MIT Press, 1988.

Morris, Colin. *The Discovery of the Individual, 1050–1200.* New York: Harper and Row, 1972.

Mortimer, Nigel. *John Lydgate's "Fall of Princes": Narrative Tragedy in Its Literary and Political Contexts.* Oxford: Clarendon Press, 2005.

Morton, Timothy. *Hyperobjects: Philosophy and Ecology after the End of the World.* Minneapolis: University of Minnesota Press, 2013.

———. *Realist Magic: Objects, Ontology, Causality.* Ann Arbor, MI: Open Humanities Press/MPublishing, 2013.

Murphy, James J. *A Short History of Writing Instruction from Ancient Greece to Twentieth-Century America.* Davis, CA: Hermagoras Press, 1990.

Myers, Robin, and Michael Harris. *A Millennium of the Book: Production, Design & Illustration in Manuscript & Print, 900–1900.* Winchester, DE: St. Paul's Bibliographies and Oak Knoll Press, 1994.

Nash, Susie. *Between France and Flanders: Manuscript Illumination in Amiens.* London: British Library and University of Toronto Press, 1999.

National Humanities Center. "Autonomy, Singularity, Creativity: A Project of the National Humanities Center." *National Humanities Center,* May 2007. http://onthehuman.org/archive/more/.

Negarestani, Reza. *Cyclonopedia: Complicity with Anonymous Materials.* Melbourne: re.press, 2008.

———. "Memento Tabere: Reflection on Time and Putrefaction." http://blog.urbanomic.com/cyclon/archives/2009/03/memento_tabi_re.html

Nelli, René. *L'érotique des troubadours, tome II.* Paris: Union Générale d'Éditions, 1974.

Nelson, Jan A., ed. *La Chanson d'Antioche.* Tuscaloosa: University of Alabama Press, 2003.

Newman, Barbara. "What Did It Mean to Say 'I Saw'? The Clash between Theory and Practice in Medieval Visionary Culture." *Speculum: A Journal of Medieval Studies* 80.1 (2005): 1–43.

Noble, Richard. *Shakespeare's Use of Song with the Text of The Principal Songs.* London: Oxford, 1966.

Nolan, Maura. *John Lydgate and the Making of Public Culture.* Cambridge: Cambridge University Press, 2005.

Norinaga, Motoori. *The Poetics of Motoori Norinaga: A Hermeneutical Journey.* Translated by Michael F. Marra. Honolulu: University of Hawai'i Press, 2007.

Noys, Benjamin. *Malign Velocities: Accelerationism and Capitalism.* Hants, UK: Zero Books, 2014.
Obeyesekere, Gananath. *Cannibal Talk: The Man-Eating Myth and Human Sacrifice in the South Seas.* Berkeley: University of California Press, 2005.
Oliver, Kelly. "Fatherhood and the Promise of Ethics." *Diacritics* 27.1 (1997): 45–57.
Oliver, Kelly, and Lisa Walsh. *Contemporary French Feminism.* Oxford: Oxford University Press, 2004.
Osborne, Lawrence. "Does Man Eat Man? Inside the Great Cannibalism Controversy." *Lingua Franca* (April/May 1997): 28–38.
Osborne, Peter. *The Politics of Time: Modernity and the Avant-Garde.* London: Verso, 1995.
Pearsall, Derek. *John Lydgate.* Charlottesville: University Press of Virginia, 1970.
The Petropunk Collective [Eileen A. Joy, Anna Kłosowska, Nicola Masciandaro, and Michael O'Rourke], eds. *Speculative Medievalisms: Discography.* Brooklyn, NY: punctum books, 2013.
Phelan, Peggy. *Unmarked: The Politics of Performance.* London and New York: Routledge, 1993.
Plassard, Jean. *Rouffignac: Le Sanctuaire des Mammouths.* Paris: Editions du Seuil, 1999.
Plassard, Marie-Odile, and Jean Plassard. *Visiter la Grotte de Rouffignac.* Luçon: Editions Sud Ouest, 1995.
Price, Merrall Llewelyn. *Consuming Passions: The Uses of Cannibalism in Late Medieval and Early Modern Europe.* New York: Routledge, 2003.
Pugliatti, Paola. *Beggary and Theater in Early Modern England.* Burlington, VT: Ashgate, 2003.
Read, Piers Paul. *Alive: The Story of the Andes Survivors.* Philadelphia: Lippincott, 1974.
Renoir, Alain. *The Poetry of John Lydgate.* Cambridge, MA: Harvard University Press, 1967.
Rigg, A. G. Rev. of Fleur Adcock, *Hugh Primas and the Archpoet. Speculum* 71.4 (1996): 925–26.
Rolle, Richard. "Ego Dormio." In *Richard Rolle, the English Writings,* edited by Rosamund Allen. New York: Paulist Press, 1988. 132–41.
———. *Richard Rolle: Emendatio Vitae; Orationes Ad Honorem Nominis Ihesu.* Edited by Nicholas Watson. Toronto: Pontifical Institute of Mediaeval Studies, 1995.
———. "Song of Love-Longing to Jesus." In *English Writings of Richard Rolle,* edited by H. E. Allen. Oxford: Oxford University Press, 1963. 37–40.
Romano, Claude. *Event and World.* Translated by Shane Mackinlay. New York: Fordham University Press, 2009.
Rouse, Mary A., and Richard H. Rouse. *Authentic Witnesses: Approaches to Medieval Texts and Manuscripts.* Notre Dame, IN: University of Notre Dame Press, 1991.
Rudnytsky, Peter L. *Freud and Oedipus.* New York: Columbia University Press, 1987.
Sabine, Ernest. "Butchering in Mediaeval London." *Speculum* 8 (1933): 335–53.
Said, Edward. *Humanism and Democratic Criticism.* New York: Columbia University Press, 2004.
Savage, Fred. "Mac and Dennis: Manhunters." Season 1, episode 4. *It's Always Sunny in Philadelphia* [Television], 2008.
Scala, Elizabeth, and Sylvia Federico, eds. *The Post-Historical Middle Ages.* New York: Palgrave Macmillan, 2009.
Scalia, Giuseppe. "Il *Testamentum Asini* e il *Lamento della leper.*" *Studi Medievali* series 3. (1962): 129–51.
Scarry, Elaine. *On Beauty and Being Just.* Princeton, NJ: Princeton University Press, 2001.
Schirmer, Walter F. *John Lydgate: A Study in the Culture of the Fifteenth Century.* Berkeley: University of California Press, 1961.
Scholes, Robert. "The Humanities in a Post-Human World." *PMLA* 120 (2005): 724–33.
Seabrook, William. *Jungle Ways.* New York: Harcourt, Brace and Co., 1931.
Serres, Michel. *The Parasite.* Minneapolis: University of Minnesota Press, 2013.
Serres, Michel, with Bruno Latour. *Conversations on Science, Culture, and Time.* Translated by Roxanne Lapidus. Ann Arbor: University of Michigan Press, 1995.

Serres, Olivier de. *Le théâtre d'agriculture et mesnage des champs.* Paris: Abr. Saugrain, 1603.

Seymour, M. D., ed. *The Bodley Version of Mandeville's Travels*, EETS o.s. 253. London: Oxford University Press, 1963.

Shakespeare, William. *Twelfth Night.* In *The Norton Shakespeare*, edited by Stephen Greenblatt, Walter Cohen, Jean E. Howard, and Katherine Eisaman Maus. 2nd ed. New York: Norton, 2005. 1793–1846.

Shannon, Laurie. *The Accommodated Animal: Cosmopolity in Shakespearean Locales.* Chicago: University of Chicago Press, 2013.

Shaviro, Steven. *The Universe of Things: On Speculative Realism.* Minneapolis: University of Minnesota Press, 2014.

Shaw, David Gary. *Necessary Conjunctions: The Social Self in Medieval England.* New York: Palgrave Macmillan, 2005.

Shukin, Nicole. *Animal Capital: Rendering Life in Biopolitical Times.* Minneapolis: Minnesota, 2011.

Silver, Lee. *Remaking Eden: Cloning and Beyond in a Brave New World.* New York: Avon, 1997.

Singer, Peter. *Animal Liberation.* New York: Random House, 1975.

Smalley, Beryl. *The Study of the Bible in the Middle Ages.* Notre Dame, IN: University of Notre Dame Press, 1964.

Smith, D. Vance. "Irregular Histories: Forgetting Ourselves." *New Literary History* 28.2 (1997): 161–84.

Snediker, Michael. *Queer Optimism: Lyric Personhood and Other Felicitous Persuasions.* Minneapolis: University of Minnesota Press, 2009.

Solomon, Don. "Interview with N. Katherine Hayles: Preparing the Humanities for the Post Human." *National Humanities Center*, May 2007, http://onthe human.org/archive/more/interview-with-n-katherine-hayles/.

Soper, Kate. *Humanism and Anti-Humanism.* London: Hutchinson, 1986.

Sophocles. *The Oedipus Tyrannus of Sophocles.* Edited by Richard Jebb. Cambridge: Cambridge University Press, 1887.

Southern, R. W. *The Making of the Middle Ages.* New Haven, CT: Yale University Press, 1953.

Sparrow, Tom. *The End of Phenomenology: Metaphysics and the New Realism.* Edinburgh: Edinburgh University Press, 2014.

Spence, Tim. "The Prioress's Oratio Ad Mariam and Medieval Prayer Composition." In *Medieval Rhetoric: A Casebook*, edited by Scott D. Troyan. New York: Routledge, 2004. 63–90.

Srnicek, Nick, and Alex Williams. "#ACCELERATE: Manifesto for an Accelerationist Politics." May 2013. http://accelerationism.files.wordpress.com/2013/ 05/williams-and-srnicek.pdf.

Stahuljak, Zrinka, Virginie Greene, Sarah Kay, Sharon Kinoshita, and Peggy McCracken. *Thinking Through Chrétien de Troyes.* Suffolk: D. S. Brewer, 2001.

Stallybrass, Peter. "The Mystery of Walking." *Journal of Medieval and Early Modern Studies* 32.3 (2002): 571–80.

Stanton, Anne. *The Queen Mary Psalter: A Study of Affect and Audience.* Philadelphia: American Philosophical Society, 2001.

Steel, Karl. *How to Make a Human: Animals and Violence in the Middle Ages.* Columbus: The Ohio State University Press, 2011.

Steel, Karl, and Peggy McCracken, eds. "The Animal Turn." Special issue, *postmedieval: a journal of medieval cultural studies* 2.1 (2011).

Stein, Robert M. *Reality Fictions: Romance, History and Governmental Authority, 1025–1180.* Notre Dame, IN: University of Notre Dame Press, 2006.

Steiner, Emily. *Documentary Culture and the Making of Medieval English Literature.* New York: Cambridge University Press, 2003.

Stekel, Wilhelm. "Cannibalism, Necrophilism, and Vampirism." In *Sadism and Masochism*, translated by Louise Brink. New York: Grove, 1965. 248–330.

Stock, Brian. *The Implications of Literacy: Written Language and Models of Interpretation in the Eleventh and Twelfth Centuries*. Princeton, NJ: Princeton University Press, 1983.
Stock, Gregory. *Redesigning Humans: Our Inevitable Genetic Future*. Boston: Houghton Mifflin, 2002.
Stockton, Will. *Playing Dirty*. Minneapolis: University of Minnesota Press, 2011.
Strohm, Paul. "Postmodernism and History." In *Theory and the Premodern Text*, edited by Strohm. Minneapolis: University of Minnesota Press, 2000. 149–62.
———. *Social Chaucer*. Cambridge, MA: Harvard University Press, 1989.
Tattersall, Jill. "Anthropophagi and Eaters of Raw Flesh in French Literature of the Crusade Period: Myth, Tradition, and Reality." *Medium Aevum* 57 (1988): 240–53.
Taylor, Charles. *Sources of the Self: The Making of the Modern Identity*. Cambridge, MA: Harvard University Press, 1989.
Taylor, Chloë. "The Precarious Lives of Animals: Butler, Coetzee, and Animal Ethics." *Philosophy Today* 52 (2008): 60–72.
Taylor, Jerome. Introduction. *The Didascalicon of Hugh of St. Victor*. New York: Columbia University Press, 1991. 3–39.
———, ed. *The Didascalicon of Hugh of St. Victor*. New York: Columbia University Press, 1991.
Temple-Raston, Dina. "Experts Aim to Explain Spike in LA Hate Crimes." *All Things Considered*. National Public Radio, 25 November 2008.
Teskey, Gordon. *Allegory and Violence*. Ithaca, NY: Cornell University Press, 1996.
Thacker, Eugene, and Alexander Galloway. *The Exploit: A Theory of Networks*. Minneapolis: University of Minnesota Press, 2007.
Thomas, Calvin. "Cultural Droppings: Bersani's Beckett." *Twentieth Century Literature* 47.2 (Summer 2001): 169–96.
Thomas, Keith. "The Meaning of Literacy in Early Modern England." *The Written Word: Literacy in Transition*, edited by Gerd Baumann. Oxford: Clarendon Press, 1986. 97–131.
Thomas, Lou. "Review, Nirvana's *Nevermind*." BBC. 23 April 2007, http://www.bbc.co.uk/music/release/f8dp/.
Todorv, Tzvetan. *The Imperfect Garden: The Legacy of Humanism*. Princeton, NJ: Princeton University Press, 2002.
Truitt, E.R. *Medieval Robots: Mechanism, Magic, Nature, and Art*. Philadelphia: University of Pennsylvania Press, 2015.
Turner, Henry S. *Shakespeare's Double Helix*. London: Bloomsbury, 2008.
Tyler, Tom. *Ciferae: A Bestiary in Five Fingers*. Minneapolis: University of Minnesota Press, 2012.
Tyrrell, Robert Yelverton. *Latin Poetry: Lectures Delivered in 1893 on the Percy Turnbull Memorial Foundation in John Hopkins University*. Boston: Houghton Mifflin, 1895); 147; partially cited by Arthur L. Keith, "A Virgilian Line," *The Classical Journal* 17.7 (1922): 398–402.
Vendler, Helen. *The Music of What Happens: Poems, Poets, Critics*. Cambridge, MA: Harvard University Press, 1989.
Vint, Sherryl. *Bodies of Tomorrow: Technology, Subjectivity, Science Fiction*. Toronto: University of Toronto Press, 2007.
Virilio, Paul. *The Great Accelerator*. Translated by Julie Rose. Cambridge: Polity, 2012.
———. *The Information Bomb*. Translated by Chris Turner. London: Verso, 2000.
———. *Open Sky*. London: Verso, 1997.
———. *Speed and Politics: An Essay on Dromology*. Translated by Mark Polizzotti. New York: Semiotext(e), 1986.
Vom Wesen der menschlichen Freieit: Einleitung in die Philosophie. Edited by H. Tietjen. Frankfurt: Klosterman, 1982.
Waddell, Helen. *The Wandering Scholars*. London: Constable, 1966.

Watson, Nicholas. "Censorship and Cultural Change in Late-Medieval England: Vernacular Theology, the Oxford Translation Debate, and Arundel's Constitutions of 1409." *Speculum* 70.4 (1995): 822–64.

———. Introduction. *Richard Rolle: Emendatio Vitae; Orationes Ad Honorem Nominis Ihesu*. Toronto: Pontifical Institute of Mediaeval Studies, 1995. 1–30.

Wenzel, Siegfried. *Preachers, Poets, and the Early English Lyric*. Princeton, NJ: Princeton University Press, 1986.

Wharton, David. "*Sunt lacrimae rerum*: An Exploration in Meaning." *Classical Journal* 103 (2008): 259–79.

Whigham, Frank. *Ambition and Privilege: The Social Tropes of Elizabethan Courtesy Theory*. Berkeley: University of California Press, 1984.

White, Carolinne. Rev. of Fleur Adcock, *Hugh Primas and the Archpoet*. *Medium Aevum* 65.1 (1996): 118–19.

White, Hayden. *The Content of the Form: Narrative Discourse and Historical Representation*. Baltimore: Johns Hopkins University Press, 1990.

White, Randall. *Prehistoric Art: The Symbolic Journey of Humankind*. New York: Harry N. Abrams, 2003.

Whitman, C. H. *Sophocles: A Study of Heroic Humanism*. Cambridge, MA: Harvard University Press, 1951.

Whitman, Jon, ed. *Interpretation and Allegory: Antiquity to the Modern Period*. Leiden: Brill, 2000.

Wieck, Roger S. *Painted Prayers: The Book of Hours in Medieval and Renaissance Art*. New York: George Braziller, 1997.

———. *Time Sanctified: The Book of Hours in Medieval Art and Life*. New York: George Braziller, 1988.

Winner, Langdon. *The Reactor and the Whale: The Search for Limits in an Age of High Technology*. Chicago: University of Chicago Press, 1987.

Wolfe, Cary. *Animal Rites: American Culture, the Discourse of Species, and Posthumanist Theory*. Chicago: University of Chicago Press, 2003.

———. *Before the Law: Humans and Other Animals in a Biopolitical Frame*. Chicago: University of Chicago Press, 2012.

———. Introduction. *Zoontologies: The Question of the Animal*, edited by Wolfe. Minneapolis: University of Minnesota Press, 2003. ix–xxiii.

———. *What Is Posthumanism?* Minneapolis: University of Minnesota Press, 2009.

Woods, Marjorie C. "The Teaching of Writing in Medieval Europe." In *A Short History of Writing Instruction from Ancient Greece to Twentieth-Century America*, edited by James J. Murphy. Davis, CA: Hermagoras Press, 1990. 77–94.

Wright, John. "*Lacrimae rerum* and the Thankless Task." *Classical Journal* 62.8 (1967): 365–67.

Yates, Julian. "Accidental Shakespeare." *Shakespeare Studies* 34 (2006): 90–122.

———. *Error, Misuse, Failure: Object Lessons from the English Renaissance*. Minneapolis: University of Minnesota Press, 2002.

Yoda, Tomiko. "Fractured Dialogues: *Mono no aware* and Poetic Communication in the *Tale of Genji*." *Harvard Journal of Asiatic Studies* 59.2 (1999): 523–57.

Ziolkowski, Jan. *Talking Animals: Medieval Latin Beast Poetry 750–1150*. Philadelphia: University of Pennsylvania Press, 1993.

Žižek, Slavoj. *How to Read Lacan*. NY: W. W. Norton and Co., 2007.

———. *On Belief*. London and New York: Routledge, 2001.

———. *The Plague of Fantasies*. NY: Verso, 1997.

Zupančič, Alenka. *The Shortest Shadow: Nietzsche's Philosophy of the Two*. Cambridge, MA: MIT University Press, 2003.

Zylinska, Joanna. "Bioethics Otherwise, or, How to Live with Machines, Humans, and Other Animals." In *Telemorphosis: Theory in the Era of Climate Change*. Vol. 1. Edited by Tom Cohen. Ann Arbor, MI: Open Humanities Press/MPublishing, 2012. 203–25.

———. *Minimal Ethics for the Anthropocene*. Ann Arbor, MI: Open Humanities Press, 2014.

CONTRIBUTORS

JEFFREY JEROME COHEN is professor of English and director of the George Washington University Medieval and Early Modern Studies Institute. The author of numerous books and articles on the meeting of the posthumanities with the distant past (including *Of Giants* and *Medieval Identity Machines*), his most recent work includes the edited collection *Prismatic Ecology: Ecotheory beyond Green* (University of Minnesota Press, 2013) and *Stone: An Ecology of the Inhuman* (University of Minnesota Press, 2015).

CRAIG DIONNE is professor of literary and cultural theory at Eastern Michigan University. He specializes in Shakespeare and popular culture, early modern literacies, and cultural studies. He has coedited *Disciplining English: Alternative Perspectives, Critical Perspectives* (with David Shumway, SUNY Press, 2002), *Rogues and Early Modern English Culture* (with Steve Mentz, University of Michigan Press, 2005), *Native Shakespeares: Indigenous Appropriations on a Global Stage* (with Parmita Kapadia, Ashgate, 2008), and *Bollywood Shakespeares* (with Parmita Kapadia, Palgrave, 2014). He was senior editor of *JNT: Journal of Narrative Theory* for ten years. In 2010 he coedited the inaugural issue of *postmedieval: a journal of medieval cultural studies*.

MICHAEL JOHNSON is assistant professor of French at Central Washington University. He has published essays on the *Romance of the Rose* and Alan of Lille's *Plaint of Nature*. In addition to collaborating with Christopher Taylor on an edition and translation of Prester John letters from the British Isles, he is currently revising a book entitled *The Medieval Erotics of Grammar*.

EILEEN A. JOY is a specialist in Old English literary studies and cultural studies, with interests and publications in poetry and poetics, historiography, ethics, affects, embodiments, queer studies, the politics of friendship, speculative realism, object-oriented ontology, the ecological, and the posthuman. She is the coeditor of multiple volumes, including *The Postmodern Beowulf* (University of West Virginia Press, 2007), *Cultural Studies of the Modern Middle Ages* (Palgrave, 2007), *Dark Chaucer* (punctum books, 2012), *Speculative Medievalisms* (punctum books, 2013), and *On Style: An Atelier* (punctum books, 2013), among others. She is also the lead ingenitor of the BABEL Working Group, coeditor of *postmedieval: a journal of medieval cultural studies*, director of punctum books: spontaneous acts of scholarly combustion, and associate director of punctum records.

DANIEL T. KLINE is professor and chair of English at the University of Alaska, Anchorage. He has published on Middle English literature and culture, literary and cultural theory, and digital medievalism, focusing especially on children, violence, and ethics in late medieval England. He edited *Medieval Children's Literature* (Routledge, 2003), the *Continuum Handbook of Medieval British Literature* (Continuum, 2009), and *Digital Gaming Re-Imagines the Middle Ages* (Routledge, 2014), and coedited, with Gail Ashton, *Medieval Afterlives in Popular Culture* (Palgrave-Macmillan, 2012). Kline is the author/webmaster of *The Electronic Canterbury Tales* <www.kankedort.net>.

ANNA KŁOSOWSKA is professor of French at Miami University. She wrote *Queer Love in the Middle Ages* (Palgrave Macmillan, 2005) and edited *Madeleine de l'Aubespine, Selected Poems and Translations* (Chicago, 2007) and is the editor/coeditor of several volumes of essays and journal issues (including recently a cluster on "Fault" in the journal *postmedieval*) and author/coauthor of articles on queer theory in medieval and early modern French texts. She is finishing a Mellon-supported book on Renaissance table games. With Eileen A. Joy, she cotaught a seminar on "Premodern Foucault" at the Newberry Library.

DANIEL C. REMEIN is assistant professor of English at the University of Massachusetts, Boston. His current book project focuses on ecologies and cosmologies of wonder and ornament in medieval poetics and mid-twentieth-century literary medievalism. Relevant publications include "Auden, Translation, Betrayal: Radical Poetics and Translation from Old English" (*Literature Compass*, 2011), the introduction to Thomas Meyer's translation of *Beowulf* (punctum books, 2012), a defense of poetics in Aranye Fraydenburg's *Staying Alive* (punctum books, 2013), as well as poems and translations in a number of journals. Remein is also a coeditor of *eth press: postmedieval poetries*.

MYRA SEAMAN is professor of English at the College of Charleston. She has published on medieval romance, textual scholarship, conduct literature, medieval film and historiography, posthumanisms medieval and modern, and Chaucerian dream visions. She coedited *Cultural Studies of the Modern Middle Ages* (Palgrave, 2007), *Dark Chaucer* (punctum books, 2012), and *Burn After Reading* (punctum books, 2014), and is a founding editor of *postmedieval: a journal of medieval cultural studies* and founding member of the BABEL Working Group. Her current work focuses on pedagogical affective object ecologies in a late-fifteenth-century English literary anthology.

JEFFREY SKOBLOW is professor of English language and literature at Southern Illinois University, Edwardsville. He is the author of two books, *Paradise Dislocated: Morris, Politics, Art* (University of Virginia Press, 1993) and *Dooble Tongue: Scots, Burns, Contradiction* (University of Delaware Press, 2001), as well as numerous articles on William Morris and on Robert Burns or other Scottish poets, as well as separate articles on LeRoi Jones, Bob Dylan, and pedagogy. *In a Trance: On Paleo Art*, a monograph on his own and other recent efforts to come to terms with prehistoric images on cave walls, appeared in 2014 (punctum books).

About the Contributors

TIM SPENCE teaches Latin to teenagers for Roanoke County Public Schools in Southwestern Virginia. Before moving to Virginia, he cofounded the Ragtag Cinema and its affiliated nonprofit, Ragtag Programming for Film and Media Art in Columbia, Missouri. His research focuses on the rhetoric of prayer, technologies of self, and lyrical mysticism. He lives with his wife and two sons on their hobby farm in the mountains of Floyd, Virginia, where they raise goats, chickens, ducks, and a miniature donkey named Stormy Fred.

KARL STEEL is associate professor of English at Brooklyn College, CUNY. He is the author of *How to Make a Human: Animals and Violence in the Middle Ages* (The Ohio State University Press, 2011) and coeditor (with Peggy McCracken) of *postmedieval*'s special issue on "The Animal Turn." He has also published on such topics as feral children, Middle English worms, medieval vegetarian philosophers, and skin, and has articles forthcoming on spontaneous generation, biopolitics and the medieval forest, and the radical passivity of oysters. He is a longtime coblogger at In the Middle (www.inthemedievalmiddle.com).

INDEX

Abbate, Carolyn, 144, 144n39
Acampora, Ralph, 27, 189
accelerationism, 9n26, 52n1, 53n12, 54
Adam of Saint Victor, 20, 67. *See also* Hugh of Saint Victor; Victorines
Adams, Carol J., 180n20. *See also* Donovan, Josephine
Adcock, Fleur, 78n42
advenant, 58, 64
Aeneas, 2. See also *Aeneid* (Virgil); Virgil
Aeneid (Virgil), 2. *See also* Aeneas; Virgil
Aers, David, 54n13
aesthetics, 3–4, 15–16, 22, 27–28, 64, 113, 114n48, 131–33, 136–50, 158, 164, 189, 223, 225–43
affect, 2, 13–14, 18, 87n66, 89n71, 100, 148, 218, 220, 226
Agamben, Giorgio, 24, 116n57
Ahl, Frederick, 197n16
Alaimo, Stacy, 5n11
Albert the Great, 177
Alford, John A., 89n69
Alighieri, Dante, 85, 97, 109–10, 120n65, 160
allure, 21, 106, 115–24
Altschul, Nadia, 11n29. *See also* Davis, Kathleen
Amphioun, King, 205, 209, 213
animals, 5n11, 6–7, 9n22, 16–18, 22–25, 27, 28n61, 34–50, 98, 104, 108, 132–40, 148, 152–60, 170–92, 204, 215, 224, 225n5, 239. *See also* aninormality; critical animal theory; dogs; horses
Animal Studies Group, 182n27
aninormality, 22–23, 140–50. *See also* animals
Ankersmit, F. R., 8n21

Antony, Saint, 136
Anthropocene/anthropocentric, 23, 136, 139, 159, 239–43
anthropophagy, 24–25, 177–85
Apollinaire, Guillaume, 173
Apuleius, 28
Archpoet, 78
Arens, William, 178n13
Aristotle, 197, 219
Aristoxenus, 30
Arthur, King/Arthurian, 56–62, 100–101, 122, 140–41, 146–48. *See also* Camelot
assemblage, 19, 57, 60–62, 189, 224
Astell, Ann W., 213n48, 214n49
Attridge, Derek, 225–26, 228, 235–38
Augustine, Saint, 18, 180
Aurignacian Period in Paleolithic art, 39
Auschwitz, 48
Avanessian, Armen, 52n1, 54n12. *See also* Mackay, Robin
Avdeevo, 39
Avrich, Jane, et al., 78n45

BABEL Working Group, 12n32, 27, 151
Badiou, Alain, 115, 237n24
Bahn, Paul, 35, 39, 49
Baker, Steve, 133, 182n27
Bakhtin, Mikhail, 166
Bamber, Linda, 232
Barad, Karen, 191
Barker, Juliet, 207n42
Barthes, Roland, 96–97, 102
Bartram, Rob, 74
Bassus, Constantine Cassianus, 158n13

271

Bataille, Georges, 17, 33, 36, 133
Battle, Dominique, 202n33, 216n53, 217
Baudrillard, Jean, 10n28, 24, 161, 174
Bauman, Zygmunt, 9n26, 18, 52
beauty, 1–2, 22, 43, 60–64, 130–34, 137–40, 143–49, 203. *See also* aesthetics
Bec, Pierre, 152, 163–65, 167n28, 168n32, 174
Beck, Ulrich, 18, 52n3, 53, 56n22. *See also* Beck-Gernsheim, Elisabeth
Beck-Gernsheim, Elisabeth, 18, 52n3, 53, 56n22. *See also* Beck, Ulrich
Beckett, Samuel, 16, 20–21, 95–100, 106, 109–10, 118–25
Bede, the Venerable, 140. See also *Ecclesiastical History of the English Peoples* (Bede)
Beguine movement, 20, 76–77
Bell, Kimberley, 11n29. *See also* Joy, Eileen A.; Ramsey, Mary; Seaman, Myra J.
Belle et la Bête, La, (Cocteau), 29. *See also* Cocteau, Jean
belletrism, 224
Belsey, Catherine, 225
Benjamin, Walter, 87n66
Bennett, Jane, 5n11, 59, 87n66, 89, 132n6
Berger, John, 182n29
Bergerac, Cyrano de, 29–30
Berman, David, 79
Bernifal Cave, 45
Bersani, Leo, 51, 131n5
Bergson, Henri, 191
Biddick, Kathleen, 11n29
Binski, Paul, 70n18. *See also* Panayotova, Stella
biopolitical theory, 16
Bisclavret (Marie de France), 148. *See also* Marie de France
Blade Runner (Scott), 156–57. *See also* Scott, Ridley
Blanchot, Maurice, 96, 116, 118
Bloch, Marc, 8n21
Bloch, R. Howard, 97, 165n27
Blumstein, Alex, 178n15
Blurton, Heather, 179n16
Bober, Phyllis Pray, 176n3
Bogost, Ian, 5n11

book of hours, 19, 66n6, 67–68, 70, 80–84, 94
Booth, Stephen, 228n11
Bororó people, 49
Bostrom, Nick, 10n28
Boswell, John Eastburn, 204n39
Bourdieu, Pierre, 75, 79
Bowie, David, 86–88
Boyarin, Daniel, 71n19
Boyle, T. Coraghessan, 145
Bracciolini, Poggio, 25, 177
Braidotti, Rosi, 5n11, 10n28, 191
Bratton, Benjamin, 9n26
Braudel, Fernand, 8n21, 14
Breton, André, 133–34, 173
Brewer, Derek, 70n19
Brock, Isaac, 79. *See also* Modest Mouse
Brownrigg, Linda L., 70n18
Brownstein, Oscar, 183n31
Brutus, 142–44
Bryant, Levi, 5n11. *See also* Harman, Graham; Srnicek, Nick
Buc, Philippe, 179n16
Buhle, Mary Jo, 194n5
Burger, Glenn, 11n29, 130n1. *See also* Kruger, Steven F.
Burns, E. J., 165n27
Butler, Judith, 4, 27, 181n26, 182, 187, 194n5, 225
Bynum, Caroline Walker, 67n8

cabbage, 29–30
Caillois, Roger, 16, 22, 130n1, 133–41, 147
Calarco, Matthew, 180n22
Callas, Ivan, 7n18. *See also* Herbrechter, Stefan
Camelot, 18–19, 57–62. *See also* Arthur, King/Arthurian
cannibalism. *See* anthropophagy
Canterbury Tales, The (Chaucer), 209. *See also* Chaucer, Geoffrey
Caputo, John D., 4, 64
Carruthers, Mary, 67n8, 68n12, 85
Cederberg, Carl, 221n71
Chambers, Iain, 10, 13–14

Chanson d'Antioche, La, 25, 177
Charnes, Linda, 56n21
Chartier, Roger, 8n21
Chasseguet-Smirgel, Janine, 160, 173n37, 174
Chaucer, Geoffrey, 84, 89n67, 201–2, 209n44. See also *Canterbury Tales, The* (Chaucer); *Knight's Tale, The* (Chaucer)
Chauvet Cave, 17, 35, 37, 39, 48–49
Chevallier, M. A., 159n16
cheveral consciousness, 238
child/childhood, 26–27, 92, 146–47, 160–61, 193–222
chivalric romance/chivalric narrative, 16, 185–87
Chrétien de Troyes, 20–22, 30, 95, 97–98, 100–102, 106, 107n31, 110, 114–15, 121–22, 125. See also *Perceval* (Chrétien de Troyes); *Yvain* (Chrétien de Troyes)
Chrétien Girls, 102, 110, 121
Chrulew, Matthew, 180n22
Clanchy, Michael T., 70n19, 84–85
Clanchy, Thomas, 76
Clarke, Bruce, 225n5
Classen, Albrecht, 182n30
Clottes, Jean, 35, 37–38
Cloud Atlas, 185
Cocteau, Jean, 29. See also *Belle et la Bête, La*, (Cocteau)
Cohen, Esther, 181n26
Cohen, Jeffrey Jerome, 7n18, 9, 11, 12n32, 16, 22–23, 54–55, 176n3, 225. See also Duckert, Lowell
Cole, Andrew, 11n29, 12n32, 55n17. See also Smith, D. Vance
Colebrook, Claire, 5n11
College of Sociology, 133
commonality, 22, 137
Connolly, William E., 5n11, 51n1, 55
Constable, Giles, 66n3
Constans, Léopold, 26, 199–201. See also *Légende d'Oedipe, La* (Constans)
contingency of art, 28, 174, 235, 238
Coole, Diana, 5n11. See also Frost, Samantha
Copeland, Rita, 70n17
Coton, Alfonso Eanes do, 166

courtly love, 164–65, 232
Crane, Susan, 133
Crary, Jonathan, 51n1
Creech, Jim, 118
Cretaceous Period in Paleolithic art, 42
critical animal theory, 180n20. See also animals
Cummings, Brian, 73n24
Curtius, Ernst Robert, 67n7

d'Aurenga, Raimbaut, 171
Daniel, Arnaut, 166, 168–74
Davis, Kathleen, 11n29. See also Altschul, Nadia
de Certeau, Michel, 54
DeLanda, Manuel, 61
Deleuze, Gilles, 10n28, 21, 60–61, 102, 104–5, 109, 134n11, 188–89. See also Guattari, Félix
Dels Petz Sobeirana (Sovereign Lady of Farts), 165
Delvoye, Wim, 152, 173
Derrida, Jacques, 13, 16, 25, 133, 180–81, 188n41, 189–92, 197n15, 232n13
Desana people, 49
Descola, Philippe, 98n13
Despres, Denise Louise, 70n18. See also Kerby-Fulton, Kathryn
deterritorialization, 61–63, 188
devotional manual, 16, 94
dialectic of desire, 229
Diamond, Cora, 27
Diamond, Jared, 190
Dickinson, Emily, 115
Dinshaw, Carolyn, 11n29, 12n32, 19, 54n13, 189n46
Dionne, Craig 7n18, 16, 27–28, 241n32. See also Joy, Eileen A.; Mentz, Steve
Dives and Pauper, 184
Dobyns, Stephen, 71
dogs, 25, 179n18, 183, 186–91. See also animals
Dolni Věstonice, 39
Donovan, Josephine, 180n20. See also Adams, Carol J.
Dronke, Peter, 81n51

Duchamp, Marcel, 173, 225. See also *Nude Descending the Staircase* (Duchamp)
Duckert, Lowell, 7n18. See also Cohen, Jeffrey Jerome
Duffin, Ross, 229n12. See also Orgel, Stephen
Dutoit, Ulysse, 51, 131n5
Dylan, Bob, 76

Eagleton, Terry, 238
Ecclesiastical History of the English Peoples (Bede), 140. See also Bede, the Venerable
Edward of York, 25, 177
Eissler, Kurt, 194n4
El Castillo Cave, 39, 43
Elmer, Jonathan, 186n37. See also Wolfe, Cary
Empedocles, 104–5
Entre Nous: Thinking-of-the-Other (Lévinas), 195n9, 196n12, 203n37, 203n38, 204n40, 205n41. See also Lévinas, Emmanuel
Eshleman, Clayton, 37–41, 48
Etiocles, 215–16
Event and World (Romano), 58n24. See also Romano, Claude
evential hermeneutics, 16, 19, 58–59, 62. See also Romano, Claude
excremental, 23–24, 152–57, 160, 165–74
Excremental Lady, 166–72
exteriority, 23, 27, 58, 61, 152–58, 179, 221

face, 16, 37, 39–41, 44–45, 48–50, 61–64, 95, 102, 113–19, 192, 196, 203
Faidit, Gaucelm, 165n26
Fall of Princes (Lydgate), 202n34, 210n45. See also Lydgate, Thomas
Farina, Lara, 69n14, 72n22
fascism, 226
Febvre, Lucien, 8n21
fecal playfulness, 172. See also excrement
Feerick, Jean E., 7n18. See also Nardizzi, Vin
Feher, Michel, 15
Fenton, James, 130–31
Ferrante, Joan, 165n27
fin'amors, 24, 162–64, 167
Finucane, Ronald C., 218n61
Flaubert, Gustave, 136

Folcuin of Lobbes, 25, 185–88
Font-de-Gaume Cave, 45
Formalism, 231–32, 235n19
Foucault, Michel, 13, 15, 96–97
Fradenburg, L. O. Aranye, 11n29, 12n32, 54n13
fragments, 15, 17, 21, 29, 35, 37, 47, 49–50, 95, 98, 100–101, 106, 109–10, 117, 120–21, 124–25, 168, 239
Fraiman, Susan, 191n54
Frank, Claudine, 134
Frank, Thomas, 77n38
Freccero, Carla, 192n56
Freud, Anna, 194n4
Freud, Sigmund, 16, 23–24, 26–27, 106, 121, 153–54, 156, 160–63, 166, 173, 178, 183, 193–222. See also *Interpretation of Dreams, The* (Freud)
Frost, Samantha, 5n11. See also Coole, Diana
Fudge, Erica, 182n27, 182n29
Fukuyama, Francis, 9n26
Fulton, Rachel, 67n9, 68n12, 69n14
Fumerton, Patricia, 239, 240n29, 241, 242n32
fundamentalist, 223

Gabillou Cave, 38, 46
Gallop, Jane, 194n5
Galloway, Alexander, 9n26. See also Thacker, Eugene
Galloway, Andrew Scott, 81n51, 221n71
Gamble, Clive, 50
Gaselee, Stephen, 78n43
Gaunt, Simon, 165n26, 165n27
Gawain, 57, 100, 112. See also *Sir Gawain and the Green Knight* (Pearl-poet)
Gay, Peter, 201n31
Geller, Jay, 201n31
Geoffrey of Monmouth, 23, 25, 140–48, 176. See also *History of the Kings of Britain* (Geoffrey of Monmouth)
Gergen, Kenneth, 9n26
Giddens, Anthony, 18, 51–53
Giffney, Noreen, 5n11, 133. See also Hird, Myra J.
Gilman, Sander L., 198n19, 201n31
Gilquin, Gaëtenelle, 181n23. See also Jacobs, George M.

Golden Legend (Voragine), 175. *See also* Voragine, Jacobus de
Goliards, 20, 78
Goodhart, Sandor, 197, 219–20
Goux, Jean-Joseph, 195
Grabes, Herbert, 233
Gravettian Period in Paleolithic art, 39
Green-Lewis, Jennifer, 131–33. *See also* Soltan, Margaret
Greenblatt, Stephen, 234n18
Greene, Virginie, 102n18
Gregory, Saint, 69, 70n16
Greimas, Algirdas Julien, 108n31, 108n33, 117n59, 117n60
Grey's Anatomy, 92
griffades d'ours, 42–45
Grosz, Elizabeth, 99n14, 133, 134n11, 136, 137n25, 189n47
Grusin, Richard, 5n11
Guattari, Félix, 61, 104n24, 109, 188–89. *See also* Deleuze, Gilles
Guigemar (Marie de France), 148–49. *See also* Marie de France

Hacking, Ian, 27, 225
Hadewijch of Brabant, 77n36
Halberstam, Judith, 10n28. *See also* Livingston, Ira
Halliwell, Martin, 10n27, 14. *See also* Mousley, Andy
Hanawalt, Barbara, 228n61
Hanks, D. Thomas, 57n23
Hanna, Ralph, 70n18
Hanning, Robert, 54n13, 143n38
Haraway, Donna, 10n28, 78n45, 133, 181n25, 188–90, 225
Harman, Graham, 5n11, 21, 105n26, 114–16. *See also* Bryant, Levi; Srnicek, Nick
Harris, Jonathan Gil, 55–56, 133
Harris, Michael, 70n18. *See also* Myers, Robin
Haug, Walter, 73
Hayles, N. Katherine, 6–7, 9, 11, 27, 133, 225
Haymo of Auxerre, 176n3
Heath, Joseph, 77n38. *See also* Potter, Andrew
Hedwig and the Angry Inch, 87–88, 92

Heidegger, Martin, 20–21, 59, 96, 98, 102–5, 112–18, 124–25, 210
Heng, Geraldine, 179n16
Henry of Hesse, 105n27
Herbert, Zbigniew, 20, 71. *See also Mr. Cogito* (Herbert)
Herbrechter, Stefan, 7n18. *See also* Callas, Ivan
heroic quest, 16
hip-hop, 77–78
Hird, Myra J., 5n11, 133
Hiroshima, 48
Hirsh, John C., 81n51
historical saga, 16
historicism, 8–11, 15, 129–32, 235
historicism ("history as costume drama"), 225
History of the Kings of Britain (Geoffrey of Monmouth), 23, 25, 140–48, 176. *See also* Geoffrey of Monmouth
Holder-Egger, O., 185n36
Hollywood, Amy, 11n29
Holsinger, Bruce, 11n29, 55n17, 69n15. *See also* Knapp, Ethan
Homo neanderthalensis, 35
horses, 17, 25, 35–37, 43–44, 47–49, 63, 99, 122, 185–190. *See also* animals
Howie, Cary, 56, 148n43
Huchet, Jean-Charles, 167
Hugh of Saint Victor, 20, 67, 68n12, 80, 90n73, 90n74. *See also* Adam of Saint Victor; Victorines
Hugh Primas, 78
Hulme, Peter, 178n13
humanist close reading, 231
humanities, 4–8, 12–13, 27, 131, 151–52, 224–25, 232
Hunt, Elizabeth Moore, 70n18
Huyssens, Andreas, 8n21

Ickstadt, Heinz, 227
incest, 26–27, 178, 198–204, 217–218
incubus/incubi, 146, 149
inhuman, 4, 16, 21–23, 64, 77, 98, 105, 110, 132, 134, 140, 145, 148, 150, 152, 154–56, 164–67, 171–74, 213

interiority, 23, 71, 152–56, 179
Interpretation of Dreams, The (Freud), 198–200, 214n50, 215n52. *See also* Freud, Sigmund
iPod, 16, 19–20, 65–66, 72, 75, 79–84, 88, 91–94
Irigaray, Luce, 221n73
Irwin, Alec, 179n17
Ishiguro, Kazuo, 223, 226–27. *See also Remains of the Day, The* (Ishiguro)
It's Always Sunny in Philadelphia, 175
Itinerant existence, 241

Jacobs, George M., 181n23. *See also* Gilquin, Gaëtenelle
Jaeger, Werner, 90n74
Jameson, Fredric, 28, 56n20
Jensen, Anders Thomas, 177n10
Jewers, Caroline, 168n32
Jocasta/Iocasta, 197n17, 198–204, 208, 215–19. *See also* Laius/Layus; Lydgate, John; Oedipus/Edippus; *Oedipus Rex/Edippus* (Sophocles/Lydgate); Sophocles
Johnson, Steven, 79n45
Jones, Melissa, 223n1
Joy, Eileen A., 7n18, 11n29, 12n32, 18–19, 225n5. *See also* Bell, Kimberly; Dionne, Craig; Neufeld, Christine; Petropunk Collective; Ramsey, Mary; Seaman, Myra J.

Kac, Eduardo, 10n28
Kantian *Ding an sich*, 227
Katz, Claire Elise, 221n71
Kaueper, Richard W., 207n42
Kaufmann, Walter, 195n7
Kay, Sarah, 100n16, 102n18, 165n27
Keen, Maurice, 207
Keith, Arthur L., 2n3
Kempe, Margery, 90n72
Kempster, Hugh, 82n53, 89
Kennedy, George A., 67n7
Kerby-Fulton, Kathryn, 70n18. *See also* Despres, Denise Louise
Key, Ellen, 193
Kilgour, Maggie, 178n15

King, C. Richard, 179n17
Kinoshita, Sharon, 102n18
Kinsey Reports, 33
Klein, Melanie, 178, 221n72
Kłosowska, Anna, 7n18, 20–21, 97, 108n31, 110n39. *See also* Petropunk Collective
Knapp, Ethan, 11n29, 55n17, 69n15. *See also* Holsinger, Bruce
Knight's Tale, The (Chaucer), 202, 209n44. *See also* Chaucer, Geoffrey
Knox, Bernard, 195
Kohn, Eduardo, 98–99
Koestenbaum, Wayne, 144n39
Kristeva, Julia, 179
Kruger, Steven, 11n29, 130n1. *See also* Burger, Glenn
Kurzweil, Ray, 10n28
Kuspit, Donald, 173n37

La Fontaine, Jean de, 28–30
La Marche, 48
Lacan, Jacques, 21, 23–24, 34, 36, 97n7, 121, 133–34, 136, 152–53, 161–62, 165n27, 221n72
LaCapra, Dominick, 8n21, 15
lacrimae rerum, 1–3, 21
Laistner, Ludwig, 199
Laius/Layus, 193, 196–208, 214, 217–220. *See also* Jocasta/Iocasta; Lydgate, John; Oedipus/Edippus; *Oedipus Rex/Edippus* (Sophocles/Lydgate); Sophocles
lapidary, 137–38, 147
LaPorte, Dominique, 151–52, 156–59
Larkin, Peter, 177n6
Lascaux Cave, 38
Lash, Scott, 18, 52–53, 56
Laskaya, Anne, 187n40. *See also* Salisbury, Eve
Latham, Rob, 179n17
Latour, Bruno, 54, 133
Lawlor, Leonard, 189n48
Le Guillou, Yanik, 35, 37
Le Guin, Ursula K., 105
lectio divina, 69–70, 72,
Légende d'Oedipe, La (Constans), 199, 201. *See also* Constans, Léopold
Lepetz, Sébastian, 186n38

Leroi-Gourhan, Andrei, 37
Les Combarelles Cave, 40, 45
Lévinas, Emmanuel, 26–27, 118–119, 191, 195–97, 203–5, 210, 221–22. See also *Entre Nous: Thinking-of-the-Other* (Lévinas); *Otherwise than Being, Or Beyond Essence* (Lévinas)
Lewis-Williams, David, 38
Lewis, Charleton T., 108n31. See also Short, Charles
Lingis, Alphonso, 40–41, 133
literacy, 76, 84–86, 90
Livingston, Ira, 10n28. See also Halberstam, Judith
Lombard, Peter, 176n3
Long, John, 229n12
Low, Anthony, 54n13
Lucas, George, 16, 24, 154–56
Lydgate, John, 26–27, 196–97, 201–22. See also Laius/Layus; Jocasta/Iocasta; Oedipus/Edippus; *Oedipus Rex/Edippus*; *Siege of Thebes* (Lydgate)

MacCormack, Patricia, 5n11
Mackay, Robin, 52n2, 54n12, 105n28. See also Avanessian, Armen
Mackinlay, Shane, 58n24, 58n25, 60n30, 64n36
Magdalenian Period in Paleolithic art, 40, 44–45, 48
Make Room! Make Room!, 185
Malkmus, Stephen, 77n38, 79
Malory, Sir Thomas, 18, 51, 56–59, 61–64, 89n67. See also *Morte darthur* (Malory)
Malthrop, Stuart, 76n33
Mandeville, John, 25, 177
Mannoni, Octave, 183
Manzoni, Piero, 172–73
Marie de France, 23, 30, 108n31, 148, 185. See also *Bisclavret* (Marie de France); *Guigemar* (Marie de France); *Yonec* (Marie de France)
Martin of Laon, 68n12
Mary/Maria of Jerusalem, 175n2
Masciandaro, Nicola, 7n18, 95n1, 113–14. See also Petropunk Collective
Masson, Jeffrey M., 193n2, 194n3, 194n4

Maupassant, Guy de, 177
McCarthy, Paul, 173
McCracken, Peggy, 7n18, 102n18. See also Chrétien Girls; Steel, Karl
McDonald, Nicola, 179n16
McLuhan, Marshall, 79n45
McVitty Book of Hours, 82–84, 93 fig. 1
Mechthild of Magdeburg, 77n37
Meens, Rob, 185n36
Meillassoux, Quentin, 5n11, 105n28
melancholy, 28, 228, 238, 240, 242–43
Melville, Herman, 178n13
Mentz, Steve, 241n32. See also Craig Dionne
Merlin, 57, 146–49
Meyer-Lee, Robert J., 202n33
Migne, Jacques Paul, 70n16, 81n50, 176n3
mimicry, 134, 136, 140, 233
Minnis, A. J., 213n49
mirror stage, 136. See also Lacan, Jacques
Mitchell-Boyask, Robin, 198–200
Mitchell, J. Allan, 7n18, 58
modes of being, 79
Modest Mouse, 20, 65, 79. See also Brock, Isaac
Mohen, Jean-Pierre, 38
Molloy (Beckett), 16, 20–21, 95–100, 105–6, 109–10, 112, 115–16, 120–24. See also Beckett, Samuel
mono no aware, 2–3, 18, 21
Montaigne, Michel de, 152, 157–59, 173
moon, 3, 47, 101, 105, 107, 118n62, 124, 146
Moran, Jacques, 99, 112, 123. See also *Molloy* (Beckett)
Moravec, Hans, 10n28
Morris, Colin, 54n13
Morte darthur (Malory), 18, 56–64. See also Malory, Sir Thomas
Mortimer, Nigel, 202n33
Morton, Timothy, 5n11
Mos Def, 78. See also hip-hop
mother, 29, 64, 97, 99–100, 119, 121–22, 149, 193, 198–200, 202, 204, 208n43, 211, 216–18
Mousley, Andy, 10n27, 14. See also Halliwell, Martin

Mr. Cogito (Herbert), 20, 71, 92. See also Herbert, Zbigniew
Murasaki, Lady, 3. See also *Tale of Genji* (Murasaki)
Murphy, James J., 90n74
Myers, Robin, 70n18. See also Harris, Michael

Nardizzi, Vin, 7n18. See also Feerick, Jean E.
Nash, Susie, 70n18
natality, 100, 204, 206, 222
National Humanities Center, 5–7
Negarestani, Reza, 21, 102n20, 105n27
Nelli, René, 152, 162–65, 174
Nelson, Jan A., 177n7
neoconservative politics, 27, 224
Neufeld, Christine, 7n18, 223n1, 225n5. See also Joy, Eileen A.
new materialism, 5n11, 27, 98–99, 114n48, 235, 240
Newman, Barbara, 66n5, 67n8, 69n14, 80
Noble, Richard, 240n30
Nolan, Maura, 202n33
Norinaga, Motoori, 3
Normans, 141, 143
Notorious B. I. G., 78. See also hip-hop
Novalis (Georg Philipp Friedrich Freiherr von Hardenberg), 103–4
Noys, Benjamin, 9n26, 52n1
Nude Descending the Staircase (Duchamp), 225. See also Duchamp, Marcel
Nunn, Trevor, 27, 243

Obeyesekere, Gananath, 178n12, 178n13
object-oriented studies, 5n11, 99, 114, 242
Oedipal complex, 26–27, 121, 193–204, 207–8, 211, 214–15, 218n59, 219–21. See also Freud, Sigmund
Oedipus/Edippus, 16, 26–27, 193–222. See also Freud, Sigmund; Laius/Layus; Jocasta/Iocasta; Lydgate, John; *Oedipus Rex/Edippus* (Sophocles/Lydgate); Sophocles
Oedipus Rex/Edippus (Sophocles/Lydgate), 26, 193–222. See also Laius/Layus; Lydgate, John; Jocasta/Iocasta; Oedipus/Edippus; Sophocles
Oliver, Kelly, 194n5, 222n75. See also Walsh, Lisa

On Beauty and Being Just (Scarry), 131. See also Scarry, Elaine
Orgel, Stephen, 229n12. See also Duffin, Ross
O'Rourke, Michael, 7n18, 12n32. See also Petropunk Collective
Osborne, Lawrence, 178n13
Osborne, Peter, 8n21
Othello (Shakespeare), 56
Otherwise than Being, Or Beyond Essence (Lévinas), 196. See also Lévinas, Emmanuel

paleolithic images, 17, 35–50
Panayotova, Stella, 70n18. See also Binski, Paul
paradox, 26, 155, 194, 200–1, 206, 230. See also Oedipus/Edippus; Sphinx
parasite, 239
patricide, 26–27, 198, 218
patronage, 232, 234, 242
Pearl-poet, 89n67. See also *Sir Gawain and the Green Knight* (*Pearl*-poet)
Pearsall, Derek, 202n33
Pech-Merle Cave, 39
Perceval (Chrétien de Troyes), 20–22, 30, 95–102, 106–13, 115, 119, 121–25. See also Chrétien de Troyes
Péret, Benjamin, 162
Petropunk Collective, 7n18, 12n32. See also Joy, Eileen A.; Kłosowska, Anna; Masciandaro, Nicola; O'Rourke, Michael
Phelan, Peggy, 34n4
Pierre, Antoine, 158
plant, 98, 99n13, 108, 160, 188
Plassard, Jean, 42–43, 45–47
Platonic Form, 227, 230, 232n13
pluralist aesthetic, 141, 221, 227
Poe, Edgar Allan, 73–74
Polish, Jessica, 192n56
Polo, Marco, 25, 177
Polynieces, 202, 215–16
Porete, Marguerite, 77n37
posthuman, 1–16, 23, 27–28, 98, 133–34, 151, 155, 191, 223–43
poststructuralism, 97, 196n15, 231–32
postsustainable, 240, 243
Potter, Andrew, 77n38. See also Heath, Joseph

Pound, Ezra, 2, 110
prayer book, 19–20, 69, 79–94
prayer, 19–20, 66–67, 82, 91
Price, Merrall Llewelyn, 175n2
professionalism, 231
Psalter, 66n6, 69n13, 70n18, 81, 85
Psyche, 28, 30
psychoanalysis, 26, 121n69, 167, 195, 201
pubic triangles in Paleolithic art, 35–37
Public Enemy, 20, 77–78
Pugliatti, Paola, 242n32
purgatory, 97n10, 106, 110, 124
Pythagoras, 30

queer, 19, 27, 98–99, 119, 121, 123, 129n1, 224

Ramsey, Mary, 11n29. See also Bell, Kimberley; Joy, Eileen A.; Seaman, Myra J.
Read, Piers Paul, 178n12
Remains of the Day, The (Ishiguro), 223, 226-7
Renaissance humanism, 23, 151, 223, 234
Renoir, Alain, 202n33
Richard Coer de Lyon, 25, 176–77, 179n16
Riddle of the Sphinx, The, 199
Rigg, A. G., 78n42
Riparo de Vado all'Arancio, 48
Road, The, 185
Rolle, Richard, 20, 66n5, 76, 79, 81, 85, 88–90, 92
Romain de Balain, Le, 63n34
Roman de Thebès, Le, 199, 201
romance, 16, 25, 56n20, 60–64, 96, 100, 102, 110, 118, 120–21, 130, 141, 145, 176
Romano, Claude, 16, 19, 58–62, 64n36. See also *Event and World* (Romano)
Rouffignac Cave, 17, 41–48
Rouse, Mary A., 70n18. See also Rouse, Richard H.
Rouse, Richard H., 70n18. See also Rouse, Mary A.
Rudel, Jaufre, 171
Rudnytsky, Peter L., 201n30
Ryder, Richard, 179

Sabine, Ernest, 183n31
Sagawa, Issei, 177n12
Said, Edward, 4
Salisbury, Eve, 187n40. See also Laskaya, Anne
Santner, Eric L., 8n21
Scalia, Giuseppe, 179n18
Scarry, Elaine, 131–33, 137n28. See also *On Beauty and Being Just* (Scarry)
Schirmer, Walter F., 202n33
Scholes, Robert, 27–28, 223–26
Scott, Ridley, 156
Seabrook, William, 178n12
Seaman, Myra J. 11n29, 12n32. See also Bell, Kimberley; Joy, Eileen A.; Ramsey, Mary
Serrano, Andres, 173
Serres, Michel, 56n20, 73n25, 239
Serres, Olivier de, 158
Seymour, M. D., 177n9
Shakespeare, William, 16, 56, 226–29, 234, 239. See also *Othello* (Shakespeare); *Twelfth Night* (Shakespeare)
Shannon, Laurie, 7n18
Shaviro, Steven, 5n11
Shaw, David Gary, 19, 54n13
Short, Charles, 108n31. See also Lewis, Charleton T.
Shukin, Nicole, 189
Siege of Thebes (Lydgate), 26, 196–97, 202–18. See also Lydgate, John
Silver, Lee, 10n28
Singer, Peter, 179n19
singularity, 5–7, 16, 27, 55, 191, 223, 227–28, 233, 235–36
Sir Gawain and the Green Knight (Pearl-poet), 22, 132. See also Pearl-poet
Sir Gowther, 24–25, 187–91
"slow" historical perspective, 14–16
Smalley, Beryl, 69n16, 90n74
Smith, D. Vance, 11n29, 12n32, 55n17. See also Cole, Andrew
Snediker, Michael, 113
Solomon, Don, 6n16
Soltan, Margaret, 131–33. See also Green-Lewis, Jennifer

Solutrean Period in Paleolithic art, 39
Soper, Kate, 13
Sophocles, 26, 193, 195n7, 197–99, 204–8, 211, 213, 215–16, 218–20. *See also* Laius/Layus; Jocasta/Iocasta; Oedipus/Edippus; *Oedipus Rex/Edippus* (Sophocles/Lydgate)
Sorcerer in Paleolithic art, the, 35, 38–39
South Park, 160
Southern, R. W., 54n13
Sparrow, Tom, 5n11
speculative realism, 5n11, 99, 102, 104, 116
Sphinx, 26, 194–200, 208–15
Srnicek, Nick, 5n11, 54n12. *See also* Bryant, Levi; Harman, Graham; Williams, Alex
Stahuljak, Zrinka, 100n16, 102n18, 110n38, 122n70. *See also* Chrétien's Girls; Greene, Virginie; Kay, Sarah; Kinoshita, Sharon; McCracken, Peggy
Stallybrass, Peter, 211
Stanton, Anne, 66n6, 69n13, 70n18
State and Empire of the Moon (Bergerac), 29. *See also* Bergerac, Cyrano de
Statius, 201
Steel, Karl, 7n18, 13, 24–26, 133. *See also* McCracken, Peggy
Stein, Gertrude, 73–74
Stein, Robert M., 130–31
Steiner, Emily, 76, 81n51
Stekel, Wilhelm, 177n12
stewardship, 223–28, 234–35, 243
Stock, Brian, 76
Stock, Gregory, 10n28
Stockton, Will, 152n3
stone, 2, 22, 39, 47–48, 61, 98, 101, 107, 109, 133–34, 137–40, 146–50
Stonehenge, 138, 147–48
Strohm, Paul, 11n29, 19n45, 54n13
sublimation, 23–24, 76, 88, 91, 152–54, 161–66, 173–74
surplus value, 130n1, 136, 148, 163, 243
surrealism [search also for: surreal-], 16, 74, 133–36, 162

"Tale of Balyn and Balin," 18–19, 51, 56–64. *See also* Malory, Thomas; *Morte darthur* (Malory)
Tale of Genji (Murasaki), 3. *See also* Murasaki, Lady
Tattersall, Jill, 177n7
Taylor, Charles, 54n13
Taylor, Chloë, 182
Taylor, Jerome, 66n4, 68n12, 80n49, 90n73, 90n74
techno-bureaucratic culture, 223
Temple-Raston, Dina, 68n11
temporality, 11, 15, 19, 26, 54–58, 69, 73–75, 97, 129, 130, 141, 144, 151, 159, 194–95, 210, 212–14, 222, 226
Teskey, Gordon, 213
Thacker, Eugene, 9n26. *See also* Galloway, Alexander
Thebes, 196, 201–7, 215–17
Thebiad, 201
Thomas, Calvin, 121n67, 121n69, 123
Thomas, Keith, 233n17
Thorpe, Lewis, 146n41
Three Essays on Sexuality (Freud), 214n51. *See also* Freud, Sigmund
THX 1138 (Lucas), 16, 24, 154—Todorov, Tzvetan, 10n27
Totality and Infinity: An Essay on Exteriority (Lévinas), 203n37. *See also* Lévinas, Emmanuel
tree, 49, 108, 113, 203–4
Trois-Frères Cave, 38, 46
Trojans, 143–44
troubadour, 16, 23–24, 152–56, 162–74
Tru Master, 78. *See also* hip-hop
Truitt, E. R., 12n32
Tudor Poor Laws, 241–42
Turner, Henry S., 7n18
Twelfth Night (Shakespeare), 27–28, 223, 226–43
Tyler, Tom, 8n20
Tyrrell, Robert Yelverton, 2n3

Uther Pendragon, 147

vagabonds, 242
vegan, 28–30
vegetal, 22, 29–30, 108–9, 112, 136
vegetarian, 30

Vendler, Helen, 130–31
Ventadorn, Bernard de, 167, 170–71
Venus of Brassempouy, 39
Vico, Giovanni Battista, 73
Victorines, 20, 67
Villon, François, 1
Vint, Sherryl, 79n45
violence, 25–26, 60, 77, 114, 145–46, 160, 181–91, 194–209, 212–13, 216–17, 220, 225
Virgil, 2, 21. See also *Aeneid* (Virgil)
Virginia Tech massacre, 71–72
Virilio, Paul, 9n26, 51n1, 74, 87n66
Voragine, Jacobus de, 175n2. See also *Golden Legend* (Voragine)
Vortigern, 145–47

Waddell, Helen, 78n42
Wainwright, Geoffrey, 138
Walbiri people, 49
Wales, 138
Walsh, Lisa, 194n5. See also Oliver, Kelly
waste, 23–24, 121, 151–74
Watson, Nicholas, 80n47, 81n52, 82n53, 86n64
waywardness, 240–41
Weather Underground, 20, 76
Weber, Max, 86–87
Wenzel, Siegfried, 81n51

Wharton, David, 2n1
White, Carolinne, 78n42
White, Hayden, 8n21
White, Randall, 35n5
Wieck, Roger S., 69n14
Williams, Alex, 54n12. See also Srnicek, Nick
Wolfe, Cary, 1, 5n11, 8–10, 13, 25, 27, 34, 133, 186n37, 189n48, 225. See also Elmer, Jonathan
Woods, Marjorie C., 90n74
Wright, John, 2n2
Writing of Stones, The (Caillois), 134n14, 136n21, 137, 138n30, 139n32. See also Caillois, Roger

Yates, Julian, 7n18, 133, 225, 242, 243n33
Yeats, William Butler, 224
Yoda, Tomiko, 3n4, 3n6
Yonec (Marie de France), 23, 149–50. See also Marie de France
Yourcenar, Marguerite, 134n14, 136n21
Yvain (Chrétien de Troyes), 95–96, 114, 116–20. See also Chrétien de Troyes

Žižek, Slavoj, 23, 152–153, 183
Zupančič, Alenka, 24, 16i, 162n21, 174
Zylinska, Joanna, 5n11, 29–30, 191

INTERVENTIONS: NEW STUDIES IN MEDIEVAL CULTURE
Ethan Knapp, Series Editor

Interventions: New Studies in Medieval Culture publishes theoretically informed work in medieval literary and cultural studies. We are interested both in studies of medieval culture and in work on the continuing importance of medieval tropes and topics in contemporary intellectual life.

Fragments for a History of a Vanishing Humanism
EDITED BY MYRA SEAMAN AND EILEEN A. JOY

The Medieval Risk-Reward Society: Courts, Adventure, and Love in the European Middle Ages
WILL HASTY

The Politics of Ecology: Land, Life, and Law in Medieval Britain
EDITED BY RANDY P. SCHIFF AND JOSEPH TAYLOR

The Art of Vision: Ekphrasis in Medieval Literature and Culture
EDITED BY ANDREW JAMES JOHNSTON, ETHAN KNAPP, AND MARGITTA ROUSE

Desire in the Canterbury Tales
ELIZABETH SCALA

Imagining the Parish in Late Medieval England
ELLEN K. RENTZ

Truth and Tales: Cultural Mobility and Medieval Media
EDITED BY FIONA SOMERSET AND NICHOLAS WATSON

Eschatological Subjects: Divine and Literary Judgment in Fourteenth-Century French Poetry
J. M. MOREAU

Chaucer's (Anti-)Eroticisms and the Queer Middle Ages
TISON PUGH

Trading Tongues: Merchants, Multilingualism, and Medieval Literature
JONATHAN HSY

Translating Troy: Provincial Politics in Alliterative Romance
ALEX MUELLER

Fictions of Evidence: Witnessing, Literature, and Community in the Late Middle Ages
JAMIE K. TAYLOR

Answerable Style: The Idea of the Literary in Medieval England
EDITED BY FRANK GRADY AND ANDREW GALLOWAY

Scribal Authorship and the Writing of History in Medieval England
MATTHEW FISHER

Fashioning Change: The Trope of Clothing in High- and Late-Medieval England
ANDREA DENNY-BROWN

Form and Reform: Reading across the Fifteenth Century
EDITED BY SHANNON GAYK AND KATHLEEN TONRY

How to Make a Human: Animals and Violence in the Middle Ages
KARL STEEL

Revivalist Fantasy: Alliterative Verse and Nationalist Literary History
RANDY P. SCHIFF

Inventing Womanhood: Gender and Language in Later Middle English Writing
TARA WILLIAMS

Body Against Soul: Gender and Sowlehele *in Middle English Allegory*
MASHA RASKOLNIKOV

www.ingramcontent.com/pod-product-compliance
Lightning Source LLC
Chambersburg PA
CBHW030108010526
44116CB00005B/150